Centre Stage

DATE DUE FOR RETURN

This book may be recalled before the above date.

D0494146

AMSTERDAMER PUBLIKATIONEN ZUR SPRACHE UND LITERATUR

in Verbindung mit

PETER BOERNER, BLOOMINGTON; HUGO DYSERINCK, AACHEN;
FERDINAND VAN INGEN, AMSTERDAM; FRIEDRICH MAURER†,
FREIBURG; OSKAR REICHMANN, HEIDELBERG

herausgegeben von

COLA MINIS†
und
AREND QUAK

137

AMSTERDAM - ATLANTA, GA 1999

Centre Stage

Contemporary Drama in Austria

Edited by

Frank Finlay
and Ralf Jeutter

ISBN: 90-420-0525-4
©Editions Rodopi B.V., Amsterdam - Atlanta, GA 1999
Printed in The Netherlands

CONTENTS

PREFACE

The majority of the papers in this volume were presented at a conference on contemporary Austrian drama held at the Manchester Metropolitan University. The generous support of the Austrian Institute, London, the German Consulate, Manchester, and the cooperation of the *Goethe Institut*, Manchester enabled us to bring together scholars and practitioners from Austria, Germany and the UK. In particular we were able to integrate theatrical performances and readings into the programme, one of which is documented in photographs here.

All the papers for this volume were revised extensively and three additional contributions were commissioned. The editors would like to thank all the contributors for their cheerful and constructive response to our various suggestions and their patience in the face of a number of difficulties we encountered when making the papers and photographs well and truly 'camera ready'.

We wish to point out that the opinions expressed in the various contributions are those of their authors and are not necessarily shared by the editors or the institutions which supported the original conference.

We want finally to record our gratitude to our respective universities for their help and support, in particular colleagues in the Department of Languages and the Department of Drama of the Manchester Metropolitan University, and Anne Croasdell, Administrative Secretary to the Department of Modern Languages of the University of Bradford for her good–humoured assistance in providing the final print–out. Special thanks to Michaela and Sally.

Frank Finlay & Ralf Jeutter

CENTRE STAGE:
CONTEMPORARY DRAMA IN AUSTRIA

FRANK FINLAY & RALF JEUTTER

Scene I
In the autumn of 1955, the twin temples of high culture on Vienna's
Ringstraße, the State Theatre (*Burgtheater*) and the Opera (*Staatsoper*)
opened their doors to audiences for the first time in over a decade, following
extensive restoration occasioned by wartime damage. The attendant
celebrations were designed as the cultural climax to a momentous year,
which had seen Austria granted its political sovereignty after a decade of
postwar occupation and, in the process, its citizens gain the official status as
the 'first victims' of National Socialism. By the time the last Allied soldier
had left the country in October, the National Assembly of the new Second
Republic — Austria's first truly democratic one — had pledged itself to
'permanent neutrality' and was preparing itself for membership of the
United Nations in time for Christmas.

Whilst the *Staatsoper* offered a performance of Beethoven's *Fidelio*,
extensive discussions and ministerial interference were required before
Goethe's *Egmont* was finally rejected in favour of the Austrian Franz
Grillparzer's *König Ottokars Glück und Ende*, as the most appropriate work
to re–open the *Burgtheater*. First performed in 1825, this paean to Austria's
glorious imperial past ('es ist ein gutes · Land [...] Wo habt Ihr
dessengleichen schon gesehn?'), with its closing lines of 'Hoch Österreich!
Habsburg für immer!'[1] was significant not least because it set the tone for
the conservative and exclusive play policy of Austria's publicly funded
theatres for almost three decades to come.[2] Here, as in the wider literary
sphere, there was a general, albeit selective adherence to the canon of great
literature which predated the 'diversions' of the Nazi hiatus, and to the
'Austrian' tradition, in particular. In the inflamed climate of the Cold War,
cultural politicians and practitioners alike followed — often to the letter —

---

[1]Quoted from the Reclam edition, pp. 65 and 112.

[2]In addition to the *Burgtheater* and the *Staatsoper*, the smaller houses of Vienna's
Akademietheater and the *Volksoper* form a state theatre conglomerate, reminiscent of
the situation in the socialist German Democratic Republic. See Gerhard Scheit, 'Theater
in Österreich', in Horst A. Glaser (ed.) *Deutsche Literatur zwischen 1945 und 1955*,
Bern/Stuttgart/Vienna: 1996, p.528. Full details of the publishers of secondary literature
are provided in the bibliography only.

the rallying call of the future head of the Austrian PEN–Club, Alexander Lernet–Holenia:

> In der Tat brauchen wir nur dort fortzusetzen, wo uns die Träume eines Irren unterbrochen haben, in der Tat brauchen wir nicht voraus–, sondern nur zurückzublicken.[3]

This restorative process of 'looking back', however, to the time before 1938 conveniently skated over the fact that the 'mad man' in question, Adolf Hitler, was an Austrian, whose criminal undertakings received the enthusiastic and active support of many of his countrymen. Austria's official efforts at 'coming to terms' with its Nazi past thus seemed for many years to consist primarily in denying or concealing its own severely compromised role, as the following example taken from Robert Menasse's essay on Austrian identity illustrates. In 1960 when preparations were underway to bring Adolf Eichmann to trial in Jerusalem, the government in Vienna went to extraordinary lengths to avoid the international embarrassment of an Austrian citizen being condemned as a Nazi war criminal in the eyes of the world; it simply revoked Eichmann's citizenship and thereby his nationality. Menasse puts the implications of this act in perspective:

> Fünf Jahre nach der Erlangung der staatlichen Souveranität hat die Zweite Republik Österreich bereits die innovative Bedeutung seines Nationsbegriffs demonstriert: nämlich eine Staatsnation zu sein, die ihren Bürgern *historische Unschuld* garantiert.[4]

In the literary sphere, this attitude was encouraged by the promotion of conservative writers, such as Albert Paris Gütersloh, Heimito von Doderer, and Lernet–Holenia himself, whose works seemed to offer a national distinctiveness in their nostalgic celebration of what has since become known in literary history as the Habsburg Myth.[5] As far as the writers of the inter–war years were concerned who had been reviled and in many cases persecuted by the Nazis, there was also myopia. In the case of the theatre, for example, this meant that the important radical innovations of the German stage works of the Weimar period, such as Erwin Piscator's multi–media experiments remained off–limits. Brecht, whose theories had such major international impact after the war, was actually boycotted in Austria, whilst the international Avant–garde went largely ignored. Attempts to revive the

---

[3]Quoted in Wendelin Schmidt–Dengler, 'Vorwort', in Petra Nachbaur and Sigurd Paul Scheichl (eds.), *Literatur über Literatur. Eine österreichische Anthologie*, Graz: 1995, p.11.

[4]Robert Menasse, *Das Land ohne Eigenschaft. Essay zur österreichischen Identität*. Frankfurt/M.: 1995, p.27.

[5]The seminal coinage of this term was Claudio Magris' monograph *Der habsburgische Mythos in der österreichischen Literatur*, Salzburg: 1966.

critical and ultimately highly influential plays of the Austrian dramatist Ödön von Horváth were abject failures, and it was to be another twenty years or so before a number of radio and television productions led to his being rediscovered.[6]

The officially sanctioned Austrian theatrical landscape was, therefore, effectively a local variant of that of West Germany's in the 1950s and early 1960s: it largely resembled 'a desert strewn with the incongruous remnants of a misunderstood and maltreated tradition.'[7] Innovative work by contemporary Austrian artists — one thinks of the neo–Dadaists and surrealists of the *Wiener Gruppe* and political satirists such as Helmut Qualtinger — struggled for many years to find a larger public forum, whilst the talents of a generation of already active writers and fledgling authors, who had been driven in fear of their lives into political exile, went largely ignored. Indeed, a reluctance to welcome back those who had fled the Nazis was one of the striking features of Austrian literary life in the early years after 1945.[8]

Scene II

Over thirty years later, in the autumn of 1988, the *Burgtheater* was once again to play a pivotal, albeit far from affirmative public role, during another season of commemorative events. This time the occasion was more sombre: the fiftieth anniversary of the *Anschluß*, Austria's annexation by the National Socialists in March 1938, and of the notorious pogrom against Jewish citizens all over German–controlled territories, on 9th November of the same year. Press revelations of the Nazi past of the country's President, Kurt Waldheim during his ill–tempered campaign for election to the highest office of state in 1986, had triggered off a period of debating Austria's role during the Third Reich[9] and guaranteed that the country's great, so–called 'year of reflection' would be controversial.

The *Burgtheater*'s contribution to the acts of remembrance was a specially commissioned play by the nation's arguably most famous living writer, Thomas Bernhard. Named — with weighty connotations — after the nearby square on which thousands of Austrians had enthusiastically

---

[6]Wendelin Schmidt–Dengler, *Bruchlinien. Vorlesungen zur Österreichischen Literatur 1945 bis 1990*. Salzburg and Vienna: 1995, p.269.

[7]See W.G. Sebald, 'Surveying the Scene — Some Introductory Remarks', in his *A Radical Stage. Theatre in Germany in the 1970s and 1980s*, Oxford/New York/Hamburg: 1988, p.1.

[8]See Anthony Bushell, 'Austria's Political and Cultural Re–emergence: The First Decade', in Anthony Bushell (ed.) *Austria 1945 – 1955. Studies in Political and Cultural Re–emergence*. Cardiff: 1996, p.5f.

[9]See Erika Weinzierl, and Anton Pelinka (eds.): *Das große Tabu. Österreichs Umgang mit seiner Vergangenheit*. Vienna: 1987.

welcomed Hitler in 1938, Bernhard's *Heldenplatz*, in a production by the outspoken German, Claus Peymann, Director of the *Burgtheater*, provoked a quite predictable and major public scandal for its characteristically polemical allegations of the durability of Nazi sentiments in modern–day Austria. Peymann and Bernhard had skilfully manipulated the media for months in advance and succeeded, not least via selective leaking of some of the play's most controversial sections,[10] in proving even before the première just how reactionary sections of Austrian society were; the two men were inundated with hate–mail, death threats — Peymann wasted no time in publishing examples, together with the 'highlights' of the press coverage — and there was a concerted and vitriolic campaign of protest against them.[11] Attempts were made to get the production halted, the opening night saw rival demonstrators clash in front of the theatre, and claques even tried to disrupt the actual performance. The ensuing theatrical triumph was arguably also pre–programmed.

In the context of the essays collected here, this occasion is important not so much as a *succès de scandale* but because it perhaps marked most graphically the climax of a development, which began in the 1960s — not least, as several of our contributors document, with the experimental orientation of writing emanating from the provincial city of Graz — and which saw works by a younger generation of dramatic artists take their rightful place at the very centre of the nation's most celebrated stage. As if to ironically underscore the point, Bernhard's location of his play's second scene, which contains many of the speeches to excite such public outcry, required the *Burgtheater* itself to be the central element of the set design.

The Present Volume

Behind the two set pieces which we have offered in our opening scenario, there is, of course, a far more complex narrative of dramatic regeneration and the establishing of a vibrant, contemporary theatrical landscape. The task of the essays, which make up *Centre Stage: Contemporary Drama in Austria*, was to provide a contribution to that narrative for both scholars and university students. It was also our hope that, by combining contributions

---

[10]The following extract from one of Professor Robert's diatribes in Scene Two caused perhaps the greatest stir: '[...] *er schaut in Richtung auf das Burgtheater*: Was diesem armen unmündigen Volk geblieben ist/ist nichts als das Theater/Österreich selbst ist nichts als eine Bühne/auf der alles verlottert und vermodert und verkommen ist/eine in sich selber verhaßte Statisterie von sechseinhalb Millionen Alleingelassenen/sechseinhalb Millionen Debile und Tobsüchtige die ununterbrochen aus vollem Hals nach einem Regisseur schreien/Der Regisseur wird kommen/und sie endgültig in den Abgrund hinunterstoßen.' Thomas Bernhard, *Heldenplatz*, Frankfurt/M.: (Bibliothek Suhrkamp) 1988, p.89.

[11]*Heldenplatz. Eine Dokumentation*, Burgtheater Wien (ed.), 13.1.1989.

from academics with those from theatrical practitioners and translators, we would be able to provide information for theatre professionals interested in introducing works by Austrian dramatists to a wider English–language audience.

In order to avoid some of the pitfalls and endless disputes that occur whenever a nation's name is applied in an essentialist way to its literature, we define contemporary drama in Austria in strictly pragmatic terms, namely as dramatic writing produced by writers who were either socialised in, or who at some time hold or held, citizenship of Austria, in any of its twentieth century incarnations. The 'contemporary' aspect is reflected in the fact that the bulk of the playwrights dealt with began to have their work performed from the late 1960s onwards. It is also reflected in the broader view we take of what constitutes dramatic writing, which acknowledges the growing importance for the contemporary writer of the more modern media of radio, film and television.

The focus of all of the chapters is on individual dramatists, ranging from playwrights with an established international reputation, such as Peter Handke, Thomas Bernhard, Wolfgang Bauer, Elfriede Jelinek and Peter Turrini, to less well–known writers, such as Gerhard Roth, Marlene Streeruwitz, Werner Schwab and the 'action artist', Hermann Nitsch. Discussions of plays by Elias Canetti, Fritz Hochwälder and Jakov Lind reflect the long overdue re–assessment of the work of at least some of the emigrés, which has taken place in Austria in the past ten years.

We have deliberately eschewed structuring the volume along chronological lines, rather it is our hope that the order of chapters will highlight, from their respective author's differing perspectives and methodologies, some of the important themes, preoccupations and forms of Austrian drama at the end of the twentieth century. The ordering of the contributions was made only after much deliberation and with an awareness that other constellations might have been equally valid. It was never our intention to provide a complete survey of the contemporary dramatic landscape in Austria, and there are some obvious omissions: we regret, for example, that despite strenuous efforts, we were unable to include more contributions on stage works written by women.

The collection opens with Julian Preece's discussion of the self–styled *enfant terrible*, Werner Schwab, who became the German–language theatre's most exciting new discovery during the short period from the première of his first play *Die Präsidentinnen* (1991) until his death at the age of only thirty–five in January 1994. Preece argues that for all the deliberate exaggeration of Schwab's carefully cultivated public persona, of which his personal aversion to political convictions was an important part, the details of the prolific dramatist's biography which have emerged since his death are a challenge to his audiences and interpreters to confront the fact that the themes of his plays are rooted in social reality. Critics have, for example, been slow to recognise Schwab's 'modernist' concern with utter alienation and the inability to overcome it. Schwab also merits our attention for his high degree of linguistic and dramatic invention. Preece's subsequent survey of form, structure and genre in Schwab's *oeuvre* identifies the astounding variety of styles he deployed, and reveals how familiar he was with the 'modern' traditions of the international Avant–garde in general, and with some of the local Austrian 'actionist' manifestations, in particular.

Werner Schwab also features prominently in Chapter Two, in Mike Rogers' comparative discussion of the theme of disorder, which he traces through three generations of Austrian writers. Rogers' analysis, which also acts as a bridge to Anthony Waine's discussion of Wolfgang Bauer in Chapter Three, seeks to establish a typology of disorder as it emerges in Schwab's plays, and in Elias Canetti's *Hochzeit* and Bauer's *Magic Afternoon*. Rogers maintains that all three dramatists set out in different ways to confront the 'order' of the complacent bourgeois world with the omnipresent 'disorder' that is veiled only by hypocrisy, pretension and self–deceit. Rogers highlights the writers' awareness that by using the medium of the theatre — itself a bourgeois institution — their staging of disorder can collude dialectically in maintaining the very order they seek, albeit implicitly, to undermine. Both Canetti and Bauer, however, accept the confines of the theatre, claim no universal validity, and leave the audience to draw their own conclusions, whereas Schwab, at least in *Die Präsidentinnen*, goes beyond the protest–for–protest-sake of most of his own plays and, by focusing on the 'order' of 'disorder', is able to bring to his play the social dimension to which Preece has already drawn our attention.

Since the end of the Second World War there has been an historic shift in modes of social and economic behaviour, perceptions of reality, aesthetic and cultural values, and consequently also a change in subjectivities — the manner in which individuals feel about themselves and one another. These changes are often brought together under the elusive and hotly debated banner of 'postmodernism'.[12] Writers and artists are, to use Peter Conrad's phrase, 'the interpreters of their age and also its memorialists'.[13] Accordingly it is possible to look to works of art for differing degrees of evidence of social and cultural change. The next three chapters all deal with some of the different ways in which contemporary Austrian stage works

---

[12]An excellent anthology of essays which documents the postmodernist, literary debate in the German–speaking world can be found in Uwe Wittstock, (ed.): *Roman oder Leben. Postmoderne in der deutschen Literatur*, Leipzig: (Reclam) 1994.

[13]Peter Conrad, *Modern Times, Modern Places. Life and Art in the 20th Century*, London: 1998, p.8.

have reflected in content, style, and the refashioning of aesthetic and theatrical traditions key aspects of postmodernism.

Anthony Waine invites us to view Wolfgang Bauer as someone whose 60s trilogy *Magic Afternoon, Change* and *Party for Six* contains already 'postmodern' sentiments or 'moods' before they were actually expressed as such. As Waine demonstrates cogently, Bauer as a writer of fiction and not theory, was able to circumvent some of the conceptual pitfalls associated with the term postmodern and which have provided a battle–ground for heated discourses within and across disciplines. Drawing on a rich, native Austrian tradition of popular drama in the previous century which had satirised the bourgeoisie in works by, for example, Nestroy and Raimund, as well as on a matrix of quotidian pastimes of 'popular' or 'pop' culture, Bauer provides an anatomy of our postmodern condition. In particular, his characters' cultural identities are revealed to embody the aesthetic at the heart of postmodernity: heterogeneity. Waine holds that it is precisely because Bauer's own problems, pleasures and dreams form the point of departure for his work and lend them a credibility, authority and legitimacy, that they reveal a serious moral core, albeit a purely personal one which does not subscribe to a hierarchically or vertically ordered set of values. It is to this extent that in Waine's view, Bauer's postmodernist 'moods' do not block or obscure 'morals'; a conclusion which raises urgent questions about the often disputed critical value of the newer art.

Allyson Fiddler's subsequent discussion in Chapter Four of Marlene Streeruwitz also alights on elements of the postmodern. Fiddler locates her analysis in the context of Streeruwitz's critique of the Western classical theatrical tradition and the feminist dimension of her work. The dramatist's application of the term 'classical' theatre is broad enough for it to include Pinter, and she dismisses it as not only 'phallic' in its preoccupation with a usually male central character, but also because it reflects inadequately the torn condition of a time and society which lack totalising systems for making sense of the world — the same hierarchical sets of values which Bauer rejects.

Fiddler focuses on two thematically–linked plays, *New York. New York.* and *Tolmezzo.* to explore Streeruwitz's 'mission' for the theatre; the espousal and practical realisation of a new, more appropriate — and therefore 'realistic'— aesthetic model for drama in which characters enact central elements of the postmodern condition, in particular its view of history and of the disunity and fragmentation of the humanist subject. Whilst rejecting the world–view that informs classical drama, Streeruwitz is happy to exploit its conventions as organising structures and as ludic gestures. Moreover, like Bauer, she also draws on elements of the Theatre of the Absurd in her act of theatrical subversion. The settings, for example, acknowledge its influence, as does the farcical humour. To these staples of an arguably 'modernist' theatrical tradition, Streeruwitz also harnesses some of the aesthetic forces of postmodernism, such as intertextuality, which is characteristic of an 'open' form and which relies on associative techniques and the ability and willingness of the audience to construct their own meanings. Accordingly, classical, literary, popular and filmic quotations abound in her plays. However, Fiddler argues that Streeruwitz's drama, for all the latter's demands for a new aesthetics in the theatre, and the absence of any overt political analysis, is not apolitical. Most evident in this regard is the feminist dimension in Streeruwitz's thinking.

The work and concerns of another radical, feminist writer, Elfriede Jelinek, are examined in Chapter Five by Jenny Lanyon. Lanyon focuses on the ways in which female subjectivity is (de)constructed in *Krankheit oder moderne Frauen* and situates the play first within the context of trends in women's writing. Lanyon argues, however, that Jelinek differs from the early orthodox feminist assumption in the conviction that female subjectivity does not exist outside its patriarchal construction. Moreover, she maintains that, for Jelinek, patterns of subjectivity are linked crucially to wider structures of oppression. Lanyon then proceeds to examine how *Krankheit oder moderne Frauen* can be interpreted within the framework of the psychoanalytic theories of Freud, which Jelinek satirises, and those of postmodern French thinkers, Jacques Lacan and Michel Foucault. She argues that no attempt is made to dramatise the conflicts of individuals in their efforts to understand gender conventions. To this extent the play's characters embody different discourses of male and female subjectivity. Nevertheless, Lanyon proposes that the play, far from being a 'book drama', is highly theatrical and, like Streeruwitz's work, playfully intertextual, although ultimately its dystopian view offers no explicit political alternative to the issues it raises.

One of the important new trends which was a feature of the regeneration of the contemporary German–language theatre, particularly in the late 1960s and early 1970s, was the so–called *neues Volksstück*. This termed was used to describe the neo–verist approach of writers such as Rainer Werner Fassbinder, Franz Xavier Kroetz and Martin Sperr, who took as their inspiration the tradition of the parodic 'folkplay' as propagated in the late years of the Weimar Republic by Horváth, Marieluise Fleisser and the less well–known Jura Soyfer. A contemporary writer, who can be located broadly in this same tradition is Felix Mitterer, whose dramatic works are the subject of Victoria Martin's analysis in Chapter Six. From the point of view of a linguistic researcher, Martin examines the role which dialect plays in Mitterer's *Volksstücke*. Specifically, she explores the communicative and social function of dialect as it emerges in Mitterer's plays, which were written with a local Tyrolean audience in mind. She then proceeds to examine in detail his four–part television series, *Die*

Piefke–Saga, and illustrates how, in the context of an Austrian and German television co–production aimed at viewers in the two respective countries, Mitterer deploys dialect in what is, in effect, his extended meditation on the complex and often fraught relationships between Austria and Germany, whereby his Tyroleans 'speak' for all Austrians. By focusing on the clash between standard and dialect, Mitterer is able to convey information about power relations and demonstrate that the inability to communicate is symptomatic of a wider failure to understand one another's values and cultures. Thus economic, social and cultural tensions are literally given voice by the use of different varieties of the German language.

Chapter Seven addresses another trend which has been particularly vibrant in Austria. Julie Wilson–Bokowiec provides an introduction to Hermann Nitsch, a performance artist who is hardly known in Britain and the US, although notorious, admired, defamed and celebrated in his home country. Wilson–Bokowiec brings to the work of Nitsch the double perspective of scholar and practitioner. In the first part of her essay, she reflects on the ideas and traditions which have influenced Nitsch in his belief that art serves a similar function as religion, in that it articulates the essential, non–rational intensity of life. In the second part of her essay, she provides a report of her preparation and staging with drama students and professional actors of Nitsch's *1st Abreaction Play*, which received its British première (13.9.1995) at the conference that formed the point of departure for the present volume. Peter Smith's photographs of the production, generously sponsored by the Austrian Institute, add to the documentary nature of this contribution.

The subsequent two chapters examine the work of writers who, having been driven into permanent exile, found themselves between two worlds and, in the case of Jakov Lind, as discussed by Silke Hassler in Chapter Eight, between two languages. The fact that Lind wrote a considerable amount of his work in English, once he had made his début in 1962, has undoubtedly influenced its late reception in his homeland. Clearly the possibilities for an author exiled in Britain who continued to publish in the German language were extremely limited, with the result that like the majority of exiles, he was under a particularly great pressure to assimilate his language.[14] As the US-emigré, Fleming, declares in Hilde Spiel's novel *The Darkened Room* 'a writer without a language is no less ridiculous than a banker without capital'.[15] Unsurprisingly, it is not an uncommon fate of such

---

[14]Gabriele Tergit, 'Die Exilsituation in England', in Manfred Durzak (ed.), *Die deutsche Exilliteratur 1933-1945*, Stuttgart: 1973, pp.135-44 (p.138).

[15]Hilde Spiel, *The Darkened Room*, London: 1961, p. 86; German edn: *Lisas Zimmer: Roman*, Munich: 1965, p.132.

work that it features rarely in literary histories.[16] However, a more significant factor was that the radical content of Lind's work did not blend easily with the politically restorative landscape, which, in the absence of a radical student movement in the 1960s, obtained far longer in Austria than in Germany. Accordingly, it has been Lind's fate — one he shares with many Austrian artists — that his work had to receive initial recognition in Germany before it could be 're-imported' into the country of his birth. It is Silke Hassler's contention that, in view of the large number of film treatments and adapations for radio which Lind produced of his own work, he was as equally at home in the dramatic mode as he was in the narrative, for which he is currently better known. Her chapter offers detailed analyses of two plays of the 1960s, *Die Heiden* and *Ergo* — the latter work was only premièred in German in 1997. Hassler's discussion locates these two stage works in the context of the Austrian 'folk play' tradition of Nestroy and Horváth, on the one hand, and of parallel developments in the German–language theatre of the 1950s and the 1960s, on the other. In so doing, she draws attention to similarities to the dramas of, for example, Friedrich Dürrenmatt, and identifies ways in which Lind adumbrates aspects of younger dramatists' work, such as Wolfgang Bauer's.

Unlike his fellow emigré, Jakov Lind, Fritz Hochwälder was a writer whose stage works have been frequently performed. Indeed, *Das heilige Experiment* (*The Strong are Lonely*), which he wrote in his Swiss exile in the early 1940s (premièred at the Zürich Schauspielhaus[17] in 1943), was a huge success during the immediate postwar years and gained a wide international reputation. The critical enthusiasm which greeted this archetypal 'well–made' drama of the downfall of the Jesuit 'experiment' of a utopian state in eighteenth–century Paraguay, also established, as Axel Schalk argues in Chapter Nine, a number of clichés, which have been applied with tenacity to the prolific playwright's subsequent work. Schalk maintains that the reception of this early play has blinded critics to Hochwälder's considerable talents, leading to his work falling into neglect from the 1970s onwards. Schalk demonstrates in his discussion of a number of dramas and Hochwälder's one posthumously published novel, that standard interpretations which regard this now sadly 'forgotten' dramatist as merely a 'Catholic' producer of 'historical' or 'folk' plays are in need of revision. In particular, Schalk draws our attention to the 'political' topicality

---

[16]See Waltraud Strickhausen, 'Schreiben in der Sprache des *Anderen*: Eine Vorstudie zu den Publikationsmöglichkeiten und der Wirkung englischsprachiger Exilwerke in Großbritannien', in Dieter Savin (ed.), *Die Resonanz des Exils: Gelungene und mißlungene Rezeption deutschsprachiger Exilautoren*, Amsterdamer Publikationen zur Sprache und Literatur, vol. 99, Amsterdam: 1992, pp.369-96 (p.379).

[17]The only major German–speaking forum for drama in mainland Europe to escape Nazi control.

of Hochwälder's historical dramas, which, for the writer, took precedence over considerations of aesthetic form.

In regarding the theatre as the locus for the presentation of social ills, Hochwälder is writing in a tradition in German–language theatre with a long history; the view that the stage should function as a 'moral institution', for example, goes back at least as far as the Enlightenment. In the twentieth century, a large body of what might be termed 'political' stage works has been produced by writers such as Bertolt Brecht, Carl Zuckmayer, Peter Weiss, Martin Walser, Heiner Kipphardt, Rolf Hochhuth, and the Swiss playwrights, Friedrich Dürrenmatt and Max Frisch. Despite many individual differences — both political and aesthetic — dramatists such as these nevertheless shared a number of common values and beliefs pertaining to the function of the theatre as an educator and promoter of social progress. Whilst never as strong in Austria, it is this tradition, that also informs the activities of Peter Turrini, as Frank Finlay demonstrates in Chapter Ten.

Finlay traces the various stages in Turrini's career and shows how, following the early successes of a number of 'critical folk plays', the dramatist came to regard the theatre as an unsuitable medium for his declared aim of giving a voice to society's disadvantaged and suppressed. Breaking out of what Turrini termed a narrow and élitist 'cultural ghetto', he placed his faith in the power of mass communications as a potential instrument of social enlightenment and change. However, his own experience of the mass medium of television, particularly the hard lessons learned during the aborted *Arbeitersaga* TV project, together with unease at the impact of technological change and the advent of new media such as video, led him to return to the theatre. Finlay shows how one important theme of *Die Minderleister*, the first new play since his self–imposed absence from the stage, is of how 'das wirklich Ungeschminkte', the unvarnished reality of life in contemporary Austria, is submerged in a deluge of mass media images. Moreover, *Die Minderleister* also constitutes an important new departure from an aesthetic point of view, with the linguistic realism of Turrini's early *Volksstücke* giving way to an altogether more experimental form.

The next two chapters concentrate on the dramatic output of the contemporary Austrian writers, whose many plays have been most frequently performed in German–language theatres — significantly in productions by Claus Peymann —, and who enjoy the widest international reputation: Thomas Bernhard and Peter Handke.

Ralf Jeutter begins in Chapter Eleven by documenting the international reception of Bernhard's prose works and contrasts it with the more ambiguous response which his stage plays have met, not least those which have been performed in translation in the UK. Jeutter identifies two themes — polarity and breathing — which run through the whole of Bernhard's *oeuvre.* By concentrating mainly on two of his shorter plays or *Dramoletten*, Jeutter's chapter attempts to find the imprints of Bernhard's real–life illness in his works. In so doing, he tries to reveal, by comparison with some of the prose works, the desire for unity which he argues lies behind Bernhard's untiring effort to set up polarities; his insistence on showing his characters to be inescapably caught up in contradictions.

In a recent literary history, Peter Handke is credited somewhat extravagantly with having single–handedly initiated a new era of dramatic writing in Austria with the international success, in 1966, of his play, *Publikumsbeschimpfung,*[18] which was followed by a series of highly regarded dramas, such as *Kaspar* and *Der Ritt über den Bodensee.* Whilst such attempts at periodisation of literature are always to be treated with circumspection, there can be no doubting Handke's status as a major literary figure. Like many authors of his generation, Handke is at home in a number of media, and it is his collaboration with German director, Wim Wenders, on the script for the film *Der Himmel über Berlin* (*Wings of Desire*) on which Fritz Wefelmeyer alights in his discussion, in Chapter Twelve, of the concept of the 'verlichtete Erzählung'. Beginning with a brief survey of the history of the drama from Classical times, Wefelmeyer defines the 'verlichtete Erzählung' in opposition to both the Epic Theatre of Brecht and classical theories of genre, which rigidly separate the dramatic and the narrative mode. He proceeds to explore central motifs and their allegorical realisation in both the film, the 'dramatic poem' *Über die Dörfer*, and the play *Das Spiel vom Fragen oder Die Reise zum Sonoren Land.*

The penultimate chapter in this volume is a survey by Uwe Schütte of the development as a playwright of Gerhard Roth, in whose oeuvre — unlike Bernhard and Handke — drama plays only a minor role. Indeed, Schütte's point of departure is the paradox of a playwright who uses the image of 'operating on a living corpse' to condemn writing for the stage as outdated and altogether insignificant. Nevertheless, Schütte maintains that Roth's dramatic development mirrors three distinct phases in the development of his prose works. He locates the overriding theme and key concern of Roth's dramatic productions in the difficulty of reconciling the theoretical nature of abstract concepts with stage representation and its demands of concretisation and visualisation. He then analyses in some detail why Roth's plays have been critical failures, with particular reference to Roth's deployment of mythical imagery and Jean Dubuffet's theory of *art brut* — deliberately 'badly–made' art. Schütte's conclusion places Roth in the wider context of a critique of reason, and asks whether negative responses to his plays by reviewers and the subsequent indifference of

---

[18]Alfred Barthofer, 'Neue Dramatiker in Österreich', in Horst A. Glaser (ed.), *Deutsche Literatur zwischen 1945 und 1995*, Bern/Stuttgart/Vienna: 1997, p.447.

academics is the inevitable fate awaiting any play that seeks to undermine the very foundations on which both professions are built: the enlightenment ideology of reason, institutionalisation, social conformity, and state subsidy.

The collection closes with a timely and practical reminder that the international reception of stage works depend crucially on their being translated in order that they might be offered to the largest possible audience. This is perhaps particularly true of the plays of dramatists from a relatively small country such as Austria. Accordingly, the success or failure of any work of literature when it is transferred to a target language can be determined on how well the author has been served by his/her translator. In Chapter Fourteen, Penny Black draws on her extensive theatrical and translation experience in her talk, which charts the practical and linguistic challenges as well as the potential pitfalls that face dramas on their journey from 'German page to English stage'.

FORM, STRUCTURE, AND POETRY IN THE VARIED PLAYS OF WERNER SCHWAB

JULIAN PREECE

When Werner Schwab was found dead, slumped in an armchair after another excessive drinking spree, on New Year's Day 1994, he was thirty–five years old and had been the undisputed star of the German–speaking stage for barely two years. He had won several of the most prestigious prizes in those two years, and theatres competed for the rights to première his latest works, which seemed to flow from his pen with miraculous ease. While it can hardly be claimed that he lacked recognition in his lifetime (his breakthrough had been quick and painless, effortless even, once he had turned his hand to writing), theatre critics and audiences alike were understandably unsure how to assess his achievement at the time of his death. His bizarre manipulation of the German language, which often went unappreciated because of its originality, his calculated dramatic extravaganza (the performance or 'actionist' element in his plays), and his carefully crafted public persona all seemed to many quite possibly fraudulent. Those who called the value of his work into question implied that his fame rested on little more than calculated self–presentation and a tried and tested formula of staged sex and taboo–breaking. As there was always so much 'hype' associated with Schwab, many felt that he would disappear from public view, like the fading rock star he was said to resemble, once the media had lost interest. Peter Iden stated boldly in his obituary for the *Frankfurter Rundschau* that in three years' time we would have forgotten all about him.[1] Schwab's biographer, Helmut Schödel, explains that this media image was indeed part of a carefully staged act, but that it formed part of a strategy of survival once he found himself catapulted into the limelight of TV screen and press interviews:

> Schwab erfand sich ein Double, das zu diesem Alptraum paßte. Er modellierte die dunklen Seiten seiner Person heraus und verkaufte den Schatten als den Dichter Werner Schwab. Mit weit ausholenden Schritten, Fliegerstiefeln, wehendem Trenchcoat und blonder Haarsträhne eroberte ein böser Großstadtcowboy unsere befriedete Theaterlandschaft. Das war, was er selber das *Projekt Schwab* nannte

---

[1]Quoted by Franz Wille, 'Das wirkliche Vorspiel für die weichgekochte Liebe: das Sterben', *Theater heute*, May 1995, pp.13–17.

[...]. Wie ein Sid Vicious der Literatur sollte Schwab wirken, vom Himmel gefallen wie ein Meteor, nur um einzuschlagen.[2]

Schödel clears up a number of misconceptions regarding both the man and the playwright: he reveals that Schwab's assertion that his father had been employed by the Nazi 'Lebensborn' project, as an Ayran 'stud' to produce genetically pure members of the Master Race, was pure fabrication;[3] and that his dismissive attitude to the theatre, particularly his claim that he had hardly ever been to see a play, concealed a knowledge of twentieth–century dramatic tradition as profound and dynamic as that of any of his contemporaries.

Iden's prediction has already been disproved, and interest in Schwab has shown no signs of abating: the remaining unperformed plays, no fewer than six in January 1994, duly received their premières; the third volume of plays appeared in late 1994, finally supplemented by *DER REIZENDE REIGEN nach dem Reigen des REIZENDEN HERRN ARTHUR SCHNITZLER* eighteen months later; Schödel published his biography in October 1995; academic articles have begun to appear on both sides of the Atlantic (there are surely more to follow); and the 'Nachlaß' established in Graz has begun to catalogue his papers.[4]

Of these events Schödel's thoroughly researched book is the most significant since it makes many convincing links between life and work and endeavours to present the man behind the mask. Schwab emerges as a self–taught intellectual and individualist artist whose own profoundly unhappy life, an impoverished, fatherless childhood followed by a failed marriage and a decade spent on the breadline in deepest Styria, provided him with his dramatic material. Future critics will probably take issue with Schödel's autobiographical interpretation of the plays (he turns up numerous real–life models for the dramatic characters), but it will be harder for them to deny that Schwab's themes are rooted in social reality.

---

[2]Helmut Schödel, *Seele brennt. Der Dichter Werner Schwab*, Vienna: 1995, pp.121–22.

[3]His former wife, Ingeborg Orthofer, explains the psychological causes of this invention: 'Der Werner hat seinen Vater zweimal im Leben gesehen und von seinem Tod aus der Zeitung gelesen. Das war ein massives Problem für ihn. Und wie immer, wenn etwas schrecklich war, hat er es noch schrecklicher gemacht, bis es erträglich wurde. Irgendwas mußte er ja machen mit seinem Schmerz' (Schödel, ibid., p.31).

[4]The plays are published in three volumes: *Fäkaliendramen* (1991); *Königskomödien* (1992); and *Dramen. Band III* (1994). All by Droschl, Graz/Vienna. Abbreviated references (F.D., K.K., and D.B.) are made after each quotation in brackets, followed by the page number.

Schwab was born into the lowest social class in post–war Austria to a single mother obliged to leave him unattended in a basement flat while she worked as a 'Putzfrau und Hausmeisterin'. Drawings in the 'Nachlaß' testify to this scarring experience. As a child Schwab ran out of control, found an early taste for alcohol, screaming drunkenly in a forest while staying with his aunt, or running his head against a wall until it bled. Schödel interprets his actions as a plea for attention from inadequate carers: 'Ein Junge, noch ein Kind, säuft im Mostkeller der Tante, macht zu hause die Schnapsflasche leer, torkelt schreiend durch die Wälder und wird trotzdem nicht wahrgenommen.'⁵ At the same time he had access to books through a certain Professor Simchen whom a second aunt had married, which meant that her young nephew could move between the world of the basement where he lived and the Bel Étage of Simchen's apartment. These class relations within a single house are reproduced exactly in his most famous play, *VOLKSVERNICHTUNG ODER MEINE LEBER IST SINNLOS*.

Schwab's reading in adult years displays some of the eclecticism of the autodidact, but places him nonetheless in the mainstream of the twentieth–century Avant–garde in its particular Austrian variation. Schödel mentions Fritz Mauthner, *Beiträge zu einer Kritik der Sprache*, and Elias Canetti, *Masse und Macht*, Thomas Bernhard and Oswald Wiener, Pasolini and Beckett: 'Schwabs Bibel aber, das war Elena Kapraliks Artaud–Biographie: *Antonin Artaud. Leben und Werk des Schauspielers, Dichters und Regisseurs*.'⁶ The biography also challenges us to confront the themes which emerge in his plays: the social and racist vindictiveness of repressed provincial life (it is no coincidence that characters by the name of Haider⁷ feature in two plays); the sadistic depravity that can pervade personal and family relations and destroy lives before they have properly begun through sexual abuse or other forms of violence; and the impossibility of achieving the basic prerequisites of social or domestic happiness despite profound yearning for the simplest blessings of life. The ambition expressed by 'der junge Mann' in *PORNOGEOGRAPHIE* is the ideal of many of Schwab's characters; 'Ich will heiraten. Ich will ein Einfamilienhaus absondern und einen Garten voll leibeigener Kinder sekretieren. Ich will überhaupt nicht verloren sein' (D.B., 140). His chances of fulfilling this most ordinary of dreams are effectively non–existent. The play ends with an exchange between two male characters over the corpse of the ritually

---

⁵Op. cit., p.23.
⁶Op. cit., p.15.
⁷The name of the leader of Austria's increasingly neo–Nazi liberal party (FPÖ) is Jörg Haider.

murdered 'junge Frau', which spells out, if it still needs spelling out, the sense of the title:

> Der ältere Herr: Man könnte ja auch geschlechtlich verkehren mit der Leiche.
> Sowas bringt Glück, wie man bei uns zuhause sagt.
> Der junge Mann: Wo sind Sie denn zuhause?
> Der ältere Herr: Überall (D.B., 195–96).

Utter alienation and an inability to overcome it are expressed by numerous other figures, and the causes are at least implicitly social.[8] *ESKALATION ORDINÄR* and *ANTIKLIMAX* in particular, both published in the third volume, mark a possible turn to social exploitation. Helmut Brennwert and Mariedl belong in the dramatic pantheon of the downtrodden.

Contrary to the view expressed by Iden and other critics, Schwab deserves to be taken seriously as a dramatist for the originality of his dramatic and linguistic depiction of this modernist theme. Schwab's plays evince, too, an astounding variety of dramatic styles. A brief survey of elements of form, structure, and genre will also help place him in the modern dramatic tradition.

It is striking that three of his later plays, *REIZENDE REIGEN*, *TROILUSWAHN UND CRESSIDATHEATER*, and *FAUST: MEIN BRUSTKORB: MEIN HELM*, are based on canonical texts, which, if his critics and detractors who called his dramas 'refuse' ('Wortmüll' was a very popular epithet) will allow nothing else, demonstrate a precise knowledge of the originals. These three re–workings of Shakespeare, Schnitzler, and Goethe establish Schwab very much as a man of the theatre, fascinated by

---

[8]There is already a tendency in writing on Schwab to de–politicise the social content of his work because he fails to slot into the critical 'Volksstück' tradition. While he is clearly not a moralist with a message and there is no ideological programme in his critique of class antagonism, it does not necessarily follow that class exploitation is a redundant factor. Stephan Zimmermann thinks so: 'Was Schwab macht, ist also kaum mit Sozialkritik zu verwechseln. Wenn Michael Merschmeier (*Theater heute*, Heft 3, 1991, S.46) Schwab in die Tradition von Horváth und Kroetz stellt, greift das zu kurz. Wenn Schwab "von Geburt an Verdammte" zeigt, dann geht es eben nicht um Verletzungen, "die eine proletarische oder kleinbürgerliche Welt" schlägt. Schwab behandelt nicht die Probleme einer Schicht, sondern etwas, das er für allgemein menschlich hält'. 'Werner Schwab', *Kritisches Lexikon zur deutschsprachigen Gegenwartsliteratur.* See also Hannelore Schlaffer, who argues, quite breathtakingly, that his settings are 'sozial ortlos', 'Die Wörter des grotesken Körpers. Der Dramatiker Werner Schwab', *Merkur* Heft 3, 1994, pp.265–71; and Jutta Landa, whose main point is in effect that Schwab fails to carry on the work of Peter Turrini and Wolfgang Bauer, "Königskomödien" oder 'Fäkaliendramen'? Zu den Theaterstücken von Werner Schwab', *Modern Austrian Literature* 26 (1993), pp.215–229.

its workings and manifestations as well as its past. His adaptation of Schnitzler is the most important of these because it is so close to its model: Schwab updates the *succès de scandale* for the current *fin de siècle*. His figures are now so detached from their sexuality that they remove plastic pudenda to perform the sexual act. Their desires, like their sexual organs, are entirely autonomous of their personalities which are nonetheless in thrall to them.

Up to now the possibly finer points of composition were not at the centre of anyone's critical attention: it was the spectacle, the apparently obligatory *tour de force* of outrageous behaviour, invariably involving liberal spillage of bodily fluids, or, failing those, mustard or animal innards, that drew applause or criticism, or simply bafflement. These dumb sequences of violent action, the 'performance' element, seemed to be more or less unmotivated, inserted gratuitously into the action which has hitherto consisted exclusively of dialogue. It was as if in grotesque distortion they took over the role of the classical intermezzo, though the debris they generated remained either on stage or plastered to the actors' clothes. Whatever else they achieved, these scenes and the resultant slimy mess provoked comment and soon came to define the Schwab style. It is highly significant that all these fluid substances are organic in one way or another and are thus related closely to the textual theme: either food (mustard and 'Schmalz', a lard–like substance), which is about to pass into the body, or liquids the body produces or contains, especially blood.[9] Schwab never worked with dry substances such as sand, for instance. His other defining feature was, of course, his language, which was linked to the first because of the frequent discussion of bodily functions, which often served as a source of imagery and metaphor. There are, however, as many subtle variations in his characters' speech and use of language as there is variety in Schwab's approach to form and genre.[10] Each play, for instance, has its own distinct core of imagery and vocabulary which singles it out as an independent aesthetic entity.

While Schwab's unusual use of language unifies all his work and immediately demands attention, what has often escaped notice is that his plays are dramatic poems in the tradition of verse drama, centring on a

---

[9]Here Schwab is deploying some of the staples of the 'Actions' of Hermann Nitsch, which are discussed by Wilson–Bokowiec in Chapter Seven of the present volume.

[10]For an analysis of his language, see Julian Preece, 'The Uses of Language in the Dramas of Werner Schwab: Towards a Definition of "das Schwabische"', in Arthur Williams, Stuart Parkes, and Julian Preece (eds.), *Contemporary German Writers, their Aesthetics and their Language*, Bern/Berlin/Frankfurt/New York/Paris/Vienna: 1996, pp.267–82.

particular circumscribed field of imagery and vocabulary. The oddity of the 'Schwabisch' recedes if one lets the poetry of his language speak for itself. The quality of the poetry in turn depends on what is happening on stage and consequently his most expressive language is to be found in those plays where his suicidal pessimism is expressed comically and where his more abstract concerns collide head–on with social reality. This is far less the case when he concentrates on art (*HOCHSCHWAB, ENDLICH TOT ENDLICH KEINE LUFT MEHR, TROILUSWAHN UND CRESSIDATHEATER, DER HIMMEL MEIN LIEB MEINE STERBENDE BEUTE*, for example). In these and other instances his abstract idea is explained rather than demonstrated. Two plays, however, *ÜBERGEWICHT, unwichtig: UNFORM* and *ANTIKLIMAX*, the first an uproarious cannibalistic comedy, the second a study of the destruction of an individual by family and social predators, reveal his poetic talent at his height.

The plot of *ÜBERGEWICHT, unwichtig: UNFORM* is straight–forward to re–tell. Two exquisitely dressed, fabulously rich Yuppies ('das schöne Paar') stray into a forlorn 'Prolo–Kneipe' visited each evening by the same group of depraved and desperately unfulfilled regulars. Schwab recreates the social setting with an accuracy which can only have been born of observation. There are working–class drinking pubs like this all over the German–speaking world, strictly off–limits to outsiders: Schwab mildly exaggerates the language and behaviour. The social tension mounts all through the first act during which 'das schöne Paar' stare into each other's eyes with no regard to their surroundings save to produce 'eine hohe Banknote' (F.D., 78) when asked for money for the jukebox, until in a frenzy of aggression they are declared to be unworthy of life and are attacked, dismembered, and eaten by the others. In the second act their attackers reflect rather absent–mindedly on their deed before the third and final act takes us back to the moment their victims entered the locale where they are treated as welcome guests. Schödel remarks that 'Eskalation' is Schwab's most important dramatic principle and 'aus' is his most significant stage direction:

> Alles beginnt wie ein Kleinbürgeralltag. Dann eskaliert es. Dann ist es aus. Dann beginnt alles wieder von vorn. Manchmal kommen Alltag und Eskalation auch in zwei Schüben. Erst dann beginnt alles wieder von vorn. Der Anfang ist immer das Nachspiel einer Eskalation.[11]

ÜBERGEWICHT, unwichtig: UNFORM is a simply but very tightly constructed play: each act confronts the same characters with a radically

---

[11]Schödel, op. cit. p.108.

different situation and forces audiences to reflect differently on the action that has preceded it. The crime of unpremeditated killing and ritualistic, eroticised cannibalism is of course at its centre. This crime has two overlapping resonances: one is political, the other religious. These wholly marginalised citizens are linked by their deed with post–war Austria and its rulers — and indeed with the rest of the contemporary Western world. One of them makes this connection, remarking that 'Das Tote ist jetzt am Leben und regiert die Luft wie ein ganzes Land sich regieren muß' (F.D., 96). She indicates that there is nothing remotely unusual in their actions because society at large is founded on similar collective blood–guilt. This was precisely the sort of point 'performance' theatre often sought to make by provoking an outraged reaction from the audience: the mass murder of unfit life had become an everyday, officially sponsored occurrence in the recent past, and the type of people who had committed these deeds were likely to be those now sitting in the audience denouncing the on–stage actions. As his 'Lebensborn' fantasy illustrates, the Third Reich was still very much a part of everyday reality for Schwab — allusions to it and to everyday Austrian participation in National Socialism are legion in his work. Act II ends with an apocalyptic vision of steppe landscape, an Eastern Front emptied of people who, through some process of transmogrification, have become natural artefacts, their individuality melted into the environment. This dystopia is wholly depopulated:

> Es ist freilich eine schöne Landschaft mit Kanten an der richtigen Stelle, mit Vertiefungen, die nicht an offene Gräber erinnern, und mit sanften Erhebungen, die keine Grabhügel in den Menschen wachrufen. Es ist ein von den Menschen befreites Land, es ist ein ausgestorbener Landstrich ohne Leichen (F.D., 105).

It is typical that this image is expressed through negation: life is an absence of death; peace an absence of war; a beautiful landscape shows no signs of mass graves.

The poetic meaning of the play begins to emerge if we focus on the groups of recurring key words which dominate the exchanges: 'Brot' and 'Wurst', which are used antithetically; 'Familie', 'Kinder', 'Menschheit', 'Gemeinschaft', 'Verantwortung'; 'Vernunft' and 'Gewissen'. The middle set are largely redundant, since none of the couples has children and the only community is that forged by their dreadful deed. Penetrative sex is generally anally centred and is never reproductive in Schwab's world: like Jürgen, Schweindi is impotent and his wife's repeated desire for children will remain unfulfilled. Characters in other works find fulfilment in masturbation, particularly 'Mariedls Bruder' in *ANTIKLIMAX*, signalling their social and sexual autism. Violence and domestic fighting determine the natural order of things; the clubbing of the weaker by the stronger, the female by the male. Family units are predicated upon violence born of frustration. Yet there exists a hope for a better life ('Ich gehe mit mir weg, anderswo ist es der bessere Ort', says Hasi, F.D., 117) and a realisation that only people cause other people's misery through rampant individualism ('Kein Mensch ist einem Menschen einen Menschen wert', ibid.). Hasi's account of their plight and her dream of something better degenerate into inarticulacy, which is the experience of all Schwab's characters when they fumble for an all–embracing meaning. Were she able to formulate her partially worked–out thoughts, she would give her life some shape and sense. Schwab's characters are only allowed that privilege in death. At the beginning of her speech she demolishes the meanings which have accrued to the word 'Brot' by associating it with sexuality, her miserable sex life in marriage, 'mein Brotelend' (F.D., 116), and her memories of childhood sexual abuse by her father, 'das riesige Menschenbrot' (F.D., 117): 'Brot ist der Täglichkeitskampf' (F.D., 116) rather than the symbol of redemption and loving sacrifice. 'Brot' is the most important word because it links the text to the play's title. It is no coincidence that the exclusion of 'das schöne Paar' from the community is justified by reference to their alleged denigration of the communal activity of breaking bread. Moments before the attack begins Schweindi announces:

> Das sind niederträchtige Menschen und keine Staatsbürger, das sind Kriegsverbrecher, die höchstwahrscheinlich die Ansicht vertreten, daß Brot ein Scheißdreck ist, daß Brot ein Nichts ist, daß unsereins ein Nichts ist (F.D., 83).

The sub–title, 'ein europäisches Abendmahl', endows the eating of bread with sacral significance and links it symbolically with cannibalism. The collective murder and cannibalism are thus both a reflection on Nazi genocide and a perverted religious ritual. In the first act, where meanings are introduced along with the characters, Jürgen, the teacher and would–be representative of the Enlightenment values which fail so utterly, muses on the cultural bonding engendered by that most Germanic item of food, 'Wurst':

> Man stelle sich das einmal vor das geistige Auge: Mehl, Blutplasma, Speck, Geschmacksverstärker, Phosphate etcetera; keinerlei lebensnotwendige Vitamine. Aber muß der Symbolwert so einer Wurst sich rechnen lassen können. Das Wurstel als Metapher für eine kulturelle Solidarität, wissen Sie, als billiger, massenhafter Zugang zum tierischen Eiweiß (F.D., 65).

By association all symbolic spiritual significance is stripped away from bread, too. There are no higher values in Schwab's world, no ideals, no spirituality, no unmotivated acts of kindness or solidarity, only urges and repressed urges. The dumb 'performance' sequences enact this grim vision of humanity just as the convoluted linguistic excesses, which threaten to smother all life out of the characters, express it.

The other strand of word–imagery is carried principally by the part–time teacher Jürgen, 'unsere Intelligenzbestie' (F.D., 110), as Schweindi introduces him, and centres on the Enlightenment, by which Schwab means civilised values, the rule of law, the curbing of destructive instincts through education and reasoned argument; in short all those things a democratic society is supposed to embody. Yet when Schweindi speaks of 'der Endsieg der menschlichen Vernunft' (F.D., 64), the unintentional oxymoron immediately reveals the unsound foundations of these Enlightenment values. At the moment of crisis they are cast aside as primitive instinct and bloodlust take their place: 'dieses wunderschöne Tötenmüssen, dieses immer wieder aufs neue alte Maulstopfen der Vernunft durch die Lust am Blut' (F.D., 86). Discussion of these ideas takes up most of the first two acts; animal appetites hold full sway, which is demonstrated by a combination of language and action.

In *ANTIKLIMAX* humanity is stripped bare and reduced to its animal state. The language revolves around the body, the substance and origin of our animal nature, and the key words are consequently 'Fleisch', 'Blut', and the other 'Flüssigkeiten' which the body produces. Human beings are no more than their bodily functions, as Mariedl identifies: 'Wasser abschlagen, Blut abschlagen und Milch abschlagen' (D.B., 288), where 'Milch' is more likely to be a synonym for semen. Now it is 'Schmalz' which unifies the activity, which Mariedl's mother smears on the sideboard, then eats, before applying the substance liberally between Mariedl's sore legs and her 'menschenvereinigungsausscheidungsorgan' (D.B., 300). That sexual gratification is dependent on the same parts of the body as those which expel bodily waste is never lost on Schwab. We are made of flesh ('Fleisch') and live off meat (also 'Fleisch'). Our orifices are our openings to, and interface with, the world; the 'Schmalz' thus links eating with sex, with excretion, and us with material objects. Mariedl, who has been regularly abused by her father, is the scapegoat for all the family's ills. When her mother suggests ridding themselves of her, she makes the obvious proposal:

> Wir müßten sie eben herrlich unauffällig umbringen, die schlecht gewachsene Mariedl, töten, braten, und aus dem Kopffleisch und den Innereien eine ewige Dauerwurst, das ginge schon irgendwie (D.B., 299).

When the police inspector informs this most dysfunctional family that they are causing a public nuisance, he does so by using the same terms, turning metaphorical speech into a literal statement, like so many of Schwab's figures:

> Unverhohlene Randale im Herzen eines ruhigen Zinshauses, und Dreckschweine sollen sie auch noch sein ... unisono.
> [...]
> Ihre privatistischen Flüssigkeiten quellen angeblich aus der blutigen Türritze hervor. Ihr ethnisch ungesäuberter Schleim soll bisweilen schon an die öffentliche Sicherheitsstraße gekrochen sein, vorbei an einem von Ihnen verursachten Exkrementalismus im Treppenhaus. Nun? (D.B., 289).

The body is the central feature in Schwab's work, both linguistically and theatrically.

A brief glance at his use of dramatic form and structure will show how, in his better plays, the poetic fields of imagery which unify the disparate dramatic elements are supplemented by his manipulation of dramatic conventions, in turn dependant on generic expectations. The first two volumes, *Fäkaliendramen* and *Königskomödien*, or 'Klomödien' as he sometimes called them, show in their titles an awareness of genre and the social status of drama, from low to high art, from new to old, from the gutter to the court — the posthumous volume, *Dramen. Band III*, rather breaks the sequence, although that may have been the author's intention. His generic descriptions of his plays tell us something of his understanding of his art: in *Fäkaliendramen* they range from the descriptive 'drei Szenen' (*DIE PRÄSIDENTINNEN*) or 'Das Schauspiel. Vier Szenen' (*MEIN HUNDEMUND*) to 'eine Radikalkomödie' (*VOLKSVERNICHTUNG*) and the ritualistic 'ein europäisches Abendmahl' (*ÜBERGEWICHT, unwichtig: UNFORM*). In the next volume we have (in the following order) 'eine Komödie' (twice: *OFFENE FENSTER OFFENE GRUBEN*; *HOCHSCHWAB*), 'eine Variationskomödie' (*MESALLIANCE ABER WIR FICKEN UNS PRÄCHTIG* — because of the three endings), 'Selbstverfreilicht eine Komödie' (*DER HIMMEL MEIN LIEB MEINE STERBENDE BEUTE*) and, finally, 'ein Theaterzernichtungslustspiel' (*ENDLICH TOT ENDLICH KEINE LUFT MEHR*). In *Dramen Band III* he experiments with linear progression in two instances: *PORNOGEOGRAPHIE* is presented in 'sieben Gerüchten' and *ESKALATION ORDINÄR* is 'ein Schwitzkastenschwank in sieben Affekten'. Because language and spectacle both enjoy a special prominence, the conventional plot of the 'well–structured' play with its twists, turning points, unexpected entrances, peripetea, absences, and subtext takes a backseat. That does not mean, however, that Schwab neglects exposition, climax, dénouement, or surprise finale; even though he deplored definite endings because he felt closure was untrue to the tortured repetitive round of existence, his plays generally possess a beginning, a middle, and (at least one) end.

In *MESALLIANCE aber wir ficken uns prächtig*, where the first most obvious 'misalliance' is to be found in the two parts of the title, the skeletal dramatic structure is highly conventional. At the end of the first act, after most of the characters and themes have been introduced, Anna Pestalozzi, daughter to the central figures, Herr and Frau Pestalozzi, and younger sister to the terrible twins around whose birthday the play centres, Johannes and Johanna, appears quite unexpectedly for the first time with the following stage direction: 'Anna tritt auf und zieht schluchzend einen toten Hund hinter sich her. Johannes und Johanna lachen laut auf' (K.K., 142). In the second act the remaining characters, Herr and Frau Torti and Herr and Frau Haider, duly make their appearance, enriching the suburban social setting and the theme of adultery and sexual conflict. The act ends with a 'Steigerung' of the first:

> Eine riesige Schlägerei zwischen den drei Paaren beginnt, jeder gegen jeden. Johannes und Johanna betrachten amüsiert die Schlacht und feuern die Beteiligten an. Plözlich steht Anna mit einem Nylonsack auf der Bühne und holt einen Totenkopf ans Licht. Die Raufenden halten inne (K.K., 161).

The third act provides a climax, as the tables are now turned on the twins, the haughty orchestrators and observers of the adulterous quarellings, as their mother enters at the end of the brief act which has featured them alone on stage to discover them in a kneeling embrace: 'Es ist ein Inzest. Der dritte Weltkrieg brennt innen bei uns. Inzest, Inzest, Inzest. Die Fleischblumen haben ihre Blumen vertrieben' (K.K., 169). Their social and domestic status is now reversed. There then follow three possible endings, the first and the third involving violence. In the third and final ending Sepp Miok, the postman, plays the role of 'reitender Bote' and rescues the twins from a grisly fate, a parodic *deus ex machina*. The theme of this distorted 'Volksstück', stuffed with crude political apercus, where the characters present a microcosm of Austrian society, is domestic strife, the oldest theme of all in comedy. *MESALLIANCE*, 'eine Variationskomödie', is indeed a variation on this.

DIE PRÄSIDENTINNEN revolves around the number three: three characters, three scenes, three wishes. The endless flow of speech in the play belies its very tight structure; its proportions are almost classical. While the title of *VOLKSVERNICHTUNG ODER MEINE LEBER IST SINNLOS* inevitably suggests thoughts of the Holocaust (*Killing People* the proposed title for the unpublished and unperformed English translation gives an altogether different ring),[12] it is another 'Radikalkomödie', with elements of melodrama, a murder story without the mystery since the fact that Frau Grollfeuer kills everybody is the dramatic surprise. The second act in the Kovacic flat is a skit on a TV situation comedy. Again entrances and exists serve conventional dramatic purposes; the exposition of theme and character is carefully managed before the shock of the poisoning party.

After three, seven is Schwab's favourite number, traditionally loaded with as much symbolism. His linear or epic plays, *ESKALTION ORDINÄR*, *PORNOGEOGRAPHIE*, *ENDLICH TOT ENDLICH KEINE LUFT MEHR* all have seven scenes (it does not matter that they are called 'Gerüchte' or 'Affekte'), as does *OFFENE GRUBEN OFFENE FENSTER*, if one discounts the silent eighth which serves as a kind of epilogue. The linear development in each of these leads to a ritual death, suicide or murder. The fourteen scenes of *ANTIKLIMAX* are constructed according to simple principles: first silence (one); then Mariedl's soliloquy (two and three); entrance of brother (four); brother and father (five); brother, father, and mother (six and seven). After the family come the representatives of the state in the shape of the doctor (eight), the police inspector (nine), the pastor (ten), who duly depart to leave the family once more alone with one another. As there is no community, no solidarity of feeling, there is dramatic suspense in the lines which announce the entrance of the non–family members:

> Mariedls Bruder: Das müssen die Menschen sein.
> Mariedls Mutter: Das sind die Menschen.
> Mariedl: Die Menschen kommen (D.B., 284f.).

In *ESKALATION ORDINÄR* Schwab draws attention to the episodic, picaresque nature of Helmut Brennwert's story by the subtitle of 'Schwitzkastenschwank'; the six different roles played by Nieroster in the first six scenes, 'Wurstbudenbesitzer, Polizist, Cafetier, Parkwächter, Showmaster, Zeitungskioskinhaber (kurz: das öffentliche Auge)' have clear Brechtian overtones. At the end of scene two, after Brennwert, who in the very final sequence lives up to his name by pouring a flammable substance all over himself and setting himself alight, has been maltreated in the most abominable manner, verbally and physically abused for the sin of

---

[12]Translated by Michael Robinson for the National Theatre in 1993. Like all Schwab's plays this awaits an English performance.

unemployment, there is something reminiscent of *Woyzeck* in his brief speech:

> Es ist schon alles richtig in der Ordnung eingerostet. Der Morgen dämmert doppelschwarz herauf, zerstört den zuckerfreien Himmel und stürzt sich als Aschenregen auf die sichtbare Welt. Der Abend friert den hochzerfetzten Morgen ein und legt ihn eine Weile lahm. Die Welt hat mir umfangreich bewiesen, daß sie einen Fehler aufgebrochen hat, als sie mich todesäugig in die Sparkasse geboren hat (D.B., 218).

These are the horizons of the Schwab cosmos. It is remarkable that an author who is said not to have cared about politics or society should have written such a parable of exploitation, which was always one of his principal subjects. Moreover the ending, which is final in this case, as it is in his other linear plays, is the dramatically consistent consequence of the action.

Approached in this way, Schwab becomes a master of styles and genres, an adept technician of plot and structure. The impression of sameness is engendered merely by his language; here the variations are subtle. His rootedness in the theatre is explicit, too, in the manner that all his plays are, in one way or another, highly self–conscious works of art, which draw attention constantly to their own artifice and artificiality; to their status as performances. There is nothing essentially new or 'postmodern' about this. Of course, the very first alienating feature, which tells us this is not real life, is Schwab's language which destroys from the outset any semblance of naturalism. For Schwab, speech is always performance, simply because it exceeds the functions of dialogue and communication, which he finds in themselves so fraught and problematic. The alternate or multiple endings stress, too, that everything is 'a play within a play'. At the end of *Die Präsidentinnen*, or rather at the end of the second end, since at the end of the first end Erna and Grete had murdered Mariedl, play and world, players and spectators merge:

> Vorhang: und geht wieder hoch. Drei hübsche junge Frauen agieren auf der Bühne und spielen das Stück *Die Präsidentinnen* bösartig, übertrieben und kreischend. Das dargestellte Publikum lacht und gibt Szenenapplaus.
>
> Erna, Grete und Mariedl, die sich im Publikum befinden, stehen bald auf und wollen den Saal verlassen, was sich schwierig gestaltet, weil sie in der Mitte einer Reihe sizten. Erna gelingt der Ausbruch zuerst und sie rüttelt an einer Saaltür, die verschlossen ist. Grete findet auch keine offene Tür. Erst Mariedl wird fündig. Sie stürzt zu Grete und zerrt sie zur offenen Tür. Grete macht sich los, stürzt zu Erna und zerrt sie zur offenen Tür. Alle drei verschwinden. Auf der Bühne wird noch eine geraume Zeit *Die Präsidentinnen* gespielt. (aus) (F.D., 58).

From a linguistic point of view what is striking in the stage directions is their precision and conciseness.

Schwab became notorious for quantities of slimy substances on stage, for simulated masturbation and sexual intercourse, as well as ritual murder. It is true that through his choice of explicit subject matter allied to his apparently obscene language he sets out to offend and confront everyday notions of good taste, depicting scenes of orgiastic cannibalism and exhibitionism, human sacrifice, self–immolation, death after sexual excitement, mutual food smearing, bathing in blood and so forth. This type of theatricality can be subsumed under the heading of 'performance'. A purist might argue that a decent dramatist has no need to be so physically explicit, that there is more horror and a greater range of emotion in Racine, say, who relied exclusively on language.[13]

In *PORNOGEOGRAPHIE* death, entwined fatally with desire, weighs heavily on the text; sex, in the shape of the frustrated relationship between the impotent 'Hausbesitzer' and his wife, fails to fulfil its functions. Sex equals sterility which leads to violence; the 'Hausbesitzer's impotence is a foretaste of death. His wife remembers one occasion when he almost managed an arousal:

> Am einunddreißigsten Dezember des vorigen Jahres hat es geschneit und zugleich hat die Sonne ihren Senf hinzugefügt, und der Purzel wäre beinahe einer Erektion anheimgefallen. Erinnerst du dich, Purzel? (D.B., 174).

The significance of the New Year would be that it symbolises new life, new hope, a new beginning, a secular Easter. In the play's closing sequence, 'die junge Frau', who has been the object of the pornographic films and who is about to be ritually executed on stage by the 'Hausbesitzer' uses a negated Easter motif in her valedictory words (her 'letzte verwerfliche Meldung'). Imagery and action, speech and gesture go together; the murder by strangulation of 'die junge Frau', which is put on as part of the 'Grundfilm aller Filme' (D.B., 194), as if it were a circus act or feat of strength, is dramatically and thematically necessary; everything leading up to it has prepared us for it. Ritual murder provides the climax to *DIE PRÄSIDENTINNEN*, *ÜBERGEWICHT*, *unwichtig: UNFORM*,

---

[13]Despite an apparent determination to *épater les bourgeois* in time–honoured fashion, Schwab singularly failed to do so, as Stephan Zimmermann notes: 'In den meisten Kritiken, die zu Aufführungen seiner Stücke erschienen sind, sah man ihn vor allem als Bürgerschreck, der mit Fäkalien, Sex und Kannibalismus nur provozieren will, ohne daß ihm das noch recht gelingt: 'Offenbar haben auch die Grazer begriffen, daß sich nur noch Spießer über einen Spießerschänder wie Schwab ereifern'', schrieb *Der Spiegel* 1992'. The answer must be that the shock–effect was not his primary purpose.

HOCHSCHWAB, VOLKSVERNICHTUNG, MESALLIANCE, and *ENDLICH TOT ENDLICH KEINE LUFT MEHR.* For Schwab all movement is downwards towards death.

The dumb sequences enacting these dramatic insights are remarkable first of all for the precision of the theatre directions. Because there is no speech, no 'Schwabisch' of any sort being spoken, it is clear that something very different from dialogue is being performed. In *ÜBERGEWICHT, unwichtig: UNFORM* something quite separate from the rest of the play is clearly happening — the sudden absence of speech signals a leap in a new direction.

(Karli tritt hinzu und gibt der schönen Frau eine Ohrfeige. Die Wirtin entreißt Schweindi die fremde Hand und führt sie sich zwischen die Beine. Hasi pirscht sich heran, gibt im Vorbeigehen dem schönen Mann eine Ohrfeige und führt sich Karlis Hand zwischen die Beine. Jürgen kommt hinzu, kniet sich vor die agierende Menschengruppe nieder und bettelt: bitte nicht, bitte nicht. Herta steht und schaut kühl, sie erzeugt mittels eines Kaugummis eine große rote Blase, die sie schließlich über ihrem Gesicht zerplatzen läßt. Man reißt das schöne Paar auf den Boden nieder und die Kleider vom Leib.

Karli macht Anstalten, die schöne junge Frau zu vergewaltigen. Schweindi zieht dem schönen jungen Mann glucksend die Hosen aus. Die Wirtin zieht ihre Kleiderschürze hoch und setzt sich auf das Gesicht des schönen Mannes. Hasi wartet hinter Schweindi auf dessen Erektion, um sie für sich ausnützen zu können. Das schöne Paar ist jetzt völlig unter den zugreifenden Leibern begraben. Schließlich spritzt Blut). Ende des ersten Aktes (F.D., 84f.).

This is the dramatic turning point of the play, the 'Abendmahl' of the title. Action here speaks louder than words; in moments of crisis Schwab's otherwise loquacious characters renounce speech and act out repressed urges. Up to this point the violence and crudity have been purely linguistic; for each action now, a number of metaphors, allusions, or statements can be found from earlier in the text. The actions described in the stage directions may appear quite random or interchangeable. However, an audience which has just witnessed the rest of the first act will recognise how in character all the actions of the various figures are. Schwab is simply making his words flesh, demonstrating graphically and physically the sense of his text.

The dramatic effect of the 'performance' intermezzo is arguably greatest in *ÜBERGEWICHT, unwichtig: UNFORM.* The 'beautiful couple', have sat aloof from the other socially disadvantaged inhabitants of this archetypal working–class pub, totally, narcissistically absorbed with one another. Their silent, motionless presence right through the first act, during which they are all but ignored by the other characters, in fact broods over every word that is spoken and every gesture that is enacted. The tension finally breaks with the eruption of violence. This sequence is a visual representation of a dramatic theme. When 'die Frau des Regisseurs' in *PORNOGEOGRAPHIE* first has to lick off soup from the corpse of a dog and then eat the dog her actions also reinforce the verbal imagery of that play.

More significantly from a theatrical point of view, each of these sequences is essential for the dramatic progression of the action; they may not in themselves be what one expects in conventional drama but dramatically the purpose they serve is conventional. If Schwab has achieved something new in this respect it is his incorporation of 'performance' set–pieces into a dramatic structure.

DIE ORDNUNG DER UNORDNUNG:
EIN VERSUCH ÜBER CANETTI, BAUER UND SCHWAB

MIKE ROGERS

In erster Linie konzentriere ich mich auf drei Werke: Canettis *Hochzeit*, Bauers *Magic Afternoon* und Schwabs *Die Präsidentinnen*. Es geht mir dabei nicht darum, eine chronologische Entwicklung dar– oder festzustellen, sondern eher darum, die Werke miteinander zu vergleichen, um zu einigen allgemeinen Schlüssen über die dramatische Darstellung der Unordnung innerhalb des kleinbürgerlichen Milieus österreichischer Prägung zu kommen.

Meine Wahl von Schwab erklärt sich von selbst, sowie die Wahl von Bauer aus der vorhergehenden Theatergeneration als Vergleichsgegenstand. Bei Canetti muß natürlich eingeräumt werden, daß seine Stücke erst in den letzten fünfundzwanzig Jahren überhaupt und dann spärlich aufgeführt worden sind, als theaterpraktische Erprobung der Kassenwirkung eines Nobelpreises auf das Stammpublikum, so daß das vorpeymannsche Burgtheater sich zu der Uraufführung von *Komödie der Eitelkeit* aufraffte. Immerhin bietet ein Stück wie *Hochzeit* interessante Vergleichs–möglichkeiten.

Kurze Inhaltsangabe: in einem dem Dialekte nach in Wien gelegenen Mietshaus wird eine Hochzeit gefeiert, und zwar die Hochzeit von der Tochter des Bauherrn des Hauses. Eine Hochzeit, als formelle Bestätigung der bestehenden gesellschaftlichen Ordnung, als öffentliche Verkündung der Rechtskräftigkeit einer sexuellen Liaison und der Erbberechtigung der daraus entsprießenden Kinder, dürfte der Verherrlichung der bürgerlichen Verhältnisse dienen, indem sie die geschlechtlichen Triebe durch vertragsmäßig aufgelegte Pflichten bändigt oder wenigstens einengt und diese womöglich sonst wilden und zerstörerischen Energien der Erhaltung und Vermehrung des Besitzes und, als Sammelbecken des Besitzes, der Familie, zuführt.

Auf dieser Hochzeit aber werden sexuelle Begierden unverblümt besprochen und befriedigt. Es ist, als würden die Masken nicht bloß gelüftet, sondern einfach weggeworfen. Wenn Schnitzler sogar in *Reigen* immer noch um den heißen Brei herumgeht, sitzen wir in *Hochzeit* mitten im brodelnden Topf. Die sexuellen Wünsche, die ohne Scheu geäußert werden, werden auch ohne Schock gehört und meistens ohne Zögern erhört, abgesehen von der üblichen Komplikation, daß A B will, während B C will, usw. Die angestrebten Liaisons widersprechen nicht nur allen ehelichen Pflichten, sondern auch den altersmäßigen Erwartungen, z.B. eine 14jährige mit einem 79jährigen.

Kein Wunder also, daß das ganze Haus wortwörtlich zusammenstürzt, in einer Apokalypse, die schon im Vorspiel angekündigt wurde. Handelt der Hauptteil des Stückes vom Eros, so muß Thanatos naturgemäß im Vorspiel seine Aufwartung machen. Es liegen im Sterben nämlich nicht nur die Hausbesitzerin, deren eine Enkelin, die Toni, sie ständig besucht, um sich das Erbe zu sichern, sondern auch die Frau des Hausmeisters, über die ihr Mann ständig die Bibel vorliest, und zwar die Stelle, in der der gefangene und geblendete Simson das Haus der Philister niederreißt. Das letzte Wort im Stück hat der Papagei der Hausbesitzerin, mit dem schon im Vorspiel wiederholt vorkommenden Schrei 'Haus. Haus. Haus.', was die zentrale Rolle des Besitzes neben dem Geschlechtstrieb unterstreicht, sowie den Symbolwert des Hauses als Verkörperung der bürgerlichen Gesellschaftsstruktur.

Die bürgerliche Ordnung wird also unterminiert und zerstört, teilweise indem die vermeintlichen unterschwelligen Motivationen aufgedeckt und mit der für den bürgerlichen Konformismus typischen Selbstverständlichkeit und Selbstzufriedenheit geäußert werden, teilweise durch die symbolisch ausartende Handlung, die die ihrem Wesen nach in sich gefangene und verfangene bürgerliche Welt durch die von außen kommende und unvermittelt auftretende Apokalypse relativiert und transzendiert. Selbst im Untergang weigern sich die Bürger, etwas anderes als ihre eigene Welt anzuerkennen, aber wenigstens für das Publikum ist das einengende Gerüst des Hauses auseinandergebrochen.

Damit hat Canetti vermutlich gemeint, die zweideutige Publikumswirkung von Brechts *Dreigroschenoper* zu vermeiden, wie er sie bei der Uraufführung erlebte:

> Es war der genaueste Ausdruck dieses Berlin. Die Leute jubelten *sich* zu, das waren sie selbst und sie gefielen sich. Erst kam *ihr* Fressen, dann kam ihre Moral, besser hätte es keiner von ihnen sagen können, das nahmen sie wörtlich.[...] Gegen die süßliche Form der Wiener Operette, in der die Leute ungestört alles fanden, was sie sich wünschten, war hier eine andere, Berliner Form gesetzt, mit Härten, Schuftigkeiten und banalen Rechtfertigungen dafür, die sie sich nicht weniger, die sie sich wahrscheinlich noch mehr als jene Süßigkeiten wünschten.[1]

Durch diesen Kommentar unterstreicht Canetti das bürgerliche Element des Theaters überhaupt: die Selbstbestätigung, die im Anschauen der vermeintlichen eigenen Handlungsweise erfolgt. Der Theaterbesuch selbst kann (besonders im abonnierten deutschsprachigen Raum) als bürgerliches Ritual der kulturellen Liebedienerei aufgefaßt werden, dem am wirksamsten durch die totale Verkehrung der Voraussetzungen entgegenzuwirken ist, wie

---

[1]Elias Cannetti, *Die Fackel im Ohr*, Frankfurt/M.: 1982, S.285-6.

im Fall von Handkes *Publikumsbeschimpfung.* Canettis realistischer Ansatz mit symbolischem Ausgang läßt sich auch in diesem Sinne deuten, als bewußte Enttäuschung der Erwartungen des Publikums, für das die reale Welt mit ihren Realkanzleien und Realitäten die einzige ausschlaggebende bleibt. Mit dem gleichen Zweck persifliert auch Bauer die dramatische Form, indem er das Stück *Party for Six* im Vorzimmer einer Grazer Wohnung spielen läßt, so daß wir nur das Nebensächliche der Handlung beobachten dürfen und vom vermeintlichen Hauptsächlichen ausgeschlossen sind.[2]

Die bürgerliche Welt liefert also nicht nur bestimmte allgemein anerkannte Regeln, gegen die ihre Mitglieder im geheimen verstoßen, während sie sie in der Öffentlichkeit predigen und aufrechterhalten, sondern auch eine greifbare Struktur der Erwartungen und der Voraussetzungen, die, indem und obwohl sie angegriffen und unterminiert wird, dennoch zwangsläufig die Struktur der ihr entgegengesetzten verkehrten anti–bürgerlichen Welt bedingt und bestimmt. Auch die Unordnung wird mit einem bürgerlich anmutenden Ordnungssinn und Konsequenzdrang beschrieben und ausgekostet.

Hat Canetti in *Hochzeit* die Kehrseite der sexuellen Ordnung zuoberst gekehrt, arbeitet Bauer in *Magic Afternoon* mit dem Begriff der Ordnung der Gegenstände im Raum. Es ist vielleicht nicht zufällig, daß diese räumliche Ordnung in ihrer äußersten fast zwanghaft–neurotischen Form von zwei österreichischen Klassikern der bürgerlichen Literatur des neunzehnten Jahrhunderts besungen und beschworen wird. Ich denke hier an Grillparzers *armen Spielmann,* der durch einen Kreidestrich auf dem Boden die ärmliche aber reinliche Ordnung in seiner Hälfte des geteilten Zimmers von der Unordnung des meistens betrunkenen männlichen Bettgeherpaars in der anderen Hälfte trennen will, aber noch mehr an jene Stellen bei Stifter, wo die Ordnung als Wert an sich dargestellt wird, wo jedes Buch gleich nach der Lektüre wieder an seinen Platz im Bücherschrank zurückgestellt, die Tür des Schrankes zugesperrt, der Vorhang am Glasfenster der Schranktür, damit das Sonnenlicht dem Einband nichts anhaben könne, gezogen wird. In diesem Zusammenhang gesehen wirkt die Bücherschlacht in *Magic Afternoon* (S.26) nicht nur als ein Trick, um dramatisches Geschehen auf die Bühne zu bringen, ohne wieder auf sowas von Bürgerlichem wie eine Handlung rekurrieren zu müssen, sondern auch als ein direkter Angriff auf die bürgerliche Ordnung, die die Bücher erst dann gutheißt, wenn sie in ordentlichen, womöglich alphabetisch geordneten Reihen nebeneinander auf schöngeschnitzten Regalen stehen. Das wahllose und ziemlich zwecklose

---

[2]Wolfgang Bauer: *Magic Afternoon, Change, Party for Six,* München: 1972. Siehe in diesem Zusammenhang den Beitrag von Waine im dritten Kapitel des vorliegenden Bandes.

Auffressen des eingemachten Obstes im Stück stellt auch einen Angriff auf die bürgerlichen Ideale des Sparens und der aufgeschobenen Befriedigung dar.

Aber das Projekt, der bürgerlichen Überdeterminiertheit durch eine vollkommene Zweck– und Ziellosigkeit entrinnen zu wollen, artet in totaler Entscheidungsunfähigkeit aus und gipfelt in einem zufälligen Mord, vor dem sich Charly (bloß Zeuge, nicht Täter) auf eine wörtliche aber unpraktische und daher symbolische Weise versteckt, indem er sich in den Kasten einsperrt. Vorhang.

Diese (wie ich sie sehe) moderne Version von Schillers *Räubern* macht alles schon in den anfänglichen Regieanweisungen klar: die Personen sind 22 bis 30 Jahre alt, aber, wie wir später erfahren, haben sie noch keine richtigen Berufe, leben also von dem Geld ihrer bürgerlichen Eltern. Ort der Handlung ist 'Ein absichtlich ungeordnetes Zimmer. [...] Man kann kaum herumgehen, ohne etwas umzustoßen. Die Unordnung ist nicht genial, nicht angenehm, sie ist nervös'.

Der allgemeine Zynismus, der sich nie zu einem bürgerlich ausbeutbaren Witz aufrafft, die Atmosphäre der sexuellen Freiheit, die nie über ziemlich lieblose aber angeblich unverbindliche Beziehungen hinausgeht, das angeblich 'höhere Blödeln', das unter dem Einfluß von Haschisch zustandekommt, und zu dem Versuch führt, die Weltkugel im Klo hinunterzuspülen ('Geht net abi! Die Wölt is ewig!' lautet die Konstatierung dieser symbolischen Handlung Raimund'scher Prägung), sowie zu dem gemimten Stiergefecht, dessen Männlichkeitsritual und Vergewaltigungsdrohung Joes Tod durch Birgits Messer herbeiführen, sind nur Produkte dieser gewollten Unordnung, die als verzweifelte aber vergebliche Antwort auf die aufgezwungene Ordnung der bürgerlichen Welt zu verstehen ist.

Konzentrieren sich Canetti auf die sexuelle Unordnung und Bauer auf die physische, so wendet sich Schwab mit Vorliebe den menschlichen Ausscheidungen zu, wie aus dem Titel seines ersten Sammelbands hervorgeht: *Fäkaliendramen.*[3]

Nascimur inter faeces et urinam: das wissen wir alle. Einige Autoren, wie Swift, nehmen diese Tatsache und den naturnotwendigen Gang sowie die Erzeugnisse des menschlichen Verdauungsprozesses als guten Grund, die Menschheit zu verabscheuen, oder wenigstens als wirksames Mittel die Abscheulichkeit der Menschen darzustellen, die doch schließlich um so tierischer sind, je mehr sie sich für etwas Besseres auszugeben versuchen. Schwab richtet sich aber in erster Linie gegen das bürgerliche Nichtwahrhabenwollen der körperlichen Funktionen, diese Weigerung, sich

---

[3]Werner Schwab, *Fäkaliendramen*, Graz/Wien: (Droschl) 1991.

zu den eigenen Produkten zu bekennen. Nicht nur die Unaussprechlichen sind unaussprechlich. Es geht aber nicht nur um die bürgerliche Heuchelei und das Leugnen der bestehenden Verhältnisse. Daß er, Schwab, von diesen Dingen spricht, ist weniger eine Demaskierung des Bewußtseins, als eine regelrecht gewollte Beleidigung der bestehenden Normen und ihrer Vertreter, die von den Machtverhältnissen der Eltern–Kind–Beziehung ausgeht. Das erste, was das Kind von den Eltern lernt, ist, wie, wo, und wann man das Verlangte, das sich aber sofort in das Verpönte verwandelt, von sich zu geben hat. Die Eltern, die Älteren, die Stützen der Gesellschaft, setzen die Normen, denen sich die Natur unterjochen muß.

Aber das wäre schon eine allzu positive Deutung. Denn die Scheiße stinkt ja doch, und der freie Stuhlgang macht bei weitem nicht den freien Menschen aus. Während Schwab das Bürgertum mit Kot bewirft, weiß er doch auch um die geheime Faszination, die dieser Gegenstand ausübt, besonders weil er notwendigerweise die infantile Position bezogen hat, um gegen die Elternfiguren rebellieren zu können. Er suggeriert, daß die Älteren dieses infantile Stadium auch nicht überwunden haben, so daß sie ihre Faszination mit dem Tabu verheimlichen und auf verdeckte und verdrängte oder transferierte Weise ausleben müssen. Ich werde am Ende dieses Versuches in meiner Analyse vom Schluß der zweiten Szene der *Präsidentinnen* näher darauf eingehen. An dieser Stelle aber möchte ich die Folgen von Schwabs konsequenter Lausbubenposition im Vergleich mit Canetti und Bauer weiter ausarbeiten.

Canettis verkehrte Ordnung bleibt zwar von der normalen obwohl im Stück nicht vorhandenen bürgerlichen Ordnung abhängig, aber er gibt uns durch das biblische Zitat sowie durch die conferencierartigen (d.h. nicht charakterbedingten) Zwischenrufe von Horch, die die Apokalypse interpunktieren, 'Sehen Sie, hören Sie, was werden Sie für Ihr Liebstes tun?', unabhängige, nicht stückinterne Maßstäbe, an denen wir das Geschehen messen und deuten können. Der ironische Titel und der bewußt als abgeschieden und abgeschlossen dargestellte Schauplatz von Bauers *Magic Afternoon*, zu dem die Hälfte der Charaktere durch Anruf und Auto gebracht werden müssen, von dem zwei Drittel der noch Lebenden akustisch vernehmbar wieder abfahren, deuten auf die Existenz einer anderen theaterexternen Welt, einer Vielfalt von anderen möglichen Geistespositionen, die zwar alle für die Personen im Stück nicht oder kaum in Frage kommen, wenigstens solange sie auf der Bühne sind, aber immerhin einen Ausweg für das Publikum darstellen, dem dadurch die Möglichkeit gegeben wird, sich von den Personen des Stückes abzugrenzen. Bei Canetti und Bauer also wird die Begrenzung des theatralischen Raumes als Begrenzung der Tragweite des Angriffs auf die bürgerliche Ordnung benutzt, um dem Publikum den zur Reflexion nötigen Abstand vom Geschehen zu gewähren.

Bei Schwab aber beruht ein Großteil der Bühnenwirksamkeit gerade auf dem Absolutheitsanspruch seiner Texte, in denen das Normale mit einem leichten Achselzucken als das erst recht Unnatürliche abgetan wird. Immerhin bleiben seine Versuche, sich von der Abhängigkeit des Negativen zu emanzipieren, sehr oft im Schwulstigen des Expressionistischen stecken. Ich denke hier an die kaum variierten Wiederholungen von *Mein Hundemund*, an das 'Musikstück' in *Hochschwab* und an die Gespräche der Geschwister Johannes und Johanna in *Mesalliance aber wir ficken uns prächtig*. Das Bestreben, die Formen der normalen bürgerlichen Sprache zu vermeiden, führt zu einem absichtlichen Verzicht auf das Interessante und sich Entwickelnde, vor allem weil vor dem zynischen und alles persiflierenden Geist von Schwabs Stücken so etwas unmöglich bestehen könnte.

Dieser Geist, der alles durchschauen und vernichten will, (wohlweislich stellen Canetti und Bauer keine Ansprüche auf absolute Gültigkeit, weil die Einsichten, die ihre Werke vermitteln wollen, sonst einer allgemeinen Skepsis allen wie immer gearteten Feststellungen gegenüber zum Opfer gefallen wären) trägt auch zu dem ambivalenten Verhältnis bei, das Schwab zu seinen eigenen Erzeugnissen (oder sagen wir besser, Ausscheidungen) hat. Er stellt in zwei Stücken aus den *Königskomödien* 'Künstlergeschichten' dar, *Der Himmel mein Lieb meine sterbende Beute* und *Endlich tot endlich keine Luft mehr*. Das erste behandelt Aufstieg und Fall des Schöpfers der Schleimfiguren (unbemannt und abwaschbar), Herrmann Wurm, ('Kunstmaler, Klumpfuß, grotesk und verloren wirkend, mehr ist dazu nicht zu sagen'). Hochgepriesen und ausgebeutet, wird er von seinem Galeristen, Axel Dingo, fallengelassen, sowie von der hochstehenden Dame, Cosima Grollfeuer, die ihn nur künstlerisch interessant findet und zum Schluß ein Verhältnis mit Dingo anfängt. Aber selbst das Pathos, mit dem der verlassene Künstler sich in den Schoß seiner Mutter zurückkriecht, wird persifliert: 'Erinnerst du dich, Mama? Du mußt dich erinnern können, auch wenn du nicht dabei warst, Mama. [...] Du bist halt meine liebe gute alte Drecksau, gell, Mama?'[4]

Das zweite Stück zeigt um so eindringlicher, wie das Schockierende an neuartigen Stücken von dem Theaterbetrieb (Schauspieler, Regisseur, Bühnenbildner, Minister) einvernahmt wird, bis der Dichter selbst sich mit dem Ausspruch zurückzieht: '[...] die Mittelmäßigkeiten heiligen den unmäßigen Zweck.'[5] Aber nichts wird ernstgenommen. Mit der infantilen Lust am Niederreißen wird jede halbe Aussage persifliert oder sonstwie

---

[4]Werner Schwab, *Königskomödien*, Graz/Wien: (Droschl) 1992, S.233f.
[5]Ebenda, S.277.

entwertet. Nach dem Mephistophelischen Ausspruch, daß alles, was entsteht, wert ist, daß es zugrundegeht, wird in Schwabs Stücken vorgegangen, bis nichts mehr übrigbleibt, als der Ekel des Lebens an sich selbst, dessen dionysische zerstörerische Kraft sich partout keine beschönigende apollonische Maske vor den Mund nehmen will.

Als Theaterkenner und –könner arbeitet Schwab auch mit den gleichen Mitteln wie Canetti und Bauer, um das gutbürgerliche, gutgebaute Stück zu unterminieren. Aber er persifliert auch die Persiflierung. Am Ende von *Hochschwab* sieht sich das künstlerische Liebespaar von Pianistin und Komponisten ertappt von den gewöhnlichen Menschen. In echt melodramatischer Weise hat das Paar den Impresario zum Fenster hinausbefördert — eine gewalttätige Handlung, die der gewalttätigen Sprache der Schwab'schen Stücke entspricht. Der Mäzen (scharf auf die Pianistin) und die Sängerin (scharf auf den Komponisten — also eine echt Racine'sche Liebhaberkette) haben diese Tat beobachtet und der Preis ihres Schweigens ist eben Besitz der Angebeteten. Das mysteriöse, todesrauschende, expressionistisch–inzestuöse Verhältnis der zwei Künstler (man denke an Trakl, man denke an Johannes und Johanna in *Mesalliance*) wird zerbrochen, zugunsten der Alltagswelt, wie der Komponist das in einem Faust–Zitat ausdrückt: 'Die Welt, sie hat uns wieder.'[6]

Aber auch dieses Ende wird durch die zwei Polizisten unterminiert, die auftreten und konstatieren: 'Es war sicher Selbstmord'.[7] Der dramatischen Form wird Genüge getan, der Krimi tritt in seine Rechte, Tricks werden als Tricks entblößt. Der Infantilismus als Grundeinstellung kennt keine Grenzen, will keine Ordnung anerkennen. Das Politische wird nicht kritisiert, sondern verulkt, wenn ein Ehepaar Haider in *Mesalliance* auftritt, oder eine Putzfrau namens Haider in *Endlich tot endlich keine Luft mehr*. Würde Schwab sich ernstlich mit Politik auseinandersetzen wollen, so hieße das wenigstens einige der bürgerlichen Kategorien anerkennen, die er doch total ablehnt.[8]

Zu diesen Kategorien gehört unter anderem auch Konsequenz. Um den Schein davon zu erzeugen, läßt Schwab gleichnamige Charaktere in verschiedenen Stücken auftreten, was den Absolutheitsanspruch seiner Welt bekräftigt, obwohl die Charaktere nur oberflächlich miteinander verbunden sind und die Verbindung eigentlich zu keiner besonderen Einsicht führt, wie der oft erwähnte Fleischhauer Wottila, oder die Tatsache, daß 'Grollfeuer' in zwei Fällen als der Name einer vornehmen und arroganten Dame benutzt wird. Das hat natürlich etwas zu sagen; nur ist das, was es zu sagen hat, genauso unwichtig, wie alles andere auf dieser Welt. Die Aussage von

---

[6]Ebenda, S.118.
[7]Ebenda, S.119.
[8]Vgl. hierzu die Ausführungen von Preece im vorigen Kapitel, S.15.

diesen Stücken ist nicht einmal die, daß man keine Aussagen machen, sondern eher daß alle Aussagen — auch diese — eigentlich sinnlos sind. Auch die rebellische Geste ist nur eine Geste. Alle Kreter seien Lügner, sagte mir einst ein Kreter.

Die Kunst lebt aber eher von Vieldeutigkeit als von Bedeutungslosigkeit. Konsequenz und Ordnung sind nicht an sich das Böse oder das Bürgerliche oder das Unkünstlerische. Das zeigt sich z.b. in Schwabs *Die Präsidentinnen*, wo ein ersprießlicher Grad an Zusammenhang mit der Wirklichkeit hergestellt wird. Die Personen entwickeln sich auf eine konsequente aber gleichzeitig übernatürliche Weise von ihren Anfängen in der realistischen Welt. Das Moment der bürgerlichen Heuchelei, das durch das Wort 'Präsident' mit seiner unverkennbaren Anspielung auf Waldheims Präsidentschaft[9] und das ihn unterstützende österreichische Bürgertum mit dem historischen Geschehen verbunden wird, erfährt in den drei Personen des Stückes, den Präsidentinnen, ihre Apotheose in Verbindung mit der fäkalen Faszination. Die Außenwelt wird hier in Schwabs Privatwelt einbezogen und zu einem Teil dieser Welt gemacht, ihren Gesetzen unterworfen.

Das gilt nicht nur für den Stoff sondern auch für die Form. Fand Canetti den unheimlichen Sinn der *Dreigroschenoper* in der Selbstbejubelung und Selbstverherrlichung des durchtriebenen Publikums, so sehen wir in dieser Szene, wie die drei alten Frauen miteinander in der Darstellung ihrer Wunschträume wetteifern. Das Dramatische liegt in dem Wettstreit, in dem Bestreben einander ständig zu überbieten, wächst also aus dem Zusammenhang und gibt ihm gleichzeitig eine Gestalt. Dieser Wettstreit ist an sich eine dramatische Form, wie das gemimte Stiergefecht in *Magic Afternoon*, die aus sich selber entsteht und aus sich selber besteht, ohne mit irgendeiner bürgerlich weiterführenden Story verbunden zu sein. Diese strenge Linienführung unterscheidet das Stück von den absichtlichen Willkürlichkeiten der anderen, die durch die ständige Wiederholung der gleichen Strategie der Persiflage schließlich ihre Wirkung einbüßen.

In dieser Aneinanderreihung von sich gegenseitig übertrumpfenden Wunschträumen entwickelt das Unflätige schließlich einen Sinn, der nicht mehr bloß in der infantilen Verletzung der Normen besteht, es zeigt ein Reichtum an Bedeutungen. Mariedl, die leicht jüngere Frau, die Dumme aus dem Dorf, die bereit ist, ohne Scheu mit bloßen Händen verstopfte Klos wieder freizumachen, verklärt in trinitärer Wiederholung diese Tätigkeit, und demütigt dabei (immer noch in Schilderungen) die zwei älteren und gesellschaftlich höher stehenden Damen, mit denen sie den Wettstreit der Wunschträume führt.

---

[9]Siehe hierzu die Einführung in den vorliegenden Band, S.3.

Mariedl beschreibt die eigene Apotheose:[10]

Und wie steht die Mariedl da? Gewonnen für alles steht sie da, mit strahlendem Unterleib. Und der Stuhl der Menschen auf ihrem Körper verwandelt sich in einen Goldstaub. [...] *Inzwischen sind Erna und Grete aufgestanden und begutachten die Küchenmesser in Ernas Kredenz. Erna geht kurz hinaus und holt einen Eimer und einen Fetzen.* [...] Hoch und höher schwebt sie, die Mariedl. Da unten ist Lourdes, so groß wie eine Zündholzschachtel. Und da fliegt die Jungfrau Maria, die schon wieder jemandem erscheinen muß...nicht größer als eine Wanze. Gütig schaut sie drein, das arme Hascherl. *Entschlossen und sehr sachlich treten Erna und Grete an Mariedl heran. Sorgfältig schneiden sie ihr den ganzen Hals durch. Erna ist gleich mit Eimer und Fetzen zur Stelle, um eine größere Schweinerei zu verhindern.* ERNA: Riechen tut so etwas schon komisch, so ein Mensch von innen. Daß der Mensch aber auch so viel Blut haben muß im Fleisch. Und die da hat auch sicher einen Stuhl im Kopf.

Was mir an dieser Stelle so sehr imponiert ist die Ordnung der Unordnung. Schwab zeigt nahtlos den Übergang von der Grausamkeit zur bürgerlichen Tugend: um eine größere Schweinerei zu verhindern, ist Erna mit Eimer und Fetzen zur Stelle. Ohne andere Wörter als gutbürgerliche benutzen zu müssen, untergräbt er den ganzen Habitus des bürgerlichen Ordnungswahns. Was ihm in anderen Stücken durch die totale Mißachtung der Regeln nicht gelingt, gelingt ihm hier durch die peinlich genaue Befolgung der Regeln, durch den übertriebenen Konformismus, den er darstellt und entlarvt, wie in der letzten Zeile dieser Szene wieder einmal klar wird, auch diesmal wieder mit einem unüberhörbaren Anklang an das Zeitgeschehen, der aber in vollem Einklang mit der sprachlichen und gedanklichen Form steht. Erna weiß, wo die Ordnung zu suchen ist, die man doch schließlich zu wahren hat:

Die graben wir im Keller ein, weil die feinen Leute sagen ja auch immer: Jeder Mensch in diesem Land hat seine Leich im Keller.[11]

[10]Werner Schwab, *Fäkaliendramen*, a.a.O., S.55.
[11]Ebenda, S.56.

POSTMODERN MOODS AND MORALS IN WOLFGANG BAUER'S SIXTIES TRILOGY: *PARTY FOR SIX, MAGIC AFTERNOON* AND *CHANGE*

ANTHONY WAINE

The term 'postmodern' denotes an historic shift in modes of social and economic behaviour, perceptions of reality, aesthetic and cultural values, and consequently also a change in the manner in which individuals feel about themselves and one another. The German philosopher Wolfgang Welsch crystallised this epochal change with admirable succinctness: '"Postmoderne" signalisiert eine Umstellung unserer Grundorientierung'.[1]

It is worth noting that the term was used for the first time carrying some of these connotations in 1947,[2] when a post–second world war western civilisation began to reflect more sceptically on approximately a century of uninterrupted modernisation, innovation and progress, indeed to reflect critically on the very concept of civilisation itself. For accompanying the progressive social, political and technological features of the years 1850 to 1950 (from free education to voting rights for women, from trade unions to parliamentary democracies, from skyscrapers to aeroplanes), were symptoms of decay, fatigue, alienation, cynicism and rebellion, which the overarching ideological systems of the thirties and the second descent into doctrinally driven barbarism this century in the guise of World War Two had finally brought to the surface. The author of the first full length study of Wolfgang Bauer sees this bipolar cultural heritage stretching back even to the eighteenth century:

> Fortschrittspessimus und Kulturskepsis, wie Bauer sie hier in verschlüsselter Form zum Ausruck bringt, haben eine lange Tradition. Spätestens seit Rousseau mischen sich derlei Moll–Töne immer wieder in die hellen Klänge, die den Gang der Industrialisierung, die Entwicklung der Naturwissenschaften, den Sieg von Vernunft und Aufklärung, den kulturellen Prozeß schlechthin instrumentieren, und

---

[1]Wolfgang Welsch, *Postmoderne – Pluralität als ethischer und politischer Wert*, Cologne: 1988, p.21.

[2]Cultural historians concur that it was in the 1947 abbreviated edition of the six volume *A Study of History* by the British historian Arnold Toynbee that the term is first used in the context of profound cultural and historical change.

nach dem Zweiten Welkrieg hören sich diese Töne eine Zeit lang besonders dumpf und bedrohlich an.[3]

Little wonder, therefore, that the Theatre of the Absurd should take root in many European societies in those very years post–Auschwitz, post–Hiroshima, post–Gulag. Some scholars, but not all, mapping the postmodern cite the spiritual wastelands of Beckett, Ionesco and Adamov as establishing the early contours of the postmodernist literary landscape.[4] It was their bewildering, uncertainty–inducing parables which were to rewrite the literary idiom for the next ten years by allowing us to see the writer's own mind as the site of the narrative; by displaying all the dramatic figures as projections of the multifarious personae lodging in that same mind, their neurotically disordered and circular dialogues and especially monologues as the authentic 'voices' of the author; by their puncturing of the stage's illusion of representing a reality and their invitation to the spectator to accept the manifest fictitiousness of the performance; by ironically teasing the spectator regarding the sense or non–sense, the earnestness or farcicality, the profundity or pure absurdity of the spectacle; and, finally, by the irreverent collage of the downright banal and the sacred texts of theology and 'high' art in an act of subversive relativism, strongly recalling the Dadaists. In the context of Wolfgang Bauer, the phenomena associated with the Theatre of the Absurd are certainly worth enumerating, as it is an accepted fact that his earliest inspiration came from this direction.[5]

These introductory remarks have deliberately avoided giving a cast–iron definition of the term 'postmodern', for the very simple reason that no such definition has ever been formulated and, more to the point, agreed on.[6] Searching for such an agreed formulation is as elusive and counter–productive as positing an all–encompassing description of 'popular culture', a term with which postmodernism, certainly since the late sixties, has become to be closely associated.[7] One very obvious reason for the reluctance of the concept 'postmodern' to cede an immediate and incontrovertible meaning is that it has been appropriated by so many different disciplines, each of them bringing along their own premises and

---

[3]Gerhard Melzer, *Wolfgang Bauer: Einführung in das Gesamtwerk*, Königstein/Ts: 1981, p.12.

[4]See Steven Connor, *Postmodernist Culture: An Introduction to Theories of the Contemporary*, Oxford: 1989, p.110.

[5]Manfred Mixner, 'Die Lust auf Unvernunft' in Gerhard Melzer (ed.), *Wolfgang Bauer: Werke in sieben Bänden*, Vol 1, Graz and Vienna: 1986–1995, pp.306–308.

[6]For an understanding of some of the difficulties see Brenda K. Marshall's *Introduction to Teaching the Postmodern: Fiction and Theory*, New York and London: 1992, pp.1–18.

[7]For example John Docker, *Postmodernism and Popular Culture: A Cultural History*, Cambridge: 1994.

their own polemical intentions. For, indeed, the term has become a veritable battle–ground for heated discourses within and across disciplines. Thus, from being first employed by a British historian in the late 1940s, it reappeared a decade later as part of elitist literary debates in the United States; spread in that same country to wider cultural debates, as the elites were swept along by, as well as willingly participating in, the new mass movements, styles and fashions of the 1960s and 1970s. By then, the visual arts, but in particular architecture, were not only debating theoretically the issues but translating them into actual forms and styles. Finally, the seeds that had germinated within the humanities and the arts now took root in cognate disciplines, such as philosophy and the social sciences, especially sociology. The fact that Wolfgang Bauer, born in 1941, spent most of the 1960s closely involved with a multi–media grouping of young creative artists and writers centred around the so–called Graz Group[8] will have exposed and sensitised him to the cerebral, sensuous, eclectic and polyvalent ethic of the postmodern.

Before examining some of his early work in relation to this ethic, it is still necessary to comment further on references made in this tentative opening scenario, to confront some of the deliberate omissions, and to identify certain paradoxes. For example, with the exception for one usage of the epithet 'postmodernist', I have so far deliberately referred to the phenomenon of the 'postmodern', without clarifying whether I regard this as a period or as a style. In other words, should we talk of 'postmodernity' or of 'postmodernism'? If we choose to see it as the former, a period, then we are struck by an inherent contradiction. Far from modernity having ceased at some point in the middle of the twentieth century, or gone into some kind of terminal decline, it has continued to proceed apace. Not least of all in the area of mass communications and in the continuing internationalisation of taste, habit and style. Yet it is not hard to perceive that side by side with the standardising of various basic facets of our national societies and cultures, there has also been a breaking down of consensus, patterns of conformism and shared cultural pursuits. New and powerful cults, sub–cultures (or merely cultures?!), movements and parties (e.g. the Greens, Women, Anti–Nuclear Campaigners), in which age, gender, social background, sexual orientation, ethnic origin have been given legitimate expression, have arisen, leading to what Wolfgang Welsch has called a 'radikale Pluralität'[9] and which for him constitutes the ethical core of postmodernity. Similarly, postmodernism might best be viewed not as a rejection of, or antithesis to, modernism with its search for new styles to express the perceived *Zeitgeist*

---

[8]See Peter Laemmle and Jörg Drews (eds.), *Wie die Grazer auszogen, die Literatur zu erobern*, Munich: 1975.
[9]Welsch, op. cit., p.23.

but as a greater feeling of freedom in finding one's own personal style and thus expressing one's own individualistic, idiosyncratic sense of difference and uniqueness.

However, this claim to be individualistic and idiosyncratic has not always met with approval from other writers and intellectuals, especially German ones belonging to an older generation. They have seen in such an allegedly 'anything goes' climate, subjectivity, solipsism and the danger of anti–social or asocial attitudes growing.[10] Postmodernism as a stylistic carte blanche was seen by such critics as the artistic pendant to the hedonism and narcissism of late capitalist societies, and postmodernism, therefore, as late capitalism's very own *Weltanschauung*. Such a view, certainly in the German–speaking world, was consistent with a sociological–philosophical attack on contemporary culture which was first articulated by left–wing commentators in the Weimar Republic and which formed the basis of the Frankfurt School's critique of a society, whose culture reinforced the status quo by keeping the mass of the population entranced, entertained, but essentially unenlightened. The United States of America, which leading thinkers like Max Horkheimer and Theodor Adorno experienced at first hand during their years of exile from National Socialism, were seen as the embodiment of such a society in which a completely industrialised and commercialised culture had colonised the consciousness of a nation and was, moreover, all set to colonise the hearts and souls of the rest of the globe. The left–wing cultural critic and poet, Hans Magnus Enzensberger, postulated an almost identical thesis for the 1960s in his highly influential and readable essay 'Bewußtseinsindustrie', but with one key difference.[11] Unlike the ethereal Frankfurt philosophers, he did not claim to be outside the industrialised mind–set but an inescapable inhabitant of it, in much the same way as the American Marxist critic Frederic Jameson was to argue twenty years later regarding his own position.[12]

'Das omnipräsente Phänomen der Massenkultur',[13] as highlighted by several presenters to Germany's first major edition of essays devoted to the

---

[10]One of the most swingeing attacks was penned in 1969 by Martin Walser (born 1927), one year after Leslie Fiedler's much reported lecture tour of West Germany, in which he called for a bridging of the gap between 'low' and 'high' literature. At the time of writing, Walser was moving towards a radical left position, close to Marxism: 'Über die neueste Stimmung im Westen' in *Wie und wovon handelt Literatur*, Frankfurt/M.: 1973, pp.7–41.

[11]Hans Magnus Enzensberger, *Einzelheiten I*, Frankfurt/M.: 1962, pp.7–17.

[12]'The point is that we are within the culture of postmodernism to the point where its facile repudiation is as impossible as any equally facile celebration of it is complacent and corrupt.' Quoted in Steven Connor, op. cit., p.50.

[13]Christa Bürger, 'Die verschwindende Kunst: Die Postmoderne–Debatte in den USA', in Christa and Peter Bürger (eds.), *Postmoderne: Alltag, Allegorie und Avantgarde*, Frankfurt/M.: 1987, p.35.

subject, has certainly helped to further muddy the waters of the debate. The fact alone that the German language has two main but sullied equivalents for the Anglo–Saxon concept of 'popular culture', which despite attempts to abuse it, still retains a relatively value–free set of connotations, has not helped to bring clarity to the waters either. The term 'Massenkultur' emphasises in German three negatives: the trivialisation of the product; the widespread consumption of it; the lack of any intrinsic artistic value. All these negatives conveniently coexist in the quintessentially Germanic coinage of the 1880s, 'Kitsch' – a foretaste of the 'Massenkultur' just around the corner. The other word available in the language has a similar history of opprobrium, for the term 'Volkskultur' evokes either the pre–industrial traditions, customs and artefacts of the ordinary rural working people — and therefore at best a suitable case for anthropological treatment — or, more negatively, the attempts by the National Socialists to resurrect a 'Blood and Soil' ('Blut und Boden') identity for the 'Aryan' tribes. It has consequently been very difficult, at a purely linguistic level, to discuss the cultural plurality of postmodern German–speaking societies in a critically considered way, which is perhaps one more good reason to analyse the plays of a non–theoretical writer such as Wolfgang Bauer.

First, as an Austrian, he has been arguably less exposed, historically speaking, to the dichotomous nature of 'Bildung' in Germany, where one set of tastes has been privileged over that of another. Second, a concomitant of this first point, the Austrian theatre in particular has a rich tradition of popular (and therefore widely assimilated) drama which actually satirises the pretensions, hypocrisies and self–deceit of those very people who claim to represent elites and their mores. Furthermore, these dramatists have drawn positively on folkloristic elements but in particular on the 'Alltag' in which they have grown up and which they have also helped to colour. This particular word is also one which most effectively connates with our own 'popular culture', for it designates that matrix of everyday encounters, dialogues, productive activities, domestic and at the workplace, pastimes and festivities, in which the 'people' (Latin: *populus*) create their values, sense of self and traditional ways of life. Third, Bauer, with his instant access to the contemporary arts in Graz (and of course other Austrian cities such as Klagenfurt and Vienna) will have grown up with another key, early product of a postmodern levelling of values: Pop Art.

In evaluating this, some German critics have wisely avoided the emotionally charged and intellectually pejorative terms discussed earlier: 'Die Pop Art, in Europa zuerst als Kritik der Warenwelt mißverstanden, riß gerade die Barriere zwischen Alltag und Kultur nieder [...]'.[14] 'Alltag' is

---

[14]Hans Belting, *Das Ende der Kunstgeschichte: Eine Revision nach zehn Jahren*, Munich: 1995, p.55.

here employed as the neutral and legitimate counterpart to 'high' culture or 'Kunst', as one German term would describe it. Fourth, Bauer belonged to that first generation of children of the affluent society who grew up appreciating the material freedoms of this epoch, without necessarily feeling guilty about the 'pleasures' attached, and therefore morally obliged to denounce such values as firmly as that older generation of dramatic writers, such as Dürrenmatt, Frisch, Walser and Weiss, had done. Finally as a writer of fiction and not theory, Bauer was able to circumvent those conceptual pitfalls I have referred to earlier. Indeed, as his nineteenth century predecessors, Nestroy and Raimund, and his much admired near contemporaries, Artmann and Jandl did, he was able to take the concepts and expose them, implicitly and even explicitly, to iconoclastic mockery. As one of his figures is permitted to say, tongue firmly in cheek, 'Bildung ist ja was Schönes!'[15] surrounded by the much cherished trivia of the affluent society!

This attitude and others implicit in his sixties trilogy invite us to view him as a writer already expressing postmodern sentiments before they were acknowledged as such. Before I focus on the sentiments, however, I should like to explain why I have chosen to look at them under the headings of 'morals' and 'moods'. I have chosen to look at moral impulses within this work for two reasons: first, when his trilogy of plays was first performed between 1967 and 1969 their ambience was so very different from that which had prevailed in the German–speaking theatre since approximately the mid–fifties (i.e. dating from the gradual rehabilitation of Bertolt Brecht) that he was viewed as at best anarchic and at worst amoral. This instantaneous assessment needs revision. Second, his plays' heterodox presentation of 'morality' needs also to be seen in the context of two centuries of the German stage functioning as an orthodox moral institution, a tradition which had maintained its pre–eminence despite the great social and political changes which the introduction to this chapter documented. Expressionism, Dadaism and the cabaret were the exceptions, but otherwise in this century Brecht and Zuckmayer, Frisch and Dürrenmatt, Kipphardt and Weiss, Walser and Hochhuth, despite many individual differences, all shared a number of common values and beliefs pertaining to dramatic literature and the function of the theatre. They believed that the stage could and should possess an educative function. They assumed that the spectators were willing to learn and to accept that the theatre was providing not just entertainment but instruction about the way society worked, about how society could be improved and about the role which each individual could

---

[15]Wolfgang Bauer: *Magic Afternoon, Change, Party for Six*, Munich: 1972, p.25. All further references to the plays are based on this edition and employ the abbreviation MA followed by the page number in brackets.

play in promoting progress.[16] Little wonder that the parable play has been such a prominent genre, even with those contemporaries of Bauer who did try and break free from the socially critical, didactic tradition. One thinks of Handke, Plenzdorf, Kroetz and Sperr. One might say that a meta–narrative based on the individual's inherent rationality, sense of responsibility and capacity for making the right moral judgements has been operational in the German theatre right up to the time when Bauer's plays were first performed.

Bauer, anti–ideological, sceptical, and realistic, refashions and reinterprets that tradition. But his plays differ in another fundamental way from the Brechtian and post–Brechtian stereotype. The rationale of this type of play was that, in order for its ideas and ideals to be grasped, the audience needed to be kept, so to speak, at arm's length from the stage through two stylistic devices in particular: distancing effects ('Verfremdung') and irony, satire and the grotesque. Such a strategy, aimed at encouraging the spectators to maintain a high degree of emotional, psychological self–control and to deny themselves passionate pleasure and visceral involvement, ran contrary to almost all other cultural experiences on offer to the same spectator: a Wagnerian opera, a football match, a private or public celebration, a television soap, a thriller, a comic strip, an erotic film, a classical concert, a political debate. All of these 'high' and 'low' genres are intended to be an experience, eliciting sensations, mobilising emotions, subtly or crassly manipulating moods, reminding us that we have bodies as well as minds, nervous systems as well as consciences, 'ids' as well as 'egos'.

It is that vague yet pregnant word 'moods' which seems so redolent of the modern *Zeitgeist*, indeed may even be equated with that term which conjures up some invisible yet palpable sense of what an epoch 'feels' like. Moods also have to do with the more involuntary activation of our senses, the often arbitrary fluctuations in our self–awareness and states of consciousness, the ephemeral and random 'moments' in our lives, as well as the more planned and conscious stimulation of our nerves with chemicals, foods and drinks. Moods are therefore subjective, affective, localised. In a post–industrial, leisure–based, media–saturated, consumption–oriented age, individuals have been freed to pursue their moods more systematically than ever before and at the same time have been subjected to more and more pressures from external agencies to induce, alter and savour what Rolf Dieter Brinkmann has called the 'kleine(n) augenblickliche(n) Erregung'.[17]

---

[16]Finlay places Peter Turrini in the same theatrical tradition in his introduction to Chapter Ten of the present volume.

[17]*Der Film in Worten. Prosa, Erzählungen, Essays, Hörspiele, Fotos, Collagen (1965–1974)*, Reinbek bei Hamburg: 1982, p.263.

Bauer has registered this epochal change in our non–rational, biochemical behaviour more radically than most contemporary writers. And he has decoded those wider mood swings in the public domain and made visible their cultural foundations.

Bauer's particular anatomy of our postmodern condition, as presented in the three very different plays *Party for Six*, *Magic Afternoon* and *Change* will be discussed under the following rubrics: culture and social intercourse as *Fest*, masquerade and post–religious rite; human intercourse as bound by anatomical habits and needs, and Bauer's scanning of his private sphere for the forces of gender and sexuality at work; the style and techniques of the author in relation to his seemingly gratuitous indulgence in overt displays of bad taste as a constituent of his levelling down of cultural values; and the underpinning of all the above tenets by the happy eclecticism and heterogeneity implied and expressed in dialogue, sound effects, music, games, as well as other non–verbal activities, like the rolling and smoking of a 'joint'.

One could justifiably say that the festive moment, so central to Bauer's presentation of contemporary mores, is encapsulated in the very title of *Party for Six*, written in 1964 and premièred in 1967, in his home city of Graz. The party is, by the standards of what is to follow in *Magic Afternoon* (1968) and *Change* (1969), a relatively innocuous affair, but it does nevertheless, literally and figuratively, set the mood. A student, Fery (who then appears in *Change*), has invited two male friends and three female friends to his parents' home for some drinks, snacks and to listen to music. The friends arrive one by one, the atmosphere changes as the music and intoxicating drinks begin to relax the characters, little flirtations occur, a neighbour rings to complain about the noise, and the play ends with a scene the next morning as some of the guests help to clean and tidy the rooms. What makes this playlet so unusual is the dramatic perspective, for the main action, namely that which takes place in the living room, is in fact never seen by the spectators! They only see the comings and goings in the hallways between the front door and the living room door, and only hear, or overhear, random snatches of conversation taking place offstage at the heart of the party. They are, in other words, voyeurs and eavesdroppers, experiencing pleasure vicariously, pleasure (that of the actors) which itself is not real but 'performed' and therefore second–hand. They become aware — thanks to the dramatic trick of placing the party *huis clos* — of how a mood is artificially induced on stage as if the playwright were a magician manipulating his audience.

This ironic awareness of stage trickery, of the sleight of hand, of the stratagems for gaining spectator involvement, sharpens one's own sense of how other cultural spectacles and experiences may also be based on a deception, and therefore be a deliberate ploy to deceive people. In fact, the idea of culture as confidence trick is at the very core of *Change*, in which Fery, the original host of the party for six, is an avant–garde painter who devises a scheme for turning another more traditional painter of landscapes into a celebrity, then engineering his death through suicide in order to cash in on the publicity resulting from this:

Fery: [...] man macht überhaupt eine große Künstlerpersönlichkeit aus ihm ...
Reicher: Wie ...
Fery: Vastehst net, was i man ... i man, man müßte ihn richtig aufbaun ...
Reicher: Der manipulierte Mensch, hehe.
Fery: Genau.
Reicher: Statt, daß du was arbeitest, willst jetzt manipulieren ... (MA, 56).

The tone of this exchange is indicative of a changing perspective on culture. It is a charade in which individuals have designs on others in order to further their own sense of worth, their material advancement, and their need for pleasure, however dubious or perverse that might be. Reicher summarises this perception later in the exchange with Fery: 'Das Absurde an dem Kunstbetrieb ist, daß ich bei a bisserl Schmäh den guten Blasius Okopenko gut verkaufen könnte' (MA, 57).

The Viennese word 'Schmäh' here is apposite for it expresses both the idea of a confidence trick and a sarcastic joke. Fery and his fellow intellectual Reicher stand for the cynicism of what is rightly perceived by them both as a 'Betrieb' — that is, a routine commercial undertaking producing material goods — a far cry from the modernist avant–garde belief that art could still maintain its autonomy from economic and commercial intrusions. The quasi–festive framework in which most of the following scenes in *Change* take place helps to further demonstrate how art and culture are embroiled in a world in which the public is perceived as just so many consumers to be manipulated whilst the artists and intellectuals (Fery, Reicher — the material connotations of his name! — and Okopenko) sell themselves or are sold to their audience with all the marketing savoir faire of an agency promoting a Hollywood star.

Magic Afternoon also reveals a morally and artistically bankrupt intelligentsia, which confronted with its own impotence in a world already providing the whole gamut of entertainment and escapism demanded by its citizens, joins the global party in a seemingly non–stop orgy of 'sex, drugs and rock 'n' roll'. That these really are global 'fashions' of which one is a 'dedicated follower' is captured perfectly in the Anglo–American titles chosen for all three plays, a linguistic act of homage to the pioneers of the cultural revolution, which, thanks to mass communications, was reaching even the provincial pulse of small, central European states. In this atmosphere, mood is of paramount importance, for it is the secular equivalent of the spirituality which was pursued by men and women living in a religious age:

> Der kulturelle Einfluß, den Religion ausübte, war jedoch für Jahrhunderte mehr als eine bloße Vorherrschaft. Sie verschaffte ihren Anhängern genauso gut bedeutende Anstöße und Anregungen, vermittelte ihnen universell verständliche Themen und Gegenstände (damit meine ich die *Biblia pauperorum*), Hingabe und Begeisterung für göttliche Erleuchtung und eine genau definierte Anleitung für den vollendeten Umgang mit Kunst und Literatur [...]. Kunst und Literatur, so wie sie sich heute darstellen, sind durch Gottverlassenheit charakterisiert. Zumindest was das Gebiet der Ästhetik angeht, hat sich Nietzsches Prophezeihung also erfüllt, sei es nun zum Guten oder zum Schlechten.[18]

The dead or vanished gods, or the Godots for which Beckett's and Bauer's characters are seemingly waiting, are meanwhile replaced in this postmodern requiem by The Beatles, The Rolling Stones, James Brown and Wilson Pickett, by film stars and by other surrogates, such as pills, alcohol and hallucinogens, which give the mind that feeling of intoxication which is integral to the sense of being involved in an eternal festivity.[19] But whereas the believer in a still religious age celebrated the wonders of God and Nature and man–made wonders too, the new celebrants turn inwards and celebrate themselves, the artificial and the *ersatz* and the machine–made gadgetry. It is a hedonistic world, and as if to symbolise the self–centred, at times even narcissistic nature of the individuals inhabiting this micro–universe, Bauer sets all three plays emphatically within flats, houses and the built–up urban world. And when the magic afternoon finally comes to an end, as it does with the killing of Joe in self–defence by Birgit, the remaining male member, Charly, creeps into a cupboard, unable to face the reality of a world where the mood is no longer 'hyped' or 'hip'.

The behaviour of all the characters in the trilogy is revealed as habitual, repetitive, boredom–inducing. Bauer's exceptionally self–aware characters regularly give expression to their sense of an existence moving in circles rather than progressing forwards in a linear fashion: 'Das Leben ist eine Gewohnheit wie das Zigarettenrauchen!' (MA, 14), declaims Charly, whilst Birgit muses, 'Ich kann mir gar nicht mehr vorstellen, daß ich arbeite ... unmöglich ... i fühl mi recht wohl, obwohl i zu nix Lust hab ... (MA, 15). One senses the omnipresence in such remarks of the Absurdists with their often repeated theme of the impossibility of saying or producing anything

---

[18]Ferenc Fehér, 'Der Pyrrhussieg der Kunst im Kampf um ihre Befreiung', in Christa and Peter Bürger (eds.), op. cit., p.15.

[19]See Anthony Waine, 'Recent German Writing and the Influence of Popular Culture', in Keith Bullivant (ed.), *After the "Death" of Literature: West German Writing of the 1970s*, Oxford/New York/Munich: 1989, pp.69–72.

new. It has been done and said already, and therefore one can only reiterate and endlessly reproduce the known, the experienced, the *déjà vu* and *déjà fait*. Man's entrapment within a cycle of almost biologically predetermined drives is expressed at every stage of the trilogy through the concentration on the basic acts of consuming food, imbibing liquids and, of course, urinating and defecating. In few other works does the toilet feature in such a central 'role' as it does in Bauer's trilogy. Throughout the course of the party in *Party for Six*, the spectator, who sees so little but hears so much, watches the party celebrants cross the hall of the flat (which is the main stage), enter the toilet, flush and return. Though comical, it also vividly reminds us of the basic functioning of our physical natures, seemingly Bauer's only concession to the presence of 'nature' in the world. When Fery in *Change* is finally defeated by the very person whom he had hoped to manipulate for his own ends, Blasi, he goes to the toilet and hangs himself there. The last exchange of the play is:

> Blasi:　Aufgehängt hat er sich?!
> Guggi:　Ja. Am Klo (MA, 119).

If Bauer stresses the anatomical fixedness of the individual through the survival patterns of eating, drinking and excretion, then he emphasises a further anatomical determinant of human nature through the frank exposure of the sexual drives of his characters. The erotic pervades his plays as another layer of mood upon which his characters are fixated and which affects a great deal of their behaviour. But a great change can be discerned between his treatment of this theme in *Party for Six* — where the 'Six' can easily be misconstrued as 'Sex' — where the audience was indeed titillated but never shown anything too explicit or shocking, and the two late sixties plays where Bauer engages fully and frankly with some of the great issues of the liberalisation of western societies in the age of the Pill, free love, promiscuity and hedonism, celebrated in pop songs, advertising, films and the mass media. *Magic Afternoon* has one of the most sexually explicit opening scenes of any modern play (or musical, where one thinks of *Hair* and *Oh! Calcutta!*). We are told in the opening stage direction that 'Ein großes Bett steht schief in der Mitte' and we immediately see two young people who are only partially dressed. Middle class audiences, particularly the 'Abonnenten', were shocked by such scenes and, in the Hamburg production of 1970 which I saw, at least a third of the audience had walked out after the opening twenty minutes of the performance, slamming the auditorium doors behind them in disgust.

Bauer in this respect, too, signals a turning away from the German–language theatre's examination of the great public issues of German and European history, such as war and the Holocaust (Hochhuth's

Der Stellvertreter and Weiss's *Die Ermittlung)*; economic insecurity and collective morality (Dürrenmatt's *Der Besuch der alten Dame)*; science, nuclear warfare and the responsibility of the intellectual (Dürrenmatt's *Die Physiker* and Kipphardt's *In der Sache J. Robert Oppenheimer)*; or mass prejudice and individual victimisation (Frisch's *Andorra* and Sperr's *Jagdszenen aus Niederbayern*). His three plays foreshadow that paradigmatic 'change' (perhaps even alluded to in the title of one of them) from the sublimely political to the shamelessly personal. For other writers, perhaps following Bauer's example and the nascent women's movement, were soon to show how the 'private is the political' and to make gender an important social and cultural configuration for analysis. Gender is already a significant issue for Bauer, especially in *Magic Afternoon* and *Change*. In the former we have many strong instances of male bonding between Charly and Joe, of records being chosen by them which feature artists well known for 'machismo' posturing such as 'Wicked' by Wilson Pickett, or the Rolling Stones' notoriously misogynistic 'Back Street Girl'; of the men's primitive and threatening taunting of Birgit, whilst 'stoned', using various objects as phallic symbols. But it is the easily aroused violent proclivities of these two men which Bauer spotlights at almost every stage of the play, so that the bloody and tragic climax is utterly convincing and contains a veiled message from the author that, whilst culture has changed quite profoundly, human nature has not. In *Change*, the battle of the sexes is, if anything, even more pessimistically presented as the two principal females in the play, Guggi and her mother, Frau Selacek, are literally the objects of the males' naked sexual lust, their machinations and their gratuitous brutality, which in one instance results in Guggi losing her unborn child.

This incident is one spectacular but not isolated example of Bauer's provocative exhibition of bad taste, through which he is wishing to distance himself from the 'bürgerlich' canon of acceptable manners, morals and codes:

> Bauer setzt sich bewußt den Ehrgeiz, das Schlechteste, das Vulgärste zu bieten, indem er die oralen, analen, phallischen Regressionen ritualisiert.[20]

One might claim that bad taste was a taboo waiting to be broken, in much the same way as the Beats in the United States and Pop Artists in the Anglo–American world were already at work subverting the hallowed divide between what was ART and what was KITSCH or trash. Perhaps these models were at least subconsciously in Bauer's mind when he chose to give all three plays such un–Germanic titles, which might also have been anathema to the custodians of 'high' culture. Reference has already been

---

[20]Marec Przybecki, 'Wolfgang Bauer's Theater gegen den Strich', in *Studia Germanica Pasnanicnsia* 6 (1977), p.44.

made to the linguistic proximity of 'Six' to 'Sex', but it was the title of his second and best known play, *Magic Afternoon* which would have raised eyebrows due to the covert presence of 'After' meaning of course 'anus'. And, in view of the omnipresence of toilets in all three pieces, Bauer's mission to rid the Austrian theatre of any vestigial petit–bourgeois prudishness is clearly visible.

To dwell, however, on the play's anal and genital references would overvalue the significance of the author's undoubted fixation on this area and encourage a psychoanalytical approach which would be surely fallacious. For one has to understand these scatalogical facets as part of a much broader cultural patterning of his plays. I would contend that this trilogy represents one of the first serious undertakings in German literature to effect a horizontalisation of cultural values: the author no longer wishes, implicitly or explicitly, to subscribe to a set of values which are hierarchically, i.e. vertically ordered. In his anti–canonical value system the mind, 'Geist', is not automatically privileged over the body and the physical senses, nor is reason valued as being superior to emotion, nor is the individual artistic work held to be morally more beneficial than a mass produced and transmitted piece of popular art, such as a comic. Bauer compels us to engage in this critical re–evaluation of our preferences, priorities and pre–judgements by presenting us with three milieux involving educated, intellectual coteries and asking us to observe and indeed judge their actual behaviour. The author lays bare their quotidian concerns, juxtaposes academic interests with trivial pursuits, allows them to converse rationally one minute and speak infantile gibberish the next, enthuse about the cinema and dismiss the classics ritually as 'Scheiß–Goethe', 'Scheiß–Schiller'. In short, Bauer de–intellectualises his protagonists and de–mystifies the ambience in which they work and spend their leisure time. They are simultaneously shown as inhabiting a levelled down culture and contributing to this very process themselves.

They come in fact to embody that aesthetic at the heart of postmodernity; heterogeneity. Their cultural identities are amalgams, conglomerates, montages; unfixed, un–certain, un–focused, full of apparent contradictions, inconsistencies, paradoxes, juxtapositions. The three texts therefore read like a cross between an encyclopaedia of modern art and a newspaper's weekend colour supplement. Here is an abbreviated and genre–specific list of groups of references found in the course of the trilogy: Jerry Cotton, Saul Bellow, Ionesco, Konrad Bayer, Wittgenstein, Beckett, Joyce and Lawrence Sterne; 'Penny Lane', Wilson Pickett, 'Sgt. Pepper's Lonely Hearts Club Band,' 'Back Street Girl', 'The Crazy World of Arthur Brown', Paul McCartney, Gerry Mulligan, Kurti Schmiderer, Charlie Mingus, Tchaikovsky's 'Pathétique', Herb Alpert, Udo Jürgens and Bill Haley; Art–Club, Pop, Jazz, totale Kunst, Münchner Volksoper,

Damen–und–Herrenboutique, objet trouvé, Avantgarde–Zeit and Hollywood–Regisseur; Malboro, Coca Cola, Hash and Gin; Mickey Maus, Gustav Gans, Danie Düsentrieb and Ede Wolf. As the list illustrates, the author's eclecticism is undisguised, but also playful, ironic, especially when the references are made in a South Austrian vernacular, a fact which also shows the cross–fertilisation of the parochial and regional with the cosmopolitan and international.

Small wonder, therefore, that one of Bauer's close contemporaries and colleagues, Rolf Schwendter, had no hesitation in declaring:

> Auf keinen Fall dürfte jedoch die Annahme 'postmodernen' Schreibens vor dem Entstehen postmoderner Mode ('Ideologie' würde er selber sagen) so sehr zutreffen, wie auf Wolfgang Bauer.[21]

Yet as this statement rightly makes clear, Bauer did not opportunistically opt for a postmodern agenda and then write accordingly — another reason why this essay did not attempt to be specific and prescriptive about what postmodernity 'is' and, by going through the credentials, to prove Bauer's membership of that particular club. If Bauer does write in a style which is recognisably postmodern then he does so, perhaps like most other genuine contemporary artists, at least in those early days, by chance as much as choice. He writes from experience and he writes about his self so that his work has the unmistakable aura of autobiographical authenticity. It is in fact that very authenticity which lends his works their credibility, authority and legitimacy, in a literary and also, I would argue, in a moral sense.

He sets out from his own problems, his own conflicts, but also his own pleasures and dreams. In the process he avoids giving opinions, making statements, taking sides. But this does not result in his works being 'jenseits der Moral', as one early review was headlined.[22] These plays reveal a serious moral core, but one which eschews the traditional categories of ethics and morality. In this respect they may be read as an early refutation of the personal and provocative hypothesis which was posed a decade and a half later by Frederic Jameson in the conclusion to his famous essay *Postmodernism and Consumer Society*. My own conclusion here must take the form of a question about the critical value of the newer art. There is some agreement that the older modernism functioned against its society in ways which are variously described as critical, negative, contestatory, subversive, oppositional, and the like. Can anything of the sort be affirmed

---

[21]*Wolfgang Bauers Werke in sieben Bänden, Bd. 6. Mit einem Nachwort von Rolf Schwendter*, p.275.

[22]Quoted by Helmut Schödel in 'Nachmittags als die Gespenster kamen', *Die Zeit*, 19 February 1982, p.41.

about postmodernism and its social moment? We have seen that there is a way in which postmodernism replicates or reproduces — reinforces — the logic of consumer capitalism; the more significant question is whether there is also a way in which it resists that logic. But that is a question we must leave open.[23]

The essential force of Bauer's work derives from his honesty about his own life and feelings and the refusal to pretend any differently. Thus, by equating sexuality with lust, ritual and aggression, he compels us to think about the absent values of affection, commitment and spontaneity. By admitting to male fantasies of violence, commodification and power, he provides evidence for the feminist claims of chauvinism and misogyny in male–female relationships. By showing artists, intellectuals and critics as neurotic and fallible he encourages in audiences a healthy scepticism towards elites and induces an attitude of taking responsibility for our own destinies rather than depending on others to tell us how to think and to behave. And finally, by showing the endgame–mentality and rituals of those addicted to all–out consumption and flagrant hedonism he forces us to reconsider our own seducibility and vulnerability. Bauer's postmodernist 'moods' do not block or obscure 'morals'. They re–perspectivise them.

---

[23]Frederic Jameson, 'Postmodernism and Consumer Society', in Hal Foster (ed.), *Postmodern Culture*, London and Sydney: 1985, p.125.

MODERNIST OR POSTMODERNIST?
THE ABSURD QUESTION IN MARLENE
STREERUWITZ

ALLYSON FIDDLER

Marlene Streeruwitz and her 'Mischon' for the theatre

Marlene Streeruwitz has been described by the journal *Theater heute* along with dramatists Peter Handke, Botho Strauß, Elfriede Jelinek, Peter Turrini, Heiner Müller, and Rolf Hochhuth, as one of the 'Vielgespielten, Oftgenannten', and was chosen as best 'Nachwuchsdramatikerin' in *Theater heute*'s poll of 1992.[1] It is surprising, then, that German literary studies have yet to accord Streeruwitz's work much attention at all.[2] It is my intention here to offer an initial reading of Streeruwitz's work and outspoken dramatic programme. This reading will detail the author's critical reflections on Western classical theatre and the feminist dimension in her work. Streeruwitz's work defies easy categorisation, displaying affinities with the Absurd and using the eclectic and playful intertextuality so characteristic of the postmodern.

Some preliminary remarks about the playwright and her *oeuvre* indicate why we perhaps have not heard too much about her. Streeruwitz was born in 1950, the daughter of the then mayor of Baden, near Vienna. She is the divorced mother of two children, whom she raised on her own. Streeruwitz studied law and Slavonic studies and wrote a doctoral thesis on Soviet theatre. Many of the reviews and short journalistic pieces on Streeruwitz mention her main employment of writing for an ecology magazine called 'Natur ums Dorf'.[3] It is obvious, then, that Streeruwitz has followed the typical female labour pattern of raising children first before embarking on her own 'career'. To date, nine of her plays have been published — all of them in the 1990s.[4]

---

[1] Franz Wille, 'Farewell, my lovely? An den Grenzen der Aufklärung', *Theater 1993*, *Theater heute* yearbook (1993), pp.29–51, p.30.

[2] To the best of my knowledge this is the case at the time of writing this article.

[3] See Wolfgang Huber–Lang, 'Balanceakt ohne Netz', *Wochenpresse*, 11 February 1993, pp.62–63.

[4] These are: *Ocean Drive.* (Frankfurt/M.: Suhrkamp, 1991); *Waikiki–Beach. Sloane Square. Zwei Stücke* (Frankfurt/M.: Suhrkamp, 1992); *New York. New York. Elysian Park. Zwei Stücke* (Frankfurt/M.: Suhrkamp, 1993); *Tolmezzo.* (Frankfurt/M.: Suhrkamp, 1994); *Bagnacavallo. Brahmsplatz. Zwei Stücke* (Frankfurt/M.: Suhrkamp,

The stage history of Streeruwitz's work is a rather typically Austrian one. Like the early dramas of Elfriede Jelinek, Streeruwitz's premières have also taken place in Germany (in Munich, Cologne, and Berlin), where productions have been very well attended. Reviews have been mixed — from the very enthusiastic *Süddeutsche Zeitung* to the *Wiener Zeitung*'s reference to *New York. New York.* as 'dieses ordinäre, literarisch bedeutungslose Stück'.[5] Streeruwitz also works as a director in her own right and has produced plays in Cologne and Vienna by, for example, Garcia Lorca and Jean Genet.

The titles of Streeruwitz's plays hint at exotic promise: *Waikiki–Beach.*, *New York. New York.*, *Elysian Park.*, *Ocean Drive.*, and so on. But these titles are the first sign of Streeruwitz's playful irony, since most of the plays do not have anything to do with, or indeed even mention, the faraway locations of their titles.[6] In the following discussion I will illustrate my comments on Streeruwitz's drama by focusing mainly on two plays, *New York. New York.* (written 1988, published 1993) and *Tolmezzo.* (1994). These two works belong together thematically and should arguably be read as a pair.[7] I have three main reasons for doing so here. Firstly, both plays are set in Vienna: *New York. New York.* in the gentlemen's toilet at the Burggasse 'Stadtbahn' station (now route number 6 in Vienna's underground system), and *Tolmezzo.* in and outside a café described as resembling the famous literary haunt, the Café Central. Secondly, both plays stage Streeruwitz's conception of history, a conception which, as I shall

---

1996). The radio play, 'Kaiserklamm. und. Kirchenwirt.' was published in Christian Fuchs (ed.), *Theater von Frauen: Österreich* (Frankfurt/M.: Eichborn, 1991). Streeruwitz's novel, *Verführungen*, was written before her plays but only published in 1996, by Suhrkamp.

    [5]Thomas Thieringer, 'Mensch — kaputt: Marlene Streeruwitz *New York. New York.* in München', *Süddeutsche Zeitung*, 1 February 1993, p.12, and Paul Wimmer, 'Kein Bedarf an der Bedürfnisanstalt: *New York. New York.* im Volkstheater', *Wiener Zeitung*, 14 May 1994, p.4. Although Wimmer is reviewing the Viennese Volkstheater production, not the Munich production, he makes it clear that his criticism is mainly of the play, not [of] the 'eindrucksvollen schauspielerischen Leistungen'.

    [6]*Sloane Square.* and *Elysian Park.* are possible exceptions since they are set in the eponymous London underground station, and in a town park by a motorway flyover, hardly, therefore, an Elysium.

    [7]Wolfgang Reiter also sees *Tolmezzo.* as the 'Komplementarstück zu *New York. New York.*' in his review, 'Die Rückkehr der Geschichte als Farce: Die Dramatikerin Marlene Streeruwitz — und zwei Wiener Inszenierungen', *Neue Zürcher Zeitung*, Fernausgabe, 11 June, 1994, p.40. Streeruwitz's classification of her plays is in terms of five plays with Anglo–American titles to be followed by five with Italian titles. These plays, therefore, do not 'belong' together in the author's own categorisation. See Stephan Dedalus, '"Shakespeare ist ein echter Langeweiler": Gespräch mit Marlene Streeruwitz — Ihr neues Stück *Elysian Park.* wird heute in Berlin uraufgeführt', *Die Welt*, 17 June 1993.

argue, is informed by theories of the postmodern. Finally, both *New York.*
New York. and *Tolmezzo.* feature the character of Professor
Chrobath/Krobath, who functions as something of a mouthpiece cum
agitator in Streeruwitz's 'mission' for the theatre and her critical reflections
on Western culture more generally.

Criticism of the State Theatre (*Burgtheater*), that symbol of 'high'
Austrian drama and marker of establishment theatre is hardly anything new.
In this regard, Streeruwitz has a long line of Austrian predecessors, from
Karl Kraus to — in more recent times — Thomas Bernhard, Erich Jandl,
and Elfriede Jelinek; indeed it has become almost *de rigeur* for any
self–respecting oppositional or experimental author to satirise the
Burgtheater. Streeruwitz's hilarious and calculatedly provocative proposal
in a newspaper article that Arnold Schwarzenegger be appointed its next
director and the theatre turned into a sauna, gymnasium and cinema, would,
she argues, foster a much more honest use of the building in a city, 'die das
Theater immer mehr zur Beruhigung hatte als für das Drama'. At the end of
her article, having mooted this new–style *Burgtheater*, she muses:

> 'Mission accomplished', sagt Schwarzeneggers Terminator, nachdem er so oft 'Sis
> wiil nod helb auer mischon' sagen mußte. Wäre das nichts. An accomplished
> Viennese mission. Anstrengungslose Freizeitglorie statt lästigem
> Auseinandersetzungszwang. Nehmen wir einmal wenigstens die Zukunft ernst und
> fragen wir ehrlich. 'Wozu die ganze Plag, die dann keiner mag'. Sis *wiil* helb auer
> mischon. Schurli.[8]

Streeruwitz's objections are to the *Burgtheater*'s preferred repertoire
of classical theatre, in her opinion a phallocentric and outdated mode of
drama. Streeruwitz's invective is aimed at classical Greek, Shakespearian,
Schillerian and at more recent twentieth–century models, in the main for
their attempts at psychological realism, for sentimentalising and being
worlds apart from the realities of late–twentieth–century life. Shakespeare
serves Streeruwitz in this regard as a good example, and in an appropriately
irreverently titled interview with Stephan Dedalus, 'Shakespeare ist ein
echter Langeweiler', she wonders what on earth the playwright is doing on
the contemporary stage when his work is 'absolut realitätsfern in unserer
entfremdeten Welt'. Pondering the role of Juliet, for example, she
concludes: 'Was hat eine so konstruierte Frauenrolle noch mit einer Frau
von heute gemeinsam? [...] Nichts!', although notably she fails to ask
whether Juliet and the women of Shakespeare's day had anything in
common.[9] She describes the theatre against which she is reacting as 'phallic'

---

[8]Marlene Streeruwitz, "Helb auer mischon!"*: Schwarzenegger for Burgtheater',
Frankfurter Rundschau, 29 February 1992, [my emphasis].

[9]Streeruwitz quoted in the interview with Stephan Dedalus, op. cit. Streeruwitz
also advances an economic argument here: since theatres do not have to pay such 'dead

in its preoccupation with the decisions and actions of an individual (usually male) central character. Streeruwitz does not gloss her own critique of classical theatre in psychoanalytic terms, as some feminist theorists have done. Tragedy, for example, has been deemed phallocentric due to its composition of '[...] foreplay, excitation and ejaculation (catharsis). The broader organisation of plot — complication, crisis and resolution — is also tied to this phallic experience'.[10] It is not only a feminist argument which Streeruwitz is advancing. Her feeling is that this model of drama does not reflect the 'Zerrissenheit des modernen Menschen',[11] that fragmentary subject which at the very latest since structuralism has replaced the unitary and unified subject of liberal humanism. As Streeruwitz bemoans:

> Es handelt sich im klassischen Theater [...] immer um Augenblicke der Entscheidung. Es gruppiert sich immer um den Augenblick, in dem der Held, heute auch Heldinnen, entscheiden. Es geht immer um dieses phallische Durchsetzungsprinzip der Männerwelt, den Entscheidungsaugenblick. Ich denke hingegen, daß das Leben ja auch für die Männer dazwischen stattfindet [...].[12]

Ironically, then, Streeruwitz is proposing a more 'realistic' dramatic mode; one more appropriate to the (post)modern condition. Streeruwitz's open and fragmented texts are designed to be analogous to the contemporary human condition. Born of uncertainty, of rupture, of a time and society which lack totalising systems for making rational sense of the world, this postmodern condition is enacted by Streeruwitz's characters. 'Wahrscheinlich ist es eine der unerträglichsten Lasten unserer Zeit,' Streeruwitz maintains, 'daß wir mit den Sehnsüchten des vorigen Jahrhunderts ausgestattet werden und dann ein ganz anderes Leben zu bestreiten haben'.[13]

Vienna — an Absurdist location?

Streeruwitz's plays are not driven by plot, intrigue, dilemma, or indeed action. Mostly, they present banal, one might say, 'everyday' situations: waiting for an underground train in *Sloane Square.*; hanging around outside a café and having a drink in *Tolmezzo.*; or the nocturnal activities in a men's

men' copyright, Streeruwitz suggests a tax on the classics which would raise revenue for staging modern, experimental authors.

[10]For a discussion of this, see Sue–Ellen Case, *Feminism and Theatre*, Basingstoke: 1988, p.129.

[11]Wolfgang Huber–Lang, 'Balanceakt ohne Netz', *Wochenpresse*, 11 February 1993, p.63.

[12]Streeruwitz quoted in Ulrich Fischer, 'Ein verheißungsvolles Debüt: Autorin Marlene Streeruwitz', *Neue Zeit*, 9 August, 1992, p.34.

[13]Streeruwitz quoted in Wolfgang Huber–Lang, 'Balanceakt ohne Netz', *Wochenpresse*, 11 February 1993, p.63.

toilet in *New York. New York.* [14] The dramatic situations are not unlike those of Absurd drama or of existentialist writing, only they are ruptured many times by the intrusion of surreal characters and by sudden, unmotivated, violent acts. Franz Wille aptly terms her plays 'Endzeitcollagen' and notes her predilection for 'symbolisch aufgeladene Durchgangsstationen für Figuren am Ende aller Fragen'.[15] Nor does Streeruwitz's writing cast off conversational dialogue or points of reference within the 'drama' altogether, as do some exponents of postmodern art. Whereas 'authors such as Peter Handke, Michel Vinaver, Samuel Beckett, and Heiner Müller no longer attempt to imitate speakers in the act of communication',[16] Streeruwitz retains some of the mechanisms of meaningful communication. Her plays are not dramatised novelistic texts as found in certain plays by her compatriots Handke, Bernhard or Jelinek.[17]

The setting of Vienna for *Tolmezzo.* and *New York. New York.* is itself cast not so much as a place but as a state; it is an 'äußerst präzise Lokalisierung und Überall–Nirgends als Ort des Monströsen'.[18] The reason Streeruwitz gives for choosing Vienna as the setting for *Tolmezzo.*, is that it is 'als Ort der Weltbeschreibung geeigneter [...] als jeder andere in Deutschland: eine imperialistische Hauptstadt, die 1917 ins Marmelade–Glas gesteckt wurde — und oben zu und nichts mehr weiter!'[19] Vienna, then, has a certain universal quality; 'Wien ist überall'.[20] In terms of any Austrian specificities of the play's setting, the playwright's argument here conjures up theories of the 'Habsburg Myth' in Austrian literature, according to which Austria's literati and intellectuals are seen as lamenting the demise of the Habsburg monarchy in 1918 and the happy and harmonious 'good old days'.[21] *New York. New York.* and, to a certain extent

---

[14]The genre description, 'Klomödie', coined by Werner Schwab, is highly appropriate for Streeruwitz's play. See the contributions to the present volume by Preece and Rogers.

[15] Franz Wille, 'Wen der Berg ruft', *Theater heute*, no. 2 (1994), pp.32–33.

[16]Patrice Pavis, 'The Classical Heritage of Modern Drama: The Case of Postmodern Theatre', *Modern Drama*, no. 1 (1986), pp.1–22, p.8.

[17]Jelinek examples of this style would be *Wolken. Heim.* (Göttingen: Steidl, 1990) and *Totenauberg* (Reinbek: Rowohlt, 1991).

[18]Siegfried Kienzle,'Die Austro–Berserker. Werner Schwab, Harald Kislinger, Marlene Streeruwitz — drei neue Stückeschreiber aus Österreich brechen über die Theater herein. Schon die Titel dampfen und ächzen', *Die deutsche Bühne*, no. 9 (1992), pp.12–15, p.15.

[19]Streeruwitz in Michael Merschmeier, 'Schrecklich schön. Marlene Streeruwitz über das Theater im allgemeinen und die Nicht–Uraufführung ihres Stückes *Elysian Park* im besonderen', *Theater Heute*, no. 8 (1993), pp.34–35, p.34.

[20]Streeruwitz in Thieringer, 'Mensch — kaputt: Marlene Streeruwitz *New York. New York.* in München', *Süddeutsche Zeitung*, 1 Feb. 1993, p.12.

[21]See Claudio Magris, *Der habsburgische Mythos in der österreichischen Literatur*, Salzburg: 1966.

Tolmezzo., might reasonably be seen to ironise this very Austrian preoccupation with, or nostalgia for, the Habsburg era.

New York. New York. sees a toilet attendant, Frau Horvath, concerned with the cleanliness and routine of her job. When not cleaning, this 'Klofrau' is busy with her knitting and listening to popular Viennese melodies or opera arias. A prostitute (with whom Frau Horvath has been discussing men's feelings about having sex during menstruation) is murdered by her boyfriend and pimp and then sexually interfered with by a man passing himself off as a doctor. There is no reaction from the toilet attendant. Her deaf–mute companion, a homosexual prostitute, brings a client into the toilets. A pregnant woman, frustrated by the blocked ladies' toilets which she desperately needs to use, is unable to make the deaf mute open the door until she realises that she must pay him a fee before he will do so. The toilet itself, having been left unrenovated since Imperial days and with the corresponding standard of sanitary installations, is a popular destination for Herr Sellner, a tour guide. Sellner brings his groups of Japanese tourists (dressed, of course, in Austrian national costume) to take photographs of the Imperial coat of arms. Sellner's yodelling is the cue for Frau Horvath to hang this on the wall, and the Japanese in turn delight in chorusing the words of their tour guide: 'It was very beautiful. I was very pleased', a poor translation of the words which Sellner alleges had been spoken by the Kaiser when he used the toilet in 1910. The stage directions tell us, '(*Sellner nimmt seine Position als Fremdenführer ein. Er spricht Englisch mit Wiener Akzent mit einem Hernalser "L"*)':[22]

> SELLNER: Gentleman. I want to show you. No. Not this. [he points at the dead prostitute] ... Yes, you. With the many cameras ... Yes, please. Here you can see. You are in an antique WC. This toilet is built 1910 and was opened by the last Emperor of Austria, Franz Joseph (*Fraantz Tschosef*). It is told that he pissed in here and said: ''It was very beautiful. I was very pleased'' (*New York. New York.*, scene 5, 19f.).

One final and very important piece of 'action' revolves around Herr Prometheus, symbol of 'tortured mankind' (scene 20, 81) whom Frau Horvath is nursing in the back room of the toilet and whose urine bottles we see her emptying from time to time. Herr Sellner clinches a deal with Frau Horvath and pays her a lot more money for the 'Japs' (scene 20, 79) to be allowed to photograph Prometheus, but, after solving the three questions Prometheus demands of the assembled lavatory audience, what is revealed to the eruption of flashlights from their cameras, is in fact a horse's cadaver dripping with blood.

---

[22]Hernals is a district of Austria's capital city which gives its name to one variety of Vienna's urban vernacular, distinguished from others not least by its users' pronunciation of the 'l'–sound.

History and the postmodern subject in *New York. New York.*

Although there is only limited linear development in Streeruwitz's dramatic scenarios, they are not just a random web of actions, either; the point is that the action begins plausibly in all her plays, but that it is then deliberately undercut and playfully thwarted, prevented from becoming 'classical' by Absurd purposelessness, and violent 'non–sense' actions. Patrice Pavis writes of 'the classical moment of a self–evident meaning' which might be present even in a modern text.[23] It is this sense of 'classical' theatre which Streeruwitz is at pains to subvert. The conventions of classical drama, on the other hand, are used both as organising structures and as ludic gestures. Streeruwitz's plays adhere — at least on the surface level — to the unities of time and place. New 'scenes' are usually motivated by an entrance or exit. In *New York. New York.* a Japanese chorus (not a Greek one) recites verses from Kleist.

The simultaneous presence of both order and chaos is one of a number of contradictions and unresolved ideas in Streeruwitz's work which can be seen as deliberate postmodern strategies. In her analysis of the poetics of postmodernist fiction, Linda Hutcheon talks of a

> [...] deliberate contamination of the historical with didactic and situational discursive elements [...]. What fades away with this kind of contesting is any sure ground upon which to base representation and narration, in either historiography or fiction. In most postmodern work, however, that ground is first inscribed and subsequently subverted.[24]

Something similar is in play here. Streeruwitz's theatre is not just a degeneration into non–meaning, a denial of politics and history as identified and criticised in some postmodern writing.[25] What Streeruwitz's texts do produce is a highly fragmented and 'open' theatre which relies very much on associative techniques and on the willingness of the audience to try to construct meaning from the disparate pieces which make up the whole. Streeruwitz outlines her desire for this to happen in a paragraph which precedes her play *New York. New York.*:

> Wir können unser Jetzt besehen. Auch auf dem Theater. [...] Aber damit das Drama ist, muß es sich aus jedem Realismus lösen. Zeit muß über die formale Lösung in Gegenwart verwandelt werden. [...] Das Publikum kann wieder an der Vision teilnehmen. Kann sie mitschaffen und bleibt nicht Zuschauer. Spontane Zugänglichkeit muß diese Gegenwart verdichten. Die Sinne können auch ganz sinnlos angesprochen werden. Sogar um den Preis, daß es unterhaltsam wird. Das

---

[23]Patrice Pavis, op. cit., p.4.

[24]Linda Hutcheon, *A Poetics of Postmodernism: History, Theory, Fiction*, London and New York: 1988, p.92.

[25]See Pavis' summary of this tendency in postmodern theatre in Patrice Pavis, op. cit., p.18.

Ganze zu Einzelteilen zerbrochen und ein anderes Ganzes werden lassen. Der Verwissenschaftlichung unserer Lebenszusammenhänge über Lust entfliehen. Ordnendem Denken den Inhalt entziehen und über Chaos Chaos bewältigen' (*New York. New York.*, 2).[26]

The way in which 'characters' are conceived in Streeruwitz's plays reflects poststructuralist notions of the disunified, fragmentary subject and deliberately works *against* the unified dramatic hero or heroine of the classical model. In the dramatis personae of *New York. New York.* we are informed that the 'Klofrau' is 'die einzige Person, die eine eindeutige Identität durchhält' (8). As for the others, the three strippers 'turn into' three furies and chase out the 'Streetworker' who has metamorphosed into a priest; the eighteen–year–old schoolboys ('die Drei von der Maturafeier') turn into sixty–year olds after their fight in the toilet cubicle. The most extreme example is that of the deaf mute who is momentarily nursed into language and recites falteringly some Rilke poetry (scene 12, 43). This constructedness of identity and the subject's lack of coherent, linear direction is reflected in the intertextual tags describing some of the characters: for example, 'Der Taubstumme, 20, Stricher, Mick–Jagger–Typ'; or in *Ocean Drive.* where the yeti is described as '70 Jahre, er trägt Schuhe in Form von Yeti–Füßen. Er ist Graf Karl Bühl für den 2. und 3. Akt des "Schwierigen" in Abendkleidung'.[27] It is difficult to imagine how the audience is expected to identify these references, unless the programme for the play also contains this information.[28] But there are other, more obvious intertextual references in the characters' names. In calling her toilet attendant, 'Frau Horvath', and her prostitute, 'Lulu', Streeruwitz, of course, directly signals Horváth and Wedekind. Equally, the name Pozzo for one of the characters in *Ocean Drive.*, is there to evoke Beckett (*Waiting for Godot*), indeed the 'real' name of Gabriele d'Annunzio,[29] and the comic characters and products such as Spiderman and the Ken and Barbie dolls of *Tolmezzo.*, all mobilise certain connotations, though these may be different for each reader and member of the audience.

This plethora of quotations and allusions promotes an emphasis on fictionality, constructedness and anti–realism which is common in postmodern art. Hutcheon cites Michael Riffaterre's theories to demonstrate how this self–reflexivity impacts on the presentation of history in

---

[26]Also in Marlene Streeruwitz, 'Passion. Devoir. Kontingenz. Und keine Zeit', *Theater 1992, Theater heute*, yearbook (1992), pp.34–37.

[27]Marlene Streeruwitz, *Ocean Drive.*, Frankfurt/M.: (Suhrkamp) 1991, p.7.

[28] I am conscious of my analysis looking only at these plays as texts rather than as performance. With Streeruwitz's copious and elaborate stage directions, it is tempting to see her theatre as written to be read or staged in the reader's mind.

[29]D'Annunzio also features in *Clara S.* by Elfriede Jelinek, in *Theaterstücke*, ed. Ute Nyssen, Cologne: (Prometh) 1984.

postmodern fiction. According to these theories, 'reference in literature is never anything but one of text to text and [...] therefore, history [...] could never refer to any actual empirical world, but merely to another text. At best, words refer, not to things, but to systems of signs that are 'ready–made textual units".'[30] Streeruwitz's use of 'ready–made textual units' ranges from musical 'texts' to literary and historical 'texts'. Scene 9 of *New York. New York.* is particularly interesting in this regard. Here, the deaf and dumb male prostitute 'plays' Duke of Gloucester to a recorded text from Shakespeare's *Richard III* while the pregnant woman 'responds' — again in playback recording — not with the words of Lady Anne but with those of a hard–to–get lover in a Raymond Chandler adaptation (à la *Murder My Sweet*). The horse's cadaver at the end of the play may be a reference to Francis Ford Coppola's film *The Godfather*, and there is certainly a *King Kong* reference in scene 6 when the pimp has an 'ape' fight with the deaf mute (complete with relevant sounds), and carries off Lulu over his shoulder.[31]

History, time, and politics in *Tolmezzo.*

Tolmezzo. does not necessarily function as a piece of 'strategic misinformation',[32] since, for many readers or audience members the title will hold no connotations at all. Others whose knowledge of history is better, may recognise Tolmezzo as the site of a First World War battle. The play is given the genre subtitle 'eine symphonische Dichtung' and uses a lot of different musical codes or intertexts (as do all Streeruwitz's plays). The stage directions of both *New York. New York.* (itself a musical allusion) and *Tolmezzo.* require the use of popular songs, modern Viennese classics and opera arias. *Tolmezzo.* includes songs such as 'Dann geh' ich ins Maxim', even 'Singing in the Rain', and snippets of Haydn and Mozart sung by 'die drei alten Sängerknaben'. In scene 25 one old choir boy tries to sing all three parts of a trio at the same time — an extreme example of the

---

[30]Linda Hutcheon explains Riffaterre's theory in *A Poetics of Postmodernism*, op. cit., p.143.

[31]Streeruwitz does not concentrate on one intertext like Botho Strauß, for example, in *Der Park*. Strauß models his drama on one (classical) intertext (Shakespeare's *A Midsummer Night's Dream*) and provides a recontextualisation of it for the present. 'Und so wie keiner von uns sein *eigenes* Leben führen kann, sondern immer nur eines, das tausenderlei übergeordneten und untergründigen Vorbedingungen, "Strukturen", Überlieferungen gehorcht, sind auch jene Zeitgenossen, die hier auftreten, Abhängige und Ideologen unter der zauberischen Herrschaft einer alten, unergründlichen Komödie.' Munich: (dtv) 1993; first published Munich/Vienna: (Carl Hanser) 1983.

[32]Manfred Pfister uses this term for titles which are calculated to evoke a certain set of connotations which are then contradicted or are not relevant in the play itself. See Pfister, *The Theory and Analysis of Drama*, transl. John Halliday, Cambridge: 1988.

fragmented subject. The 'symphonic' quality of *Tolmezzo.* might be traceable in the recurrence of a number of themes. The central theme is provided by the nostalgic reminiscences of the main character, Manon Greeff,[33] a seventy–year–old Austro–American emigrée who is visiting Vienna with her daughter Linda. Greeff's monologues consist of recollections of her flight from Austria/Germany, of how her family were able to get passports, and how she met her husband, who later drank himself to death. They are repeated in different scenes, are varied several times, and are spoken in chorus in one scene by two other female characters. These speeches are grafted onto the other goings–on, the nonsense rhymes, surreal activities and Wilhelm Busch stories of Spiderman, Luise and the Ken and Barbie dolls, and the antics of three drunken men, one of whom runs the café and is enabling his friends to carry on drinking despite the lateness of the hour. In addition to this element of 'personal' history, the stage directions provide for historical noises: '(*Güterzüge werden verschoben. Anschwellend näher)*' (*Tolmezzo.*, scene 19, 59). These allusions to the *Second* World War and to the transportation of Jews in the Holocaust, reach their most incongruous expression in the 'Miss Soldierbride' beauty competition (scene 21), in which the Barbie dolls (who in scene 9 have had a sex change)[34] are pitted one to one against the 'real' women of the play. Each time it is a Barbie doll who is chosen, with much whistling and applause from the sound track, although the stage directions make it clear that '(*sie wurden für eine abendliche Massenvergewaltigung ausgesucht. Dementsprechend sträuben sie sich und werden gewaltsam hinausbugsiert)*' (*Tolmezzo.*, 66). This conflation of historical time and references with the present textual time of the play demonstrates Streeruwitz's appeal to contemporary drama cited above: 'Zeit muß über die formale Lösung in Gegenwart verwandelt werden'.

Although her statements on the need for a new aesthetics in the theatre and her criticisms of the classical paradigm are not accompanied by overt political analysis, it would nevertheless be wrong to read her work as apolitical. A fusion of references and chronologies which allows a beauty–competition–meets–Nazi–Holocaust scenario outside a Viennese café may be taken by some as highly distasteful, not to mention apolitical or irresponsible. But this would be to fail to recognise the new image created by this provocative cocktail. This very texture of chaotic simultaneity,[35] of textual and historical references is mobilised in Streeruwitz's drama to

---

[33]This name, too, looks intertextual; it is possibly some kind of portmanteau incorporating Manon from Puccini's *Manon Lescaut.*

[34]A difficult transformation on stage if ever there was one: '*Sie haben keine Busen mehr. Glatzen. Keine Schuhe... Große feuchte Flecken auf den Röcken hinten'* (*Tolmezzo.*, scene 9, p.27).

[35]Siegfried Kienzle, op. cit., p.15.

generate political connections. This practice and the playwright's criticism of realism are not as radical as those of Heiner Müller but are certainly reminiscent of them. Carl Weber comments of Müller being 'increasingly doubtful that a linear concept of history, as Marx, and before him Hegel, constructed it, can encompass and/or define the complex situation contemporary mankind finds itself in'.[36] Streeruwitz, too, is searching for a more appropriate dramatic mode and would certainly agree with Müller's rhetorical complaint of the audience 'that refuses to accept that the theatre has a reality of its own and doesn't portray, mirror, or copy the reality of the audience? [...] Naturalism nearly killed the theatre with this strategy of doubling [reality]'.[37]

The concluding lines of *Tolmezzo*. demonstrate the kind of political connections which are offered up to the reader. The ending of Manon, in her sentimentalising melancholy, reflects how she is glad that she is old: 'Ich bin froh, daß ich alt bin. Und wenn einem alles zugestoßen ist. Dann muß man keine Angst mehr haben. Wenigstens. *Die Güterzüge fahren [...]* ' followed by one of the refrain–style repetitions from the mouth of 'Die grantige Frauenstimme aus dem Fenster': 'Gusch. Tschusch. Nazi' (*Tolmezzo.*, scene 27, 77). This is an amusing but frightening conflation and inversion — 'Nazi' and an abusive racist term, 'Tschusch', directed at one and the same person. This kind of contemporary and 'everyday' latent fascist behaviour is also highlighted in *New York. New York*. Frau Horvath ignores the chaos and violence around her, maintaining her capitalist stance in the face of it all ('immer schön kassieren,' scene 7, 27). She remains obsessed with cleanliness, with 'wiping clean' the signs of human excretion and blood, and is portrayed by Streeruwitz as an instrument of modern oppression. It comes as no surprise that it is the 'Deutschlandlied' which Horvath sings when Sellner asks her to 'sing for us our Bundeshymne' (*New York. New York.*, scene 20, 85). Frau Horvath is not so much caught up in the Imperial as in the Nazi past.

The feminist dimension in Streeruwitz's politics is more evident. In her consideration of a number of German–speaking women playwrights, Katrin Sieg maintains that they:

[...] offer resistance to the 'theater as it is', motivated by their feminist politics. Their plays, to some degree, supply the political conscience of postmodern theater, a theater largely occupied with the deconstruction of the Western, male, humanist

---

[36]Carl Weber, 'Introduction: The Pressure of Experience', in Heiner Müller, *Hamletmachine and other texts for the stage*, ed. and transl. Carl Weber, New York: (Performing Arts Journal Publications) 1984, pp.13-14.

[37]Müller quoted in Carl Weber, ibid., p.19.

subject yet unwilling to stage anything but that subject–in–demise. [...] They confront the classical traditions from the perspective of the Other.[38]

Sieg's appraisal of these dramatists' inability or unwillingness to stage anything other than that male, humanist subject in demise is certainly correct for Austrian women writers such as Marlene Streeruwitz and Elfriede Jelinek. The means of parody which Streeruwitz employs is often put to feminist ends. There is, however, no feminist triumph, and the victims are most often women[39] — the two murdered women in *Waikiki–Beach.*, for example, and the murdered prostitute in *New York. New York.* Streeruwitz usurps and inverts the pietà image to feminist ends in both *Waikiki–Beach.* and *New York. New York.* Conveniently, the playwright describes her *tableaux vivants* as pietàs in the stage directions, so that the 'body of Christ' is now a dead woman being cradled by a man.

Professor Chrobath, or, the Fall of the West

Streeruwitz's use of humour and her emphasis on metafiction or metatheatre are two of the factors in her particular staging of the humanist subject in demise. The character of Professor Chrobath both helps to re–enforce the metafictional and self–referential nature of Streeruwitz's writing and is consciously employed by the playwright to effect her own 'mischon' for the theatre. Chrobath is thus an *intra*–textual reference in his own right. Professor Chrobath first appears in *New York. New York.* in scene 15, where he makes his creeping entrance 'in guter alter Indianer–Spiel–Manier' (57), wearing a jogging suit. University Professor Chrobath is a kind of Spengleresque doomsday prophet, but one who is engaged in trying to precipitate the demise of 'das Abendland' (the Occident).[40] His particular way of doing this is through his quest to destroy all the toilet bowls in the public toilets — by karate–chopping them. The toilet — an aptly ironic Streeruwitzian symbol for the Western world — is something which Frau Horvath is understandably very keen to preserve (her livelihood after all depends on it). Chrobath insists:

Schauen Sie. Frau Horvath. Ich weiß schon. Sie können das alles nicht verstehen. Aber ich sage Ihnen, es muß sein. Ich habe fast alle schon. Und jetzt ist die Burggasse an der Reihe. [...] Sie wissen gar nicht, wie das Nichts im Kopf weh tut.

---

[38]Katrin Sieg, *Exiles, Eccentrics, Activists: Women in Contemporary German Theater*, Ann Arbor: 1994, p.110. Streeruwitz is mentioned at this point in Sieg's study.

[39]See in this context Jenny Lanyon's discussion of Jelinek's play, *Krankheit oder moderne Frauen* in the next chapter of this volume.

[40]Oswald Spengler's *Der Untergang des Abendlandes*, 2 vols, Munich: 1918–1922 is another likely intertext for this character in *New York. New York.* The Japanese tourists are an ironic marker of the ascendancy of Asian power.

Und sich selbst nie erreichen. Sie können es nicht wissen. (*New York. New York.*, scene 15, 59f.).

Frau Horvath replies: 'Nein. Kann ich nicht. Aber mir ist das Abendland ja auch gleich. Ich will mein Häusl in Ordnung. Und die Leute, die hierherkommen, wollen es auch' (60).

The deployment of this post–Faustian man is confusing. On the one hand, Streeruwitz appears to be ridiculing his existentialist 'angst'; his fear of 'das Nichts', and she does so by using feminist parody. After all, Chrobath does not poke out his own eyes — à la Oedipus — Streeruwitz pokes them out for him with Frau Horvath's knitting needles (57).[41] On the other hand, it is precisely the cultural baggage of the male, Western world that Streeruwitz is herself trying to hasten towards its own demise. Chrobath, then, could be construed as a kind of Streeruwitzian hero. In the end, he succeeds in getting his toilet bowl, and the myth of Promethean man is exploded by the Absurd symbol of the dead horse. In her review of the play, Heike Kruschinski concludes that 'der Untergang des Abendlandes ist perfekt: Prometheus wird an die Japaner verscherbelt und die kaiserlich–königliche Kloschüssel von einem verrückten Professor zerschlagen'.[42] In one sense, this is, of course, correct, but in another, Western civilisation is not so much destroyed as debunked. Frau Horvath has been keeping Prometheus fed and watered, she has been keeping her faith in humanity alive. The ending looks to be an Absurdist position: there is no Prometheus, no Christ to bolster one's faith, or, to quote Streeruwitz, 'wir haben keinen Himmel, auf den wir warten sollten'.[43] Theorists are divided as to whether to position the Absurd as a modernist or as a postmodernist phenomenon. For Patrice Pavis, it is quite firmly 'a modernist [...] manifestation, since its nonsense still makes sense and recalls an interpretation of the world.' She substantiates this argument by citing Adorno for whom even 'so–called absurd literature [...] has a stake in the dialectic: that there is no meaning and that negating meaning maintains nonetheless the category of meaning'.[44] To this reader, Streeruwitz does not so much negate meaning as parody the quest for meaning. In her reading of the poetics of postmodernism, Hutcheon promises that the reader will not find 'any apocalyptic wailing about the decline of the west under late

---

[41]In *Ocean Drive.*, the film star, Elizabeth Maynard, does this to her would–be biographer with a Swiss army knife.

[42]Heike Kruschinski, 'Geschichten aus dem Wiener Klo: Marlene Streeruwitz *New York. New York.* bei Mühlheimer Theatertagen', *Recklinghausener Zeitung*, 22 May 1993.

[43]*New York. New York.*, p.2; also in Marlene Streeruwitz, 'Passion. Devoir. Kontingenz. Und keine Zeit', *Theater heute*, *Theater 1992*, yearbook (1992), pp.34–37.

[44]Patrice Pavis, op. cit. pp.7–8.

capitalism'.[45] It may not be the stated intention of the playwright, but the effect of Streeruwitz's writing is to ironise precisely this facet of some postmodernist thinking.

In *Tolmezzo.*, Professor Krobath (here with a 'K'), is an ex-university professor, now drunken landlord of a café, trying to escape reality through copious quantities of alcohol. Occasionally he stops capering with his two drinking friends and delivers one of his little lectures:

> Wir werden von einer Grammatik beherrscht, die im Konjunktiv die Möglichkeit der Realimagination besitzt, die aber, durch die Formverarmung, indikativisch ausgedrückt wird. Damit indikativ geworden. Die Absicht des Ausdrucks von der Form des Ausdrucks. Abgetrennt. Entfremdet. [...] Die durch den Indikativ hergestellte Versprechung auf ein real mögliches Ganzes eine Lüge durch das Begraben des Konjunktivs im Indikativ (*Tolmezzo.*, scene 5, 19–20).

For Krobath the death of the subjunctive, the appropriation of the possible by the indicative mode, is yet another symptom of the demise of Western culture. Again, it is not certain whether Streeruwitz is condemning, condoning or merely poking fun at Krobath's desire to keep 'the possible' alive; the realm of the idea, the utopian. At first sight, his linguistic nostalgia may seem to be another metaphor for Austria's harking back to its past. But it seems more likely that Krobath and Streeruwitz are pleading here for the pursuance of some kind of Musil–style 'Möglichkeitssinn'. 'Als eine "große Versuchsstätte" denkt Ulrich sich das Leben, Musil sich die Dichtung', Albrecht Schöne tells us.[46] For Streeruwitz, too, the 'possible', the subjunctive, is not a linguistic form but a poetic, or dramatic form. Full stops are used in the above passage as throughout Streeruwitz's writing not as aposiopesis, as some reviewers have thought, but as a type of estranging device.[47] They do not signal tension or doubt in the speaker's intentions, rather they should force the actor to speak what are in much of Streeruwitz's work quite ordinary, everyday lines in a distanced and non–natural manner. Where Krobath and Streeruwitz are clearly at one is in their condemnation of the *Burgtheater* and of Austria's cultural prostitution. In *Tolmezzo.* Krobath is made to echo the sentiments of the playwright on the state of the *Burgtheater* today. Krobath laments: 'Das *Burgtheater* ist das größte

---

[45]Linda Hutcheon, op. cit., p.ix.

[46]Albrecht Schöne, 'Zum Gebrauch des Konjunktivs bei Robert Musil', *Euphorion*, no. 55 (1961), pp.196–220, p.219. I am grateful to Fritz Wefelmayer for suggesting this analogy.

[47]See, for example, Franz Wille, 'Wen der Berg ruft', *Theater heute*, no. 2 (1994), pp.32–33. Aposiopesis is the rhetorical device of breaking off in the middle of a sentence and is meant to signal an unwillingness to continue. If the actors' lines came over in this manner, it is, of course, hardly surprising that the reviewer saw them in this light. The play title 'Kaiserklamm. und. Kirchenwirt.' demonstrates clearly that there is more to Streeruwitz's full stops than this.

Bauerntheater der Welt. [...] Das deutsche Theater war einmal ein Instrument der Aufklärung. Eine Stätte des Geistes. [...] Heute herrscht doch nur noch sentimentales Geschluder' (*Tolmezzo.*, scene 18, 54). Krobath's wife, on the other hand, stands for the stereotyped, conservative, Viennese audience. She has been put off going to the 'Burg' by the productions which are 'zwar aktuell. Aber die Kostüme. Die waren aus dem 3. Reich. Ich gehe da nicht mehr hin. Klassiker müssen klassisch bleiben' (*Tolmezzo.*, scene 18, 55).

When Streeruwitz's characters become sentimental, or want to express grandiose feelings which are out of line with their late–twentieth–century lives, the playwright makes them have recourse to 'high', or mainstream culture: the tramp in *Waikiki–Beach.* sings an aria from *Tosca*, Frau Horvath also listens to opera music. Equally, hearing Mozart prompts Manon in *Tolmezzo.* to sentimentalise: 'Wenn es das nicht gäbe. Man müßte vollkommen. Einfach gar nichts.' Krobath is predictably as damning of Mozart as he is of the *Burgtheater*. He labels it, 'Zirkusmusik. Zirkusmusik für touristische Vermassung. Sentimentalisierungsvehikel.' Mozartkugeln, the popular Austrian confectionery, are for the American Linda, 'too big to put into the mouth and too small to bite into. They are so. So. Inbetween'. Their size is deliberate, Krobath, explains: they are designed to be stuffed into the mouth in order to silence the critical voices: 'Die werden auch hergestellt, um den Mund zu stopfen'. Krobath asks himself rhetorically, 'Im Rahmen des Untergangs dieser Kultur. Soll ich nur zuschaun?' (scene 8, 24).

The two plays considered here, *New York. New York.* and *Tolmezzo.*, stand as the playwright's own answer to this question. Like Professor Krobath, Streeruwitz too has a mission. To quote Krobath, this 'mischon' is to be 'aktiv tätig. Für den Untergang dieser Kultur' (*Tolmezzo.*, scene 8, 25). Streeruwitz's plays share many features with the theatre of the Absurd: the settings acknowledge its influence and the farcical humour is also a familiar trait. Whether or not Streeruwitz shares the 'sense of metaphysical anguish at the absurdity of the human condition' manifested by the Absurdists is a more difficult question to answer.[48] A preliminary examination of her work would suggest that for Streeruwitz the senselessness of the human condition is no longer a source of anguish but a focus of postmodern irony. As a textual strategy this lack of purpose pays due homage to the theatre of the Absurd.

---

[48]Martin Esslin, *The Theatre of the Absurd*, 3rd edition, Harmondsworth: 1980, pp.23–24 (first published 1962). In the additional chapter, 'Beyond the Absurd' Esslin sees Austrian avant–gardists, Peter Handke, Wolfgang Bauer, and Thomas Bernhard as deriving from the 'innovations of Beckett, Ionesco, and Genet'(p.434). See also the comments in the previous chapter by Waine, p.42.

THE DE(CON)STRUCTION OF FEMALE SUBJECTIVITY IN ELFRIEDE JELINEK'S PLAY *KRANKHEIT ODER MODERNE FRAUEN*

JENNY LANYON

Elfriede Jelinek has been writing and publishing since the late 1960s. Whilst perhaps best known for her novels, particularly *Die Klavierspielerin* and *Lust*, which brought her to the attention of a large reading public and resulted in the award of a number of prestigious literary prizes, she has also written several controversial works for the stage. In this chapter I intend to focus on one play, *Krankheit oder moderne Frauen*,[1] which was published and first performed in 1987, and analyse its treatment and dramatisation of the theme of female subjectivity. Subjectivity is 'identity' in the psychoanalytic sense of the word and describes the total image we have of ourselves as rational and emotional beings, and the way in which we relate to the society in which we live.[2] The quotation from Jelinek's play which provides part of the title of this chapter, an appropriation of the Cartesian 'cogito', suggests that female subjectivity, at least as it is constructed within patriarchal structures, is in questionable health.[3] I shall first locate the play within the context of trends in women's writing, before examining how some of its main ideas resonate with postmodern and poststructuralist theories of subjectivity, particularly those of Jacques Lacan and Michel Foucault. In my conclusion, I will evaluate the extent to which it is justifiable to speak of female subjectivity as 'diseased', and assess Jelinek's contribution to the feminist concern with the redefinition of conventional femininity.

---

[1]Elfriede Jelinek, *Krankheit oder moderne Frauen*, Cologne: (Prometh) 1987. All further references to the play are based on this edition and employ the abbreviation K followed by the page number in brackets.

[2]Charles A. Rycoft defines identity as 'the sense of one's continuous being as an entity distinguishable from others'. *Critical Dictionary of Psychoanalysis*, London: 1968, p.68. A further useful definition is provided by Chris Weedon in her *Feminist Practice and Poststructuralist Theory*, Oxford: 1987, p.88: "Subjectivity" is used to refer to the conscious and unconscious thoughts and emotions of the individual, her sense of herself and her ways of understanding her reaction to the world.'

[3]As Regine Friedrich in her *Nachwort* to the Prometh edition argues, to be female is to suffer from what she terms '[...] die bei der Geburt erworbene Krankheit 'Frau'". Op. cit., p.84.

Subjectivity in German Women's Writing

The literature which arose out of the Women's Movement of the sixties and seventies reflected a wide range of issues affecting women. Its central preoccupation, from approximately 1975 onwards, was with female subjectivity,[4] and texts expressed typically a desire for self–determination, for the radical redefinition of a female identity which, it was felt, had been imposed on women by men. This emerges powerfully in one of the best known feminist texts in German, Verena Stefan's *Häutungen*, in which the image of colonisation is used to express the crisis of identity:

> Die erste kolonisierung in der geschichte
> der menschheit war die der frauen durch die männer. seit jahrtausenden
> leben wir in massenghettos, bis heut im exil.
> unsere Wege vorgeschrieben, eingezäunt.[5]

Female social oppression is constructed by Stefan as an act of violence against women, condemning them to situate their lives within a limited framework of acceptable models for female behaviour. The path to personal and political liberation, as developed in *Häutungen*, is through self–analysis, the radical reevaluation of female sexuality, and the development of a feminist consciousness. The conclusion of the main character's search coincides with her rebirth as a new, autonomous version of her former self. Stefan's image of the colonisation of female subjectivity, however, postulates the existence of a female territory waiting to be reclaimed, if only the conquering male can be driven out. The conceptualisation of female subjectivity as an entity available for discovery, located beneath layers of patriarchal prescriptions is a recurrent theme in German women's writing of the 1970s and early 1980s, and many of the (predominantly autobiographical) texts published during this period thematise self–discovery, frequently expressed as a process of disentanglement from an unsatisfactory relationship[6] or from a repressive family background.[7] The

---

[4]See Richarda Schmidt, 'Arbeit an weiblicher Subjektivität: Erzählende Prosa der siebzieger und achziger Jahre', Gisela Brinkler–Gabler (ed.) *Deutsche Literatur von Frauen. Zweiter Band: 19. und 20. Jahrhundert*, Munich: 1988.

[5]Verena Stefan, *Häutungen*. Munich: 1975, p.39.

[6]See, for example Brigitte Schwaiger, *Wie kommt das Salz ins Meer?* Reinbek bei Hamburg: 1979, and Svende Merian *Der Tod des Märchenprinzen*, Hamburg: 1979. For an overview of trends see Ricarda Schmidt, op. cit.

[7]See, for example, Elisabeth Plessen, *Mitteilungen an den Adel*, Munich: 1979 and Helga M. Novak's *Die Eisheiligen*, Frankfurt/M.: 1979 and its sequel *Vogel federlos*, Darmstadt: 1982. For a discussion of other works on this theme see Renate Wiggershaus, 'Feministische Aufbrüche: Neue Tendenzen in der Bundesrepublik Deutschland, in Österreich und in der Schweiz', in Hiltrud Gnüg and Renate Möhrmann (eds.), *Frauen — Literatur — Geschichte: schreibende Frauen vom Mittelalter bis zur Gegenwart*. Stuttgart: 1985, pp.415–433.

redefinition of female subjectivity, however, has revealed itself to be a far more complex undertaking than these early texts suggested. By simply reversing the polarities of masculine and feminine, attributing a new, positive value to qualities which had hitherto been viewed as typically feminine, and therefore inferior, there was a failure to break new ground. This is summarised cogently in a critical review of Stefan's book:

> Frau hat, darf sie Verena Stefan's 'Häutungen' glauben, wenig Aussicht auf Veränderung. Schon in 'Brehms Tierleben' könnte sie erfahren, daß bei dem Prozeß der Häutung zwar eine neuere und bessere, doch bis ins Detail gleiche Haut nachwächst. Die Oberfläche mag in Verena Stefan's Fall neu sein, kurze Haare statt lange, Bauernhof statt Großstadt, Frau statt Mann, aber immer noch gilt die gleiche Biologie: die der Frau als Mädchen, Blondine, Mutter und Natur, dumm und unsicher ihren Emotionen ausgeliefert, von pflanzenhafter Passivität und Trägheit. Das Bild, das man und nun auch frau von frau machen, ist fast deckungsgleich.[8]

Thus is seems that the female writer's attempt to loosen the grip of a patriarchal structure tends to project her back into the arena from which she had sought to escape, a phenomenon which, as Ricarda Schmidt has noted, is frequently to be observed in German women's writing in the period under consideration:

> Im Gefolge von *Häutungen* und durch die Selbsterfahrungsgruppen der autonomen Frauenbewegung ermuntert, persönliche Erfahrungen wichtig zu nehmen und zu veröffentlichen, um die weibliche Gesichtslosigkeit zu beenden, schrieben die Frauen autobiographische Texte, die wieder und wieder die Loslösung aus einer entfremdeten Beziehung zu einem Mann als Weg ihrer Selbstfindung schilderten. Statt aber das Autobiographische als Form subversiv zu nutzen, verdoppelten die meisten Texte die schlechte Realität, ohne ihr neue Aspekte abzugewinnen.[9]

The resolution of the dilemma lies perhaps in the recognition that this bleak observation regarding female subjectivity is an accurate one: 'Das Subjektsein des Mannes steht nicht grundsätzlich in Frage. Für die Frau jedoch gilt es zu allerserst zu entdecken, daß ein weibliches Subjekt noch existiert'.[10]

In Elfriede Jelinek's work, on the other hand, and in *Krankheit oder moderne Frauen* in particular, no attempt is made to present feminine gender in a favourable light: female subjectivity does not exist outside its patriarchal construction. Further, Jelinek demonstrates that individual patterns of subjectivity are linked crucially to wider structures of oppression

---

[8]Britgitte Classen and Gabriele Goettle, ''Häutungen'' — eine Verwechslung von Anemone und Amazone', in Gabriele Dietze, *Die Überwindung der Sprachlosigkeit: Texte aus der neuen Frauenbewegung*, Frankfurt/M: 1979, p.105.

[9]See Ricarda Schmidt, op. cit., pp.462f.

[10]Ibid., p.460.

within a capitalist and patriarchal society. The portrayal by the 'radikale Pessimistin',[11] of her two main female characters as vampires who have no mirror image echoes Schmidt's rejection of the concept of the female subject. Whereas some of the early feminist texts referred to briefly in the foregoing appeared to suggest that the 'true' female mirror reflection may be restored by removing carefully the layers of false patriarchal images, Jelinek's technique is first to deconstruct the workings of the mirror, and then to smash it altogether. Before turning to a detailed analysis of *Krankheit oder moderne Frauen*, I should now like to establish recent critiques of the individual subject as an interpretative framework for it.

Subjectivity and Postmodernism
A central critical focus of postmodernist and poststructuralist thought is the Cartesian notion that the individual consciousness is the source of all knowledge about the world (*cogito ergo sum*):

> Not only is the bourgeois individual subject a thing of the past, it is also a myth: it never really existed in the first place: there have never been autonomous subjects of that type. Rather this construct is merely a philosophical mystification, which sought to persuade people that they 'had' individual subjects and possessed this unique personal identity.[12]

It is argued that there is no core of truth at the centre of the cosmos to be unearthed by means of philosophical enquiry. Moreover, the status of consciousness itself is questioned. In contrast to the stable, fully–present self of the 'cogito', the postmodern subject is theorised as diffuse, constantly in process and constituted out of social rather than personal meaning, as Patricia Waugh, echoing Foucault, argues:

> Postmodernism situates itself epistemologically at the point where the epistemic subject characterised in terms of historical experience, interiority, and consciousness has given way to the 'decentred' subject identified through the public, impersonal signifying practices of other similarly 'decentred' subjects.[13]

The displacement of the autonomous self of the Enlightenment is the result of the assaults from a number of directions. Influential theorists in this respect are Jacques Derrida, who criticised and rewrote Ferdinand de Saussure's 'structuralist' linguistic theory of the sign, and therefore of meaning; Michel Foucault, whose discourse theory asserted that the language of subjectivity is inscribed by the power of relations at work in

---

[11]Regine Friedrich, op. cit., p.85.
[12]Frederic Jameson, quoted in Patricia Waugh, *Feminine Fictions: Revisiting the Postmodern*. London: 1982, pp.1f.
[13]Waugh, op. cit., p.7.

society as a whole; and Jacques Lacan, who, following Freud, stressed the instability of identity which is continually threatened by repressed, unconscious psychic material.

Jacques Lacan's controversial psychoanalytical theories have been particularly influential for feminist explorations of subjectivity. Lacan argues that subjectivity is linguistically constructed.[14] The acquisition of subjectivity is initiated by the mechanisms of the so–called mirror stage, the point at which an infant (usually at the age of about six months) becomes aware of its reflection in the mirror.[15] Before this stage, according to Lacan, the child's experience of itself is one of fragmentation. The moment of recognition of its reflection in the mirror is the first step towards the development of a unitary self–image. However it is also a misrecognition — the child believes and desires its reflection to be its actual self, rather than just a representation. The infant, then, irresistibly drawn by the apparent solidity of its mirror image, adopts a 'false' self as its real 'self', prefiguring the fundamental cleavage which will occur in its identity when it enters the Oedipus complex.[16] This is initiated when the child begins to speak at around eighteen months of age, using the pronoun 'I' for the first time to describe itself. However, repeating and developing the experience of the mirror stage, the use of 'I' denotes not presence, but lack, as, by naming itself, the child acknowledges its irrevocable separation from the oneness with its mother. The desire for a return to pre–Oedipal unity with its mother is sublimated by the child into demands articulated through language. The demands, however are merely a substitute for what is really wanted. The 'I' used in language, therefore, can never be the same as the 'I' which is really meant. As Belsey explains:

> [...] entry into the symbolic order liberates the child into the possibility of social relationship; it also reduces its helplessness to the extent that it is now able to articulate its needs in the form of demands. But at the same time a division within the self is constructed. In offering the child the possibility of formulating its desires the symbolic order also betrays them since it cannot by definition formulate those elements of desire which remain conscious. Demand is always only a metonymy of desire.[17]

In Lacanian terms, then, the self is fundamentally and irrevocably alienated from itself.

A link between the Lacanian theory of subjectivity and the work of other poststructuralist theorists is in their insistence on the centrality of

---

[14]Jacques Lacan, *The Four Fundamental Concepts of Psychoanalysis*, trsl. Alan Sheridan, London: 1979, pp.196–200.

[15]Jacques Lacan, *Écrits: A Selection*, trsl. Alan Sheridan, London: 1977, pp.1–7.

[16]Ibid., pp.22–25.

[17]Catherine Belsey, *Critical Practice*, London & New York: 1980, p.65.

language in the construction of subjectivity. Lacanian theory follows the main contours of Freudian theory. For both Lacan and Freud the major mechanism through which the infant is exploded out of dyadic unity with the mother is that of the Oedipus complex. In the Freudian account of the complex, the father intervenes in the relationship between mother and child, introducing into the family dynamic a triangular configuration.[18] The infant is thus opened out to relationships with family members other than the mother and, by extension, to society as a whole — it becomes a social being. However, in the Freudian Oedipus complex the underlying motivation is provided by the child's biological drives, whereas Lacan shifts the emphasis into the linguistic and cultural sphere.[19] For Lacan, the resolution of the Oedipus complex results in the human subject's entry into language, which he terms symbolic order. However, there is a further twist to the construction of the subject's sense of self which is inherent in language. According to Lacan, language is not neutral, rather it is structured by the rules and codes for behaviour of the society out of which it originates.[20] Subjectivity, therefore, is 'over determined' by the prevailing conventions for the construction of self in the social network in which the subject is placed. The individual is not free to invent herself.

For women this is particularly problematic as, according to Lacan, the structuring principle of the symbolic order is what he terms the Name–of–the–Father, or the phallus.[21] The phallus is the primary signifier, designating the symbolic father of the Oedipus complex who interposes himself between mother and child, bringing about the subject's entry into language. Thus, being able to speak at all necessitates acceptance of the laws of patriarchy. For women a double dislocation occurs in the necessity for them to be subjected to patriarchal authority if they are to have a speaking voice at all. Their relationship to language, to the symbolic order, as Lacan termed it, is fundamentally ambivalent: they speak the 'father' rather than the 'mother' tongue. Elisabeth Grosz has described this phenomenon as follows:

> In one sense, in so far as she speaks and says 'I', she too [the girl] must take up a place as a subject of the symbolic [representational system]; yet, in another, in so far as she is positioned as castrated, passive, an object of desire for men rather than a subject who desires, her position within the symbolic must be marginal or tenuous: when she speaks as an 'I' it is never clear that she speaks [of or as] herself. She speaks in a mode or masquerade, in imitation of the masculine, phallic

---

[18]'Das Ich und das Über–Ich' in Sigmund Freud, *Gesammelte Werke*, vol. 13, Frankfurt: 1966.

[19]Grosz, op. cit., p.284.

[20]Jacques Lacan (1977), op. cit., p.284.

[21]See in particular the chapter 'The Signification of the Phallus', ibid., pp.281-291, here p.287.

subject. Her 'I' then ambiguously signifies her position as a [pale reflection of the] masculine subject.[22]

What could be referred to as the 'Name–of–the–Mother', the lost unity with the mother (Lacan calls it the 'Other'), is repressed into the unconscious mind. The Other is the source of desire in the human subject, the motivating force in life. But desire can never be satisfied and moves from one object to the next in search of fulfilment: 'The phallus is the privileged signifier of that mark in which the role of the logos is joined with the advent of desire.'[23] For the woman, the effect is that any act of speaking involves further alienation — in addition to that present for all speaking subjects — because she has to take up temporarily the phallic position to make any utterance at all. It can be argued then, that language, as many feminist theorists have pointed out, is man– rather than woman–made.[24]

Krankheit oder moderne Frauen
The plot of Jelinek's play is hardly one of everyday Austrian folk. Three of the four main characters are derived from other literary sources, reflecting both their representative function and the intertextuality which is a major feature of the play.[25] Carmilla, described as 'Hausfrau, Mutter und Vampir, österr.' is the eponymous anti–heroine of Sheridan Le Fanu's short story, published in 1872, and also set in Austria. Dr Heidlkliff, 'Fachartz für Kiefer– und Frauenheilkunde', is derived from the rugged Heathcliff of Emily Brontë's famous novel, *Wuthering Heights*. Ironically the second female character, Emily, 'Krankenschwester und Vampir', is based on Heathcliff's own creator, although, like that other famous literary character Frankenstein, she is ultimately destroyed by her creation. The fourth main protagonist is Benno Hundekoffer, 'Steuerberater und Carmilla's Mann', who towards the beginning of the play visits the practice of Dr. Heidkliff. The latter has just become engaged to his practice nurse, Emily. The occasion is the birth of Carmilla's sixth child, who is born before the doctor's arrival. Carmilla dies in childbirth, a fact initially ignored by the two men but immediately noticed by the lesbian vampire, Emily, who promptly bites Carmilla, thus turning her into a vampire. The two then escape to Emily's graveyard–bedroom, where they sit in a double bed

---

[22]Grosz, op. cit., p.72.

[23]Lacan (1977), op. cit., p.287.

[24]Two examples of the feminist concern with the patriarchal structure of language are: Mary Daly, *Gyn/Ecology: The Metaethics of Radical Feminisim*, London: 1979, and Dale Spender, *Man made Language*, London: 1980.

[25]The intertextuality which is a dominant characteristic of Jelinek's work can be linked to the author's reading of Roland Barthes, and her knowledge of the montage techniques of Pop Art. See Marlies Janz, *Elfriede Jelinek*, Stuttgart: 1995.

consisting of two coffins. At the same time, Carmilla has killed several of her children, divided them into portions and deep–frozen them in two freezers marked 'Familie'. Emily and Carmilla's illicit bliss results in a furious attack on them by their men–folk. Heidkliff and Benno soon take on the canine behaviour of the hunting dogs which accompany them on their mission, as their own speech degenerates into volleys of barking. They acquire a huge arsenal of weapons and finally shoot and kill Emily and Carmilla, who have merged to form a huge double–headed woman, ironically reminiscent of Plato's account of the origins of love.[26] The play ends with the two men sucking at the necks of the double–headed woman, like vampires, or babies, or both.

Jelinek's approach is intensely satirical and similar to Goettle's definition of satire as a ' [...] Technik zur Entlarvung des falschen und schädlichen Denkens.'[27] In the interests of the exposure of 'false and harmful' thinking in the play, no sympathetic or sisterly hand is extended, and both women and men are subjected to the full force of Jelinek's attack. Moreover, she employs techniques reminiscent of Brechtian theatre in order to deprive the audience of any opportunity for cosy identification with the events on stage. As she declared in 1983: 'Ich will keine fremden Leute vor den Zuschauern zum Leben erwecken [...]. Ich will kein Theater'.[28]

In the context of our discussion of Lacan, it is highly significant that the main vehicle for Jelinek's critique is the language of subjectivity, which she distorts and exaggerates in such a way that it appears stilted and unfamiliar. Although she stages the battle of the sexes, it takes the form of a 'war of words'. The characters do not use naturalistic speech, rather they deliver lengthy monologues, composed of discursive fragments, quotations, allusions and puns. As Jelinek once stated: 'Die Schauspieler sollen sagen, was sonst kein Mensch sagt, denn es ist ja nicht Leben'.[29] The thematic focus of the majority of the utterances is the social and cultural construction of femininity, as seen from both the male and female perspectives. Masculinity is not excluded from this treatment — Jelinek also illuminates the interdependence of concepts of the masculine and the feminine.

Two versions of female subjectivity are revealed in the figures of Carmilla and Emily, both of which have a strong Lacanian resonance. In her vampirism, Emily represents the patriarchal stereotype of the liberated woman as voracious, self–centred and aggressive. The fact that she is lesbian places her beyond male control and renders her dangerous to other

---

[26]See Robert Cavalier, *Plato for Beginners*, New York: 1990, pp.104f.

[27]Gabriel Göttle, 'Schleim oder nicht Schleim, das ist hier die Frage', in Gabriele Dietze, op. cit., p.53.

[28]Elfriede Jelinek, 'Ich möchte seicht sein', in Chista Gürtler (ed.) *Gegen den schönen Schein: Texte zu Elfriede Jelinek*, Frankfurt/M.: 1990, p.157.

[29]Jelinek, in Gürtler, op. cit., p.157.

women. In a determined phallic take–over bid, which is also an ironic play on Freud's theory of penis envy, Emily enjoins Heidkliff to deploy his dentist's skill in order to make her teeth retractable:

> Ich wünsche mir diese beiden wesentlichen Zähne ausfahrbar gemacht! Sie sollen hervorlugen und wieder verschwinden können. Wie ich ja auch. Ich brauche einen ähnlichen Apparat wie ihr Männer ihn habt! Ich möchte imponieren können. Ich möchte Lust vorzeigen können! Ich habe Säfte, aber die gelten im Alltag wenig. Ich möchte nach einem Prinzip funktionieren dürfen (K, 33).

According to Freud, the way out of the 'trap' of penis envy is for the little girl to accept the fact of her own castration, and to take up her place in the female ranks, having sublimated her desire to possess a penis into the deferred desire to give birth to a baby. Her sexual desire as an integral part of the same process, is transferred from her mother to her father. However, Emily demonstrates her rejection of this traditional role in her declaration to Carmilla, 'ich gebäre nicht, ich begehre dich' (K, 21). Within Freudian theory, conventional femininity requires a woman to be the object of (male) desire. Emily, however, casts herself as a desiring subject who is outside the dictates of patriarchy. At the linguistic level, Emily's pun demonstrates her unwillingness to conform to the Oedipus complex by rejecting the maternal role, and continuing to desire the mother (in the form of mother–of–six, Carmilla). Expressed in Lacanian terms, she seizes control of language and, in rejecting her castration, assumes the mantle of the phallus.

Emily's position vis–à–vis language, the Lacanian symbolic order, represents a further dimension to her status as 'phallic' woman. At the beginning of the play, both Emily and Heidkliff reveal their respective relationships to the symbolic order. Heidkliff, representative of the phallic law, situates himself firmly within the metaphysics of presence when he declares, 'Ich bin hier, aber nicht dort', and later, 'Verrückt hat mich keiner' (K, 6). His supremacy still unchallenged, he confidently celebrates his materiality, as opposed to the insubstantiality of the woman: 'Ich bin der, an dem sich ein anderer mißt' and, later, 'Ich bin ein Maß. Ich bin ein Muß' (K, 6f.). Emily, though, is unintimidated by 'otherness'. In common with her namesake, Emily Brontë, she is a writer. Emily would appear to embody Kristeva's view[30] of the radical potential of marginality, which enables the subject, particularly through artistic practice, to both enter the symbolic order, and maintain a critical position beyond its domains: 'Ich bin hier und dort', she tells Carmilla, 'Ich spreche in der Kunst. Ich bin international. Ich bin abstrakt, dennoch tauche ich an dem einen und sofort an dem anderen Ort auf. Dann wieder bin ich absolut fort' (K, 22). Emily believes that she can 'shoot the patriarchal rapids' in her writing, whenever she feels like,

---

[30] See Toril Moi, *The Kristeva Reader*, Oxford: 1986, pp.15–156.

retreating to a space beyond the symbolic order. However, whereas Emily has evolved a speaking voice, even if it is a pale imitation of its male counterpart, Carmilla, the conventional woman has no voice at all: 'Ich bin eine Dilettantin des Existierens. Ein Wunder, daß ich spreche, Ich bin restlos gar nichts', she laments (K, 15).

Emily's claim to phallic presence is also to be observed in her subversion of liturgical language into female 'vampire–speak'.[31] Descartes claimed to have found the proof of the existence of God in his own consciousness, and, in the Cartesian world view, God functioned as a transcendental signified, the ultimate source of meaning. The anti–Cartesian theories of Lacan replaced God with the phallus as the symbol which contains and places all others. Emily usurps the position of the transcendental signified when she blasphemes: 'Ich bin der Anfang und das Ende. Von dem ich esse, der wird ewig leben' (K, 22). However, Emily's defiance appears to offer less of a threat to patriarchy, as represented by Heidkliff, than she might have imagined: 'Daß du Vampir bist, Emily, stört mich gar nicht, solange du das Haus nicht vernachlässigst', he reassures her (K, 35). Or, even more devastatingly: 'Daß du lesbisch bist, stört mich gar nicht, solange sich diese Veranlagung nicht auf mich ausdehnt und solange du den Haushalt darüber nicht aus den Augen verlierst' (ibid.). The difficulty of any effective protest against patriarchal power is a recurrent theme in Jelinek's work, and female defiance is often revealed to be yet a further refraction of the stereotypical view of women.

Carmilla represents a more conventional patriarchal fantasy of womanhood. At the beginning of the play she appears as a parody of the perfect wife and mother, on the verge of giving birth to her sixth child. To her husband, Benno, she says, 'Ich werde an dich denken, wenn das Kind herauskommt. Ich danke dir, daß du mich erneut vollgefüllt hast' (ibid.). Emily's self confidence finds its mirror image in Carmilla's almost complete lack of a sense of self; of where her boundaries are: 'Ich bin nichts Halbes und nichts Ganzes. Ich bin dazwischen. Ich bin von liebenswürdiger Geringfügigkeit' (K, 14). In Benno's eyes, Carmilla is crucially dependent on him for guidance and for the interpretation of the baffling and confusing world in which she struggles to exist. In one of several intertextual references to the myth of Theseus and the Minotaur in the play, he jokes: 'Sogar den Faden fürs Labyrinth würdest du noch irgendwo verlegen, lenkte man dich mit einem hübschen Kleid ab. Dabei lege ich dir diesen Faden jeden Tag aufs neue in deine Handtasche' (ibid.). However, Carmilla's self–effacement, in keeping with the myth to which Benno alludes, has monstrous overtones. Her rejection of the natural role of mother for the unnatural role of vampire involves, shockingly, the murder of her own

---

[31] See Marlies Janz, in Gürtler, op. cit., pp.83–86.

children. Her character satirises not only the image of mothers as sainted, self–sacrificing and completely bound up in the welfare of husband and children, but also its counterpart, namely the fantasy of the omnipotent, devouring mother. The Medea figure of the mother who destroys her own young has had a pervasive influence, even in the late twentieth century. As Marina Warner has argued, 'Medea, the child–murderer, contravenes the most fundamental criterion of femininity: maternal love.'[32] The terror evoked by this myth is an enduring one, and it is precisely the reaction that it can engender which Jelinek exploits in her characterisation of Carmilla. Benno, anxious to re–instate the conventional hegemony of patriarchy in the face of his wife's defection, also invokes Medea, if only as a reminder to Carmilla of what he considers to be her proper place: 'Carmilla, eines sag ich dir: Eine Medea wirst du trotzdem nicht. Du bist und bleibst eine Hausfrau. Wenn du nun stirbst, bist du eine tote Hausfrau' (K, 54).

Deprived of her role as mother and housewife, Carmilla fails to discover any 'true' self concealed beneath the veneer of matriarchal stereotypes. Rather, she gives herself up to a narcissistic revelling in illness revealed in her re–writing of the 'cogito' in her pronouncement, 'Ich bin krank, daher bin ich.' As she says, 'Ich bin krank und daher berechtigt. Ohne Krankheit wäre ich nichts' (K, 44). For Carmilla, illness provides affirmation of her existence. In place of the patriarchal version of healthy womanhood, Carmilla opts for the sickness of life as a vampire beyond the pale of the patriarchal structure. The character of Carmilla, the vampire in Le Fanu's original story, is interesting in this context. She, too, was often overcome by bouts of weakness and lassitude during the daytime, when she had no access to her victims, who were always young girls. Le Fanu only alludes to lesbianism in connection with the vampire, but it is nonetheless made clear that sexual attraction between women is regarded by the author as 'unnatural' and a form of sickness.[33] The lesbian relationship between the two female vampires in Jelinek's play, then, can be regarded as a further dimension of the sickness which they, as modern women, embody.

The figure of the reviled female vampire is a recurrent one in nineteenth and twentieth century fiction, and the vampire movie is one of the best known genres in the cinema's repertoire of horror films. Rosie Garland discusses the fascination which male writers have for the figure of the female vampire and, in particular, the significance of Carmilla in Le Fanu's novella. Garland argues cogently that the female vampire functions as 'an

---

[32]Marina Warner, *Managing Monsters: Six Myths of Our Time*. BBC Reith Lecturers 1994. The lecture referred to here is the first, entitled 'Monstrous Mothers: Women
Over The Top'.

[33]See Robert Tracy's introduction to his edition of the story: *In a Glass Darkly*, Oxford: 1993, p.xix.

"outsider", social rebel; sexual subversive; epitome of the threat posed to patriarchy by independent women who must therefore be brought to book.'[34] She goes on to point up the subversive potential of the defiant female vampire from a feminist perspective:

> The female vampire has not simply been thrown out of patriarchal society; she defies it [...]. The female vampire myth is about women in rebellion — and they are not alone; vampires have a social grouping and create their own interrelated networks, they have no need for heterosexual, procreative, genital sex to perpetuate their species.[35]

It is my view that this is an appropriate characterisation of the use which Jelinek makes of the vampire figure, despite the fact that, ultimately, her view of the potential of feminist vampirism is pessimistic. Although, initially, Carmilla's illness represents her celebration of the rejection of her former existence, and of a sexuality deemed perverted by patriarchal society, in her defection to the Lacanian 'Other', she is deflected back into the patriarchal camp. She has become exactly what men believed women to be if not kept firmly under male supervision. Regine Friedrich is right to maintain that 'Krankheit steht als Metapher für die Existenz der Frau schlechthin'.[36] Here it represents the patriarchal view of women who attempt to escape from their allotted subordinate role. As Benno shouts angrily from outside the door of Emily and Carmilla's bedroom, 'Ihr seid die einzige Geschichte der Krankheit. Ihr gebt es ja zu!' (K, 53). Janz is right to argue of the play that '[die] vermeintliche Opposition durch "Krankheit" wird damit als Angleichung an die männliche Ausgrenzungsstrategie dekuvriert'.[37] Patriarchy, whilst idealising women, had viewed them as 'diseased' all along. There is thus no escape for women in these terms — whichever position they take up involves their being 'ill'. Significantly, when midnight strikes and the two women burst forth from their lair, they find that their weapons are ineffective against the men — they are unable to suck their blood: 'Wir können sie nicht bluten lassen, es kommt nicht, wenn man sie anstict. Ihre Gedanken gehen bereits über uns hinaus. Sie wünschen jetzt, fremde Länder in Anspruch nehmen zu können' (K, 61). The men, to employ a Lacanian analogy, have already moved themselves to another part of the labyrinthine patriarchal symbolic order and beyond the influence of women.

Jelinek does, however, not only restrict herself to depicting the fragility of female identity. Carmilla and Emily's retreat to their women–only

---

[34]Rosie Garland, 'Suburban Vampire', in *Trouble and Strife: The Radical Feminist Magazine*, no. 20, Spring 1991.
[35]Ibid., p.40.
[36]Op. cit., p.84.
[37]Op. cit, p.90.

sanctuary produces a crisis of identity in the two men and elicits their furious response. The particular threat to the men which the two 'emancipated' women pose lies in their usurpation of the 'male' prerogative — that of lust. Benno's shock at Carmilla's abandonment of her duties as spouse and mother are matched by his outraged imaginings of her new life of untrammelled passion: 'Sie ist obszön! Grausam wütet nichts als Vergnügen in ihrem Körper. Mein Blick wird von ihrer Leere eingesogen. Mein Geschlecht streikt. Sie verführt mich nicht mehr' (K, 51). Heidkliff fears in a similar fashion that if women lay claim to passion in their own right, the male will be emasculated and rendered impotent and effeminate: 'Gebt unsere Lust wieder heraus!' he yells. 'Verbindet euch mit uns! Seid fraulich. Sonst würden wir nämlich mit der Zeit ebenfalls stumpfe Rockträger. Werdet wieder leer! Wir oder ihr!' (K, 53). Here we see the view demonstrated that patriarchy, as a discourse of masculine superiority, is crucially dependent on its 'Other'; the 'inferior' discourse of femininity. As Jelinek herself wrote in her frequently quoted essay on Ingeborg Bachmann, 'Die Frau ist das Andere, der Mann ist die Norm'.[38] Any attempt by the 'Other' to redefine itself in more positive terms, suggests Jelinek, rocks the whole patriarchal edifice in which both sexes are situated, producing an aggressive backlash and threatening the existence of both parties.

Benno and Heidkliff equate the 'unnatural' vampire–woman with environmental pollution and they embark on a campaign to clean up 'Mother' Nature. Temporarily, Emily and Carmilla flee to that ultimate women–only space, a ladies toilet where they gorge themselves on the flesh of the women inside, and when they finally emerge, they have metamorphosed into the monstrous 'Doppelgeschöpf' — a union of the liberated woman and the mother and an incarnation of yet another patriarchal fantasy and fear; the large, devouring woman.[39] Heidkliff and Benno are appalled by what they consider to be an offence against nature and promptly murder it. As Benno declares, 'Natur ohne das wär schöner' (K, 75).

As the work of Elizabeth Grosz and Judith Butler has sought to demonstrate, female subjectivity, which is, as we have seen, associated with nature, is crucially related to the patriarchal construction of the female body, and in Jelinek's figure of the 'Doppelgeschöpf' this close association is evident. It provides, for example, the context for Heidkliff's explanation of

---

[38]Elfried Jelinek, 'Der Krieg mit anderen Mitteln. Über Ingeborg Bachmann', in *Die schwarze Botin*, quoted in Gürtler, op. cit., p.8.
[39]This is a recurrent theme in feminist writing and features, for example, in the works of Fay Weldon, Jeannette Winterson and Margaret Attwood and, in the German–speaking world, in novels such as Ulrike Kolb's *Idas Idee*.

his interest in gynaecology: 'Weil ich die Natur liebe, beschäftigt mich die Frau als solche'(K, 29). Carmilla is described in similar terms: 'In der Tat handelt es sich bei meiner Frau Carmilla mehr um Natur als um irgend etwas sonst' (K, 26). Jelinek develops this aspect further in the scene in the ladies toilet; in a haphazard montage of female voices, the conflation of the concepts of female subjectivity, the female body and nature is deconstructed in a manner which is typical of Jelinek's use of language:

> Die Frau und der Körper gehören untrennbar zusammen. Geht der Körper, geht auch die Frau [...]. Die Frau ist das Kleine neben ihrem Bild. Das Vermögen der Frau ist von ihrer Größe abhängig. Die Größe des Bildes besteht in dessen Abhängigkeit von der Natur. Die Frau ist Natur. Die natürliche Frau steht vermöge ihres inneren Halts vor der Frau, welche nur als Bild auftritt. Keine Frau stellt etwas dar. Das Bild der Frau bringt Gehalt ein. Ihr Auftritt Frau. Die Natur ist das Bild. Das Bild der Frau besteht lange. Das Innere der Natur verkörpert in der Frau. Der Körper geht ins Innere. Der Körper und die Frauen gehen zusammen in die Natur. Keine Frau mehr (K, p 68f.).

Here, the deconstructive process carried out by Jelinek pivots around the terms 'nature', 'woman', 'image' and 'body'. Its purpose is to reveal that none of the terms has *a priori* status; they do not exist outside of their cultural construction, as the insistent use of the word 'Bild' suggests. There is no 'natural woman' to juxtapose with the cultural construct 'woman'. Further, if the opposition between nature and culture is deconstructed, mirroring, as it does, the polarities of feminine and masculine, that between the two genders is also undermined.

It is at this point of the play that an additional and recurrent theme in feminist theory emerges, namely the body as a point of convergence of the discourses of femininity.[40] In *Krankheit oder moderne Frauen*, the female body fights back against its marginalisation within the Enlightenment world view in which reason, the mind, rules supreme, and in which women were regarded in close relation to their bodily functions and relegated permanently to the sidelines, emerging only in patriarchal idealisations of the female body. It is those very aspects of the female body which patriarchal society regards as taboo that Jelinek foregrounds, although she eschews the idealisation that can be found in some radical feminist writing. She does not, for example, search for the hidden truth of female existence in the menstrual cycle, rather, by making the stage run with blood, she satirises both the

---

[40]This aspect is elaborated in the work of Elisabeth Groth, *Volatile Bodies*, Indiana: 1994; Judith Butler, *Gender Trouble: Feminism and the Subversion of Identity*, New York: 1990; and *Bodies that Matter: On the Discursive Limits of 'Sex'*, New York: 1993; and Moira Gattens, *Imaginary Bodies: Ethics Power and Corporeality*, London & New York: 1996.

taboos regarding menstruation and its counterpart, the mystification and idealisation of female biology.

'Weißt du, einer sagt, die Geschichte beruhe in letzter Instanz auf dem Körper des Menschen' (K, 44), remarks Emily to Carmilla, an apparent allusion to Foucault's theories of power and the body in the first volume of his *History of Sexuality*. If female history, and therefore that of female subjectivity is inscribed on the body, then it is necessary to look at how this relates to the female bodies in *Krankheit oder moderne Frauen*. Foucault describes three levels of the 'hysterisation of women's bodies', a process which began, he argues, in the eighteenth century. The first of these involved the subsuming of the female body into medical science, thereby gaining control of it. Women were then forced to rely on male experts to tell them 'truths' about their bodies. Such male medical mastery of the 'recalcitrant' female body is represented in the play by Heidkliff's gynaecological practice, and is demonstrated particularly in the surrealistic scene which follows the birth of Carmilla's baby and her subsequent death. Heidkliff displays his ability to dominate Mother Nature, when he cheerfully converses with Benno whilst rummaging around in Carmilla's body, producing organs and even inflatable plastic animals, all of which are thrown carelessly on to the floor.

A further facet of the process of hysterisation described by Foucault lay in the relegation of women to the home and to their 'natural' task; that of producing and bringing up children. In *Krankheit oder moderne Frauen*, by removing bodies from male control and the possibility of impregnation, the women offer physical resistance to the patriarchal notion that their anatomy is their destiny. Further, according to Foucault, the bodies of women were deemed to be 'thoroughly saturated with sexuality'.[41] Thus, when not subject to the regulatory force of male desire, they would give themselves up to unrestrained sensuality, as feared by the two men in the play and expressed in Heidkliff's outburst:

> Sie spotten uns aus! Auf einmal ist ihnen das Geschlecht nicht mehr tödlich und ernsthaft! Sie betrachten es nicht mehr als Körperhygiene. Es bricht aus ihnen hervor. Ein Springbrunnen. Plötzlich ist ihnen das Geschlecht nur eine Gefälligkeit unter vielen (K, 51).

Ultimately it is the grotesque exaggeration of the female body, the 'Doppelgeschöpf' which arouses an extreme of murderous rage in the two men. There is simply too much of it; it is too corporeal, it is 'Talg. Margarienhauf ... Cholesteron [...] Ein Braten in einem Netz ... Fettgranaten. Fleischbomben ... Tirolerknödel' (K, 74). The female body is idealised when

---

[41]Michel Foucault, *The History of Sexuality. Volume 1. An Introduction*, Harmondsworth: 1990, p.104.

it obeys patriarchal laws, but the flouting of these regulations reveals the deep–seated contempt and hatred which underlies the original idealisation.

Conclusion

The play *Krankheit oder moderne Frauen* engages with social and cultural constructions of female (and male) subjectivity; there is no attempt made to dramatise the conflicts of individuals in their endeavour to make personal sense of gender conventions. The *dramatis personae* are the discourses which constitute our cultural understanding of female and male subjectivity. Although Jelinek's deconstructive focus is on the language of subjectivity, this is not merely a 'Lesedrama': events on stage are not superfluous to requirements, rather the physical action of the play is a witty combination of slapstick and horror movie. In spite of the author's avowal of 'Ich will kein Theater', the play is highly theatrical — a blend of melodrama and farce. The meticulous details of the stage directions ensure that the spectators are provided with a series of richly–textured 'grausige Bilder', as Ulrike Haß describes them. These heighten, rather than detract from the play's purpose of exposing the absurdity of social convention, and revealing the power interests which it secretly represents. By drawing attention to its own artifice, Jelinek's dramatic technique exposes our certainties regarding female subjectivity to be cultural constructs.

The discourses deconstructed by Jelinek are drawn, as I have demonstrated, from a number of theoretical sources, with particular reference being made to Freud, Lacan and Foucault. It is the Freudian view of femininity which is the main target for Jelinek's satire, and the women in the play do everything possible to free themselves from its strictures. In a reversal of the mechanisms of the Oedipus complex, they assert their desire for the 'mother' (for each other). As part of the same process, they reject motherhood, symbolised by Carmilla's murder and dissection of her children. Unwilling to accept their role as the passive objects of male desire, they 'steal' male lust and make it their own, revelling in their illicit relationship. Rather than concealing the social shame of menstruation, the two vampires wallow in blood at every opportunity. However, it is their final 'obscene' gesture which pushes the men beyond their limit: Emily and Carmilla dare to occupy a larger space than is normally allotted to women in their manifestation as the monstrous 'Doppelgeschöpf' at the end of the play, by which they also flaunt their self–sufficent existence outside the sphere of influence of their men folk.

Both sexes are revealed to be victims of ideology in the play. Heidkliff's confident assertion in the opening scene, 'Ich bin der, an dem sich ein anderer mißt' is exposed in all its fragility once the women begin to take charge. The male is not as secure as he had hoped, as demonstrated by

Emily's comic attempt to conquer the phallus by making her vampire's teeth retractable. The bogus premise on which the phallic law is based (which Lacan himself had admitted) is demonstrated by the readiness with which it degenerates into self-doubt at the first sign that its bluff is being called. The play exposes the absurdity of a system of gender which is constructed on the basis of the superiority of one sex over the other. However, there is a crucial difference in Jelinek's dramatisation of the construction of male and female subjectivity. The asymmetrical balance of power between the sexes ensures that, however precarious and fragile male identity may be, the male will always be able to assert himself over the socially weaker female.

The metaphor of illness is appropriate, if also pessimistic, as a means of describing the absence of meaningful female subjectivity. The 'cogito' developed out of a social context which, for the most part, excluded women from discursive and cultural production. In common with the vampires in the play, women in Western European culture have no mirror reflection, or at least, only a false one which has been imposed on them by the patriarchal social system. Jelinek also exposes the fear which underlies the male denigration of women. The vampire figure, a strong and hopeful image for many feminists, offers little hope in this play. Women, however iconoclastic and presumptuous they may be, will eventually succumb to the brute force represented by patriarchy, whose most extreme manifestation is violence against women. However, fear of women is not accepted as an excuse for their social oppression, as it is in the work of some psychoanalytic theorists, In the light of men's greater social power, Jelinek exposes this fear as absurd.

No political programme or solution to the problem of female subjectivity is suggested by the play *Krankheit oder moderne Frauen*. There is, for example, no rebirth of an newly–empowered Emily and Carmilla, and the difficulty of constructing a viable identity beyond cultural norms is emphasised. As Emily remarks to Heidkliff, 'Die Macht ist ein Kreislauf wechselseitiger Verführung', thus alluding to the complex psychological investment which individuals make in gender conventions. Deconstruction, for Jelinek, also involves destruction. So complete is her de(con)struction of our assumptions and preconceptions about gender that she leaves no alternative to the complete redefinition of female (and male) subjectivity. Within its own framework of logic, Jelinek's dystopian view of female subjectivity can offer no reassuring blueprint for an alternative society and yet, in the very bleakness of her vision, she recalls Brecht's imperative 'Ändere die Welt! Sie braucht es!'

VOX POPULAE, VOX AUSTRIAE: LINGUISTIC VARIETIES AND THE EXPRESSION OF REGIONAL AND NATIONAL IDENTITY IN THE WORKS OF FELIX MITTERER

VICTORIA MARTIN

Dialect in the *Volksstück*

Dialect is primarily a spoken rather than a written variety, and although there is a thriving tradition of dialect poetry in Austria, its use in literary contexts has been largely confined to drama, where the written text is intended to capture to a certain degree the structure and rhythm of spoken language and will, moreover, ultimately be realised by the actors as speech. Unlike the standard language, no set of orthographic conventions exists for dialect in its written form. Dialect poets, concerned with the appearance of the word on the printed page, have long exploited this lack of orthographic conventions for aesthetic effect, devising individual solutions to the problems of representing dialect phonemes, but a text designed to be spoken does not benefit from such experimentation. Mitterer himself lays emphasis on the importance of legibility in representing dialect in the text of his plays, and employs what he describes as a 'stylised Tyrolean *Umgangssprache*', in the expectation that actors from different regions will in any case realise this in various different ways.[1] He is, therefore, not concerned with the accurate transcription of particular dialect forms, but instead provides an impressionistic representation as a basis from which the actors can work. As a result, the transcription is not systematic, and various different features are used on different occasions to indicate that a character is speaking dialect. The choice of dialect as the linguistic medium is thus based not upon the perceived characteristics of any particular dialect, but upon the communicative and social function of dialect in general.

The dramatic genre which has made the most consistent use of dialect is the *Volksstück*, although the use of dialect is not its defining characteristic. The reasons for this choice of linguistic variety are closely bound up with the nature of the *Volksstück* itself. Schmitz sums up the genre with the

---

[1] Unless otherwise indicated, quotations are taken from: Felix Mitterer, *Stücke 1/ Stücke 2*, published by Haymon Verlag, Innsbruck: 1992, and employ the codes S1 and S2 respectively, followed by the page number in brackets (here, S1, p.7).

phrase: 'Volkstheater ist Theater *vom* Volk, *fürs* Volk, *über das* Volk',[2] a typology which in turn requires a definition of *Volk*. As Schmitz himself observes, the term is used in a number of different ways in connection with discussions of the genre: '*Volk* kann ebenso den Pöbel meinen, wie den unverbildeten natürlichen Teil der Bevölkerung, es kann die große Masse meinen wie die Nation, das Proletariat wie das Kleinbürgertum'.[3] Allowing for the fact that the social groups referred to by the term *Volk* vary, Schmitz's definition of *Volkstheater* makes the claim that it is produced by people from the same social group as the intended audience and depicts characters from that same group on stage. Klotz's definition largely overlaps with Schmitz's: '*Volksstücke* sind Bühnenstücke einfacher, übersichtlicher Machart, die zweifach mit den unteren Gesellschaftsklassen ihrer Zeit rechnen: als Personen und als Adressaten'.[4] Clearly the aspect of Schmitz's defintion that Klotz does not include, namely that *Volkstheater* must be produced by the *Volk*, is also the most restrictive criterion, since it would appear to exclude productions mounted by professional companies or texts written by educated playwrights (at least as far as *Volk* in the sense of 'unverbildet natürlich [...]' is concerned). In the case of Mitterer, however, even this rather extreme criterion is fulfilled, since many of his plays were originally written for, and performed by, semi–professional drama groups rather than in professional theatres (some of these originally amateur players also appeared in television adaptations of Mitterer's works, including the four–part TV series, *Die Piefke–Saga*). In this sense, Mitterer's plays can be said to be 'by' the *Volk*, and they are 'about' the *Volk* inasmuch as the majority of them are set in rural communities and feature central characters who are usually of 'low' social status, often struggling, as in *Besuchszeit*, *Stigma* or *Kein Platz für Idioten*, with social institutions or forces against which they are powerless. Finally, his plays are 'for' the *Volk* in that the target audience was often in the first instance, not habitual theatre–goers but local people. Mitterer emphasises this aspect of his audience in his description of the first production of *Kein Platz für Idioten*:

> Zur gleichen Zeit wurde übrigens im Theater am Landhausplatz *Stallerhof* von Kroetz gespielt, gewiß das größere und auch radikalere Kunstwerk, aber mit der geringeren Wirkung. Dort im Alternativtheater saßen die Studenten, die Intellektuellen, die ohnehin und von vorneherein der Meinung des Autors waren. Hier aber, an der Volksbühne, waren die Besucher ganz normale Menschen, mit ganz normalen Vorurteilen (S1, 11).

---

[2]T. Schmitz, *Das Volksstück*, Stuttgart: 1990, p.8.
[3]Ibid., p.5.
[4]V. Klotz, *Dramaturgie des Publikums: Wie Bühne und Publikum aufeinander eingehen, insbesondere bei Raimund, Büchner, Wedekind, Horváth, Gatti und im politischen Agitationstheater.* 1976: p.41.

As this comment suggests, Mitterer's works are primarily aimed not at 'students' and 'intellectuals' but at 'perfectly ordinary people with perfectly ordinary prejudices', who by implication are not part of any social élite. It is questionable, however, how far the requirement that the play should be 'for' the *Volk*, in the sense of the uneducated or lower classes, is relevant to the contemporary *Volksstück*, though it continues to take such figures for its subject matter. In works such as Horváth's *Geschichten aus dem Wienerwald*, Turrini's *Sauschlachten* or Kroetz's *Stallerhof* the *Volk* depicted on the stage are representative of the *Volk* as a nation, and the bitter criticisms voiced are directed at the nation as a whole, rather than at specific sub–groups within the population. The educated, socially privileged audience is expected to recognise aspects of themselves, as Austrians, in the lower class characters on stage. In these plays, dialect serves two key functions. Firstly it identifies the characters as distinctively Austrian, since it is at the level of dialect that Austrian German is most distinct and because the features which separate Austrian standard German from German standard German ultimately derive from the dialect substrate. (It is no accident that the common phrase 'Mir saan mir', which Karl Kraus puts into the mouth of Das österreichische Antlitz in *Die letzten Tage der Menschheit*, becomes a meaningless tautology when translated into the standard. It is the dialect forms which indicate to which national group the pronoun refers and hence serve as a marker of national identity). Secondly, dialect evokes in the audience the Austrian stereotypes of good–humoured 'Gemütlichkeit' and 'Schmäh' which the action of the play then proceeds to subvert, revealing the violence that lurks beneath.[5] In Mitterer's works, too, but particularly in *Die Piefke–Saga*, dialect functions as a marker of national identity, and the small local communities depicted on stage are representative, by virtue of their embodiment of certain avowedly 'Austrian' characteristics, of wider Austrian society.

Dialect and Standard

The way in which the term 'dialect' is frequently used in opposition to the standard language implies that it is a monolithic speech variety which admits of no internal variation. In fact, Austrian dialects exhibit substantial structural variation, as indeed does the standard language. The conventional division of German speech varieties into standard, *Umgangssprache* ('colloquial German') and dialect obscures the fact that in Austria the dialect and the standard are linked by a continuum of linguistic features, some of which are considered to be more dialectal than others. Speakers can vary the dialectality of their speech by moving up and down the continuum as the needs of the communicative situation demand, by increasing or decreasing

---

[5]For a discussion of 'Schmäh' see Waine's chapter in the present volume, pp.49.

the proportion and the type of dialect features realised.[6] These changes may only be slight or they may be so great as to constitute a shift from one linguistic code to the other. In spite of this flexibility, however, there is a strong tendency on the part of speakers to categorise all speech as belonging to one or other of the two polar varieties, with the term *Umgangssprache* sometimes being used when the speech in question exhibits salient characteristics of both polar varieties. As a result of modern mass education, almost all Austrians are familiar with the norms of the standard language, although their competence in the standard may be largely passive.[7] For many people, particularly in rural areas, the standard language is rarely or never used in the course of daily life, and variation is restricted to the lower ends of the continuum. Dialect, or largely dialectal speech, is the variety used at home, and the standard is not learned until schooling commences, whilst the dialect remains the variety that is used in intimate and informal domains. As a result, the standard language constitutes a slightly alien variety, used only on formal, public occasions where personal feelings and wishes are repressed and an objective, neutral stance is considered appropriate. It is the language of authority, of schools, of the judiciary, of parliament and so on, but not the language of everyday discourse, so that its use by people who are primarily dialect speakers involves a degree of effort and conscious reflection that is absent when dialect is spoken.[8]

Since the majority of Mitterer's dramatic works are written in dialect, it is worth problematising the standard language and considering why his three plays written in standard German employ this variety, rather than asking why the remainder are written in dialect. In all three instances, Mitterer chooses the standard language 'aus bestimmten Gründen' (S1, 7). *Die Kinder des Teufels* (S2) is set in Austria, in 18th century Salzburg, but although it is based on authentic contemporary sources, it is not intended merely as a recreation of this particular historical event (the torture and in some instances execution of beggar children for allegedly practising witchcraft) but as an exemplification of witch trials in general. It is the exemplifying function which dictates the avoidance of dialect, since it would lend the events too specifically local a character. *Siberien* (S2), an extended monologue by an old man in a geriatric home, 'kann überall auf der Welt spielen' (S1, 7), and since dialect identifies a speaker as coming from a

---

[6]See V. Martin, 'Modelle der Umgangssprache: Überlegungen zum theoretischen Status eines linguistischen Begriffs am Beispiel des Wiener Deutsch', *Zeitschrift für Dialektologie und Linguistik* 63 (2), 1996, pp. 129–156.

[7]See S. Moosmüller, *Hochsprache und Dialekt in Österreich*, Vienna: 1992.

[8]See Christine Nöstlinger's introduction to W. Pollak, *Was halten die Österreicher von ihrem Deutsch? Eine sprachpolitische und soziosemantische Analyse der sprachlichen Identität der Österreicher.* Vienna: Institut für SozioSemiotische Studien, [1992].

particular region, it is inappropriate here. Finally, *Ein Jedermann* (S2) is set in the world of high finance, a social context in which dialect would not be spoken. The standard language is thus employed where the setting of the play is not a specifically local milieu. This is not to imply that those plays written in dialect are preoccupied with provincial concerns. Indeed, the main themes of the dramas are universal: 'wie wir Menschen miteinander umgehen' (S1, 259). However, although the overarching theme of the human condition is universal, it is treated through the medium of the specific and local.

The human condition is illustrated in the stories of particular individuals at a particular time and place, embedded in very particular social and historical contexts, which the use of dialect reinforces. Mitterer is careful to stress, for instance, that his depiction of the effects of mass tourism on local communities in *Die Piefke–Saga*, need not have been set in Austria, but could just as well have taken for its subject matter a Viennese family in the popular Italian seaside resort of Caorle, or an Innsbruck family on Lake Garda (*Die Piefke–Saga*),[9] but it is typical of his dramatic approach that a theme which is of broad, general significance should be located very precisely in a particular regional and cultural context.

The importance of the specific is pointed up by the tremendous significance that the setting plays in many of Mitterer's dramas. *Munde* (S2), which is set on a mountain peak, was originally staged on top of the Hohe Munde, a mountain near Telfs in the Tyrol; *Verlorene Heimat* (S2), which is concerned with the expulsion of Protestants from the Zillertal in 1837, is performed in the village square of Stumm in the Zillertal;[10] and *Das Spiel im Berg*, set in a mine, was first staged in a salt mine in Altaussee. In each instance, the fictional story — or, in the case of *Verlorene Heimat*, the dramatic reconstruction — is enacted in a real location, and the events are lent a greater immediacy by being presented in the actual location in which they are set. The intimate connection between the setting and the action is reinforced by the use of the local dialect, which situates the action socially, regionally and culturally with the same degree of immediacy and precision as does the setting. A dialect familiar to the audience serves to anchor the characters and action in a world that is known and directly relevant to that audience's own experience, and Mitterer is able to exploit the social and cultural cues which dialect provides as part of his characterisation:

---

[9]Felix Mitterer, *Die Piefke-Saga*, published by Haymon Verlag, Innsbruck: 1991. Henceforth abbreviated as PS, followed by the page number in brackets.

[10]The inhabitants of the Zillertal have the exclusive performance rights and plan to stage the play every ten years.

> Die Art und Weise, wie ich den Dialekt niedergeschrieben habe, war nicht immer gleich. [...] Hauptsächlich variiert die Sprache je nach dem beschriebenen Milieu [...] oder je nach den auftretenden Personen (Herkunft, Beruf, Stand) (S1, 7).

An audience familiar with the various speech varieties can instantly interpret the linguistic cues provided by the characters to locate them in social space. The couples engaged in dialogue in the four plays that make up *Besuchszeit* (S1), for example, all use dialect, and in this instance it serves to underline the helplessness that derives from their weak position in society. The husband and his dying wife in *Man versteht nichts* cannot get clear information from the doctors about her illness because they do not know the language in which to couch the questions, nor do they have the social clout to enforce a reply. As Mitterer says of the institutions in which his characters find themselves imprisoned: 'Vor allem ist der Mensch ausgeliefert, wenn er ein Mensch zweiter Klasse ist, im wahrsten Sinne des Wortes. Diejenigen, die Geld haben und Einfluß, die können sich wehren' (S1, 167). The dialect in these plays vividly conveys the characters' status as underprivileged second class citizens. Similarly, in *Stigma* (S1) the helplessness of the ignorant farm girl, Moid, in the face of her educated interrogators, the Professor and the Monsignore, is pointed up by her use of dialect, paratactic sentence constructions and limited vocabulary in contrast with their command of the standard.

In other works, certain characters, whose linguistic repertoire encompasses a wider range, code–switch between the standard and dialect, or speak a form of *Umgangssprache*. Their ability to alter their linguistic register is an indication of their ability to operate effectively in public and institutional domains as well as in intimate and domestic contexts. Franz Wechselberger, the mayor of Lahnenberg in *Die Piefke–Saga*, code–switches between the standard language in his public speeches and when talking to the German guests, and dialect when speaking to the locals in a non–official capacity. Other officials also use the standard in public, although they may switch to dialect depending on the interlocutor, as is the case with the notary, who uses the standard with his German client, dialect with the dying farmer, Andreas, and the standard again with Hans and Manfred when they interrupt the proceedings and threaten to expose him:

> Notar: [To Andreas] Jetzt tua weiter, Opa! I hab nit soviel Zeit! [...]
> [To Hans] Geben Sie diese Papiere her! [...] Wir sehen uns vor Gericht wieder! (PS, 129, 130).

Such code–switching is not always complete. Many characters speak a mixture of features drawn from the standard and features from the dialect, and this is an accurate reflection of modern Austrian speech, although

Mitterer also exploits the mix for comic effect. When norms associated with the dialect occur unexpectedly in otherwise standard speech, the result can be very funny:

> Franz Wechselberger: Ich versichere Ihnen, Herr Sattmann, Sie sind uns beim Arsch lieber als jeder Wiener beim Gesicht! (PS, 15)

Here the unexpected occurrence of the vulgar 'Arsch' in an otherwise impeccably standard utterance has a humourous effect. Wechselberger is attempting to adhere to linguistic norms other than his own and, as he flails about attempting to reassure the Sattmanns of the affection the Tyroleans feel for their German guests, he lapses briefly into his more usual style of speaking.

Code–switching is not confined to the Tyrolean dialect speakers. The Viennese reporter, Manfred Holleschek, uses pure standard when explaining the scheme by which the notary had sought to evade the law forbidding the sale of land to German citizens, but immediately afterwards his speech becomes more dialectal as he enjoys watching the consternation he has created:

> Manfred: Also: Laut Tiroler Grundverkehrsgesetz dürfen deutsche Staatsbürger in Tirol keinen Grund mehr erwerben. Um diesem Gesetz auszuweichen, suchen Sie sich Strohmänner, die als Grundkäufer auftreten. Der Strohmann unterschreibt zuerst den Kaufvertrag, ist also damit Besitzer des Grundstückes. Richtig? [...] Bin gespannt, wie Ihr aus dem Schlamassel herauskommts! (PS, 129–130).

The switch to dialect[11] conveys his satisfaction at watching his opponents squirm and reintroduces the emotional aspect of the conflict which was absent during his dry, purely technical speech about the legal implications of their actions.

The symbolic function of dialect in many of the dramas is thus more complex than a mere linear relationship between linguistic variety and class. An essential ingredient in this mix is the fact that for the earliest intended audiences, the Tyrolean dialect was their own local speech variety. This instantly creates a sense of familiarity with the characters but, more than this, it also implies that the characters and the audience share the same cultural background, the same social norms and values. The use of dialect serves to mark the characters as members of the same social group as the audience. Where the plays are translated out of dialect and into the standard — and versions in the standard exist for most of them — this crucial dimension of in–group membership vanishes. Performing the dramas in the

---

[11]This switch is conveyed in the written text by the dropping of the pronoun 'ich' and the addition of the second person plural marker –s to the verb. As spoken by the actor, the sentence contains further features of Viennese pronunciation.

standard allows them to reach a wider audience than is possible with the dialect versions, but it also ensures that those audiences will not experience the strong sense of shared identity that a dialect–speaking audience feels watching a play written in their own dialect. Since the use of dialect is largely stigmatised in all but the most intimate domains,[12] the public use of dialect is a strong marker of adherence to local values and hence of membership of the local community. Dialect speakers are 'us' not 'them', and dialect–speaking characters are instantly viewed more positively because the audience knows that an audience of out–group members, of non–dialect speakers or speakers of a different dialect, would react differently to hearing the dialect spoken on stage. The use of the local dialect in the public context of the theatre, a setting where the dialect is not normally considered the appropriate register, becomes an act of affirmation for a minority of its own sense of self.

Because the standard is, at best, the secondary language of the audience, for whom dialect is a marker of integration into the local community, the use of the standard necessarily conveys alienation from that same community. It signals social prestige and power,[13] but at the cost of relationships within the community. As a result, standard–speaking characters are instinctively distrusted, perceived by the other characters in the plays, as well as by the audience, as socially superior, but also as cold, unfriendly and untrustworthy. The most consistent standard speakers in Mitterer's plays are Germans, who are external to the community not only because they are not Tyrolean but also because they are not Austrian. The standard German they speak is not only not dialect, it is not even Austrian standard German. They are thus doubly outsiders. The contrast between Austrian villagers and German tourists is already drawn in Mitterer's first play, *Kein Platz für Idioten*, although the contrast here is fairly crass: the German tourists are pure stereotypes, who complain about the lack of a 'Tyrolean evening' and regard the village as a kind of souvenir shop. Their language is equally stilted and unconvincing, showing the stereotypical standard characteristics of over–intellectualisation and emotional distance, whilst the content of their speech is guaranteed to alienate an Alpine audience still further:

> Deutscher Gast: Mach dich nicht lächerlich! Vor dem brauchst du keine Angst zu haben! Scheint der Dorftrottel zu sein. Harmloses Individuum. Ist wahrscheinlich hochgradig debil. Solche Leute soll es ja nicht wenige in den Alpen geben. [...] durch Inzucht nehme ich an. Oder durch Zeugung im Alkoholrausch (S1, 27).

---

[12]See Moosmüller, op. cit.
[13]See H. Giles and P.F. Powesland, *Speech Style and Social Evaluation*. London: 1975.

The German guests, with their ridiculous prejudices about the Alpine population, are set up as easy targets for laughter and thus strengthen the identification of the audience with the Austrian characters. Their exaggerated *Hochdeutsch* (German rather than Austrian standard German), with its features of grammatical ellipsis ('Harmloses Individuum') and educated vocabulary ('hochgradig debil') contrasts with the villagers' dialectal vocabulary, which is coarse but lively: the Zweiter Gast calls Mandl not 'hochgradig debil' but 'a trensata Heudepp' ['a drooling moron'] (S1, 28). Behind this stereotyped portrayal of the tourist, however, lurks a moralising intent, for in fact the tourists do not complain about Mandl's presence in the inn, even when pressed to do so by the Zweiter Gast. The claim that the boy must be kept out of sight so as not to discourage tourism is merely an excuse, a projection of the community's own fears and hatreds onto the outsiders, so that the villagers need not take responsibility for their treatment of Mandl — it is being done 'for the sake of the tourists'. The audience is thus encouraged to identify with the Austrian characters only to discover that their behaviour is actually worse than that of the outsiders at whom they sneer.

It is not only Germans who employ standard speech, however. As mentioned above, although the dramas are written mainly in dialect, some Austrian characters do speak the Austrian standard, whilst others can switch between the standard and the local dialect at will. Since the use of dialect reflects adherence to local norms and values, the use of the standard can signify a rejection of those values and hence a distance from the community. Moreover, the standard is associated with a certain emotional coldness, even untrustworthiness. This is made most explicit in *Stigma*, where the scientific language of the Professor, in particular, reveals that he is alienated not only from the common people, over whose lives he has such power, but also from his own humanity. After he has examined Moid and concluded that she is no more than a hysterical epileptic, the stage directions read:

> *Der Professor geht weg, ohne Moid nur eines Blickes zu würdigen, dreht sich dann noch einmal um.* Vielleicht könnte man ihren Leichnam der Universitätsklinik zur Verfügung stellen, wenn sie ... Ein interessanter Fall immerhin ... Und alt wird sie ja sicher nicht (S1, 97).

The Monsignore is linguistically a rather more interesting figure. Whilst the Professor comes from the provincial capital, the Monsignore was born in the region in which the action is set, and so is able to speak not only the standard but also the local dialect. This becomes apparent in the course of the exorcism scene, for whilst the Monsignore's language up until now has been impeccably formal, standard German, as the prospect of the exorcism begins to excite him, so dialect features creep into his speech:

> – Beischlafsmäßig, oder wie? Unzucht! Zur geschlechtlichen Unzucht wollten sie dich verführen! (S2, 99).
> – Wollust! Unzucht! Geilheit! Los, meld di! Komm schon! I kenn di! Du kommst mir nit aus! I derwisch di schon! (S2, 101).
> – Hast ihr's Bluat hoaß gmacht, was? Hast ihr die Punzen kitzelt, was? Hast sie niedergrammelt, daß ihr Hören und Sehen vergangen is, was? (S2, 101).

Here emotions which are considered unacceptable in polite, 'civilised' society are articulated in a language which is equally unacceptable to that society. In accordance with the widespread lay belief that dialect is inherently coarse, even aggressive,[14] the Monsignore's lapse into dialect reveals the brutal interior beneath a surface of cultivated civilisation. However, it is not only because of the violent and crudely sexual emotions that surface under the demons' influence that the Monsignore's outburst is in dialect, but also precisely because it is his true emotions which are being articulated. He switches to dialect because the standard language, owing to its intellectualising, distancing function, is an inappropriate medium in which to express profoundly felt emotions of any kind. In this respect it is significant that in *Die Piefke–Saga*, it is the old farmer, Andreas, to whom the Sattmanns are able to communicate their deepest feelings, even though his speech is the most dialectal of all the characters' (and a rather archaic and hence particularly incomprehensible dialect to boot). When Heinrich's dog, Asta, is killed, it is to Andreas that he turns for help in burying him; when Gunnar's old life threatens to overwhelm him again after the police catch him accepting cannabis from Stefan, it is to Andreas that he confides (although on a purely linguistic level, the two wholly fail to comprehend one another); and when Karl–Friedrich discovers the plot to give him his building land through Andreas, his apology turns into a confession of his deepest feelings for Tyrol:

> Karl–Friedrich: Andere Leute träumen von der Südsee. Ich träum von den Bergen in Tirol. Ich liebe dieses Land. Verstehen Sie? Aber ich komm nicht hin. Ich komm nicht hin! Es gelingt mir nicht. Ich bin eben doch ein Piefke (PS, 131).

Andreas's role as recipient of these confidences stems from his position as the character with the most integrity and this in turn derives from his closeness to nature. Gunnar senses this integrity when he voices his admiration for the old man as he tries to drive the visitors away with a scythe: 'He, Mann, du bist echt stark'; Andreas is seen milking a real cow by hand, in contrast with the tourists who practise on a cardboard cut–out with rubber udders; and when his farm is destroyed to make way for a modern building with guest rooms, he sinks into an almost terminal decline. (That the rebuilding necessitates the digging up and disposal of Asta hints at

---

[14]See the remarks about dialect made by Moosmüller's informants, op. cit.

the fact that with the old farm, the old, more 'human' way of life has gone). Only when Gunnar rescues him from the hospital and brings him to Lena in the forest, does he recover — indeed, the surroundings restore him to such vigour that he and Lena finally marry. It is this closeness to nature and absolute integrity that Hans Wechselberger tries to imitate by opting for a life of poverty in Lena's hut, but Mitterer makes it clear that we cannot recapture the dignity of the past in this way. Hans appears as ludicrously under an illusion in his pursuit of the rural idyll as do the tourists with their scythes and cut–out cows. With the loss of the land to the demands of mass tourism, the old authentic way of life has gone, and with it people like Andreas and Lena, as is indicated in part by the loss of the dialect they speak.

Whereas the dialect allows the expression of personal integrity and true feeling, the speaking of standard German can be symptomatic of an emotional deadness, a lack of vitality. Indeed, Ulm Sanford suggests that the standard language is associated with dishonesty *per se*: 'Wahrscheinlich ließe sich ganz allgemein sagen, daß im gehobenen Milieu eine gewisse Unehrlichkeit in die sprachliche Ausdruckweise und auch in die Gestik einschleicht',[15] and points to *Ein Jedermann* as an example. Because the standard is associated with educated speakers, well–versed in the art of manipulating facts, ideas and people through the medium of language, it is also associated with deception. This is certainly true up to a point, as exemplified by the Professor in *Stigma*, and by the doctor and former National Socialist, Walther, in *Heim*:

> Walter: Sie gehören alle abgespritzt! Alle! Einschließlich dem da! Die ganzen Versager!
> Hilde: Was? Was heißt denn abgespritzt?
> Mike: Gekillt, Mutter! Gekillt! (S2, 159).

Here the true meaning of the Nazi euphemism 'abgespritzt' ['given a lethal injection'], an expressively neutral standard lexeme, is exposed by the honest brutality of the slang term 'gekillt'. However, the claim that standard German is associated with dishonesty overlooks the fact that in Mitterer's works, it is manifestly the case that 'eine gewisse Unehrlichkeit in [der] sprachliche[n] Ausdrucksweise' is as much present in the rural dialect–speaking milieu as it is in more elevated social circles, and that in consequence, dialect speakers can be as dishonest and manipulative as standard speakers. The usual representative of this slipperiness is the village Bürgermeister, as in *Kein schöner Land* (S1), where, after the murder of the

---

[15]G. Ulm Sanford 'Brutalität und Zärtlichkeit in Felix Mitterers Volksstück "Die Wilde Frau"', *Modern Austrian Literature* 26 (3/4), 1993, p. 168.

Jewish engineer and the defeat of the Nazi regime, he closes the play with an impassioned speech about the need to forget the past:

> Bürgermeister: Am besten is, wenn ma alles vergessen! Streich ma aus die furchtbare Zeit! Zsammhalten, lautet das Gebot der Stunde! Eisern zsammhalten! Jetzt gehts an den Wiederaufbau! Und nur, wenn ma Hader und Zwist und kleinliche Rache vergessen, könn ma des neue, zukünftige Österreich aufbauen! (S1, 362).

The politician character reaches his apogee in Franz Wechselberger of *Die Piefke–Saga*. Indeed, *Die Piefke–Saga* is from one point of view a long series of revelations of just how 'unehrlich' the average Austrian can be, so that by the end the viewer is compelled to agree with Karl–Friedrich's disgusted assessment of them as a 'hinterlistiges Bergvolk'.

Die Piefke–Saga: Dialect and National Identity

Thus far I have discussed the use of dialect in Mitterer's plays with reference to its significance for a local, dialect–speaking audience and have argued that it serves, amongst other things, to create a sense of shared norms and values. His four part television series, *Die Piefke–Saga* also makes considerable use of dialect but here the community it appeals to is not local but national, and the sense of a common identity is constructed at the national rather than the regional level. This is in part a consequence of the much wider audience that television can reach. In the case of *Die Piefke–Saga*, a co–production by the state broadcaster, Österreichischer Rundfunk (ORF) and Germany's Norddeutscher Rundfunk (NDR), the target audience was not only Austrian but German, though for the German audience it is the German rather than the Austrian characters with whom they share a language and with whom they are therefore likely to identify, whilst the Austrian viewers identify with the Tyrolean characters as fellow–Austrians, even if they come from a community that speaks a different dialect.

It is in *Die Piefke–Saga* that Mitterer concerns himself most explicitly with the question of what it is to be Austrian. The series constitutes an extended meditation on the complex and fraught relationship between Austria and Germany, on the bonds that link the two peoples together and on the vast differences that separate them. It is in comparison with the (perceived) characteristics of the Germans that the Austrian identity is thrown into sharpest relief. Precisely because the two nations are presumed to be fundamentally similar, the differences come as a greater shock. Tourist advertising suggests that Germans in Austria will feel themselves to be 'Nicht daheim und doch zuhause',[16] and at a high point in the

---

[16]An untranslateable slogan meaning 'Not at home and yet at home'.

Sattmann–Lahnenberg relations, Heinrich Sattmann refers to the Tyroleans as 'wirklich die besseren Deutschen', expressing the close sense of kinship the Germans believe they feel with their Austrian hosts. The reality is different, but it takes the Sattmanns a while before they can peer behind the carefully cultivated facade of hospitality to discover just how alien ('fremd') they really are. The Austrian characters, for all their superficial friendliness, an essential characteristic in the tourist industry, are markedly reluctant to acknowledge their German guests as individuals or to enter into anything more than an economic relationship with them. The Lahnenberg community delimits its boundaries strictly, defining itself both regionally, in opposition to the Viennese ('Wir haben mit diesem slawischen Volksstamm nichts zu schaffen, unsere Mentalität ist eine völlig andere! Wir sind stolze und fleißige Bergbewohner, die Wiener, die Ostösterreicher insgesamt sind faul, verweichlicht, verdorben und hinterhältig!' PS 54), and nationally, in opposition to the Germans. The Germans are reduced to the 'Piefkes' ('Piefke' is a derogatory Austrian term for Germans, particularly those from the north), whose main attributes are listed twice in the series, once by the jury in the Fuchsberger show (indicating that the Lahnenbergers' prejudices‣ about the Germans are shared by the rest of Austria, since the jury members speak recognisably Viennese German), and once by the mayor, who says of Karl–Friedrich:

> Vor vier Jahren, da is er an dieser Stelle gestanden und hat sich darüber beklagt, daß man seinesgleichen als Piefke bezeichnet. Aber er *ist* leider ein Piefke! Er ist alles, was man sich unter dieser Bezeichnung vorstellt: großspurig, profitgierig, arrogant und herrschsüchtig! (PS, 167).

The mayor's use of 'man' to refer to himself and the villagers indicates that, naturally, the Tyroleans and their opinions are taken to be the norm, whilst Karl–Friedrich is assigned to a group of clearly identifiable outsiders, 'seinesgleichen' ('his sort'), and it is above all through the use of language that this distinction is upheld. Tyrolean German functions as a literal marker of local identity, a shibboleth, at one point in *Die Piefke–Saga*, when Herr Körner attempts to infiltrate a meeting of the villagers to plan how to deal with the German guests' revolt. In an attempt to prove himself a local he tries to imitate the local dialect: 'Griaß di Gott, wia gehts der denn?' (Standard German: 'Grüß (dich) Gott, wie geht's dir denn?'), only to be told 'verschwind, du Flachlandtiroler' ['Get out of here, you Lowland–Tyrolean'].

Die Piefke–Saga is subtitled 'Komödie einer vergeblichen Zuneigung', the 'Zuneigung' being the love of Karl–Friedrich Sattmann for Tyrol. The first three episodes of the series are devoted to showing the impossibility of Karl–Friedrich's dream of becoming part of the land that he loves. We first encounter him sacking his sales director for failing to secure a business deal in some unspecified Arab country. When the man complains that this was impossible because of the corruption and nepotism of his trading partners, Karl–Friedrich responds furiously:

> Sie sind ein blöder, ein bornierter Deutscher! Man muß sich hineinfühlen in fremde Mentalitäten! Die haben eben andere Verhandlungsmethoden als wir! Darauf muß man eingehen! (PS, 18).

The discussion anticipates the difficulties Karl–Friedrich will encounter when dealing with the 'fremde Mentalitäten' of the Austrians, who will prove to be easily as corrupt and devious. The parallel with the sales director, who as the representative of a Western industrialised society had difficulty coping with the alien norms of his Arab trading partners, is taken up again at the end of Part 3, when the mayor of Lahnenberg describes Karl–Friedrich as a 'colonialist': 'Was kann ich dafür, wenn sich der Sattmann aufführt wie ein Kolonialist bei die Neger?'(PS, 167). This description is to some extent justified, for the relationship between the Sattmanns and the villagers has from the start been based upon economic dependency. Karl–Friedrich yearns to be accepted in Lahnenberg, but he also wants that acceptance on his own terms and is in no way willing to compromise in the demands he makes as a tourist.

The economic dependency of the region on tourists from Germany reflects the general economic dependence of Austria as a state on the more powerful German economy, and the theme of money as power runs throughout the series. When the Fuchsberger 'Piefke' episode is shown, Heinrich warns the mayor 'Wir können unsre Mark auch woanders ausgeben!' (PS, 21), and when Elsa tries to persuade the old farmer, Andreas, to let them stay the night, she employs a form of German used only for talking to foreign 'guest workers': 'Hier schlafen, Du verstehen? Viel Geld zahlen! Deutschmark!' (PS, 40). Most blatantly of all, Heinrich tries to stir up his compatriots to protest against the article 'Wer braucht die Piefkes?' by pointing out: 'Dieses Land, liebe Mitbürger, dieses Land lebt von uns! Von unseren harten und hart erarbeiteten Devisen lebt es!' (PS, 36).

Although the Germans show no hesitation in using their economic superiority to enforce deference, the Austrians are equally ruthless in the pursuit of their own interests, although the measures they adopt are quite different from the overt pressures that the Germans apply. Indeed, the approaches that the two groups take constitute a summary of the stereotypical characteristics of the two nations. The 'colonialist' behaviour of the Sattmanns is presented as a fairly typical, if humourously exaggerated example of the attitude and behaviour of German tourists in general, whilst the treatment of the tourists by the Austrians is representative of the mentality of Austria as a nation and not just of small local communities like

Lahnenberg. The Sattmans may be ignorant and arrogant, but they are honest and straightforward in their dealings with the villagers. They may be too quick to voice their displeasure but the Lahnenbergers conceal their hostility behind a cloak of superficial friendliness and 'Gemütlichkeit'. Where the demands Karl–Friedrich makes come into conflict with the needs of the locals, or even with the law, the key village figures (the mayor, the police, the priest) resort to deceit and wheeler–dealing in order to fulfil their promises, indeed they are incorrigibly underhand in all their dealings with the Sattmanns. When Karl–Friedrich asks for shooting rights they are granted over the heads of the village consortium which had previously been promised them; the chief of police takes his revenge by shooting Asta on the pretext that he might have been chasing deer. When Karl–Friedrich wishes to build a house in Lahnenberg (legally not permissible, since he has not lived in Tyrol for at least 5 years), the local authorities resort to deception, attempting to prevail upon the dying Andreas to leave the necessary land to Karl–Friedrich in his will. That this devious approach to problems is not a characteristic confined to the Lahnenberger is shown by the reaction of the state governor when he learns of the plot:

> Landeshauptmann: Geh! Sowas Ungeschicktes! *(Zu Karl–Friedrich)* [...] Sie kriegen Ihren Grund, Herr Sattmann! Auf de paar Quadratmeter kommt's a nimmer drauf an! (PS, 132).

Although it is illegal, the state governor is sufficiently influential to arrange for the law to be waived when he considers it politically expedient, and the underhandedness continues when the village council allows Karl–Friedrich to build his house in the avalanche zone which, technically, can only be used if the buildings comply to extremely strict safety regulations.

Since the Tyroleans are economically dependent on the German tourists, the latter are able to enforce an accommodation, at least in public, to their norms and values, including linguistic norms. An important factor here is the relative status of German standard German and the Tyrolean dialects, which can be described in terms of a centre and its periphery. German standard German occupies the centre, the validity of its norms is acknowledged in all areas of the German speaking world. Austrian German, by contrast, is a marginal variety, whose norms are only valid in a small region. The German attitude to the Tyrolean dialect thus reflects their attitude to Austrian German in general. It never occurs to the German characters that their way of speaking is not superior, because it is 'correct' according to universally acknowledged norms. The villagers, however, speak an obscure deviation from these norms; therefore the tourists are entitled to expect their hosts to try to speak like them, rather than the other way round. As a result, when the villagers speak to the Germans their language is less dialectal. The feelings of resentment this enforced accommodation provokes have been described by the Austrian linguist, Peter Wiesinger:

> Bei einem Urlaubsaufenthalt in Thiersee bei Kufstein in Tirol wurde ich nicht nur gefragt, wie viele *Brötchen* [Austrian: *Semmeln*] ich zum Frühstück gerne haben möchte, sondern die Gastgeberin bestellte auch beim heimischen Bäcker mit Hilfe eines Zettels täglich eine wechselnde Anzahl von *Brötchen* und nicht *Semmeln*. Ebenso mußte ich beim Einkauf im Lebensmittelgeschäft bei Verlangen von Wurst und Käse in *Deka* [abbreviation of *Dekagramm*, a unit of ten grams] die ständige nachfragende Umrechnung in *Gramm* über mich ergehen lassen sowie schließlich die Frage, ob ich zum Heimtragen eine *Tüte* [Austrian: *Sackerl*] benötige.[17]

Their economic power, and the higher status of German standard German — 'proper' German, as opposed to some charming but inferior local dialect — allows the Germans to enforce their norms on the local speakers. Significantly, in the final episode of *Die Piefke–Saga*, described by Mitterer as a 'Horrorvision zum Totlachen' (PS, 6), which is set in the future when Tyrol has become an independent state, the Japanese scientists working for the Tyrolean government speak not German standard German but Tyrolean dialect, albeit with a Japanese accent. The shift in the power relations between Tyrol and the rest of Austria and Germany has transformed the status of Tyrolean German from a peripheral regional dialect to a national language, learnt even by foreigners.

The differences between the Tyrolean dialect and German standard German not only serve to convey information about the power relations between the two nationalities. In the misunderstandings that arise between individuals, Mitterer illustrates the difficulties that the two nations have in communicating with each other. The failure of verbal communication between Germans and Austrians is symptomatic of a wider failure on the part of both groups to understand the mentality of the other. Significantly, it is Gunnar who is best able to understand the Tyrolean dialect, even the archaic variety spoken by Andreas. On several occasions Gunnar translates for his parents, for example when Andreas first discovers the uninvited guests sitting in his farmhouse:

> Andreas: Wos tats denn ös do?
> Karl–Friedrich: Wie bitte?Andreas: Wos ös do tats?!
> Karl–Friedrich: *(to Heinrich):*Ich versteh kein Wort!
> Heinrich: Wo sind denn die anderen?

---

[17]P. Wiesinger, 'Zur Frage aktueller bundesdeutscher Spracheinflüsse in Österreich', *Das österreichische Deutsch*, Vienna: 1988: p.239.

Andreas: Wos?
Heinrich: Wo die anderen sind? Wohl bei der Heuarbeit, was?
Andreas: Wos tats denn ös do?
Karl–Friedrich: Was? Was sagt er?
Gunnar: Ich glaub, der alte Fuzzy will wissen, was wir hier tun! (PS, 40).

The older Sattmanns' inability to understand the local dialect is symptomatic of their attitude to Lahnenberg, their failure to recognise that acceptance would require some adaptation on their part. The fact that Gunnar can understand the dialect suggests that his parents' failure to do so is in part deliberate, albeit not conscious. They do not see why they should have to learn this other language and insist that the villagers master their language instead. It is invariably the villagers who have to translate their thoughts into standard German, although Gunnar is occasionally obliged to find alternative renderings for his anglicisms and slang.

This willingness to compromise linguistically is indicative of a willingness to adopt local norms, hence it is Gunnar who of all the Sattmanns most nearly succeeds in becoming integrated into village life. By staying at the Rotterhof and working in the fields he earns a degree of affection from Anna's family and respect from Andreas. He is the only one of the Germans to experience first hand the harshness of life as a farmer (Herr Körner, by contrast, learns to use a scythe so that he can impress his friends by cutting his lawn with it at home). The extent of Gunnar's integration is indicated by the fact that it is he who rescues Andreas from the hospital and brings him to Lena's hut to recover; although Gunnar and Andreas frequently do not understand each other's words, this is not a barrier to communication. Ultimately, however, Gunnar, too, fails to become a part of Lahnenberg. Significantly, at the moment when Anna tells him she is pregnant, his ability to understand the dialect proves inadequate:

Anna: I bin in der Hoffnung!
Gunnar: Was bist du?
Anna: In der Hoffnung!
Gunnar: Was für Hoffnung? Versteh ich nicht!
Anna: Schwanger bin i. Von dir.
Gunnar: Warum hast du nicht ne Info zukommen lassen?
Anna: Was?
Gunnar: Warum du mir nicht geschrieben hast?
Anna: I wollt di nit in Schwierigkeiten bringen!
Gunnar: [...] Was sagt deine Mutter dazu?
Anna: Sie woaß es nit. Niemand weiß es.
Gunnar: Was? Das kann doch nicht dein Ernst sein?
Anna: I hab mi nit traut!
Gunnar: Was hast du nicht?
Anna: Nicht getraut! Angst hab i! Bevor i angfangen hab im Hotel, hat sie gsagt: aber daß du mir ja koan Piefke–Fratzen hoambringst! Sonst setz i di vor die Tür!

Gunnar: *(ahmt ihrer Sprache nach)* Piefke–Fratzen hoambringst! Was heißt denn
das nun wieder? Red doch deutsch mit mir! (PS, 80).[18]

Not only does Gunnar fail to understand the dialect at this crucial
moment, and demand that Anna use his vocabulary instead, he also, by
demanding that she speak 'German' with him, denies the 'Germanness' of
her own speech variety. As such he imposes his norms on her; by taking his
language as a model of what is real German, he sets up his own values and
lifestyle as norms, from which Anna deviates.

Sabine and Joe experience similar difficulties in their relationship;
again, their failure to communicate effectively is symptomatic of a wider
failure to appreciate their different mentalities. Joe finds working for his
father–in–law, together with marriage to a wife who is more successful than
he is, intolerable, and resorts to poaching as an outlet to his frustrations.
Sabine cannot understand why Joe is unable to conform to her father's
expectations. The differences are encapsulated in an exchange between them
that takes place at the opening of the snow canon factory.

Joe: Du bist mir abgegangen!
Sabine: Was?
Joe: No, abgangen bist mir!
Sabine versteht nicht
Joe: Furchtbar is des! Mir werdn uns nie verstehn! Gefehlt hast mir! (PS, 118)

The difficulty that the characters from the two nations encounter in
communicating with each other are symptomatic of the cultural gap that
exists between Austria and Germany. The similarities in their respective
languages mislead them into believing that they speak the 'same' language,
and, by implication that they share the same norms and values, but this
illusion can be maintained only at the most superficial level of contact. As
the relationships between the Austrian and the German characters become
deeper, so the differences between them become increasingly exposed. The
differences in the kinds of German they speak, which initially seemed no
more than an external marker of group identity (tourist or host, German or
Austrian) prove symbolic of the unbridgeable cultural gulf that lies between
them. In Part IV, the comic horror vision of the future consequences of mass
tourism, Karl–Friedrich finally achieves his dream of becoming accepted
into Tyrol, but against his will and at the cost of losing his own identity. The
Japanese scientists working for the Tyrolean government perform an

---

[18]Gunnar's demand that Anna speak 'German' to him is reminiscent of Gerhard's
demand to Mehmet in *Munde* when he hears him speaking Turkish: 'Red' gefälligst
deutsch mit mir!'. By 'deutsch' he means Tyrolean dialect, but in this particular dialogue
it is Gerhard who holds the power and is therefore in a position to define 'German'.

operation that transforms him into a robotic Tyrolean stereotype, complete
with a huge beard, a new name and a perfect mastery of Tyrolean dialect:

> Karl–Friedrich: Was hast denn immer mit dein Karl–Friedrich, Weibele? I hoaß
> decht nit Karl–Friedrich! I bin der Sepp Unterwurzacher! Schilehrer,
> Schuachplattler, Jodler, Bergführer, Bergbauer! Alles klar? Gfall i dir, ha? (PS,
> 212).

In this way the dialect, which has all along functioned as marker of
membership of the Lahnenberg community, becomes a grotesque outward
sign of Karl–Friedrich's total loss of his own identity. The dialect he speaks
is as exaggerated as the Tyrolean costume and bushy beard he now sports,
full of untranslatable stereotypical interjections such as 'hoi', 'ha' and
'eppa'. The final lines of the series underline how those aspects of Tyrolean
culture which can be profitably marketed, including the dialect, have been
completely emptied of their original significance to the community from
which they sprang:

> ALMHÜTTEN–TV–STUDIO. — Im Studio wieder der bärtige Bursche, vor sich
> Maßkrug und Jause.
> Tiroler Fernsehsprecher: *(in die Kamera)* Griaß enk, Leuteln, da bin i wieder! Der
> Schorsch vom Sender Tirol! Wir übertragen jetzt direkt an zünftigen Heimatabend
> aus unserem bekannten und beliebten Urlaubsort Lahnenberg. I wünsch enk a recht
> guate Unterhaltung! Pfiat enk derweil! *(Hebt den Maßkrug hoch und trinkt.)*

The Tyrolean identity has been reduced to its external trappings in their
most exaggerated and clichéd form, a process that is mirrored by the
emptying of the dialect of all its social and cultural significance. The dialect
has been reduced to a marketing ploy, projecting an image of Tyrolean
'Gemütlichkeit' that is as false as the layer of artificial vegetation concealing
the vast piles of rubbish that now make up the Alps.

Die Piefke–Saga thus investigates two broad themes, that of the
cultural differences between Germany and Austria, and the effects of mass
tourism upon local communities, by focusing on a community with a specific
regional and cultural identity. The Tyrolean dialect serves an important
function, both in establishing the identity of that local community and in
making it representative of a much wider group, namely the Austrian nation.
The clash of expectations and values between the Germans and the
Austrians is indicated in part by the linguistic differences which render
communication difficult, whilst the lower status of the dialect and the
insistence of the Germans that the Lahnenberger accommodate to their
norms reflects the relationship that exists between Austrian German and
German standard German, with the former seen as an inferior and degraded
version of the latter. Not only is the German attitude to the Tyrolean dialect
symptomatic of their attitude to Austrian German in general, but it is through

the dialect that the sense of a distinct, Austrian national identity is asserted. The differences between the two nations are vividly conveyed by the differences in the German that they speak, and it is at the level of the dialects that the crucial linguistic differences emerge which render Austrian German distinctive. Dialect is thus not merely a marker of identity for the local community but for the Austrian nation as a whole.

HUMAN BEINGS *IN EXTREMIS*
RECONSTRUCTING HERMANN NITSCH'S
1ST ABREACTION PLAY

JULIE WILSON–BOKOWIEC
WITH PHOTOGRAPHS BY PETER SMITH

By comparison with the exposure which his work has received in the rest of Europe, Hermann Nitsch is virtually unknown in Britain.[1] Nitsch first visited the country in 1966 in order to participate in the 'Destruction In Art Symposium' which also featured works by Gustav Metzger, Ralph Ortiz, Ivor David, Wolf Vostell, Yoko Ono and Al Hansen. Nitsch gave a lecture at the African Institute in London, entitled 'Abreaction and Criminality', and presented his '21st Action' at the St. Brides Institute.[2] According to the The *Times* (10.12.1966) Gustav Metzger, and his co-organiser of the Symposium, John Sharkey, of the Institute of Contemporary Art, London, were given a summons to appear at Guildhall Justice Room on 11 January 1967 to answer allegations of having staged an 'indecent exhibition'. After the Destruction in Art Symposium, Nitsch's work was not seen again in the UK until 1973, when photographs of a number of 'Actions' were included as part of The Austrian Exhibition at the Richard Demarco Gallery. This was the last 'substantial' exhibition of Nitsch's work in Britain.

It is my aim in this chapter to provide a brief introduction to the work and thought of Hermann Nitsch before moving on to document the British première of the so-called *1st Abreaction Play* (*Shouts, Noises and the Evisceration of the Lamb*) of 1961, which I produced with students on 13 September 1995, in the Didsbury Drama Studio of the Manchester Metropolitan University, as part of the conference which was the point of departure for the present volume.

Nitsch's large scale 'Actions' set out to relate in terms of their visual and graphic narrative, the story of Man stripped of identity, of his mythical journey from flesh and blood corporeality into symbol, iconography and incorporeality. On a deeper level, the 'Actions' 'map' or 'recreate' what

---

[1]At the time of the final copy editing of this chapter, Nitsch achieved a degree of exposure and notoriety in the British press, occasioned by the protest of high–profile French animal rights activist and erstwhile actress, Brigitte Bardot, outside his private castle where his six–day 'Orgies Mysteries Theatre' was being staged. See Kate Conolly's report entitled 'You'll Never Eat Again', in *The Guardian* (6.8.1998).

[2]For a report on this event see Jay Landsmann's account in the *International Times* (October 14-27), 1966.

Nitsch sees as the physical circumstances which affect mind and body when confronted with the experience and possibilities of 'Being' or 'Dasein'. His work aims at allowing the extended moment of existence to be felt by the participants in his 'Actions'. By introducing materials such as paint, eggs, blood, entrails, and musical and other noise–making instruments into the same environment as the participants, he provides the tools by which the actors' automatic subconscious gestures attain audible and graphic velocity.

Nitsch derived the conception underlying his 'Actions' from his interest in psychology and German philosophy, particularly the writings of Friedrich Nietzsche. Applying his training and skills as a fine artist, Nitsch took these ideas and began to explore them in terms of their potential for art and performance. However, Nitsch's artistic concern goes beyond finding merely visual 'metaphors' for philosophical ideas; it involves engagement with concepts and ideas on what might be called a 'vocational' level. As far as theatrical tradition is concerned, Nitsch prefers to align himself to the spirit of the Viennese Secession, and the 'priesthood' of artists such as Gustav Klimt. He argues that 'professing to practise art is the priesthood of a new understanding of being', and he proposes that art be 'transformed in the sense of its innermost mission', to become 'the centre of all glorification of life, a meditation',[3] a prayer, a synthetic liturgy. Given that Nitsch is perhaps more concerned with philosophy than he is with art, and more concerned with life than he is with philosophy, his aim has been to create what he calls a 'practical philosophy' which is concerned with encapsulating what he regards to be the essential intensity of life:

> Life is more than duty: it is bliss, excess, waste to the point of orgy. Everything that exists should be celebrated. Art as propaganda for life, for how it enhances it — that to BE is a ceremony, that in this word IS lies all the preconditions for celebration. The whole ascetic philosophy will be turned on its head; life will be a celebration. All metaphysics begin with the affirmation of life, which is what admits the possibility of broader–based knowledge.[4]

For Nitsch 'IS' becomes an existential mantra, a word which unlocks the doors of 'experience'. 'IS' motivates actions. The notion of 'IS' transcends words and speech, communicating directly with the senses, the instincts, and the unconscious. Unlike the Cartesian *cogito*,[5] 'IS' has no definitive beginning and end. 'To Be' is to exist within a stream of consciousness intimately connected with the movement of the cosmos. Intensive contemplation of this word, Nitsch argues, transcends the

[3]Hermann Nitsch 'The Orgies and Mysteries Theatre' (1962), manifesto reproduced in the Seville Art Expo Catalogue: 1992.
[4]Hermann Nitsch 'Das Orgien–Mysterien Theater 1960-1983', exhibition catalogue, Het Stedelijk Van Abbemuseum Eindoven: 1983. pp.44-45.
[5]See the discussion in Jenny Lanyon's chapter of the present volume, p.76.

intellectual; it moves the mind beyond the symbol, to the very heart of being. 'IS' plays a key role in Nitsch's work and places the 'self' in acute proximity to the rest of the universe: 'IS' is the primacy of the uniqueness of the moment of experience.

Through the writings of Nietzsche, Nitsch also became acquainted with the principles of ancient Greek mythology, and, in particular, with the psychological basis of the Dionysian myth which explores the nature of the animalist and instinctive side of the human psyche. Nitsch also found in the Greek tragedy a dramatic form or 'machine' which he believed was capable of processing symbolism into the type of cathartic experience which might trigger momentary sensations of 'Dasein'. Greek Tragedy and Nitsch's reading of Freudian psychology also provided the background for his appropriation of the figure of Oedipus as a possible model for experiential 'realisation'. Seeking both a dramatic and a psychological framework, he saw in this character the disposition and potential of 'Everyman' — combining the regal control of the Apollonian character, and the excessive animalistic traits of the Dionysian. The Oedipus myth also provided Nitsch with a scenario of empirical proportions. Here was an intelligent man who, despite his insecurities, despite his psychological, moral, physical and emotional 'fall' into darkness, is resurrected through a personal act of Will. Oedipus returns from crisis and psychological death, illuminated and made 'holy' by his experience. In Nitsch's view, the blind King Oedipus standing on the stage, all bloody, knowing he has slept with his mother, and killed his father, is 'one of the most important scenes in all theatre',[6] because at this moment the whole of his being is polarised and intensified.

Nitsch also conceives of his works in terms of the characters of Apollo and Dionysus. Apollo stands for the conscious logical aspect of the work; the form or structure of the piece which can be scored and which follows a set of rules, governing, for instance, duration, velocity and the way materials are positioned within the performance space. Dionysus, on the other hand, stands for the subconscious element within the work; that which can not be scored, but which happens instinctively. In other words, the characteristics of the Dionysian character are 'contained' within Apollonian structures. This is, in effect, the essence of what Nietzsche saw as an ideal aesthetic, with the vehicle of form and structure harnessing the awe and terror of the spirit of the Dionysian. It is the artistic meeting place of form and chaos, the model of which is Nature itself.

---

[6]Hermann Nitsch 'M.A.R.Z.', Darmstadt: 1969, paragraph 123.

Abreaction

In a treatise of 1968 Nitsch defined what he terms the 'abreactive event' as a 'synaesthetic' experience, stimulated by the heightening of the senses, of excess. It establishes synaesthetic relations between perceptions of touch, taste, smell and acoustic and visual registrations:

> [It] shall inspire our senses orgiastically. The accelerating activation of all senses can be compared to psychoanalysis. Instead of associating, actions are instituted which heighten the perception of the senses until the endpoint of orgiastic 'abreaction'.[7]

He goes on to suggest that what results is 'a descending into subconscious regions', into moments of uncontrolled excess. In this early treatise, Nitsch suggests that there may exist a correlation between 'abreaction' and what he imagines to have been the benefits of catharsis. He suggests that, for him, catharsis means the point at which fragments of the subconscious become partly conscious. 'Abreaction' therefore involves submerging the individual in the subconscious, thereby stimulating catharsis, which is the emergence of fragments from the subconscious into the conscious. Thus abreaction precedes and initiates catharsis. The notion of recognition, cognition and intellectual rationalism (the subconscious becoming conscious) seems to imply a verbal or language–assimilating imperative. However, Nitsch's form of 'abreaction' does not necessarily operate within the cognitive realm. For Nitsch it is the materials of the artist, paint, blood, egg, sound, etc, which provide the medium through which the individual may 'view' the pure language of the subconscious as it emerges through the automatic physical and emotional responses of the body.

It is Nitsch's view that the actual connection with life through the celebration and experience of existence on the deepest level, on the level of excess, is beyond abstract interpretation and requires no verbal realisation. In this sense, it is also beyond any notions of verbal cognition. Nitsch's relation of a particular incident is of significance in this context:

> I just received a letter from Vienna, from my girlfriend, and she writes that she just saw a birth, and that this new experience helped her to understand my work better — because my work helped her to understand the birth. The birth to her, now, blood and everything, looked beautiful, very beautiful. There was pain, we shouldn't forget it, but there was also beauty. Many of my theatre actions are like births. And a birth is like a crucifixion and resurrection together. There is blood, and meat and pain, and then comes the newly born child, and he cries, and he begins to live. That's why I work only with the senses of great intensity.[8]

---

[7]Ibid., paragraphs 52-54.
[8]Ibid., paragraph 19.

Here Nitsch associates the sight, sound, smell, pain and symbolic significance of childbirth with his own work. Considering childbirth he is struck by the colour, the sound and the intensity of emotion and labour. The combination of all of these gives the scene a kind of beauty which is derived from the sight of Nature, raw and infinite, yet meaningful while remaining beyond verbal interpretation.

Nitsch seeks to realise the same kind of authentic physicality in his own works — a creative gesture as powerful and spontaneous as child birth. However, he regarded the techniques which he had learned during his formal training as an artist as insufficiently robust to convey something so essentially and powerfully existential. In the late 1950s, therefore, he began to first explore the idea of throwing, splattering and pouring paint onto large canvases. These painting 'Actions' were performed in public places in an attempt to include the physicality of the act of painting in the art work itself; in other words to make the 'real' expression of life become 'art'. Nitsch developed the principles of his later Orgies Mysteries Theatre out of this extreme desire to match the actions of the artist to the immediacy of life lived to its fullest intensity. However, as an expression of life, paint quickly became inadequate as a material. The next step was then to employ blood, and with blood, the smells and textures of flesh. A further inclusion of fluids and organic substances added to the 'sensual' experience of the painting 'Action'.

For Nitsch, the performance area takes on what he calls a 'seismographic' quality. Rather than it being used as a 'canvas', its many 'surfaces', which include the bodies of the 'actors', function very much like a painter's smock or coat. For Nitsch this coat is:

> [...] a seismograph of the passion and reincarnation of all creatures. The hieroglyphics of chance are drawn spontaneously on the coat without the painter having to move his hand. To clean his hands the painter wipes the paint on his coat. The mark of the descent into sacrificial excess, the pit, the night of death, the cosmos, void, is blood–fresh. The passion, renunciation 'blood letting' of the painter inscribes itself onto the coat.[9]

Like the surface of the body which is 'inscribed' by the signs of ageing, the procession towards 'abreaction', catharsis, and an intensity of 'Being' in Nitsch's work is 'inscribed' in colour and action, emotion and the mounting of visual and aural textures on all of the elements, including the actors' bodies. Within the context of Nitsch's 'Actions', 'painting', whether it employs paint, blood, sound, or other forms of 'dispersal', such as that of the emotions through action, can perhaps be viewed as an alchemical

---

[9]Hermann Nitsch 'Colourful Paintings' (1990), manifesto reproduced in the Seville Art Expo Catalogue: 1992.

activity, or a form of 'putrefaction'; a decomposition of parts in order to find the 'inner' character which lies deep within the psyche.

It is not surprising that Nitsch refers to the kind of aesthetic experience he hopes to share with an audience as a 'feast'; a banquet of the senses. But more than this it is a form of communion, in which the body of the passive actor is transformed into the 'food' of the 'feast'. The body becomes the unleavened white bread and the consecrated wine, 'like the flesh and blood of God, which is at work in us as an essential, life–preserving substance of the cosmos' (ibid.) In this manifesto Nitsch argues that the tactile experiences encompassed in his 'Actions' are, in effect, the experiences of taste and tasting. Thus, in his work the body is presented as part of the sensuous banquet, on which 'all five senses, ultimately culminate in tasting' (ibid.) The aesthetic basis of Nitsch's work may be summed up as TASTE (the taking in of taste values) in the metabolic sense of the word. The body of the passive actor becomes part of a 'pure, concentrated (liturgical) meal, bearing resemblance to a sacrament' (ibid.).

Nitsch sees both the participants and the audience as guests at the communion table. All participate in the activity of consumption. Whatever state our 'palate' or capacity for determining both the delicate and the strong flavours of this meal, the feasting in Nitsch's work inevitably gains momentum developing into a devouring, gorging, drunkenness and intoxication. Nitsch suggests that the mind and body are transfigured by the feast, by the absorption of the taste values and experiences of sight, sound, smell and touch.

As the main course in this banquet of the senses, Nitsch offers the simplified, yet highly potent image of 'crucifixion'. Like Christ, the passive actor accepts his fate — he does not turn away from the 'cup', the container of blood, the cup of death, the quintessential item on the menu. In the *1st Abreaction Play* this moment is repeated time and time again, it becomes an inevitability, and an affirmation of collective will to rise above annihilation.

Nitsch impresses upon the viewer the closeness of death, and the fragility of the body in the midst of excess. He also presents us with the essential existential imperative — the image of man 'Becoming', through the realisation of his own depths. Nitsch holds that it is the extra–societal right of every person to know and experience the nature of 'Self' to the point of extinction.

Giving 'voice' to the psyche

For Nitsch the conventional spoken and written word was both a limitation, a symptom and a tool of repression. As a consequence, Nitsch required a new language of sound and action through which he might connect with 'the very core of life' and 'cast off every last vestige of repression'. This he

found in the 'shout' to which he gives primacy. As he states in his text of the
1st Abreaction Play:

> The shout is a more immediate expression of the subconscious, of the sphere of
> human urges, than the word is. The need to shout normally comes about when the
> 'ES' asserts its right, overcomes an intellectual control and allows the elemental
> drive to break through into life. The shock of torment, the sudden break–in of
> extreme enjoyment, in fact all those situations which result in a diminution of
> consciousness, cause the shock to break out. The shouts produced by direct
> ecstasies in the abreaction play should render audible the deeper psychic
> possibilities open to us. It is a matter of freeing subconscious regions of our psyche
> by means of excitement and shouting which are the concrete images of these
> stimuli. What is aimed at here is a deliberate regression into earlier states of the
> human psyche. The ego of early man was even more firmly related to the
> animal/vegetable elements of the subconscious (and therefore also to the
> mystic/religious elements).[10]

While it is clear that Nitsch, even as early as 1961, was concerned with
fleeing from the constrains of the intellect, he was also aware that this
should not be achieved at the expense of 'individual' consciousness. Whilst
the 'retrogression into the ecstasy of the shout is a communication with the
subconscious', through which 'one gives oneself up to the intoxication of
vegetative, often hectically dynamic laws', such an experience of
renunciation should not flee the constraint of the senses.[11] For this reason,
instead of developing a constantly repetitive 'meditative' trance–inducing
soundscape, Nitsch introduces silences and orchestral interruptions into
more rhythmic sequences.

Staging the 1st Abreaction Play
On 13 September 1995 a group of final year students, postgraduates, and
staff from the Theatre Studies department of Huddersfield University, joined
by two actors from Middlesex University, took part in a reconstruction of
the *1st Abreaction Play* by Hermann Nitsch under my direction. From my
personal conversations with Nitsch, it was deemed unnecessary for the
actors and orchestra to 'know' the work, in the way that one would normally
expect actors to memorise their parts in a traditionally scripted play, indeed
this level of familiarity was actively discouraged. Although there are
moments within the *1st Abreaction Play* when the participants are required
to 'act', notably within the 'Burlesque' sequences which involve the skills of
mimicry and characterisation, the bulk of the play requires that they do not
act, if 'acting' is taken to mean 'to pretend'. Of paramount importance for
Nitsch is that the participants in his 'Actions' should 'desire' to express

---

[10]Hermann Nitsch, 'MARZ', op. cit.
[11]Ibid.

rather than pretend. This is a concomitant of his view that life should not be lived under false pretences, and that one should not be satisfied with weak feelings and dull sensations.

During each of our rehearsals, the distance between the 'performed' and the 'real' widened. For example, the long episodes which called for extreme emotional release contrasted markedly with the shorter sequences of the 'Burlesque' and became more and more shocking as a very transparent type of comedy is juxtaposed with a real intensity. The plasticity of the 'actor' in the traditional sense is displayed alongside individual crisis; the actor's mask is placed next to the flesh and blood face distorted by emotion, as the 'actor' is asked to 'focus' upon their own life, and on the exploration of their own physicality and psychology.

My first task was to construct some kind of graphic score from the written accounts of the *1st Abreaction Play*. I decided to simplify and adapt Nitsch's own notation system, which sets out the 'Action' in terms of its duration in seconds and minutes, to my own needs. Each actor was allotted a 'stave' on the graph paper score so that their actions could be directed by the so–called Time–Keeper in the same way that a conductor leads an orchestra. During the familiarisation period, the accent was on understanding how the structures worked, learning how to take cues from the Time-Keeper, and building physical and emotional stamina for the piece which was approximately two hours, ten minutes in length.

Work on the play commenced in the early summer of 1995. Two days were given over to familiarising the actors with the basic structure of the piece and the kind of physical demands that the 'Action' required. The cast next met for four days immediately prior to the performance, at which point they were joined by an 'orchestra' of nine noise–makers. Large sections of the 'play' were now run in sequence. During this short period, the actors were introduced to some of the organic materials to be used in the play, such as eggs, wine, paint and raw meat. However, the actors did not encounter all the materials until they were in front of the audience, this was in order to keep intact that sense of authenticity of first contact with the materials, for the actual staging.

In Nitsch's early 'Actions' sound is articulated as merely 'noise' produced on musical instruments as well as found objects.[12] Later this was scored and instruments were given a simple pitch, duration, and three levels of velocity. Together with the noise of the orchestra, Nitsch asked that the 'actors' contribute to the sound texture; that the 'noise' produced by them should be 'real', in other words that it should be motivated by real sensations and real emotional states. It is the shouts and screams produced

---

[12]For the *1st Abreaction Play*, Nitsch suggests pan lids, wooden drums, cymbals, flutes, violins, metal containers, trombones, cow bells, tubas, and ocarionos.

by 'actors' which form the choral backbone of alternating episodes of lamentation, death and resurrection which pulse through the 'Action'. The shout or scream in Nitsch's early works is an immediate and authentically powerful expression of both death and resurrection — that only sound to be made at extreme moments of intoxicated ecstasy. In this sense, the desired sound, is not one produced through the act of 'pretence'.

The score of the *1st Abreaction Play* provides a framework into which passages of 'real' action can be injected. The strict assignment of 'time' (measured in seconds and minutes) acts as a mechanism of control. It also provides a broad rhythmic structure which propels the participants from controlled choral moments into highly charged emotional states, which are invariably accompanied by massive tides of sound produced by the orchestra. The velocity of the more extreme passages is highly confrontational; not only in terms of the severity of the images, emotions, and extreme physicality, but because the volume being produced by the orchestra comes very close to the point at which sound is painful. In addition, the audience is confronted with a group of people who are not acting, but are engaging with the material on a very 'real' and personal level. The process of how this is communicated to the audience is very complex, but I believe that it is conveyed through an atmosphere of sincerity, which generates a familiar resonance. The combination of extreme physical and emotional demands, largely the result of the massive rhythmic swings from one emotional frame to another, forces the 'actors' towards the intuitive. This is the type of intuition produced at moments of crisis and at such moments, the body responds with postures of survival. In a very real sense, the bodies of the 'actors' begin to speak in an intuitive and generally comprehensible body language of crisis and survival. The face is transformed by archetypal moments of anguish, terror, and personal torment — the body retreats into postures of submission, resistance, and sometimes complete annihilation.

Actor and Audience Response

Following the staging, I discussed with my actors their experience of the production and their responses to it, many of which throw interesting light on what Nitsch sets out to achieve in the *1st Abreaction Play*. Most of the actors, for example, speak about their deep feelings of 'responsibility' for the audience, and of the audience responses pushing them increasingly towards a 'crisis of responsibility', as the following typical account by a cast member indicates:

> Seeing her [a member of the audience] in tears, reminded me that [...] our performances could no longer be selfish [...] and that I did have some responsibility

towards the audience — to look out for them, as I was wholly aware that the cast were certainly looking out for each other.[13]

Most of the cast were unprepared for the unconventional affect that the play had on the audience. All recognised very early in the performance that both they and the audience were part of something which could not be described as 'theatre' in the conventional sense. In the discussions which followed the production, both the audience and the cast testified to the deep sensation of having experienced something 'collectively'. During the play's first twenty minutes, it became apparent that the audience was being ousted from its relatively 'safe' position as designated 'observers' and turned into active participants. There was expression of dissent and heckling, not of the actors but of fellow audience members. When items of costume, pieces of meat, 'sensuous' objects with texture and smell were passed around the auditorium, embarrassed or jovial conversation broke out. A similar reaction occurred when some of the cast walked into the audience. The 'wall' between the audience did not so much crumble as shatter within the first ten minutes. In the final sequences the shouts and screams of the audience even drowned out those of the actors:

> The wall between audience and players was broken down by the intensity of emotion on the stage. I felt drawn into the action.[14]

There seemed to be no escape for the audience, they felt either compelled or moved to join in with the actors, or were repelled by them. Because of the extreme emotional swings, there was barely any time for individual audience members to rationalise what they were experiencing. In the same way, there was no impetus or any moments within the opening structure of the first forty–five minutes of the play which might help or encourage a unified audience response. The performance structure had in effect 'divided' audience response, and the nature of each person's dilemma:

> They [the audience] were certainly taking an active part rather than remaining passive and I felt at times I was able to take a breather and watch the audience and what they were up to, it was like barriers coming down and an acceptance of what was going on [...].[15]

At some point in the middle of the play, both the actors and the audience felt a kind of transformation taking place. The audience, although still extremely active in terms of their response, began to 'enjoy' their individual engagement with the play, in the sense that they seemed to gain

---

[13]Actor testimony.
[14]Ibid.
[15]Ibid.

Figures

Fig. 1 Painting Action

Fig. 2 Mixing Liquids

Fig. 3 Shouts and Cries

some kind of strong emotional connection with the work, which was not necessarily joyful, but achieved a personal resonance. The audience, now familiar with the basic structure of soloist and chorus response, joined in the singing of some of the choral passages, many of them entering into the physical spirit of the play by standing, moving, and throwing objects and wine around in the auditorium. From the point of view of the actors, it was interesting to see how, over the space of two hours, what seemed to be a sceptical and reserved 'academic' audience had been transformed, or indeed transformed itself, into a wild rabble of shouting and laughing, demonstratively cynical, or emotionally moved and crying individuals.

It is difficult to state with certainty whether members of the cast or the audience actually experienced something approaching Nitsch's understanding of 'Dasein'. All of the 'actors' testify to a cathartic affect, to feeling extremely 'cleansed' by the experience. A number even went as far as to maintain that the experience changed their lives. What I find particularly interesting is the clear indication of the existence of a mutual 'bond' between the actors and the audience, and the audience and the actors, as the testimonies to feelings of 'responsibility', based on intimacy and sincerity demonstrate:

> After the performance I felt good within myself and exhausted; an achievement of endurance shared with fellow actors on an intimate level, but also shown and shared with a larger audience, who felt more than just 'bums-on-seats'[...].

> I felt opened up by the actions of the actors and felt very strongly that they were doing me a favour. I felt that they were shouting down all the partitions and walls that limit us, they seemed to remind me and urge me on not to succumb to small emotions.[16]

The experience of reconstructing, producing and directing Hermann Nitsch's *1st Abreaction Play* has convinced me that his 'Actions' succeed in their intention to provide space in which others can experience the extremes of life for themselves, albeit within a prescribed list of activities. This is because Nitsch, in my view, articulates a common language of experience. Certainly, evidence from my own investigations into this language and method of working does suggest to me that there is a common understanding and set of feelings and sensations with which the work 'connects'. This 'connection' lies outside what an audience would normally consider to be 'theatre' or 'art', yet it would appear to resonate somewhere in the deep region of their 'collective' instincts and emotions.

---

[16]Ibid.

IN WAHRHEIT IST JAKOV LIND EIN DRAMATIKER EIN VERSUCH ÜBER DIE KOMÖDIENTRAGÖDIEN *DIE HEIDEN* UND *ERGO*

SILKE HASSLER

Einleitung

Seit Jakov Lind 1962 mit dem Erzählband *Eine Seele aus Holz* und zwei rasch nachfolgenden Romanen[1] die deutsche Literaturszene betrat, wird sein Name mit dem eines Prosaisten assoziiert. Und dies, obwohl er sonst in den sechziger Jahren nur noch Hörspiele und Theaterstücke veröffentlicht hat.[2] Die geringere Beachtung seiner dramatischen Texte entspringt weniger deren Qualität als dem Versäumnis des deutschen und der Nichtbeachtung durch das österreichische Theater. Ähnlich zu vielen österreichischen Dramatikern hätten seine Stücke erst an deutschen Theatern erfolgreich sein müssen, um nach Österreich re-importiert zu werden. Da die Besonderheit der Lindschen Stücke weniger in der formalen als in der inhaltlichen, d.h. historischen Radikalität besteht, waren sie in einer Theaterlandschaft, die mehr von ideologischer Restauration als von zeitgeschichtlicher Diskussion geprägt war, nicht gefragt.

Es ist außergewöhnlich, wie oft die dramatische Grundstruktur aller seiner Texte — der dramatischen, epischen und autobiographischen — dazu angereizt hat, sie zu bearbeiten und in ein anderes Genre zu überführen.[3]

---

[1]Gemeint sind *Landschaft in Beton*, 1963, und *Eine bessere Welt*, 1966.

[2]*Die Heiden*, Spiel in drei Akten, 1965; *Das Sterben der Silberfüchse*, Hörspiel, 1965, *Anna Laub*, Hörspiel, 1965; *Angst und Hunger*, 2 Hörspiele, 1968; *Ergo*, a Comedy. 1968. Ab den siebziger Jahren wird er ins Deutsche übersetzt und veröffentlicht; Autobiographien und autobiographische Essays (der Rezeption ist somit ein anderes Feld geöffnet): *Counting my steps*, 1969 (dt.: *Selbstporträt*, 1970); *Numbers, a further autobiography*, 1972 (dt.: *Nahaufnahme*, 1972); *The Trip to Jerusalem*, 1973 (dt.: *Israel. Rückkehr für 28 Tage*, 1972).

[3]*Fringale*. Audiodrame de Jakov Lind. Traduit et adapté de l'allemand par Roger Richard, Réalisation de Bronislaw Horowicz, Paris. *Ergo, a Comedy*. Performed by the New York Shakespeare Festival at the Public Theater, 1968, directed by Gerald Freedman. *Fear*. Produced at Workshop of the Players Art, New York, 1973. The Silver Foxes Trilogy. Performed at the Gate Theatre Club, London. Dir. by Nicholas Broadhurst, 1983. *The Silver Foxes Trilogy*. Performed at the Everyman Theatre, Liverpool. Performance Opera based on the play *Hunger*. Composition by Carl Mansker in the Mallorquin dialect 'El Bon Senyor Karnak', Festival Music & Drama, Deia, Mallorca, 24.6.1988. *Eine bessere Welt*. Treatment zum Fernsehspiel von Jörn Thiel

124 – *Silke Hassler*

Den dramatischen Bearbeitungen durch Jakov Lind steht eine viel höhere Zahl an Adaptionen durch andere Autoren gegenüber. Schon die Titelgeschichte seiner Erstveröffentlichung, *Eine Seele aus Holz*, wurde als Theaterstück und Film adaptiert, und wird zur Zeit als Oper vertont.[4] Das Hörspiel *Anna Laub* ist als Bühnenfassung in fünf verschiedenen Inszenierungen in England, Frankreich und den USA aufgeführt worden.[5]

Als ich mich mit dem Werk von Jakov Lind zu beschäftigen begann, war ich überrascht, erstens, wie viel unveröffentlicht geblieben ist und zweitens, wie viele dramatische Entwürfe, Filmdrehbücher, Treatments und Outlines[6] er geschrieben hat. Schon dies bestätigt meine These, daß die dramatische Produktion gegenüber der prosaistischen quantitativ eine gleichwertige ist, obwohl Jakov Lind den Wechsel in dieses Genre nie richtig vollzogen hat, außer zwei Stücken keines veröffentlicht und meistens von Prosavorlagen ausgehend seine Stücke oder Hörspiele entworfen hat.[7]

---

nach dem gleichnamigen Roman von Jakov Lind, 1971. Fam. Versió catalana: Aina Bonner, Joseph M. Llompart. Música: Carl Mansker, 1982. *Counting my steps*. An Autobiography by Jakov Lind. *Being The Adventures Of A Jewish Teenager On The Run In Nazi Germany*. Treatment written by Joel N. Block, 1982.

[4]*Soul of Wood*. A play by James E. Dwyer, 1967. *Soul of Wood*. Adapted for the stage by Dana Coen. *Journey Through the Night*. Treatment from the story by Peter Javsicas Resurrection. Adapted for Television by Mordechai Richler. *Soul of Wood*. Een opera. Door Robert Heppener, Holland Festival 1996. Eine andere Kurzgeschichte desselben Bandes, 'Die Auferstehung', wurde als Fernsehspiel adaptiert: De Opstanding. Televisiespel.Vereniging van Arbeiders–Radio–Amateurs (VARA) Sendung: 3.5.1963. *Das Ende einer Saison*. Bayerischer Rundfunk, Sendung: April 1965 (3. Progr.). Hörspielbearbeitung: *Die Auferstehung*, unveröffentlichtes Hörspiel, adaptiert von Petra Kiener und Said. Süddeutscher Rundfunk, Sender Freies Berlin, Sendung: 5.11.1985. 8.30. In der holländischen Übersetzung 'Een ziel van hout' (1970) findet sich die Titelgeschichte als surrealistische Version wieder.

[5]*Anna Laub*. Audiodrama de Jakov Lind. Traduit et adapté de l'allemand par Roger Richard. Theatre de l'etrange, Paris, France Culture 1966. *Anna Laub*, produced in London, 1973. *The Ditch*. Early Street Dance Studio, Santa Fé, 1977. Dir. by Ann Scofield. *The Ditch*, adapted from *Anna Laub* and directed by Ann Scofield, produced at Theater of the Open Eye, New York, 1982. *Anna Laub*. A Screenplay by Aaron Broadhurst. London, Sept. 1988. *The Silver Foxes Trilogy*. Performed at the Gate Theatre Club, London. Dir. by Nicholas Broadhurst 1983. *The Silver Foxes Trilogy*. Performed at the Everyman Theatre, Liverpool.

[6]Im Besitz des Autors oder in der 'Sammlung Jakov Lind', Literaturhaus Wien.

[7]*Landscape in Concrete*. Treatment, unpublished *Eine bessere Welt*, Roman. *Ergo*, a Comedy. New York: (Hill & Wang) 1968. *Travels to the Enu. The story of a shipwreck: Travels to the Enu*, unpublished play. *The Inventor*. A novel: *The Inventor*, a radioplay, unpublished.

Die Heiden

Jakov Linds allererstes literarisches Werk ist ein Theaterstück, *The Pagans*, im Manuskript mitunter auch als *The Game* betitelt, welches er Ende der Fünfziger Jahre[8], also noch vor dem ersten Erzählband und auf englisch verfaßt hat. Im dritten Band seiner Autobiographie *Crossing* schreibt er:

> My idea of writing was not connected to writing a novel; my idea was to write because I was stimulated by what I heard and saw.[...] Everything that happened to me from day to day was going to be part of my story. [...] A story consisting of many stories, a theme with many variations.[...] The story I wanted to tell [...] was, of course, that of my war time experience.[9]

Die Heiden wurde von Erich Fried ins Deutsche übersetzt und 1964 am Staatstheater in Braunschweig unter der Regie von Alexander Wagner und mit Bühnenbild von Manfred Schröter uraufgeführt.

Jakov Lind führt uns in diesem Stück eine Gruppe 19– bis 40jähriger vor, Henry, seine Freundin Judy, ihre Mutter Bernice, Roger, Peter und den schwarzen Diener Abukowo. Eine Generation, die noch vor oder während des Krieges geboren wurde. Die erzählte Zeit im Stück wird als London der Gegenwart bezeichnet.

Eine Party soll stattfinden, 'keine Orgie diesmal', sondern ein Experiment über Leben und Tod, ein Spiel im Spiel, und der Spielleiter ist Henry, 'König der Sanftmütigen, Kaiser der Heiden, Fürst der Vernachlässigten' (H, 10),[10] wie er sich selbst zu Beginn des Stückes nennt. Er plant seine vermeintlich schwache Freundin Judy unter Hinzuziehung diverser Erniedrigungen und Opferrituale zum freiwilligen Selbstmord zu bringen. Aber damit dieser auch eindrucksvoll stattfinden kann, warten alle Partymitglieder mit etwas weniger als godotscher Geduld auf Oswald und vertreiben sich die Zeit mit tendenziell monologischen Selbstdarstellungen. Dieser Oswald, der mit einer Gruppe von Chelsea–Nichtstuern und Beatniks dann auch tatsächlich auftaucht, ist nicht zufällig Sir Oswald Mosley, dem Gründer und Führer der 'British Union of Fascists' nachgebildet.[11] Er bleibt aber als dramaturgische Hauptperson im Stück merkwürdig diffus und löst auch die ihm zugedachte Aufgabe, den Mord zu legitimieren, nicht ein.

Schon in der Regieanweisung werden wir in die dekadente, leicht schäbige Atmosphäre rund um diese Partygesellschaft eingeführt:

---

[8]Diese Datierung folgt einer handschriftlichen Notiz des Autors.

[9]Jakov Lind: *Crossing*. S.4, 93, 141. Sigle = C und Seitenangabe. Buchausgabe: London: (Methuen) 1991.

[10]Sigle für *Die Heiden* = H und Seitenangabe. Buchausgabe: Neuwied: Luchterhand 1965.

[11]Vgl. *Crossing*, S.16.

Henry schält eine Apfelsine und wirft die Schalen unbekümmert auf den Fußboden. Bernice küßt Henrys Fuß, der aus der Hängematte niederbaumelt, wie den Fuß eines heiligen Buddha (H, 9).

Diese an erotische Vorlieben des Dorian Gray oder Grafen Des Esseintes erinnernde Anfangsszene (H, 15) zeigt bereits eine der sich durch das ganze Stück hinziehenden Opfer–Täter–Konstellationen, welche ebenfalls durchgehend hetero– und homosexuell (H, 37) unterlegt sind.

> Judy. Hättest du etwas gegen ein kleines Spiel? — Was für ein Spiel? — Ich will Fragen stellen ... — Und? — Und du sollst die Wahrheit antworten — Was sind die Spielregeln? — Die erste Spielregel ist die Wahrheit. — Und die anderen? Die Konsequenz daraus zu ziehen. — Was für eine Art von Spiel ist das? — Wenn man es richtig spielt, kann es sehr aufregend sein. Es geht um dein Leben. — [...] Henry. Ich spiele dein Spiel jetzt schon seit drei Jahren. Aber bitte laß uns doch, bitte, Liebe spielen ... tu, was du willst, aber sei nicht grausam. [...] sei lieb zu mir und bring mich nicht um; oder bring mich um; tu, was du willst, aber sei lieb (H, 29).

Kulisse dieses Stücks ist die krankhafte, absonderliche Gemütsverfassung dieser Generation. Tatenlose Rebellen, die in betonter Gottlosigkeit und Indifferenz durch den Alltag treiben. Schon der Anfangsmonolog Henrys stimmt auf das existentielle Lebensgefühl der Gruppe ein:

> Die Zeit schält das flüssige Fleisch, die Zeit preßt unsere Träume aus ... nicht süße, sondern saure Träume; farblose, klebrige Substanz aus durchsichtiger Haut. [...] Die dunklen Stunden sind in Schlaf gebettet. Schlaf mit Ungeheuern, Schlaf mit brennenden Häusern, mit Köpfen ohne Gesichter, mit blinden Piraten, die ihre Absätze in meine schlaflosen Augen bohren. Angst vor dem Schlaf, Angst, im atemlosen Schlaf zu ersticken, nie mehr aufzuwachen, Angst zu sterben. Die Sonne geht auf, aber die übrige Zeit ist Angst (H, 10).

Die Figuren nehmen die Haltung verkannter Genies ein, reden ihre Visionen in den blauen Rauch gemeinsam konsumierter Drogen, ihre Resistenz ist passiv, ihre Auflehnung ohne Ziel.[12] Sie sind sich innerhalb der Gruppe in Qualfreudigkeit zugetan und in gegenseitige Opferungsbereitschaft verstrickt, aber statt aus diesen greifbaren Abhängigkeiten auszubrechen, fühlen sie sich von anonymen Mächten bedroht, der Atomtod bietet sich als Alibi geradezu perfekt an. Sie fühlen sich für diese Welt, in die sie hineingeworfen wurden, nicht verantwortlich; Peter meint, der einzige Ausweg wäre kollektiver Selbstmord (H, 36), aber

---

[12]Vgl. Hilde Spiel: 'Unser aller Alpdruck'. In: Programmheft zur Aufführung der 'Heiden', hrsg. von der Staatsintendanz Braunschweig, 1964, S.187.

selbst das erscheint ihnen zu human. Sie richten ihre Angriffe nur auf abstrakte Ziele, wie Gott, der nicht für tot, aber, gekoppelt mit ihrem Haß auf alles Durchschnittsbürgerliche, zu einer reaktionären Figur erklärt wird: 'Es war eine Finsternis, ich habe Gott gesehen. Er hatte eine gewisse Ähnlichkeit mit dem Papst. Er saß da in einem Armsessel und hat Formulare ausgefüllt. Schon sonderbar' (H, 12).

Sie fühlen sich unfähig zu menschlichen Beziehungen — ein angedeuteter Geschlechtsakt mit einer Puppe (H, 13) wird zum bezeichnenden Symbol — und der Welt entfremdet:

> Diese Welt ist eine Welt der Illusionen. Wenn Illusionen Geisteskrankheiten sind, dann ist Wahnsinn Wahrheit, und Wahrheit, das sind kurze Träume. Wacht auf und seht euch um. Steine sind Steine, Bäume nichts als Bäume, Menschen Augen, die nach einem Spiegel suchen, Augen, die vor sich hin starren und täglich mehr erblinden. Man starrt und sieht nichts mehr (H, 28).

Gleichzeitig beziehen sie ihr Überlegenheitsgefühl, ihre Verachtung, ihre rassistisch motivierte Abneigung gegen andere Nationalitäten und Klassen (H, 25) gerade aus dieser Undurchschaubarkeit der Welt. Ihre Angst muß seinen plakativen Ausdruck finden. Vor allem die Sprache der Anfangsszenen ist besonders stark durchsetzt mit expressionistischer Rhetorik:

> [...] Mondhöhle, Mondungeheuer, kriechende, schnuppernde, quiekende Halunken. Schlafen in Mondbetten. Rattensäuglinge saugen in geilen Rattenlöchern. Finstere Wirtshäuser voller gesegneter Rattenjungfrauen. Ich bin drin! Ich bin drin, drin, drin, und schnapp, schnapp nach Luft! (H, 15).

Dieses Pathos drückt das Gefühl der existentiellen Bodenlosigkeit nach dem Krieg aus. Es verweist auf Tendenzen der Nachkriegslyrik, die stilistisch von romantischem Irrationalismus und Wirklichkeitsverweigerung geprägt, sich größter Beliebtheit erfreute, wahrscheinlich, um das aufgerissene Ideologieloch wieder zu füllen. Da dies nunmehr mit christlichen und mystischen und nicht mehr mit faschistischen Begriffen geschieht, sagt wenig darüber aus, wie fruchtbar der ideologische Nährboden noch immer ist, und wie schnell er wieder mit politischer Rhetorik aufgefüllt werden kann: 'Was ist denn das hier? Ein Wartezimmer? Worauf warten wir? Wer kommt? '(H, 15).

Die Partymitglieder glauben, durch einen Mord endlich zu sich selber zu finden:

> [...] jetzt ist der Augenblick für Religionswahnsinnige. [...] Jeder soll sagen, was er will. Worte sind einfach Worte. Und es genügt nicht, sie nur zu sprechen, man muß sie schreien. Denn unsere Ohren machen nicht mehr mit, und sogar unsere Augen

sind nicht mehr, was sie früher einmal waren. Wenn ihr nicht die Farbe des Blutes seht, dann wißt ihr nicht, was ihr seht. Wenn Worte keinen Sinn mehr haben, Blut hat immer noch einen Sinn. Jetzt ist die Zeit für Menschenopfer (H, 24).

Dieses Grundgefühl, die eigene Angst, Feigheit und Lebensunfähigkeit könnte nur durch Gewalt und Krieg–Spielen überwunden werden, bildet eine Parallele zur aktuellen rechten Szene Deutschlands und Österreichs, die sich gerade durch das Abfackeln von Asylantenheimen und das Versenden von Briefbomben[13] Gehör verschafft.

Judy, ich weiß, ich bin unmenschlich, ich bin kein Mensch, ich bin ein Feigling. Verstehst du denn nicht? Ich habe keine Chance. Wie kann ein Feigling atmen? — Durch den Mund. — Durch den Mund? Durch meinen? Der ist vertrocknet. Zugesperrt. — [...] Wozu brauchst du Mut, nicht für ein Leben, wie du es führst. [...] Du hast alles. Geld, Freunde, Jugend. Herrgott nochmal, was willst du denn? — Du weißt nicht, was ich brauche, was ich haben will. — Nein — Etwas, was größer ist als ich (H, 19).

Die gleiche Erlösungsphantasie, das Aufgehen in einem mordenden und quälenden Kollektiv, haben auch andere in der Gruppe: 'Er wird uns segnen, mit seinem allerheiligsten Segen, und dann wird es uns gestattet sein, ihm nachzufolgen'(H, 17).

Die Thematik des Stückes, das existentielle Grundgefühl dieser Gruppe, läßt Vergleiche zum absurden Theater zu. In einer Regieanweisung findet sich die Bemerkung: 'Peter übt Kreuzigung, indem er sich ans Fensterkreuz bindet und auf und nieder hüpft' (H, 28). In der Braunschweiger Inszenierung wurden diese Motive stark hervorgehoben. Der erste Akt vermittelte, parallel zu der Handlungsunfähigkeit der Figuren, eine Art Stillstand, während die Steigerung der Handlung auf der Bühne den Eindruck eines 'Happenings' vermittelte. Ein Happening, bei dem Gott (H, 24) und ein Gruppenmitglied ermordet werden sollen, mit Alkohol herumgeschüttet und ansatzweise Geschlechtsverkehr betrieben wird. In diesen Krisenerfahrungen einer nicht mehr faßbaren Welt wird eine Parallele zu den 'angry young man', vor allem zu Edward Bond, erkennbar.[14] Diese Inszenierungspraxis weist auch voraus auf frühe Stücke von Wolfgang Bauer.

Die sozialen Befunde über die Nachkriegsgeneration, die zumeist blasphemische Verfremdung von Liedern, der Ablauf des Stückes als Nummernrevue, die Einführung eines auktorialen Erzählers, zeigen die Nähe

---

[13]Vgl. die seit 1995 anhaltende und ungeklärte Briefbombenserie einer sich selbst als 'Bajuwarische Befreiungsarmee' bezeichnenden terroristischen Gruppierung in Österreich. Vgl. Anm. 50.

[14]Vgl. Hans U. Seeber: *Englische Literaturgeschichte*. Stuttgart: 1993, S.369.

zu Brecht. Linds Beschäftigung mit Brecht ist weniger ideologisch als biographisch geprägt. In den 30er Jahren von der 'Dreigroschenoper' beeindruckt, werden die 'songs' bald eine Art des Umgangs mit der Wirklichkeit: 'Nach dem Anschluß im März 1938 [...] sang ich nur noch die Lieder von Kurt Weill und Bert Brecht. [...] Denn sonst fiel mir nichts mehr ein [...] besser konnte ich es nicht sagen.'[15]

Spannender als die Bezüge zum zeitgenössischen Theater, scheint mir die Frage, was hinter der Haltung dieser vermeintlichen Wirtschaftswunderkinder steckt: Es ist eine wehleidige, introvertierte Generation, die ihre Väter um die Tatkraft beneidet, in den Krieg gezogen zu sein. Ihre eigene Unfähigkeit rechtfertigen sie mit der Tatsache, die Welt sei auf jeden Fall zum Untergang bestimmt. Dadurch unterscheiden sie sich zunächst einmal grundsätzlich von den Söhnen und Töchtern der deutschen und österreichischen Aufbau–Generation, die ihre Aufgabe kurz nach dem Krieg noch in sozialer Gerechtigkeit und einer neuen geistigen Freiheit suchen. Gemeinsam ist ihnen die Enttäuschung, die Anfang der sechziger Jahre eintritt, verursacht durch die Haltung der Westmächte: Kalter Krieg, Aufrüstung, die Politik der Westmächte in der Dritten Welt. Nicht bewußt ist dieser Generation, unabhängig davon, ob sie in Chelsea oder woanders angesiedelt ist, wie anfällig sie für neue Faschismen ist. Die Party wird zur Kulisse, die Figuren zu Projektionen von feigen Durchschnittsbürgern, potentiellen Neofaschisten.

Aber auch die Elterngeneration kommt nicht ungeschoren davon. Sie verfallen nämlich nicht nur der Bewunderung ob ihrer Taten wie Oswald, sondern auch der Verachtung. Judy, die auf die Anwesenheit ihrer Mutter auf dieser Party angesprochen wird, kommentiert dies mit: 'Ach ja. Sie auch. Eigentlich mehr ein Zufall, nicht? Ich kenne sie gar nicht. Aber immerhin, sie ist meine Mutter' (H, 14). Auch diese Kriegsgeneration ist vollständig der Hoffnungslosigkeit verfallen und damit nicht minder anfällig für eine Reideologisierung:

An diesem brütenden Sonntagnachmittag ... der kein Ende nehmen will — ist mein Kopf leer, wie gewöhnlich. Aber mein Magen war noch nie so schwer. Oder ist das mein Herz? Herz, kein Herz, Herz, kein Herz ... Mein Gott, wenn ich nur Trauer empfinden würde oder Schuld, oder irgend etwas, dann hätte ich doch wenigstens Schuld, Trauer oder irgend etwas. Aber ich habe nichts. Gott, nichts, nichts. Ich bin ein Krater ohne Grund, für jeden da, der mich haben will. Mein Gott, nichts als ein Krater ... (H, 22).

---

[15]Vgl. Jakov Lind: 'Mein Wiener Liederbuch'. NDR, 10.2.1987 und Silke Hassler: 'Die Geschichte im Ohr — ein Wiener Liederbuch'. In: *Illustrierte Neue Welt*, Aug./Sept.1994, S.37.

Indem Jakov Lind seinen Figuren ein genau definiertes Alter gibt, markiert er auch die Nähe zu seiner Generation. Er selbst steht im Bann des Nationalsozialismus: 1938 verließ er als Kind Österreich Richtung Holland, verbrachte die letzten zwei Kriegsjahre mit gefälschten Papieren in Deutschland. Nach fünf Jahren Israel kehrt er 1950 wieder auf den Kontinent zurück, nach Amsterdam und Wien, bis er ihn 1954 wieder verläßt und nach London geht, wo er seit nunmehr vierzig Jahren lebt.

> The Jews, the Germans, the Communists, — Nazi politics for short — was the theme with many variations. Every single person I came in contact with would sooner or later start talking politics to me [...]. My view on the entire matter was as complicated to understand as my private wartime story — but I was stuck with it, there was no way out (C, 74).

Seine Erfahrungen hat er in drei Autobiographien beschrieben. Diese persönliche Ebene der Auseinandersetzung ist immer von der Frage begleitet, was die tieferen Gründe für zwölf Jahre Naziherrschaft in Europa sein könnten, die in gängigen Erklärungsbehelfen wie Massenarbeitslosigkeit, Inflation und wirtschaftliche Depression nicht aufgehen und damit schon gar nicht aus der Welt geschafft sind:

> [...] this ongoing never–ending war between ordinary decent people, pursuing their own muddle in their own lives, and the robot–minded army of terrorists, who first poison the air with slogans and then with car bombs, hijacks, hostage–taking and machine guns (C, 121).

Ein, von Canetti in *Masse und Macht* ausgeführtes Motiv, Krieg sei 'die Angst vor dem eigenen Tod' (C, 120), die Überwindung der eigenen Feigheit, ist in den *Heiden* Handlungsträger. Als 'Spiel im Spiel' wird auf der Bühne exerziert, was in der Wirklichkeit angelegt ist. Ein zweites Motiv, das auch für die persönliche Auseinandersetzung Jakov Linds mit seiner Geschichte akut wird, ist die Frage nach dem Verhalten der Opfer, warum sie sich widerstandslos ihren Mördern ergeben: 'Da liegst du vor mir, ausgestreckt. Sollte ich dich nicht schon dafür töten? Ist das nicht genug? [...] in dieser Welt ist kein Platz für die Unschuldigen':

> [...] Halt, halt. Laß mich atmen! Weiter nichts als atmen! — Weiter nichts als atmen. Das ist alles, was ich hören wollte. Weiter nichts als atmen. Keine Illusion, keine Liebe. Weiter nichts als atmen, atmen ist alles, was man braucht, atmen (H, 44/45).

Judy, die auf die perfide Rhetorik von Henry hereinfällt, ihm durch ihre Zuneigung blind vertraut, seine Andeutungen und Drohungen deswegen nie ernst nimmt, das ist die exakte Wiederholung einer politisch–ideologischen

Strategie im Mikrokosmos einer Beziehung. In diesem Fall aber, in der vollständigen Erniedrigung, in der Aberkennung des Lebens, liegt der Wendepunkt des Stücks:

> (Judy nimmt eine der Fackeln und macht einen Schritt auf Henry zu): Du brauchst Haß, was? Da hast du. Haß! Haß! Spürst du jetzt, daß es weh tut? [...] Was bewegst du dich denn nicht — Angst vor mir? Herausgefunden, daß auch ich hassen kann? [...] Wer hätte das gedacht, daß du mich nicht umbringen kannst? Das macht dir Angst? Ich hab' geglaubt, du bist ein Mann, Henry, aber du bist — ein Kind.[...] Du bist weiter nichts als ein Feigling! [...] der große Heide — ein Kind! (H, 46)

Am Ende des Stücks wird Henry von allen seinen Freunden und Mitmachern alleine gelassen — das Mordsspiel ist zu Ende, alle gehen nach Hause — nur Abukowo bleibt und fordert Rechenschaft von ihm. Er mutet in dieser Funktion an wie ein Soldat der Alliierten, der gerade einen zwanzigjährigen Wehrmachtssoldaten durch Buchenwald geführt hat, und ihn nach einer Erklärung fragt, die der ihm auch prompt liefert:

> Ich bin ein ganz gewöhnlicher Durchschnittsbürger. Nichts besonderes. Ganz gewöhnlich. Alles an mir war mittelmäßig. Ich bin wie hundert andere Leute, eine lieblose Mutter, ein Vater, der gestorben ist. Und dann kam Oswald. [...] Mein Gewissen ist so gut wie das eines jeden anderen Menschen (H, 50f.).

Abukowo setzt ihm die Pistole an und bringt ihn dazu, seine Angst, sein Entsetzen, seine Trauer zuzugeben, und überläßt ihm den Rat: 'Hab' Erbarmen mit den Blinden und den Verbrannten, und lasse sie leben. Das ist alles!' und seinem Staunen: 'Es ist wieder Tag. Sehr sonderbar' (H, 51/52).

Der Uraufführung von *Die Heiden* kann man nach dem Erscheinen von fünfzig Kritiken in den Tagen nach der Uraufführung ein hohes Maß an Interesse bescheinigen.[16] Die Zahl der Belobigungen, Verrisse und sich neutral verhaltenden Kritiken halten sich ungefähr die Waage, eine durchgängige und klare Linie der Aufnahme und Einordnung dieses Stückes in den Kontext des gegenwärtigen deutschen Theaters ist nicht ersichtlich. Die einzige konkrete Bezugnahme ist der Vergleich über die Größe des Schnurrbarts von Jakov Lind mit jenem von Günter Grass.[17] Nicht wenige Kritiker wundern sich, daß sich die Zuschauer einem Stück, das an neuralgischen Punkten ihrer Vergangenheit ansetzt, sie gleichzeitig an Defizite und Bedrohungen der Gegenwart, an ihre eigenen Ängste und

---

[16]Diese Zahl muß durch Zwei– bis Vierfachveröffentlichungen der gleichen Kritik etwas eingeschränkt werden.

[17]Diese Gleichsetzung taucht auch schon in Kritiken zu den ersten drei Prosaveröffentlichungen auf.

Verführbarkeiten erinnert, und ihnen dies in einer besonderen Form der Langeweile vorführt, wie eben diese Kritiker zähnebleckend vermerken, so bereitwillig aussetzten. Gesteigert wurde diese Konfrontation noch durch die Aufhebung der Bühnendistanz, da sich die Zuschauer bei Betreten des Zuschauerraums mitten in einer schon im Gang befindlichen Party wiederfanden.[18] Aber ihr Lustgewinn schien darin zu bestehen, am Ende des Stückes so etwas wie eine kathartische Reinigung vorgeführt zu bekommen. Günther Rühle schreibt in der *Frankfurter Allgemeinen Zeitung*: 'Das Wohlbehagen über die drakonische Reinigung des wüsten Henry war in diesem auf Gerechtigkeit erpichten Parkett nicht zu unterdrücken'.[19]

Die Uraufführung dieses Stückes fand zur gleichen Zeit statt wie die Frankfurter Auschwitz–Prozesse. Ähnlich wie sich die deutsche Selbst– und Nachkriegsinszenierung als 'Kulturnation' über die inflationäre Einrichtung von Stadt– und Staatstheatern präsentierte, könnte das große Interesse des Publikums an diesem Stück (und seinem Verfasser) auch daran gelegen sein, mit einem masochistischen Gefühl das Theater zu betreten und es durch einen theatralischen Schock, wieder ein Stück deutscher Vergangenheit abgearbeitet zu haben, wieder zu verlassen. Wolfgang Schlüter, der seine Kritik mit dem Befund: 'Jakov Lind ist ein Betroffener' beginnen läßt, hebt hervor, daß er seinen 'berechtigten Haß nicht nach außen projiziere. Er sucht die Quelle des Unheils an tieferem Orte, als sie gemeinhin gesucht wird.'[20] Bei den Deutschen, ist man geneigt, hinzuzufügen. Heinrich Mersmann betitelt Jakov Lind gar als 'sympathischen Verkünder der Toleranz'.[21]

In einer Kritik, die ironischerweise mit 'Ein schwacher Held' betitelt ist, empfiehlt Heinz–Ludwig Schneiders, daß das Stück, welches 'durch den Beifall für Ensemble, Autor und Stück offenbar theaterwirksam sei, trotz der Tendenz auch andernorts gespielt werden könnte.'[22] Mit einer Abwandlung eines Sartre–Zitats könnte man sagen: Die Nazis sind immer auch die anderen.

Ein weiterer Aspekt der Rezeption von den *Heiden* ist, daß die Prosa gegen das Stück ausgespielt wird. Christian Gneuss beklagt, daß 'die Elemente, die Linds Erzählungen auszeichneten und zu Recht ihren Ruhm

---

[18]Bei dieser Inszenierung wurde, abweichend vom Text, die Anfangsszene gestrichen

[19]Günther Rühle: 'Die Faschistenprobe'. In: *Frankfurter Allgemeine Zeitung*, 14.12.1964

[20]Wolfgang Schlüter: 'Warten auf Mord'. In: *Hannoversche Presse*, 12.12.1964.

[21]Heinrich Mersmann: 'Warten auf Oswald'. In: *Die Weltwoche*, 18.12.1964. Vgl. auch:Hans Berndt: 'Party über Abgründen'. In: *Saarbrückener Zeitung*, 16.12.1964.

[22]Heinz–Ludwig Schneiders: 'Ein schwacher Held'. In: *Handelsblatt*, 14.12.1964.

bewirkten, die jüngste Vergangenheit im Stil des Gruselmärchens' darzubieten, 'mit grausiger Phantasie, mit schwarzem Humor, all das in seinem Stück eliminiert ist.'[23] Aber auch hier sind sich die Kritiker nicht ganz einig, denn der Spiegel–Rezensent schreibt:

> Sicher ist, daß Linds zynische, desperate und jämmerliche Gestalten in der gelungenen Braunschweiger Inszenierung nicht nur zeitgemäßer, sondern auch psychologisch weit glaubwürdiger wirken als jene expressionistischen Schauermärchenhelden im Leichenhausmilieu, mit denen bislang der Erzähler Lind das Gruseln lehrte.[24]

Hermann Dannecker beklagt: 'Das Stück greift nicht wirklich in die politischen Verhältnisse hinaus und ein.'[25] Sein kritischer Klagegesang über die ihm mangelnde politische Intention des Stücks greift bald besser: Bereits die zweite Aufführung von *Die Heiden*, diesmal unter dem Titel *Die Party*, im Forum–Theater in Berlin, 1966 aufgeführt,[26] fiel durch den Raster der gebotenen politisierten Haltung deutscher Autoren. Die Party wurde als Anarchisten–Treff und die Protagonisten als politische Amokläufer kategorisiert.[27]

Ein Kritiker versucht, *Die Heiden* in die deutsche Theatertradition einzuorden, ein Befund, der im nachhinein unfreiwillig entlarvend anmutet:

> Man kann sich nun kaum noch verhehlen, daß eine neue dramatische Gattung begründet wird. Auf Realismus im Drama erpicht, von den Schocks bedrängt, die durch die Aufdeckung der Nazi–Verbrechen auch das Bild unserer Gegenwart verdüstern, sind die Autoren dabei, Symptome dieser Wirklichkeit zu sammeln, um sie durch Darstellung sichtbar zu machen.[28]

Das zeigt wohl, daß die deutsche Faschismusaufarbeitung erst ab Mitte der 60er Jahre und nur — wie durch *Die Ermittlung* von Peter Weiss — am Theater stattgefunden hat. Seine Feststellung erklärt die gesamte deutsche und österreichische Literatur, die seit Kriegsende bis zu diesem Zeitpunkt entstanden ist und sich an die jüngste Vergangenheit herantastet, als nicht existent, was sie im Bewußtsein einer breiten Öffentlichkeit auch nicht war. Von ernstzunehmenden Bemühungen um die Herausbildung eines neuen

---

[23]Christian Gneuss: 'Warten auf Oswald'. In: *Süddeutsche Zeitung*, 14.12.1964.

[24]'Würgen und winseln'. In: *Der Spiegel*, 16.12.1964.

[25]Hermann Dannecker: '*Die Heiden* von Jakov Lind'. In: *Schwäbische Zeitung*, 14.12.1964.

[26]Regie: Frank Bruckner. Bühnenbild: Horst Hödicke.

[27]Wolf Ghedini: 'Warten auf Chaos'. Florian Kienzl: 'Zum Unterschied: Warten auf Oswald'. Beide Rezensionen in der 'Sammlung Jakov Lind', im Literaturhaus, Wien.

[28]Günther Rühle: 'Die Faschistenprobe'. In: *Frankfurter Allgemeine Zeitung*, 14.12.1964.

deutschsprachigen Theaters in den 50er Jahren kann auch kaum die Rede sein, aber das ist nicht auf der Schuldenseite der Autoren zu verbuchen, sondern entspringt der kulturellen Wiederaufrüstung Westdeutschlands und Österreichs. Daß sich in den 50er Jahren kein repräsentatives deutsches Drama finden läßt, ist Indiz nicht nur der unbewältigten Vergangenheit, sondern auch einer nichtbegriffenen Gegenwart.[29] Erst mit wachsender kritischer Distanz zur reaktionären Ära, zur Wirtschaftswundergläubigkeit und den ideologischen Ausverkauf an die Westmächte, durch die Wiederaufrüstung und später die Einführung der Notstandsgesetze in Deutschland entwickelt sich ein Bewußtsein und auch die Möglichkeit für die Wirkungen der Theatersprache und Bühnenrealität.

'Kann die Welt durch Theater wiedergegeben werden?', so lautet die Frage, die Friedrich Dürrenmatt dem Darmstädter Gespräch 'Über das Theater' 1955 vorlegte. In der Debatte, die er damit entzündet, legt er nicht nur seine Position gegen Brecht fest, sondern er favorisiert auch eine dramatische Form, die diese Forderung noch einlösen kann:

> Die Tragödie setzt Schuld, Not, Maß, Übersicht, Verantwortung voraus. In der Wurstelei unseres Jahrhunderts, in diesem Kehraus der weißen Rasse, gibt es keine Schuldigen und auch keine Verantwortlichen mehr. Alle können nichts dafür und haben es nicht gewollt. Es geht wirklich ohne jeden. Alles wird mitgerissen und bleibt in irgendeinem Rechen hängen. Wir sind zu kollektiv schuldig, zu kollektiv gebettet in die Sünden unserer Väter und Vorväter. Wir sind nur noch Kindeskinder. Das ist unser Pech, nicht unsere Schuld: Schuld gibt es nur noch als persönliche Leistung, als religiöse Tat. Uns kommt nur noch die Komödie bei.[30]

Ergo

Nach den *Heiden*, drei Bänden Prosa und Hörspielen, in denen Jakov Lind versucht hat, der 'Seuche, die Mensch heißt'[31] beizukommen, wählt er in der Bearbeitung seines Romans *Eine bessere Welt* diese Gattung:

> Man könnte die Komödie auch Szenen aus meinem Vaterland nennen. [...] ERGO spielt in meinem Wien — die Koalition von Rot und Schwarz hat mich nie interessiert, sondern nur die beiden Lager von alten Sozis und alten Nazis. Und nicht einmal die Österreicher interessieren mich so sehr, als der Wahnsinn, der

[29]Vgl. Ralf Schnell: *Geschichte der deutschsprachigen Literatur seit 1945*. Stuttgart: 1993, S.320.
[30]Friedrich Dürrenmatt: 'Theaterprobleme'. In: *Gesammelte Werke. Essays und Gedichte* (Bd. 7) Zürich: 1991, S.59.
[31]Vgl. das Motto seines Romans *Landschaft in Beton*.

nicht mit Hitler verbrannt wurde. Und um es noch komplizierter zu sagen: Nicht einmal die Nazis sind mir wichtig, sondern nur der Wahnsinn schlechthin.[32]

Seine Komödie steht in der Tradition Nestroys, dramaturgisch und sprachlich. Lind bezieht sich wie Nestroy auf den nationalsprachlichen Unterbau, er schaut 'dem Volk' — aufs schon wieder weit aufgerissene — 'Maul'.[33] Auch das Bühnenbild — links Schnitt durch Wacholders Behausung, rechts Schnitt durch das Haus von Würz — erinnert an 'Zu ebener Erde und erster Stock' von Nestroy, wobei hier die Aufteilung nicht in Arm und Reich erfolgt, sondern in Verkommen und Steril, Altnazi und Wiederaufbau–Sozi.[34] Zusammengenommen entsprechen diese Äußerungsformen auch der Innenansicht der österreichischen Seele. Das Unzerstörbare, Immerwährende an ihr entspricht der Zeitrechnung im Stück:

> Was für ein Tag ist heut? — Der 25. — Der Monat [...] September. — Das Jahr [...] — Kein Jahr, es gibt kein Jahr — Mach mich nicht verrückt! Das Jahr. — Siebzehn Jahre nach dem Krieg (E, 43).

Diese Kontinuität entspricht der Gleichzeitigkeit, der simultanen Existenz scheinbar unvereinbarer Dinge:

> Das ist meine Stadt [...] Alles ist verdreht und verkehrt, aber keiner bemerkt das. Nicht hier. Eine Stadt aus Liptauer, Lippizzaner, Leberknödel und Leberkäs. Ein Reim. Eine Redewendung. Ein Sprichwort. Und vielleicht nicht einmal das [...], sondern nur die Familiengruft der Maria Theresia und des Franz Josef und ihrer Kinder Calafati, Rübezahl, Krampus und Nikolo, Christkindl und Andreas Hofer, die alle an Scharlach, Keuchhusten, Masern, Feuchtblattern und Basedow im allgemeinen Krankenhaus starben, wo der Erlöser zur Welt kam. Der Heiland vom Kahlenberg, der stromaufwärts in die Wachau ging, um Richard Löwenherz aus Mauthausen zu befreien, aber auch er ist gestorben und begraben am Zentralfriedhof und muß dort ewig schlafen neben Lueger und Seitz, Kaltenbrunner und Mozart, liegt dort bei Dollfuß und Schubert und Fey und Robert Stricker vom Zionistenverband und dem Prinzen Eugen [...] und den Helden vom Karl Marx–Hof und den Helden der Heimwehr, und keiner weiß, wieso es so eine Stadt überhaupt geben kann [...] (E, 68/69).

In dieser Kulisse werden uns zwei verfeindete Lager vorgeführt, der verkommene, schlecht aufgelegte, furzende Roman Wacholder, der seinen

---

[32]Jakov Lind: *Ergo*. Eine Komödie. Theatermanuskript des Thomas Sessler–Verlages Wien: 1995. Die Sigle für Ergo ist E und Seitenangabe. Hier wird aus Linds Vorrede zitiert.

[33]Vgl. Otto Basil: 'Die sprachliche Landschaft'. In: *Johann Nestroy*. Reinbek bei Hamburg: 1967, S.7f.

[34]Vgl. dazu den Begriff des 'epischen Nebeneinanderlebens' von Peter Szondi. In: *Theorie des modernen Dramas*. Frankfurt: 1963, S.121f.

tausendjährigen Traum noch nicht ausgeträumt hat und sich mit einem Dichter und einem Philosophen umgibt, und auf der anderen Seite der neurotische, wiederaufbaugierige Ossias Würz mit seiner Familie. Ähnlich wie in Günter Eichs Gedicht 'Inventur' vollführt Würz auch eine Inventaraufnahme seiner Existenz:

> Hier stehe ich also. Ossias Würz, 55 Jahre alt, ein Mann in mittleren Jahren [...] Ich habe eins, zwei, drei, vier, fünf, sechs, sieben, acht, neun, zehn Zehen, ich habe eine, zwei, drei, vier, fünf, sechs, sieben, acht, neun, zehn Finger. Ich habe ein männliches Geschlechtsteil der Mittelklasse mit dazupassendem Hoden. Ich habe zwei Augen, sie tasten den Raum ab, ihnen entgeht nichts: also ein Vorteil, daß sie zufällig leicht nach außen drängen. Ich habe eine Nase ... sie ist groß, breit und rund. Ja. Mein Bauch ist da. Nabel ist da. Ja. Rücken, Hintern und Fersen sind da. Alles ist vollzählig. Alles ist da. Mein rotes helles Haar von der Farbe süßer Karotten ist etwas Scheußliches. Aber Hauptsache, es ist da. Alles ist da, also bin ich da. Meine Existenz steht fest (E, 39/40).

Damit seine Existenz auch weiter feststeht, glaubt er an 'die guten Menschen in einer lieben guten Welt' (E, 119f.), numeriert die Gegenstände und die Zimmer (E, 37), geht ständig auf Bazillenjagd (E, 93), vertilgt alles ihm unrein Erscheinende (E, 97), ja selbst sein Geschlechtsakt hat etwas Akkordarbeitartiges (E, 26). Damit er seinen Verfolgern, den Wacholders davonkommt, bemalt er sich mit weißer Farbe (E, 100f), um zu verschwinden, versteckt er sich in seinem eigenen Verstand: 'Und damit mich niemand finden kann, verlier ich ihn.'(E, 108).

Wacholder, der auf der anderen Seite der Stadt in einem verdreckten Zollschuppen wohnt, ist besessen von seiner Phantasie, mit seinem überdimensionalen Schwanz eine Prostituierte ermordet zu haben. Der Schauplatz dieses Verbrechens, Chicago, das inzwischen schon 'Geschichte geworden ist, Kriminalgeschichte, wenn man so will, und durch die Verjährung nicht mehr geahndet werden kann', verwandelt sich in seinem Kopf schnell in den Heldenplatz, in die brünstige Atmosphäre des Führerempfangs bei der Heimkehr Österreichs ins Deutsche Reich:

> Ich hab was gespürt, irgendwas wollt sich rühren in mir. Und auf einmal war da der Heldenplatz und die Weiber haben die Beine gehoben und geschrien: 'Führer, wir folgen dir! Auch ins Bett!' [...] Heil Hitler! Sieg Heil! Ich bin der Führer, auseinander mit den Haxen und hinein ins Volk, in die Hur'n, die Juden, die Weiber. Ich vögel euch alle — Ich hab da was; was sonst keiner hat. Ich bin der Übermensch (E, 54f).[35]

---

[35]Vgl. dazu das Gedicht 'Heldenplatz' von Ernst Jandl als lyrischen Versuch, die sexuell aufgeladene Stimmung am Wiener Heldenplatz einzufangen.

Dies sind die Prototypen einer Gesellschaft, die sich gerade wieder als sozial–demokratisch–christlich–volksparteiliche oder kommunistische zu konstituieren versucht. Beide basteln an ihrer besseren Welt, verteidigen sie mit ausgeprägtem Fanatismus oder planen die Vernichtung der Gegenseite, um ihre Idee als die bessere zu legitimieren. Das Stück ist also nicht nur als Satire auf das Nachkriegsösterreich zu lesen, sondern auch auf das Verhältnis von West– zu Ostdeutschland. Anläßlich der 17–Jahr–Feier prangen in Würzs Haus 'rote Transparente mit weißen Aufschriften: Freiheit! Zukunft! Arbeit!' (E, 119). Vor Wacholders Haus verkündet ein Zeitungsverkäufer neben der 'Freiheit! Vorwärts. Avanti. Die Gegenwart. [...] Der Tagesanbruch' noch 'Heiße Maroni!' (E, 10). Der westliche Wiederaufbau war schon immer wortreicher. Dementsprechend lautet die profunde politische Kritik des Mannes auf der Straße auch:

> Das Volk hat zugenommen und der einzelne ist dick und fett geworden. Wir können uns nicht mehr wehren. Wir sind zu dick und behäbig, und die Sozis sind auch noch stolz drauf (E, 16).

Sie selbst sind und bleiben auf etwas anderes stolz: 'Wir sind das Volk. Weißt du, was das heißt? Das heißt, wir sind besser als die anderen, ja besser, das sag ich (=Wacholder) dir im Guten, ich kann aber auch grob werden' (E, 57). Aber sie haben noch andere Gründe, zu klagen, denn:

> [...] die Freiheit, und das mit der Demokratie, das ist oft ein Schwindel [...] Das mit dem Leben und Lebenlassen, dieses ganze Getue, das ist nichts [...] für uns. Das ist was Fremdes, was Ausländisches, [...] In dieser Welt kann man froh sein, wenn man den Verstand verliert, sonst wird man noch ganz verrückt (E, 66).

> [...] die Leut nehmen heutzutage alles gleich ernst. Das war früher anders. Da hat sich allerhand verändert. Das kommt vom siebenjährigen Mißverständnis. Das kommt vom Hitler (E, 22).

Wacholder und Würz teilen nicht nur den Fanatismus, mit dem sie von einer 'besseren' Welt träumen, sondern auch die Vergangenheit:

> Ich hab' es nicht gewollt, Aslan! Und ich konnt's nicht verhindern! Der Krieg! Er ist doch mein Freund. Ich bin und bleib ihm treu. Treu bis in den Tod, wie wir immer gesagt haben. [...] Er hat sich eingesperrt — er wird befreit. [...] wir (träumen) beide, ich in diesem Misthaufen, atemlos und ohne Luft — und er in seinem Wahn — dieser eigensinnige Dickschädel (E, 48/51).

Wacholder plant die Vernichtung seines Freundes mittels 'Hirngift', 'Nervenschaum' (E, 17). Er will ihn aushungern, die Vitamine aus dem Essen stehlen, damit er ihn unter der geschlossenen Türe herauszerren kann, ihn auf den Kopf stellen, damit seine geheimen Pläne auf das Pflaster (E,

15–18) fallen. Ossias Würz scheint ihm gefährlich und dementsprechend bedenkt er ihn auch mit Flüchen wie 'Fortschrittsbauer' oder 'Zukunftstrampel' (E, 19). Jakov Lind ironisiert mit treffsicherer Übertreibung den latenten Antikommunismus der Nachkriegszeit, aber auch das Ressentiment gegen demokratische Errungenschaften: 'Kann man sich denn auf die Elektrizität verlassen, Vater? Kann sich heutzutage irgend jemand auf die Elektrizität verlassen?' (E, 31).

Die Vernichtung von Würz soll auf zweifachem Wege vor sich gehen: Mittels einer einberufenen Konferenz zur Verneinung der Würzschen Existenz, und als vorbereitende Maßnahme, der 'Nervenschaum':

> Was für ein Schaum? — Nervenschaum, irgendein Wortgesprudel, ein Kauderwelsch; etwas, was kein Mensch verstehen kann. Etwas, das so gescheit ist, so schwer und kompliziert, daß er den Verstand verliert, wenn er den Sinn herausfinden will. [...] Nervenschaum halt, natürlich, ein Brief. [...] Was denn sonst? Ein Brief, aber so ein Brief, der mit einem derartigen Druck in ein Hirn eindringt, daß man fast krepiert — Nervenschaum. [...] Das wäre die endgültigste aller Endlösungen (E, 65f.).

Es ist nicht nur spannend, diese beiden Verrückten zu betrachten, sondern auch die jüngere Generation. Würzs Stiefsöhne verdingen sich, entgegen seiner Sauberkeitsideologie, als Strichjungen, während Aslan und Leo als Intellektuelle im verdreckten Schuppen von Wacholder Unterschlupf gefunden haben. Ihre Bemühung, den Bürgern Dreck ins Haus zu schütten, ist fast ein aktionistisches Element.

Würz reagiert, als ihm seine Familie androht, ihn zu verlassen, folgerichtig mit der Bemerkung:

> Habe ich siebzehn Jahre wie ein Narr geschuftet, waren die siebzehn Jahre nutzlos? Meine Gesundheit ist ruiniert [...] Ich bin erledigt. Ein Haus hingestellt, ein Monument gebaut [...] sie brauchen mich nicht, [...] sie werden gehen [...] Ich soll dann hier allein verkommen [...] (E, 104).

Der Schriftsteller Aslan und der Philosoph Leo wohnen mit einem alten Nazi auf engstem Raum, der ihnen allerdings verbietet, ihn zu 'bespitzeln'(E, 41), auch nur ein einziges Wort über ihn zu schreiben (E, 46). Aslan schreibt dafür Goethe und Schiller ab:

> Ich bin sehr berühmt, ich hab alle Klassiker geschrieben. Servus, Johann Wolfgang. Grüß Dich, Friedrich! Ich mag Leute nicht, die mich nur grüßen, weil ich ein paar Klassiker geschrieben habe. Mich würden sie nicht grüßen — die würden auf mich spucken (E, 44).

Leo verlegt sich darauf, die plazentale Existenzphilosophie zu entwerfen, die ihre eigene Tradition negiert und auch deren Auswirkungen:

'Schopenhauer ist tot und Bergson sitzt in einer Zündholzschachtel [...]
Nazis hat's nie gegeben. Nicht hier' (E, 56). Ihre erste Nutzanwendung ist
die Arbeit am Nichtsein von Würz. Ähnlich wie schon im Hörspiel *Hunger*
wächst sich das Stück hier als Parodie auf die deutsche Kultur aus, auf die
deutsche Philosophie, die sich in ihrer Funktion als verbale
Blickvernebelung schon immer gut mit jeder Politik vertragen hat.
Wacholder ist von ihrer Effektivität überzeugt, beruht sie ja auf dem
deutsch–österreichischen Geist (E, 64).

Der Schriftsteller Aslan ist der einzige, der sich im Verlauf des Stücks
gegen diesen Irrsinn stellt, und auf der einberufenen Konferenz[36] für die
Existenz von Würz votiert:

> Gnade, ich bitte inständig um Gnade für Würz. Ich bin auch nur aus Gnade am
> Leben. Es war an einem Tag, als das Sterben in dieser Stadt noch geläufig war. [...]
> Ich war auf einmal da, nicht aber die Stadt. Die Stadt war mit spitzen Messern
> geschlachtet, sie war verbrannt und zugeschüttet, die Terrassen waren blind, die
> Kaffeehäuser tot. Zerlumpte Gestalten zogen einer Musik nach, die von weither
> kam. Wohin man auch sah, Haufen von Gegenständen, Bilderrahmen, Stühle,
> Berge von Besteck, leere Flaschen, Notenpulte, Vogelkäfige, Bürsten, Schlüssel,
> Schlüssel, Millionen Schlüssel! — genug jetzt, genug. Wir wollen Positives hören,
> [...] das alles ist Jahre her, dafür interessiert sich kein Mensch. Hast du nichts
> Positives zu berichten? (E, 113f.).

In der Romanvorlage wird noch eine weitere Dimension dieser Polemik
eingeführt: Aslan, in seiner Funktion als fiktiver Autor, schreibt an einem
Roman gleichen Titels. Er kann nicht mit dem realen Autor gleichgesetzt
werden, vertritt allerdings ein ähnliches ästhetisches Programm, das als sehr
konkrete Polemik gegen die Literatur der sechziger Jahre gelesen werden
kann, und als weiterer Rekurs auf eine Diskussion, die in mehreren
Akzente-Heften[37] ausgetragen wurde:

> Ich bin hier um mir meinen stoff für meinen roman eine bessere welt zu holen aber
> waren die wunder auf erden selten scheint es hier überhaupt keine zu geben ...
> meine moralische entrüstung ist ja keine moralische entrüstung ich brauche die
> schuld für meine bessere welt. um sich wirklich zu entrüsten muß man mit beiden
> beinen im leben stehen als sozialist zum beispiel was sich gut macht weil keiner
> einer ist. in die grönländische ästhetik ... werde ich mich zurückziehen sobald ich
> meine schuld losgeworden bin ... österreich wird man nicht los auch wenn man
> grönländisch schreibt wie manche meiner kollegen. man macht die sache nur

---

[36]Vgl. auch die Reaktion von Schriftstellern auf die Rede von Melphin Josef Lasky,
am ersten gesamtdeutschen Schriftstellerkongreß in Berlin, 1947.

[37]'Haben die Jungen nichts zu sagen?' In: *Akzente* 5, 1966; 1 und 4, 1967. Diese
Diskussion wurde angeregt durch eine Kritik von Jakov Lind über Handkes Roman *Die
Hornissen*. In: *Der Spiegel*, 29, 1966, S.79.

unverständlicher. die stadt ist so schlecht wie ihre leute....und man kann sie wirklich nicht abschaffen. die kunstmittel dagegen richten nichts aus. eine bessere welt heißt mein buch macht man nicht indem man den dreck der hier bei uns liegt, der heute schon die gehirne verstopft mit schönen worten abstrahiert [...].[38]

Gibt es nichts Positives zu berichten? Die Ministerin für Handel und Wiederaufbau, Gertrude Böckling, die zu einer Routinekontrolle in Schuppen von Wacholder auftaucht, findet Gefallen daran, dieses 'verirrte Schaf des Hirten aus Braunau am Inn', wieder in den 'Schoß der Gemeinschaft' zurückzuführen, und sie nimmt das durchaus wörtlich (E, 131). Wacholder ist glücklich:

Hätt ich mir jemals träumen lassen, daß ich eine Ministerin vögeln werde? Und sogar ganz offiziell. [...] Eine Frau, die gut riecht, [...] und ein Philosphendoktor [...] das war schon immer was für mich. Eigentlich bin ich ein lustiger Kerl. Gar nicht schwermütig. [...] Nur dieses Land kann ich nicht leiden. Wie sie alle gleich wieder die Pratzen gehoben haben, als Leo ihnen seinen Blödsinn aufgetischt hat. So sind die Leute bei uns. Die haben sich nicht geändert. Das ist meine Heimat, die Heimat der Charakterlosen. [...] Ein Land, das seine eigenen Bürger verschickt, als wären das Karnikel für Weihnachten, das ist überhaupt kein Land. Ich halt's hier nicht mehr aus (E, 125f.).

Nach dem Verweis seiner Hörerschaft berichtet auch der Schriftsteller Aslan das Geforderte:

Wohin man jetzt blickt, sieht man in dieser Stadt Marmor und Granit und goldene Glockentürme. Dekorative Ergänzungen zur Landschaft. Das ist positiv. Die Stadt ist wieder aufgebaut worden, das habe ich fast vergessen. Die Drachen und Giftschlangen, die Aasfresser und Basilisken aber haben sich ins Unterholz verkrochen, in Erdlöcher. Sie sind mit Sprüchen und Girlanden getarnt, keiner erkennt sie, und da hausen sie [...] (E, 114).

Obwohl die deutschsprachige Erstaufführung dieses Stückes erst im Frühjahr 1997 am Wiener Volkstheater stattfand, das Stück also nie im Kontext der deutschsprachigen Literatur der 60er Jahre wahrgenommen wurde, ist es sehr ergiebig, einen Vergleich mit deutschen Theaterstücken der 60er Jahre anzustellen. Bewußt oder nicht, weist dieses Stück einige Parallelen zu ihnen auf: Formal ist es eine Erweiterung der Volksstücktradition, wie sie bisher eingehender nur bei Sperr, Kroetz, Turrini, Fassbinder untersucht wurde. Auch hier wird die Sprache derer dokumentiert, die in der sozialen Wirklichkeit Schäden davongetragen haben: Sie haben keine individuelle Sprache sondern reproduzieren einen offiziellen Jargon: Würz wird vom ideologischen Diskurs der Aufbauzeit

---

[38]Jakov Lind: *Eine bessere Welt*. Berlin: (Wagenbach) 1966, S.144.

offiziellen Jargon: Würz wird vom ideologischen Diskurs der Aufbauzeit diktiert, bei Wacholder ist es die Rhetorik der Nazis. Es finden sich aber auch Parallelen zu Stücken von Grass, Weiss und Dürrenmatt, vor allem zu jenen, die mit dem Begriff des 'Revolutionsdramas'[39] verbunden werden. In Linds *Ergo* proben aber nicht die Plebejer den Aufstand, wie bei Grass, sondern die Nazis. In den *Physikern* und *Marat/Sade* ist der Schauplatz der Handlung eine Irrenanstalt. In *Ergo* wird ganz Wien zu einer 'schalldichten Gummizelle einer Verrücktenanstalt'[40], mit einer zusätzlichen politischen Dimension: 'Wenn man bei uns jeden einsperren würde, der gewollt hat was geschehen ist, dann könnten's einen Stacheldraht um das ganze Land ziehen' (E, 54). Die Nähe zur Schaubudendramatik zeigt sich in der Vorführung dieser monströsen Irren.[41] 'Mit einem kleinen Schieber, mit einem Kanzlisten, mit einem Polizisten läßt sich die heutige Welt besser wiedergeben als mit einem Bundesrat',[42] in der Komödienwelt Linds sind daraus größenwahnsinnige und neurotische Kleinbürger, verkommene Künstler und Politiker und verzweifelte und dekadente Jugendliche geworden.

Durch die komödienhafte Übersteigerung, den österreichischen Sprachgestus und die Anknüpfung an Traditionen des Volkstheaters von Nestroy über Horváth bis Qualtinger, wäre dieses Stück in der deutschen Theaterlandschaft, welche Ende der 60er Jahre vor allem von dokumentarischen Stücken geprägt war, deplaziert gewesen. Schon die Romanvorlage war, weil sie allen von der Kritik angesagten Kriterien widersprochen hatte, im Feuilleton vernichtet worden. Es ist 1968 beim Shakespeare Festival in New York erfolgreich uraufgeführt worden. Die politischen Anspielungen des Stücks wurden in der Kritik besonders hervorgehoben, durch den unterschiedlichen Kontext vom Publikum aber anders, fast durchgehend als 'Theater of the Absurd in an Advanced Lesson' wahrgenommen.[43]

Wann immer man einen Blick auf Kritiken wirft, ob dies seine Rezeption in Österreich, Deutschland, England oder Amerika ist, merkt man, wie Jakov Linds Literatur mit Etiketten beklebt wird, gerade gängigen, gerade angesagten und geforderten. Es kann aber nicht die Rede davon sein, daß sich Jakov Lind in eines der zeitgenössischen literarischen Modelle

---

[39]Vgl. Reinhold Grimm: 'Brecht, Artaud und das moderne Theater'. In: *Nach dem Naturalismus. Essays zur modernen Dramatik*. Kronberg: 1978, S.185–202.

[40]Jakov Lind: *Nahaufnahme*. Frankfurt: (Fischer) 1972, S.103.

[41]Vgl. Thomas Koebner: 'Tendenzen des Dramas'. In: *Tendenzen der deutschen Gegenwartsliteratur*. Stuttgart: 1984

[42]Friedrich Dürrenmatt: 'Theaterprobleme', a.a.O., S.57.

[43]Richard Watts: 'Theater of the Absurd'. In: *New York Post*, 4.3.1968.

einschreiben wollte. Seine Kenntnis der deutschen Literatur beruhte auf den spärlichen Informationen, die man in London aus Zeitschriften erfahren konnte und auf persönlichen Kontakten.[44] Selbst seine Anwesenheit bei der 'Gruppe 47' leitete keine wie immer geartete Heimholung ein: '[...] no one could decide whether to make me a glorious outsider of the german literature or [...] the jewish–german Heinrich Heine'(C, 164).

Peter Turrini hat in einem Brief seine Position sehr treffend beschrieben:

> In Wahrheit ist dieser Jakov Lind ein Wiener Komödienverschreiber, ein Urenkel von Johann Nestroy, ein Jakov Nepomuk Lind, einer, den sie hinausgeworfen haben aus dem Land, aus ihrer Kultur. Und wenn ich diese Komödie lese, dann merke ich, wie sie dafür bestraft werden.[...] Die Linds leben heute in New York oder in London oder in Boston, aber in Wahrheit sind sie, diese urwienerischen Theatraliker, aus der Vorstadt nie entwichen. Sie wurden mit Prügeln und Gas aus ihr verjagt, aber im Geiste leben sie und sitzen auf jedem Dachfirst, in jedem Schanigarten und beobachten ihre Vertreiber.[45]

Jakov Lind hat aus dieser Perspektive seine literarische Besonderheit entwickelt. Wo immer er sich gerade aufhält, beobachtet er seine alten und die neuen Vertreiber. Seine Literatur ist eine rastlose, die ständige Suche nach Möglichkeiten und Formen ihrer Beschreibung. Nach *Ergo* haben sich seine Formen der Beschreibung erweitert. Die nächsten beiden Stücke, die unveröffentlicht geblieben sind, nähern sich dieser Thematik mit der Bearbeitung mythischer Stoffe, dem Golem,[46] der Mitglied einer polnischen Widerstandsgruppe ist. Und durch ein historisches Drama über die Konversion der Khasaren[47] zum jüdischen Glauben. Die dramatische Bearbeitung seines Romans *Travels to the Enu*[48] ist eine Parabel auf eine Gesellschaft, der die Atombombe bereits auf den Kopf gefallen ist, die aber dennoch nicht damit aufhört, Krieg zu führen. Der gleiche Wahnsinn beginnt wieder von vorne: mit Krallen und Fingernägeln.

Obwohl sich Wacholder am Ende des Stücks selber ein Grab schaufelt, die Hauptfigur in seinem letzten Roman *Der Erfinder* an einen imaginären Ort zurückzieht: 'wo sie von meiner Vergangenheit keine Ahnung haben. [...] Polen und Deutsche, Auschwitz und Wien, der alte Judenhaß der

---

[44]Vgl. *Crossing*, S.124.
[45]Abgedruckt in: *Der Standard*, 1.9.1995.
[46]*The Golem*, unpublished synopsis.
[47]*The Conversion and Circumcision of Bulan, King of the Khazars*, unpublished play.
[48]*Travels to the Enu*, unpublished play.

Rechten und der neue der Linken, [...]'⁴⁹ bleiben seine literarischen Bestandsaufnahmen brisant und aktuell:

> Die Knallfrösche zu unserem Krambambulicocktail der Kampfeinheit 'Graf Rüdiger von Starhemberg' waren der Auftakt zu einem unerläßlichen Maßnahmenpaket an Sie alle, die in der Frage der Fremden– und Flüchtlingsprobleme mit zu lockerer Hand engagiert sind [...] zugunsten des Panslawismus und anderer obskurer Völkerideologien die eigene Kultur einer Überfremdung ausliefern [...] Sie umgekehrt bei der Entgegennahme von Steuer– und Spendengeldern nicht gerade zimperlich, noch dazu hochprozentual auf die bodenständige, deutsche Bevölkerungsschicht zurückgreifen, und so diesen kostspieligen Wahnsinnsmittelweg für Unsere Heimat überhaupt begehbar machen [...] auf Kosten traditioneller Wesenseigenschaften einer ganzen Volksgemeinschaft.⁵⁰

Dies ist kein Brief von Roman Wacholder an Ossias Würz, sondern der Anfang eines Bekennerschreibens der 'Bajuwarischen Befreiungsarmee', die in Österreich und Deutschland mit Bomben etwas fortzuführen gedenken, was im letzten Krieg nicht ganz gelungen ist.

> Manchmal träume ich so vor mich hin: Da sehe ich eine Eislandschaft, auf der nichts wächst, wo's auch keine Menschen gibt. Das beruhigt mich. Im letzten Krieg hätten wir's fast. geschafft und dann ist am Schluß trotzdem nichts draus geworden.⁵¹

---

⁴⁹Jakov Lind: *Der Erfinder. Ein Roman in Briefen.* München: (Hanser) 1988, S.166.

⁵⁰Die Briefe der Bajuwaren. In: *Profil*, 26, 26.6.1995.

⁵¹*Eine bessere Welt*, S.87.

FRITZ HOCHWÄLDER — DER FALL EINES VERGESSENEN DRAMATIKERS

AXEL SCHALK

HORST KELLNER GEWIDMET

Hôtel du Commerce heißt ein von Fritz Hochwälder 1944 geschriebenes Stück; eine Prostituierte steht im Mittelpunkt des Konflikts, bei dem eine auf der Flucht befindliche Gruppe in die Kriegswirren der preußischen Besetzung Frankreichs 1870 gerät. Ist diese Komödie, die das für den Autor typische historische Ambiente bietet, ein Geschichtsdrama? Wohl kaum. Der Titel fungiert als Metapher für das, was real–gesellschaftlich einzig herrscht und in Hochwälders Fabel einzig den szenischen Konflikt bestimmt: das Geschäft. Die Situation, in der ein nichtauftretender preußischer Offizier die Reisegruppe so lange festhält, bis die Dame sich mit ihm eingelassen hat, demaskiert die Figuren: 'Mit welchem Recht verfügt dieses Weibsbild über ihre persönliche Freiheit?'[1] heißt es im Text, in dem die von den anderen ob ihres Berufs verachtete Hure in zynischer Dialektik zur einzig ehrenwerten Person wird. Ihr geschäftliches Ethos, das einzig auf der freien Entscheidung beruht, mündet in Patriotismus: Sie rettet alle, indem sie sich hingibt; nur sie hat eine Haltung, die anderen aber haben Interessen. Hochwälders Provokation liegt nicht nur in der Verkehrung der bürgerlichen Moral; er argumentiert grundsätzlich: Man ist gerettet und die Geschäfte gehen in 'Le Havre' (S. 164) weiter.

Unschwer läßt sich die boulevardeske Historienszene auf die zeitgeschichtliche Situation beziehen, die faschistische Besetzung: In fast Brechtscher Verfremdung wird das Drama zum unterhaltsamen Lehrstück über politischen Opportunismus. Gerade die Umfunktionierung der Komödienmechanik verschärft die Wirkung. Hier liegt eine der zentralen Absichten des Autors, verstört sie doch als gebräuchliche Form des Unterhaltungstheaters tradierte Erwartungshorizonte. Das vom Autor kritisierte kapitalistische Nützlichkeitsdenken herrscht über den Stückschluß hinaus, die Harmonisierung bleibt aus; die mutige Hure, die sogar mit dem Gedanken spielt, den Besatzer zu erstechen, bleibt die von den anderen verachtete Person. Fritz Hochwälder formuliert anders als der Didaktiker Brecht eine *konkrete* Lehre.

---

[1] Fritz Hochwälder: 'Hôtel du Commerce'. Komödie in fünf Akten. Nach Maupassants Novelle "Boule De Suif". In: F H.: *Dramen I*, Graz: (Styria) 1975 S.173. Weitere Seitenangaben erfolgen im Text in Klammern.

Die zeitgenössische Literaturgeschichtsschreibung ist ungerecht, sie muß es sein, wenn sie systematische Begriffe, Abfolgen von Schulen oder vermeintliche Zusammenhänge beschreiben will; geht sie doch immer nur von den im jeweiligen, zeitgebundenen intellektuellen Mainstream konstruierten Linien aus. Diese können aber, wenn sie es denn je konnten, und nicht immer schon chimärisch waren, gerade im 20. Jahrhundert, einem literarischen Zeitalter der Unüberschaubarkeit und Brüche, nicht mehr greifen. Dieser Sachverhalt der herrschenden Praxis mag ein Grund sein, warum einer der produktivsten Dramatiker des 20. Jahrhunderts heute weitgehend vergessen ist. Fritz Hochwälder, der bis in die Mitte der siebziger Jahre zu den international viel gespielten modernen Dramatikern gehörte, ist offenbar zwischen den Schützengräben von 'Moderne' und 'Tradition', als Vertreter einer schwer klassifizierbaren Zwischenposition trotz aller Bühnenwirksamkeit für die Literaturwissenschaft, nichtkompatibel geblieben. Der Autor hat sich 'wie kein zweiter deutschsprachiger Dramatiker der Nachkriegszeit [...] jeder modernen Strömung des Theaters versagt.'[2] Beckett und Ionesco, die Vertreter des sogenannten Absurdismus, trafen nach literaturgeschichtlicher Aussage in den fünfziger Jahren auf das epische Theater Brechts; da ist das vielfältige dramatische Schaffen Hochwälders schwerlich zu verorten. Wenn Peter Handke oder Wolfgang Bauer als Sprachexperimentierer Mitte der sechziger Jahre die Diskussion der österreichischen Gegenwartsliteratur bestimmten, so hat Hochwälder auch in dieser Theaterdebatte keinen Platz. Der Autor schreibt 1966:

> [...] Zu schweizerischen und deutschen Theaterkreisen hatte und habe ich keinerlei persönliche Beziehung, stehe gänzlich außerhalb, und meine Verbindung mit den Wiener Bühnen, vor allem mit dem Burgtheater, beschränkt sich darauf, dort uraufgeführt zu werden [...] der Autor mitsamt seinem Theater ist anscheinend nirgends zu Hause [...].[3]

Doch Hochwälders entschiedene Verweigerungshaltung, mit der er sich hier etwa gegen Dürrenmatt oder Frisch abgrenzt, deutet auf den Kern seiner antifaschistischen, politischen Position, die, mit Thomas Bernhard vergleichbar, — Hochwälder redet vom 'Ur–Nazismus' (ebenda., S. 100) Österreichs — ihn im Züricher Exil bleiben ließ. Sein literarisches Programm ist zugleich ein politisches. Der Autor steht jenseits von jeglichem literarischen Formalismus und jenseits modernistischer Formzertrümmerung; dies, die Fixierung einzig auf verhandelte Inhalte, hat ihn unbequem gemacht. Mit polemischer, undifferenzierter Schärfe

---

[2]Lutz Hagestedt: 'Fritz Hochwälder'. In: *Kritisches Lexikon zur deutschsprachigen Gegenwartsliteratur [KLG]* (ed.) Heinz Ludwig Arnold, München: 1978f., S.2.
[3]Fritz Hochwälder: 'Über mein Theater'. In: F. H.: *Im Wechsel der Zeit. Autobiographische Skizzen und Essays*, Graz/Wien/Köln: 1980, (Styria) S.87.

bezeichnet Hochwälder die zeitgenössischen Theaterautoren als 'Pseudoliteraten', die im Formalismus erstarrt wären:

> Vielfach dominiert ein verschmockter, denaturierter Kunstverstand auf einem Gebiet, das sich professionshalber gegen jede Schmockerei intolerant erweisen sollte. Das ist leider nicht der Fall, statt dessen bewundert man des Kaisers neue Kleider [...], allenthalben wächst Sterilität, die sich mit Fistelstimme als Ästhetizismus anpreist [...] nur Geduld, die Zeit der präpotenten Impotenten läuft unaufhaltsam ab [...].[4]

Hochwälders Stücke operieren jenseits von ästhetizistischen Formalismen, sprachlich einfach, metaphernlos 'unliterarisch, unprätentiös'.[5] 'Formlosigkeit', scheinbarer Traditionalismus, so verstandene gestaltete Anti–Literatur, waren von Hochwälder zweifellos politisch gemeint. Hochwälders szenische Modelle weisen dem Autor schwerlich einen Ort innerhalb der gültigen ästhetischen Modelle an, sie weisen ihn, formalistisch begriffen, sowohl als Traditionalisten wie als 'modern' aus. Doch auch die bewußt gestaltete Poesielosigkeit seiner Stücke wird dem Autor, der auf Inhalte und Positionen rekurriert, keine literaturwissenschaftlichen Auslegungsfreunde geschaffen haben. Entschiedenes Außenseitertum kennzeichnet Hochwälders Haltung. Die vom Literaturwissenschaftler zu registrierende ästhetische Unergiebigkeit, ist, so verstanden, auch eine Provokation gegen seinen Berufsstand. Die Folge war, daß der Autor auf gängige Formen, wie das 'Volksstück' fixiert wurde, diese aber, so die These, bilden lediglich eine *formale Folie* für die erörterten Inhalte. Der Autor selbst, bekennt sich 1961 zu Aristoteles:

> Nicht Pessimismus wollte oder will ich durch meine übertreibende Darstellung der drei großen Gefahren Verlust von Sprache, Gewissen und Naivität unterstützen [...] sondern geneigtes Verständnis für das zeitbedingte Sich–Versagen von Hanswurst, dessen liebstes Kind [...] die Tragödie ist [...]. Denn Tragödie ist ursprünglich, unpsychologisch; sie ist unterhaltsam [...] sie ist unverschmockt, sie reinigt das Gemüt des Zuschauers, ohne ihn zu verändern, darin gleicht sie allem Theater; sie verstrickt ihn in eine Aktion, die zwingend ist; sie hält dem neuzeitlichen Oreopithecus den blanken Spiegel vor, wenn es nichts nützt, so schadet es auch nicht, überhaupt wächst bekanntlich das Rettende bei zunehmender Bedrohung; endlich wirkt die Tragödie durch Handlung, nicht durch Charaktere, wie schon der Stagirit feststellte [...].[6]

'Naivität' mag eine der Hochwälderschen Gestaltungsmaximen sein, rekurriert sie doch auf seinen radikalen, unliterarischen Konkretismus. Die

---

[4]Fritz Hochwälder: 'Vom Versagen des Dramas in unserer Zeit'. In: *Im Wechsel*, a.a.O. S.71; ähnlich in 'Über mein Theater', S.94: 'Gegenwärtig zeigt man in stolzer Sterilität den prunkvollen Rahmen [...].'

[5]*Über mein*, a.a.O. S.93.

[6]*Vom Versagen*, a.a.O. S.79.

ästhetische Praxis allerdings der hier vorgestellten, in biederen Akten gehaltenen Stücke, ist weit davon entfernt, die kathartische Erregung und Reinigung der Leidenschaften zu predigen; die aristotelische Struktur bleibt in Hochwälders Werk formale Schablone. So sagt der ehemalige Nazi und Fabrikant in *Der Befehl* (Uraufführung [UA] 1968):

> [...] Das ist das wunderbare am Theater: man erkennt die eigene Niedertracht, läßt sich erschüttern [...] applaudiert [...] und fünf Minuten später pfeift man drauf. Das nennt man Reinigung.[7]

Stattdessen entwickeln die hier diskutierten Stücke nur einen Ausschnitt des über zwanzig Stücke umfassenden dramatischen Werks: Einen die herrschende Fremdbestimmung aufzeigenden Maschinencharakter, eine konzentrierte Dramaturgie der Reduktion, der szenischen Abläufe, die zentral auf die verhandelten Inhalte rekurriert. Es herrscht in Hochwälders 'pièces bien–faites' die Dramaturgie des Fernsehspiels, aber auch die des Ablaufs. Heiner Müllers *Die Hamletmaschine* oder Cocteaus *Maschine infernal* stehen dem Grundcharakter zumindest der hier diskutierten Stücke Hochwälders alles andere als fern. 'Hanswurst' ist für Hochwälder der Protagonist der 'altneuen' Dramenform der Zwischenposition, dessen 'Kampfruf [...] "Glückauf zum Untergang"'[8] heißt.

Hochwälders 1948 uraufgeführtes Stück *Der öffentliche Ankläger* belegt schon von der Handlungskonstruktion her, daß der Autor durchaus im modernistischen Kontext der Maschinenmetaphorik etwa eines Louis Aragon steht. Fouquier Tinville, der Staatsanwalt Robespierres, soll in der historischen Szene, die unmittelbar nach dem Thermidor spielt, ein letztes Mal mit dem Prairialgesetz ermitteln. Dieses Denunziationsgesetz, ein politisches Instrument der *terreur*, ermöglichte mit zwei Zeugenaussagen das Todesurteil. Theresia Tallien, die gute Frau vom Thermidor, fordert im Amtszimmer des Anklägers, daß ein Unbekannter vernichtet werden soll, um die Schreckensherrschaft endgültig zu beenden. Der Blutsäufer Fouquier selbst, Hochwälders literarischer Protagonist, exemplarisch für die furchtbaren Nazijuristen, wird sein eigenes Opfer sein! Er charakterisiert seine Rolle in dieser szenisch spannungsreichen Extremsituation, die bis zum Schluß offen läßt, wessen Kopf fällt, so:

> Nun ich bin nicht Verteidiger, mein Amt ist es zu töten! Ich habe alles vorbereitet, um einen Unbekannten zu vernichten. Es fehlt nur ein winziges Rad in der Maschine, wenn ich es einfüge, läuft sie von selbst, niemand kann sie mehr

---

[7]Fritz Hochwälder: 'Der Befehl'. Schauspiel in drei Akten. In: F.H.: *Dramen II*, Graz: 1975 (Styria) S.314.
[8]*Vom Versagen*, a.a.O. S.80.

aufhalten. Auch ich bin von diesem Augenblick an [...] ein Teil dieser Maschine, sie nimmt mich mit, was immer auch geschieht ...'[9]

Hier liegt Hochwälders poetisches Programm, das in überraschender Übereinstimmung mit Artaud den psychologisch gestalteten Menschen aus dem Stück eliminiert.

Die an den *Ödipus* oder Kleists *Der zerbrochene Krug* erinnernde Fabel des Stücks operiert im szenischen *Paradox* und entwickelt damit ein zutiefst modernes Weltbild, das der instrumentellen, entfremdeten Vernunft. Die klassische Finalspannung ist so angelegt, daß sich alle Aktionen des scharfen Analytikers Fouquier gegen ihn selbst richten. Sein analytisches Instrumentarium und die Geheimdienstakten, die ihn über alle auftretenden Personen omnipotent machen, sind nutzlos. Die Situation bleibt dominant. Paradigmatisch erörtert das so gestaltete Geschichtsdrama nicht nur die erlittene Gegenwart des Faschismus, es dominiert eine für das moderne Drama stilbildende Binnenmechanik, die die Subjekte zu Objekten des Ablaufs degradiert. Spiel und Gegenspiel bleiben nichts als scheinhafte Handlungsschablone, die von der Intrigenmaschinerie bestimmt wird.

Wenn das klassische Geschichtsdrama das Schicksal gestaltete, so herrschen bei Hochwälder bis in die Nuancen des geschlossenen Dramas — alle Auftretenden können Opfer werden — Abläufe. Hochwälders Stück zeigt aufklärungskritisch die Welt als verwaltete Welt, es dominiert die unpoetische Kanzleisprache in der Conciergerie. Töten, das Thema des Stücks, wird zum mechanischen Töten. Die Dialoge kreisen in sich, sie transportieren eine unparteiliche Antimoral, eine Antipsychologie, die einzig einen Fall zur Debatte stellt, ein widersinniges, tödliches System. Der Henker Sanson tritt auf, ein Bürokrat des Todes, der mit der Abfertigung der Opfer nicht mehr nachkommt:

Sanson: Ich kann nicht mehr. Ich bin erschöpft. Ich falle vom Fleisch [...]
Fouquier: Sanson Nehmen Sie sich zusammen [...] Sie können diesmal ausnahmsweise in zwei Partien fahren!
Sanson: Zweiundsiebzig in zwei Partien? Sechsunddreißig auf einem Karren? Ist das Ihr Ernst?
Fouquier *sanft*: Gut, ich sehe ein, daß das schwer möglich ist [...] in drei Partien also... [...]
Sanson [...]: Aber es wird bis in den Nachmittag dauern das sage ich ihnen gleich.
Fouquier: Bis in den Nachmittag das ist zu lang. [...] Es muß rascher gehen.
Sanson: Ich kann Ihnen nichts versprechen.
Fouquier: So fangen Sie endlich an worauf warten Sie noch?
Sanson: Auf die Reihenfolge.
Fouquier: Was für eine Reihenfolge?

---

[9]Fritz Hochwälder: 'Der öffentliche Ankläger'. Schauspiel in drei Akten. In: *Dramen I*, a.a.O. S.297; zum Maschinenmotiv vgl. auch S.266, 306, 314.

Sanson: Wenn in mehreren Partien gefahren wird, muß die Reihenfolge bestimmt werden.
Fouquier: Das überlasse ich Ihnen.
Sanson: Wünschen Sie die Partien in der Reihenfolge der Liste eingeteilt?
Fouquier: Machen Sie das, wie sie wollen.
Sanson: Bedaure die Einteilung ist Ihre Sache [...] (S. 259 f.).

Verdinglichung, Bürokratie, Funktionalität stehen statt der großen historischen Szene. Es läuft ein Uhrwerk ohne Handlungsoptionen. Täter und Opfer werden in dieser Antidialektik ununterscheidbar. Auch das für ein geschlossenes, aristotelisches Stück ungewöhnliche Ende verdeutlicht Hochwälders Haltung: Zwar ist die Handlung mit der Vernichtung Tinvilles erschöpft; die Mechanismen, die im historischen Gewand moderne Welt bedeuten, bleiben aber virulent. Theresia und Tallien, die Sieger, streiten über den Akten, die wohl schreckliche Wahrheiten enthalten. Übertragbar ist dieses Stück, das eine 'Wendesituation' thematisiert, allemal. Orientiert ist es an der Theateravantgarde, die das handelnde Subjekt zugunsten der dominanten Situation puppenhaft aufhebt.

Erlitt der heute weitgehend vergessene Dramatiker, der 1911 in Wien geborene und 1986 im Züricher Exil gestorbene Autodidakt und Tapezierermeister das Unglück des Erfolgreichen? Offenbar hat der Welterfolg seines 1943 uraufgeführten Stücks über den utopisch–plakativ gezeichneten kommunistischen Jesuitenstaat in Paraguay, *Das heilige Experiment*, den Blick für sein bemerkenswert differenziertes dramatisches Schaffen verstellt. Hochwälder selbst hat das Mißverständnis, ein 'katholischer' Autor zu sein, zurechtgerückt.

Ich bin alles eher als ein katholischer Autor. Der Irrtum, mich für einen solchen zu halten, ist [...] ohne mein Zutun entstanden, vor allem dadurch, daß eines meiner Stücke, [...] 'Das heilige Experiment' [...] im katholischen Gewand auftreten mußte. Keinem meiner anderen Stücke dürfte ein konfessionell–katholisches Bekenntnis zu entnehmen sein. ' Wenn ich die Umschreibung 'romantisch–katholisch' für eine gewisse traditionelle Hinneigung zu Klarheit und Form verwende, im Gegensatz etwa zu 'protestantisch–puritanisch' [...] dann haben diese Begriffe im landläufigen Sinn nichts mit Katholizismus oder Protestantismus zu tun.[10]

Dennoch wurde er auf die Schablone des katholisch–konservativen Autors der klassischen Form festgelegt, des Tragikers des 'gedankenhohen Schauspiels'. 'Sicher gebaute historische Dramen, Symbol– und Legendenspiele', die in einem 'Rahmen fester Wertungen und Ordnungen' stünden, lautete das Diktum Margret Dietrichs in den sechziger Jahren. Auffällig ist, daß dieses Jesuitenstück, analytisch wenig begründet, zum Maßstab für Hochwälders Schaffen wurde: 'klassizistisches Ideendrama'

---

[10] *Über mein*, a.a.O. S.89; vgl. auch S.88.

oder 'gegenwärtige Gültigkeit des Zeitlosen' sind die typischen Dikta, bis hin zum pathetischen 'Ewigkeitswert', die den Blick auf Hochwälder verstellt haben. Wie aber das zweifellos vorliegende Aristotelische Programm der 'Wahrscheinlichkeit und Folgerichtigkeit'[11] bei Hochwälder szenisch instrumentalisiert ist, wird nicht diskutiert. Beschreibbar bei Hochwälder ist eine Struktur, die lediglich Folie ist, die auf Gegenwart verweist und an der soziologischen Beobachtung, der Beschreibung der Phänomene festhält.

Selbst Bortenschläger, Autor der einzigen bisher erschienenen Monographie über Hochwälder, in der auch er vom 'immerwährenden Problem', 'rein Menschliche[m]', von 'Gewissensdrama' und 'ewiggültiger Problematik' redet, widerspricht der These vom vermeintlichen Traditionalismus: 'Was er [Hochwälder] allein fordert, ist eine theatergerechte Form [...]'; was dies aber impliziert, wird nicht erörtert. Vielmehr stilisiert er den Autor zum österreichischen Staatsdramatiker und weist seinem Schaffen alle Attribute traditionellen Schreibens wie 'zeitlose Gültigkeit'[12] zu.

Der Vorwurf der Epigonalität[13] gegen die Stücke kann schwerlich greifen; diese, mögen sie auch im aristotelischen Koordinatensystem stehen, mögen sie auch das dramaturgische Muster des Volksstücks oder, wie gezeigt, dramatische Muster der Moderne adaptieren, sie transportieren immer einen 'naiven' einen konkreten, gesellschaftlichen Bezug, stehen nie in einem ästhetizistischen Vakuum. Hier im mikrologischen, immer Gesellschaft meinenden *Konkretismus*, liegt die spezifische, unliterarische Stärke der Dramatik Fritz Hochwälders.

Wie im *Öffentlichen Ankläger* ermittelt in *Der Befehl* einer gegen sich selbst; der Kriminalbeamte Mittermayer soll den Nazimord an einem holländischen Mädchen, den er selbst begangen hat, aufklären. Der Fabrikant Pokorny, der frühere SD–Vorgesetzte Mittermayers, formuliert die Position der Verdränger:

— Wo kämen wir hin, wenn uns die Vergangenheit auf Schritt und Tritt verfolgt? Was wir getan haben, hat nichts mehr mit uns zu tun, ich lehne es ab, dafür grad zu stehn, wir waren andere damals, und die anderen auch. (S. 312)

Auch hier herrscht die Maschine, die der Bürokratie, der tatsächliche Täter Mittermayer verhört das ausgewählte Opfer. Hier wird Hochwälder

---

[11]Margret Dietrich: *Das moderne Drama. Strömungen, Gestalten, Motive*, Stuttgart: 1963, S.616; *Kindlers Literaturgeschichte der Gegenwart* Bd. 2; [Hrsg.] Hilde Spiel, Frankfurt/M.: 1980 S.373; Hans Vogelsang: *Österreichische Dramatik des 20. Jahrhunderts. Spiel mit Welten, Wesen, Worten*, Wien: 1981, S.191; 202.

[12]Wilhelm Bortenschläger: *Der Dramatiker Fritz Hochwälder*, Innsbruck: 1979, S.15; 63, 82, 113, 204.

[13]Vgl. *KLG*, S.1.

konkreter, gesellschaftlicher, ohne ein historisches Ambiente zu bemühen. So wiederholt sich Hochwälders Gerichtsdramaturgie. Der Täter bekennt sich zur Tat und wird von seinen Kollegen als nervenkrank bezeichnet, '– Wir haben Befehle empfangen und durchgeführt, zeigen Sie mir einen Abschnitt in der Geschichte, wo es anders war – [...]' (S. 312). Die Bestien von damals sind, wie der Himbeerpflücker, die Durchschnittsmenschen von heute, im szenischen Jetzt herrschen andere Bedingungen, andere Befehle. Die 'abgrundtiefe Feigheit' führt 'zum Exzeß gegen Wehrlose — schauen Sie mich an. *Ruhig.* So und nicht anders sieht der aus, der die Untat auf dem Gewissen hat' (S. 334). Die Hochwäldersche Dramatik nach 1945 erörtert in ihren wesentlichen Stücken den Faschismus. Auch wenn der Autor sich dem Aristotelischen Verfahren verpflichtet hat, sich zum Humanismus bekennt, so operiert er doch inhaltlich immer wieder in anderen Modellen: Als Geschichtsdramatiker, als Volkstheaterautor, der den autoritären Charakter untersucht oder als Situationsdramatiker, der eine Flucht szenisch darstellt. Die Klassifizierung nach Stoffen, die Bortenschläger vorlegt, bleibt aber vordergründig fragwürdig, da immer Faschismus und Gegenwart gemeint sind.

    Donadieu (UA 1953) setzt einen genau beschriebenen Schloßraum in Szene, wenn ein historisches Spektakel aus der Hugenottenzeit beginnt, das die Hochwälder vertraute Exilsituation des Verfolgtseins historisch spiegelt. Du Bosc, ein Königlicher, der Donadieus Frau tötete und für ein Hugenottenmassaker verantwortlich ist, gerät in dessen Hand. Das Problem der Bestrafung von 'Kriegsgreuln'[14] deutet auf die aktuelle Problematik hin, die der Autor in seiner historischen Modellsituation erörtert. Auch in *Der Flüchtling* (UA 5. 9. 1945), einem der meistgespielten Stücke, setzt Hochwälder eine Extremsituation in Szene; er operiert in diesem Dreipersonenstück direkter als im modellhaften Fouquier–Stück. Unbestritten dürfte dieses hermetische Drama deutlich von der historischen Stunde, in der es entstand, der Stunde des Siegs über den Faschismus, geprägt sein. Wenn Wolfgang Borchert mit *Draußen vor der Tür* das moralisierende Zeitstück entwickelte, hat Hochwälder zeitgebunden aber doch grundsätzlicher szenisch argumentiert; die Situation ist übertragbar: Ein politischer Flüchtling kommt im Hause seines Verfolgers an. Die poesielose, realistisch gehaltene Sprache, ohne poetische Bilder, Metaphern oder Symbole transportiert 'unverschmockt' das Problem der Diktatur und ihrer Folgen für den Einzelnen. Ohne Brechtisch zu didaktisieren, entwickelt der Autor seine Lehre über die immanente Dynamik von Repression, die zwangsläufig zur Denunziation führt.

---

[14]Fritz Hochwälder: 'Donadieu'. Schauspiel in drei Akten. In: F. H. *Dramen II*, a.a.O. S.41.

Zwei Haltungen stellt der Autor gegenüber, die des Opportunismus der Grenzwächter und die des Widerstands der Flüchtlinge. Bestimmt wird das Stück ausschließlich durch diese reduzierte Situation. Die Dramaturgie ist auf den einen Konflikt konzentriert, drei Menschen geraten auf Grund der politischen Lage in eine Zwangssituation; verhalten sie sich human, gefährden sie sich. Jenseits jeglicher Moral entwickelt Hochwälder eine zwanghafte, tödliche Mechanik, eine szenisch dominante Situation ohne Handlungsoptionen. Der Grenzwächter, der Verteter der 'Rechtschaffenheitslumpen',[15] der Flüchtling, die Frau, die klassische Dreieckssituation wird hier politisch umgedeutet. Am Ende muß der Grenzwächter erkennen, daß er als Mitläufer auch verloren ist:

> Ja ich war in Wirklichkeit der Flüchtling! Ich! Ich! Wer solang auf der Flucht war, der muß einmal stehen bleiben. Es kommt der Augenblick, da erkennt er, daß kein Weg weiter führt. Ich bleibe stehn. Hier (S. 120).

Der Grenzwächter, der in Selbsterkenntnis Frau und Flüchtling hat gehen lassen, stirbt im Maschinengewehrfeuer. Auch wenn Hochwälder hier vordergründig Handlungs– bzw. Entscheidungsoptionen als falsch und richtig thematisiert, sein Grenzwächter stirbt. Die Gut–Böse–Moral, selbst die Selbsterkenntnis, helfe in der Zwangslage nicht. Die Situation ist dominant.

In *Der Himbeerpflücker* (UA 1964 als Fernsehspiel im Österreichischen Rundfunk) treibt der Autor die Faschismuskritik weg von der zeitverhafteten, moralischen Agitation mit einer unentrinnbaren tödlichen Situation dem Gebrauchsstück hin zur mehr grundsätzlichen Studie des autoritären Charakters, zum alltäglichen Faschismus der Geschäftemacher und Opportunisten, zur Kritik an der nach Hochwälder nach wie vor existierenden paranoiden, kleinbürgerlichen Haltung.

> [...] Und was wäre geschehen, [...] wenn Roosevelt nicht rechtzeitig als Kommunist entlarvt worden wäre? [...] Man hätte uns in ferne, unwirtliche Gefilde verschleppt, nach Rußland und Amerika, niemand wäre verschont geblieben, die heimatliche Erde wäre verödet, und jene dunklen Gestalten, die der Himbeerpflücker noch am Leben gelassen hat, würden heute sadistisch die Knute über uns schwingen, vor meinem geistigen Auge sehe ich die triumphierende Fratze des Untermenschen, wie sie sich lustverzerrt an unserer Vernichtung weiden [...].[16]

So geriert sich die herrschende Ideologie in der Wirtshausszene. Theodor W. Adorno redet in diesem Zusammenhang vom 'Antivolksstück' und trifft Hochwälders Umfunktionierung des Suggestiven der tradierten Form im

---

[15]Fritz Hochwälder: 'Der Flüchtling'. Schauspiel in drei Akten. In: F. H.: *Dramen III*, Graz: 1979 (Styria) S.113.

[16]Fritz Hochwälder: 'Der Himbeerpflücker'. Komödie in drei Akten. In: *Dramen II*, a.a.O. S.219 f.

Kern: Die 'Abkürzung über das Abgekürzte' sagt die 'Wahrheit'.[17] Erst wenn das Publikum der Suggestion des Stücks selbst widersteht und sich dennoch dialektisch dessen Bann überantwortet, dann wird das Entsetzen des Gemütlichen spürbar.

Die Komödie, deren Konstruktion deutliche Züge des Gogolschen *Revisors* trägt, erinnert an das exemplarische Beispiel des radikal–komödiantischen österreichischen antifaschisten Dramas, *Der Bockerer* von Ulrich Becher und Peter Preses. Die Schrecken werden im überspitzten, nur folienhaft–funktional inszenierten 'Volksstück' und seinen satirisch gezeichneten Typen *qua* Übertreibung als realer gesellschaftlich–alltäglicher Vorgang entdämonisiert. Hochwälder aber entwickelt gleichsam über das Personal ein schlüssiges gesellschaftliches Modell. Das Volksstückpersonal, das in allen typischen Mustern auf der Szene agiert, hat hier nur eine einzige Funktion, eine politische; die gezeigten Handlungsmuster zielen nur auf die politische Wirkung, sie transportieren das Thema der Verdrängung. Vergleichbar mit Rolf Hochhuths politischer Tragödien– oder Dokumentardramatik trachtet Hochwälder danach, die konkrete, gesellschaftskritische Lehre zu transportieren. Doch anders als Brecht didaktisiert er nicht, sondern benutzt das jeweilige spezifisch dramaturgische Modell satirisch. Epigonal ist Hochwälder bei der Umfunktionierung des Volksstückmusters schon deshalb nicht, weil seine szenisch erzählende Epik aus der Logik der Kenntlichmachung lebt als unpoetische Materialität des tabuisierten, unangenehmen Inhalts, die das Muster lediglich formal benutzt.

Wenn George Tabori mit seinem Stück *Mein Kampf* (1986) als der zeitgenössische Dramatiker gilt, der über absurdistische Dialoge den Faschismus jenseits der Moral provokativ, tabuverletzend erörterte, so kann der Hochwälder des *Himbeerpflückers* durchaus als sein Urahn gelten. In Peter Weiss' *Die Ermittlung* herrscht die oriatorenhafte Poetisierung der Auschwitzschrecken, bei Hochwälder dagegen begegnen wir realistischen Charakteren aus Fleisch und Blut. Die permanenten Handlungsumschläge gestalten das Stück darüberhinaus unterhaltsam, die Wirkungsmächtigkeit liegt im bekannten Modell, im Volksstück, das aber den Erwartungshorizont verstört.

Die Szene, ein Gasthof in 'Bad Braunau', zeigt ein bizarr–satirisches Gruppenbild von saufenden, typisierten Honoratioren–Spießern: Arzt, Schuldirektor, Wirt, Fabrikdirektor, Rechtsanwalt, Bauunternehmer, die vermuten, daß ein im Dorfe beliebter Kriegsverbrecher, der 'Himbeerpflücker', der sich versteckt hielt, zurückgekommen sei. Wie immer beginnt der Autor in medias res mit einer überschaubaren,

---

[17]Theodor W. Adorno: 'Reflexion über das Volksstück'. In: T.W.A.: *Notizen zur Literatur*, Frankfurt/M.: 1981 (stw 355) S.693.

bühnenpraktischen Situation, in der die Domestiken parieren müssen. Wie bei Tabori in *Mein Kampf* operiert auch Hochwälder mit dem Mittel der zugespitzten Übertreibung. Ein Gast ist angekommen, ein Krimineller, der für den 'Himbeerpflücker' gehalten wird, dessen Auftreten, dem Ödipusmodell folgend, die schmähliche Vergangenheit der Figuren aufrollt. Auch das Dürrenmattmodell des *Besuchs der alten Dame* steht hier dramaturgisch Pate, durch den Auftritt einer fremden Person kommt die Szenerie in Gang. Die Hysterie beginnt, die Psychopathologie des nazistischen Kleinbürgers wird vom Autor als aktuelle gesellschaftliche Realität gesetzt: 'Ein Auftreten wie damals am Waldrand [...] Die Erscheinung, der Ton, die Hakennase unverkennbar [...] ohne Uniform freilich, das schwächt ihn ab' (S. 223). Die Verwechslung treibt die Dynamik weiter, die die Vergangenheit der Protagonisten ans Tageslicht zerrt: Der Wirt Steisshäuptl hat seinen Reichtum aus einer Kiste mit Gold, die der 'Himbeerpflücker' ihm aus dem KZ zur Aufbewahrung übergab; die Honoratioren bis hinunter zum Kellner, der denunzierte, haben alle ihre Rolle mitgespielt, der Arzt, der 'Lebensunwertes' im Altersheim abtötete, der Direktor etwa, der mit dem Schrotgewehr flüchtige Deportierte jagte. Wenn Tabori den Absurdismus des Faschismus in Nonsense–Dialogen gestaltet, liegt dieser bei Hochwälder in der realen Situation, die ebenfalls jenseits von Moral oder Anklage gefaßt wird: Die Figuren geraten in eine Maschinerie der Enthüllungen; jeder gerät im geschickt gewebten szenischen Geflecht gegen jeden, denn jeder möchte wieder ein Geschäft machen, ist doch jeder erpreßbar. Die faschistoide Haltung aber hat sich nicht verändert, die Mechanik der eigenen Ideologie hat die Possenfiguren erfaßt. Die Organisation des Spannungsbogens führt zum Aufrollen der Vergangenheit. Der Wirt und Bürgermeister Steisshäuptl, der Prototyp des von Hochwälder gezeichneten autoritären Charakters, hat das Psychogramm der 'Führernatur' (S. 230), die sich, der inneren Dynamik folgend, vor dem Wirtshauspublikum selbst entlarvt:

Steisshäuptl *elegisch*: Von Verrätern umgeben, im eignen Haus, in der eignen Stadt... (erhebt sich, holt aus einem Wandschränkchen eine Schapsflasche und ein Wasserglas, das er bis zum Rand füllt und in einem Zug leert) [...] Ja meine Herrschaften mir scheint, ihr habt's vergessen, daß wir in Brauning sind, beim Steisshäuptl (*wirft das Glas an die Wand.*) Ich bin eine Naturgewalt, gegen mich seid's ihr alle Scheißer! [...] Herhören alle! [...] Ein Held hat mich aufgesucht, heimgesucht, ein von allen Hunden Gehetzter [...] der berühmte Himmbeerpflücker vom Lager Wüstenhofen, eine Ungerechtigkeit, daß man ihn deswegen verfolgt, es war eine andere Zeit, und wo gehobelt wird, fliegen Späne [...] innerlich sind wir geblieben, was wir waren, infolgedessen möcht man annehmen, daß die Kameraden in so einer Situation wie ein Mann zusammenstehen, aber nein
Zagl stellt ihm den Bierhumpen hin; beschwörend: Herr Steisshäuptl –
Steisshäuptl: Ruhe im Hasenstall! aber nein: man verschwört sich gegen mich [...] natürlich der Doktor Schnopf (*tut einen mächtigen Zug aus dem Humpen*) der

hat's notwendig, glaubt er vielleicht, ich hab vergessen, daß er seinerzeit im Altersheim einige lebensunwerte Leben abgekürzt hat (*macht Geste des Abspritzens*) [...]
Niemand rührt sich
[...]
Zagl *flehend*: Herr Bürgermeister
Steisshäuptl: Nichts, alles muß heraus! (*Trinkt abermals ausgiebig; stellt den Humpen hin, wischt sich den Mund*) Nach'm Schnaps ist so ein Bier das einzige...(*Richtet sich auf.*) Und der Herr Doktor Suppinger [...] soll lieber drüber nachdenken, was er zusammengstohlen hat bei der Arisierung vom Herrn Hirsch, es geht auf keine Kuhhaut, dagegen bin ich mit meinen zwei Kisten Zahngold ein Kleingewerbetreibender. Millionen und Millionen! Und wenn sich der Hirsch meldt' oder seine Erben, müssen wir es wiedergutmachen aus unsern Steuergeldern [...] Ordnung machen, radikal!
Zagl *fast weinend*: Herr Ortsgruppenleiter!
[...]
Steisshäuptl, *der plötzlich volltrunken ist*: Wer ruft wie ein Donnerhall? (*Reißt sich zusammen, steht schwankend hab–acht.*) Ortsgruppenleiter Konrad Steisshäuptl! Die Kisten mit'm Gold...zu Befehl, jawohl: verwertet... (S. 256 ff.).

Hochwälders Komik ist gebrochen, sie ist auf entlarvende Wirkung kalkuliert. Der Wirt, die komische Type aus dem Volksstückspersonal, zerbricht ein Klischee und verstört potentielle Erwartungshorizonte. Das Klischee des Sichbetrinkens mündet in die Selbstdenunziation. Die Szene löst sich nach der peinlichen Klimax im 3. Akt harmonisch in Vertuschung auf, denn man ist in Brauning in Braunau, in Österreich? Die Szene schlägt in Hochwälders komprimierter Dramatik um, die Sektgläser der Honoratioren werden gefüllt. Man ist gerettet: Den kleinen Verbrecher, dessen tatsächliche Identität bekannt wird, verhaftet man. Sarkastisch zieht der Autor sein Fazit, es war wohl ein Jude; die großen Verbrecher, die Mittäter an der Ermordung Tausender, bleiben unbehelligt. Die poetische Mathematik formuliert eine bittere Erkenntnis.[18]

Wie facettenreich Hochwälders dramatische Spurensuche angelegt ist, zeigt sein Drama *Donnerstag*, das gleichermaßen an Raimunds Zauberspiele erinnert, wie es an Goethes *Faust* von der Konstruktion her anschließt. Nikolaus Manuel Pomfrit heißt der von der 'Belial Incorporation' gesuchte typische, normierte Zeitprotagonist, 'ein lebendiger Toter',[19] der laut Vertrag sich für ein garantiert leidensfreies, rein materialistisches Glück entscheiden muß. In drei Tagen, am 'Donnerstag' tritt dieses ein. Das Glück

---

[18]Bortenschlägers Lesart des Stücks wirft ein bezeichnendes Licht auf den ideologischen Umgang mit Hochwälder, wenn er schreibt: 'Nicht um die Verbrechen [...] und den Terror des NS–Regimes geht es, sondern darum, wie die "Ehemaligen", die "alten Kämpfer" damit fertig werden, wie sie in der Gegenwart damit leben können [...]'! A.a.O. S.208.
[19]Fritz Hochwälder: 'Donnerstag. Ein modernes Mysterienspiel'. In:: *Dramen III*, a.a.O. S.124.

wird durch eine elektronische Maschine simuliert, die die Leinwandsurrogate für die klerikalen Werte Glaube, Liebe, Hoffnung liefert: Kormoran sorgt für das normierte Luxuseigenheim, Perseberg, der 'Weltraumprofessor, von und zu Peenemünde' (S. 142), bietet eine Kosmosfahrt an, die Realitätsflucht; und schließlich wird Amalie von Maskeron, dem Spiegelmenschen als williges Sexobjekt, als 'die göttliche Mäly' (S. 143), projiziert.

Die symbolische Handlung endet offen, Hochwälders Skepsis an den im Fluß befindlichen Verhältnissen problematisierend. Frater Thomas, der mit der Lumpensammlerin Estrella die Gegenwelt zur technischen Glücksmaschinerie darstellt, formuliert Hochwälders kulturkritische Haltung: Auf sauber drainierten Straßen schleicht unser aller 'Ich', das wohlgenährte Untervieh, mit seinem Nasenzipfel, dem übergroßen Eiterkasten, benamst Gehirn; den rosigen Fleischklümpchen rechts und links an der Gesichtskartoffel, von unstillbarer Gier verzehrt nach Leere und Vernichtung ... (S. 167).

Hat Hans Vogelsang recht, wenn er Hochwälders Stück *Donnerstag*, (UA Salzburger Festspiele 1959) das immer wieder, auch vom Autor selbst im Untertitel, ein 'modernes Mysterienspiel'[20] genannt wurde, als ein an Hofmannsthals *Jedermann* orientiertes Werk, 'daß das Fehlen der Glaubensinhalte trotz menschlichem Glück und Wohlstand' (S. 198) als Gefahr aufzeige, interpretiert? Sicher argumentiert hier der 'katholische' Hochwälder des *heiligen Experiments*, der christliche Gläubigkeit versus gesellschaftlichen Materialismus und Triebbefriedigung setzt; doch Hochwälder formuliert eine scharfe Kritik an der herrschenden Warengesellschaft, die durch den Fortschrittsfetisch bestimmt ist: Hier schließt der moderne Mensch, 'seelenlos, genormt, prosperierend, vegetierend' (S. 150) den faustischen Pakt, der ihn 'erlösen' soll. Thematisch behandelt der Autor das Problem der Ich–Vernichtung, die für ihn gesellschaftlich durchaus real ist, weiter bringt seine vehemente, an den kulturkritischen Werfel der zwanziger Jahre anschließende, Technikkritik den Fortschrittsglauben auf den Punkt; dieser gipfelt im zynischen Begriff der 'Gottwerdung' (S. 158) der Menschheit. Die konkrete, gesellschaftliche Bestandsaufnahme, die der Autor seinem Drama unterlegt, ist schwerlich zu überlesen. Das Zauberspiel dieser Versuchsanordnung, das die Frage der 'Entproblematisierung der Existenz' (S. 284) kulturkritisch, wenn auch von der unglücklichen Konstruktion her höchst problematisch angeht, verwebt auch die Faschismuskritik ('Massenvergaser' S. 166) in diesen Kontext: 'der unteilbare Mensch erwürgte Gott [...]: Gott flog als Asche gegen Himmel' (S. 167). Jedenfalls aber setzt Hochwälder die Alternative Glauben versus Verdinglichung, ohne gesellschaftliche Bezüge zu unterschätzen. Der

[20]Peter Demetz: *Die süße Anarchie. Deutsche Literatur seit 1945. Eine kritische Einführung*, Frankfurt/Main/Berlin: 1970, S.129; Vogelsang a.a.O. S.198.

'Pionier des neuen Bauens', der Architekt Pomfrit, die 'WHO IS WHO' (S. 125) Unperson ist eine in ihrem transzendenten Trachten gebrochene Figur. Das 1964 uraufgeführte Stück *1003* demonstriert durch seine Dramaturgie zweierlei: Der Autor dürfte, und hier hat die Forschung recht, zu denen zählen, die meisterhaft die geschlossene Form beherrschen. Die Konstruktion des Vexierspiels zeugt von einer immensen Genauigkeit und Kalkuliertheit, zugleich wird die grundsätzliche Zivilisationskepsis der *Donnerstag*–Konstruktion verschärft. Andererseits ist aber dieser wirkungsmächtige Dramatiker nicht auf tradierte Linien wie das Volksstück festzulegen. Wieder dominiert, wie im *Flüchtling*, die hermetisch–statische Situation, nun aber bewegt sich der Dichter in einem imaginären szenischen Territorium.

Von Mitternacht bis zum Morgengrauen erlebt der Dichter Valmont — hier steht durchaus ein Autor wie E. T. A. Hoffmann Pate — eine Geisterstunde: Er hat eine Figur erfunden, 'die Wohlstandskreatur', die 'der Prototyp'[21] [ist] — der seines Zeitalters, der entstandenen Konsumgesellschaft? In konziser Dramaturgie entwirklicht der vermeintliche 'Traditionalist' Hochwälder zunehmend die drei Akte. Spricht Valmont in seinem Zimmer zunächst beckettisch mit seinem Tonband, so taucht unvermittelt Bloner, seine erfundene Gestalt, auf. Das Stück umkreist das Problem der Schizophrenie, der Ich–Dissoziation, denn Bloner wird zu Valmont, dieser zu Bloner in einer ausvariierten statischen Zimmersituation. Dieses zutiefst moderne Thema, — der Ich–Verlust — das noch in *Donnerstag* klerikal verbrämt wurde, kennt keine Alternativen mehr. Die pirandellesken Rollenspiele weisen Individualität, auch die des dichtenden Subjekts, als chimärenhafte Rollenspiele aus, der *homo technicus*, Fahrer eines Sportwagens mit der Nummer 1003, ist nach Hochwälders moderner Haltung ein Nichts: 'Der Nichtmensch. Projektion der eigenen Niedertracht!' (S. 245). Und, auch sprachlich, durch expressionistisch–fetzenhaft abgehackte Sätze, unterstreicht Hochwälder seine skeptische Haltung gegenüber der aufklärerischen Idee des entfalteten Subjekts, das bei ihm, im Modell des permanenten Identitätstausches, Realitätsfetzen vom Partywohlstand referiert: Individualität kann modernistisch bei Hochwälder nur gebrochen sein, ein Werfelscher Spiegelmensch trifft auf den anderen:

> Vermittle lediglich gebrauchte Ware: Abwechslung, Amüsement, Konsum, Verschleiß ... Bereuen ... Fragen Sie doch meinen Wagen, rassiges Gefährt, stadtbekannte Polizeinummer, fragen Sie den, ob er bereut [...]. Fragen Sie Nummer 1003 (S. 232).

---

[21]Fritz Hochwälder: '1003'. Stück in drei Akten. In:: *Dramen III* a.a.O. S.210.

Moral oder Ethik oder kontroverse Haltungen, gar die politische Utopie, wie im *heiligen Experiment* stehen nicht mehr zur Debatte; die Austauschbarkeit inszeniert über das leerlaufende Rollenspiel eine verdinglichte Wohlstandsgesellschaft, deren flache Ideologie dem Warenfetisch huldigt. Die Kommunikation bleibt scheinhaft.

Die Literaturgeschichte ist ungerecht; endgültig dürfte am Ende des 20. Jahrhunderts das gängige Hochwälderbild obsolet geworden sein. 'Klassisch' (S. 198) sei der Dichter nach Bortenschlägers Diktum. Noch 1992 heißt es:

> Die Wahrheit dieser universalen Weltdramatik aber ist, daß zwischen den anthropologischen Eckwerten von Lachen und Weinen, Komik und Ernst, das Leben oszilliert.[22]

Wieder ist die Rede vom dezidierten 'Verzicht auf Zeitaktualität' (S. 119), und dies wäre der Grund, warum der Autor aus den Spielplänen verschwunden sei. Grund ist wohl eher die Reproduktion falscher Klischees, die aus Unkenntnis des Werks resultieren. *Lazaretti oder der Säbeltiger* (UA 1995) hat nichts mehr von 'immanenter Katholizität', auch die alles entscheidende Stunde des 'Geschichtsdramas' spielt keine Rolle mehr; nunmehr beschäftigt sich der Autor mit dem in den siebziger Jahren aktuellen Problem des Terrorismus. Offenbar hat Fritz Hochwälder auch das Festhalten an traditionellen Formen behindert, trägt doch das Stück starke kolportagehaft–holprige Züge. Das Intellektuellenmilieu wird durchleuchtet, die Sinnfrage resignativ gestellt. Wahn und Realität werden radikal modernistisch ununterscheidbar, das Paranoide wird zu Hochwälders Thema.

Bei Professor Camenisch, der sich ins geistige Exil in der Schweiz zurückgezogen hat, trifft sein Freund, der weltberühmte Autor Lazaretti, Camenisch nennt ihn 'Lazarus' im Verfolgungswahn, ein. Er hat ein Buch geschrieben, das den Terror durch ein Bündnis militanter Anti–Terroristen ausmerzen will:

> Keine Nation, keine Partei, keine Gesinnung wird exkulpiert, aber diesmal verharre ich im Negativen, führe Gedanken bis zu Ende, die in meinem letzten Buch 'Die totale Aggression' bloß angedeutet sind. Hier im Kapitel neun, rufe ich die Jugend der Welt zur direkten Aktion gegen alle Untat auf, entwerfe ein lückenloses System des Anti–Terrors, unter dem Motto 'Man schlage ihre Fressen mit

---

[22]Walter Dimter: "Glückauf zum Untergang!". Fritz Hochwälders Theater'. In: *Das zeitgenössische deutschsprachige Volksstück*; [hrsg.] Ursula Hassel; Herbert Herzmann, Tübingen: 1992, S.120.

schweren Eisenhämmern ein' [...]. Deshalb jagt man mich parforce. [...] ich knalle jeden über den Haufen, der die Hand nach diesem Manuskript ausstreckt [...].[23]

Lazaretti formuliert hilflos das Programm der Befreiung vom Terror durch den Terror. Wie schrieb abstrakter 1970 Heiner Müller in *Mauser*: 'wissend, das Gras noch/Müssen wir ausreißen, damit es grün bleibt.'[24] Hochwälder aber argumentiert ästhetisch nicht als Dialektiker, der, wie Heiner Müller, die maschinenhaft in sich kreisende, selbstzerstörerische, permanente Revolution beschwört. Es ist die Paradoxie des Fouquier, die wieder einmal szenisch greift; in diesem Stück bleibt sie allerdings nur Behauptung, da sie ästhetisch im Konversationsstück keine adäquate Form gefunden hat. Im Stück siegt die sogenannte Vernunft, Lazaretti begibt sich freiwillig ins Irrenhaus, der Professor publiziert das Werk unter seinem Namen.

Von klassischer Harmonisierung kann die Rede nicht sein; vielmehr hat der antiintellektuelle Autor Fritz Hochwälder offenbar ein unentschiedenes Bild hinterlassen, in dem undeutlich bleibt, ob Lazarettis Wahn, der auf Veränderung drängt, nicht reale Ursachen hat — den gesellschaftlichen Ekel. Dieser wird mit entfremdeter Vernunft 'erklärt', der Psychiater Dr. Fliess tritt auf:

> Camenisch: Haben Sie sein letztes Buch 'Die totale Aggression' gelesen?
> Fliess: Noch nicht.
> Camenisch: Schade. Da steht beispielsweise, daß man potentielle Aggressoren ohne weiteres umlegen soll. Im neuen Buch, dessen handschriftliches Manuskript er mir zur Verwahrung anvertraut hat, geht er weit drüber hinaus, blendende Arbeit übrigens [...] Aber bei der Lektüre [...] bleibt einem der Verstand stehen: leidenschaftlicher Aufruf zu heimtückischem Mord, im Dienst der Menschheit! Was sagen sie dazu?
> Fliess: Paranoide Ideen (S. 271).

Erst 1995 wurde aus dem Nachlaß Hochwälders bis dato einziger Roman publiziert *Donnerstag*, in den dreißiger Jahren geschrieben. Wieder ist der Donnerstag, obwohl das Werk inhaltlich nichts mit dem Drama zu tun hat, der Tag, der nicht stattfinden wird, der Tag, an dem die Probleme der Protagonisten gelöst werden sollen — die schwarze Utopie, auf die die abgeschilderten Momentaufnahmen zulaufen. Donnerstag bleibt im Werk der summierten Augenblicke projektierter Wunsch. Dieser Text, der deutlich in der Tradition des modernen Stadtromans steht, erinnert formal an Dos Passos *Manhattan Transfer* und steht im literarhistorischen Kontext von Döblins *Berlin Alexanderplatz*. Einen Helden allerdings gibt es nicht mehr,

---

[23]Fritz Hochwälder. 'Lazaretti oder Der Säbeltiger'. Schauspiel in zwei Akten. In: *Dramen III* a.a.O. S.262.

[24]Heiner Müller: 'Mauser'. In: H. M.: *Revolutionsstücke*, Stuttgart: 1988 (Reclam) S.15.

gestaltet ist vielmehr die Gleichzeitigkeit der Momente der drei austauschbaren Tage. Ausschnitte, Realitätsfetzen des Wiens der dreißiger Jahre zertrümmern ein episches Kontinuum, das moderne Stadtwelt und ihre isolierten Existenzen *disparat* erörtert. Die Analogie zu Koeppens *Tauben im Gras* drängt sich auf; ist doch die Filmschnittechnik Hochwälders grundlegende Gestaltungskategorie, der Leser muß die Zusammenhänge konstruieren:

> Josef Zundt saß auf der Kohlenkiste. Von Warzen und Furunkeln gesprenkeltes Gesicht. Traurige Augen. Ein Anzug: Pfeffer und Salz. Zundt rückte unbehaglich hin und her. Nichts zu tun. Saublöde Zeiten.
> [...] Karl Herkens stand vor dem Haustor. [...] Weißer kühler Himmel. Herkens warf den Kopf zurück, er hatte fast einen Blähhals. Räusperte sich. [...] Ein Stimmband war kaputt, gerissen, heiser zischte die Stimme durch die Zähne, irgendwie verbrüht [...] Er war ein ausgezeichneter Redner.[25]

Ist es wirklich die literarische Sensation, wie der Verlag meint, daß Fritz Hochwälder auch einen Roman geschrieben hat? Die Nähe zu modernen Prosamustern ergibt sich konsequent aus den erörterten Dramenmustern. Hochwälder wurde schlicht nicht entsprechend gewürdigt, da er außerhalb der herrschenden Diskurse stand.

Herkens, der Vertreter einer untergehenden Partei (vgl. S. 20), Zundt, der Arbeitslose oder Bogner, der Taxiunternehmer; der Roman und sein Kaleidoskop von Protagonisten demonstriert, wie genau Hochwälder die jeweilige Zeit beschrieb. Die erzählte Stadt wird vor dem zeitlichen Hintergrund disparat, es herrscht poetisch 'unverschmockt' der Perspektivwechsel, die zeitliche Austauschbarkeit beschriebener Momente der komprimierten Prosa. Der Autor ein Seismograph seines Jahrhunderts; Augenblick reiht sich an Augenblick wie in Joyces *Ulysses*, hier allerdings ist Bloom das Medium der imaginären Vorgänge gebrochene Augenblicke, Biographiefetzen, es gibt keine durcherzählte Geschichte mehr. Der Leser selbst muß wie bei Koeppen die Zusammenhänge und Beziehungsgeflechte rekonstruieren.

Walter Höllerer hat mit seiner Reflexion des modernen Romans anhand von Joyces Epiphanientheorie Hochwälders Verfahren beschrieben:

> [...] Erscheinung = Vision, vorgestellter Moment, der die einzelne Wahrnehmung von einem anvisierten Ganzen her aufleuchten läßt. [...] Augenblick und Einzelding werden so, wie bisher kaum je, betont. Nicht ein System der organologischen Entfaltung gibt dem Roman Halt und Stütze, sondern eine Schar von

---

[25]Fritz Hochwälder: *Donnerstag.* Roman, Graz/Wien/Köln: 1995 (Styria), S.10; 12.

gegensätzlichen Augenblicken, die als Nacheinander, Nebeneinander und Miteinander von Epiphanien komponiert sind.[26]

Hochwälder hat seinem Augenblicksroman aber auch die ihn immer wieder beschäftigende soziale Frage unterlegt:

> Der Mann mochte zwischen vierzig und fünfzig sein. Er ging langsam die Straße hinunter, pfeifend, der Aufenthalt im Kaffeehaus reute ihn nicht. So war er billig zu einem zweiten Frühstück gekommen, seine Frau liebte es, bis zehn Uhr im Bett zu liegen.
> Zahlungen, kein Verdienst, allerhand probieren, nützt alles nichts, [...] (S. 13).

Dieser erzählte Augenblick, diese Kurzbeschreibung kennzeichnen die Poetik Hochwälders und die herrschende, von ihm erfaßte soziale Situation; der Mann steht für die anderen im Kaleidoskop der über einhundert Momente des Betrugs, der Verzweiflung, der sinnlosen, tristen Zeit, der trügerischen Hoffnung des Augenblicks. Das Dienstmädchen Grete wird ihr Erspartes verlieren; Ferenz wird Käthe beschlafen und ein 'glänzendes Geschäft' (S. 97) machen. Die Schauspielerin Lilli hofft auf 'Donnerstag' dann erst kann sie die Premiere spielen oder Herkens seine Rede halten.

Diese Struktur weist sicher Ähnlichkeit mit Schnitzlers noch geschlossen—schlüssigem *Reigen* auf, doch Hochwälder steht mit seinem Roman im Kontext der diskontenten Moderne; wenn er mit seinen Stücken bei der Gegenwartsabbildung formal an der Tradition festhielt, so bedient er sich in seinem Augenblicksroman des für sein Jahrhundert gültigen Romanmusters, der gebrochenen Geschichte der Maschine: 'Ja, wie das weitergehen solle, ward er gefragt. He! wie das weitergeht. Es läuft von selbst' (S. 159), heißt es am Schluß. Subjektauflösung in der Momentaufnahme, Bilder der Anonymität, der Leser als mutmaßender Detektiv; das Motiv des Telefonats, Struktur als formauflösende Antistruktur, saufende Intellektuelle als Rahmenhandlung des Romans, der in der herrschenden Gleichzeitigkeit von Präteritum zum Präsens den Helden eliminiert.

Statt einer Zusammenfassung sei aus Hochwälders Roman *Donnerstag* abschließend folgendes Telefonat zitiert; Wien ist ein Ort, der keinen handlungsmäßigen Impetus transportiert, der lediglich einen Rahmen setzt. 'Ich' ist ein jemand, es ist hier, aus dem Zusammenhang konstruiert, Kurt Langemann, der keine Biographie hat, der angekommen ist, ein anderer, ein Protagonist unter vielen. Das Erzählte beglaubigt nichts, es steht selbstreferentiell, zusammenhangslos für sich:

---

[26]Walter Höllerer: Die Epiphanie als Held des Romans (I). In: *Akzente*. Zeitschrift für Dichtung H. 2 1961 (Zit. nach Nachdruck von Zweitausendeinsvlg. Bd. II., Frankfurt/M.: 1975 S.127).

...Ja ich! ... Aus Wien, ja! ... Ich wollte dich sprechen, Riki! ... Nein, nichts Wichtiges ... Wird wohl in absehbarer Zeit nicht möglich sein. Riki ... Ich habe strikten Auftrag nach Konstantinopel zu gehen... [...] Aus Budapest ruf ich wieder an ... Das ist eine komplizierte Geschichte, kann dir das nicht so rasch erzählen ... Ja, ich habe eine Menge Geld ... Ja, ich werde mich schon durchschlagen [...] verstehst du! ... Also auf Wiedersehen (S. 38).

Hat Fritz Hochwälder die konservative Frage gestellt, wer 'Ich' denn sei? Er hat in seinem Roman jedenfalls gewiß keine konservative Antwort formuliert. Der Roman belegt, daß Hochwälder als heute vergessener Autor von dem Abschied genommen hat, was jeglichen Konservatismus kennzeichnet: ein geschlossenes Weltbild. Die Möglichkeit der Beschreibung von Stadtwelt, jenes immer wieder bemühte Motiv des modernen Romans, stellt nur Fragen an den Leser, sie formuliert keine Gewißheiten. Die beschriebenen Realitätsfetzen, die intellektuell zu rekonstruieren sind, die Mutmaßungen befördern, verweigern ausgestaltete Biographien. In medias res beginnt der Roman, beginnen die Stücke; die gewohnte Sprache der Kontinuitäten und Erklärungen, der schlüssigen Deutungen wird zum Konstrukt im Kopf des Lesers. Oberflächenphänomene, konzentrierte Augenblicke, die nur noch einen verweisenden Charakter haben, zerschlagen ein Ganzes, konstitutiv wird der Ausschnitt, das erzählte Moment.

'DAS WIRKLICH UNGESCHMINKTE': PETER TURRINI'S *DIE MINDERLEISTER* AS A CRITIQUE OF THE MASS MEDIA

FRANK FINLAY

Introduction

In this chapter my concern is with the left–wing writer Peter Turrini, who has risen to prominence from the late 1980s onwards, and whose prolific output for the stage has received high–profile premières both in Austria and in Germany. Turrini's plays, particularly those of the last decade, are almost invariably examples of political theatre. Like political plays of all ages and cultures, Turrini's share the assumption that the theatre is a public institution with corresponding responsibilities and powers. For him the audience is not a random collection of private individuals but a public group with certain common social, economic and historical experiences. His works generally seek to bring into the public sphere matters which, for whatever reasons, the ruling powers would prefer to exclude. He thus hopes to initiate and participate in public debate and, where possible, to influence public opinion.[1]

Predictably, the reception of Turrini's plays in his homeland has often been hostile, with conservative critics quick to condemn their unedifying depiction of the social and political scene. It is my view, however, that it is precisely because of his attempts to grapple with some of the major issues of our day, such as the affects of long–term unemployment and incipient racism, that Turrini is one of only a few contemporary Austrian and German playwrights to have had their work performed beyond the German–speaking world, most recently in a number of English translations.[2]

Turrini has also combined literary and political activity, intervening as essayist, speech–maker and campaigner. He was particularly vocal, for example, in the campaign against Kurt Waldheim's candidacy for the office of President in 1986. Waldheim's tenacious, albeit bungled attempts to conceal his Nazi past inadvertently triggered a period of debate in Austria

---

[1]I am following Anthony Waine's definition of political theatre in his discussion of Brecht's legacy for German–speaking playwrights in Graham Bartram and Anthony Waine (eds.), *Brecht in Perspective*, London and New York: 1982, p.192.

[2]For the challenges which Turrini provides the translator see the discussion by Black in the present volume.

about its role during the Third Reich and brought an abrupt and confrontational end to the collective lie, enshrined in the Allied declarations which paved the way for the restoration of sovereign status to the country in 1955, that Austrians were the first victims of Hitler's expansionism, and not to a considerable extent active partners in the crimes of National Socialism.[3]

Most recently, Turrini has spoken–out against the disturbing trend towards intolerance of foreigners and support for the ultra right–wing Austrian Freedom Party (FPÖ), which has lurched ever rightwards under the leadership of Jörg Haider, who took control of the party in the same year which saw Waldheim become President. Haider has made steady electoral gains since 1986, capitalising, as Melanie Sully notes, on voters' frustration with the extensive patronage of the two dominant political parties which have ruled since 1945, on growing insecurity about Austria's role in the new Europe, and xenophobia.[4] Turrini's political commitment culminated in his appearance as a speaker, alongside Salman Rushdie, at the 'Fest der Freiheit' in April 1995, a demonstration of over 50,000 people, on Vienna's Heldenplatz.[5] In a candid and provocatively titled speech, 'Liebe Mörder!' he attacked the recrudescent racism and intolerance of his compatriots.

Perhaps inevitably, Turrini has been saddled of late with the unenviable sobriquet of his nation's 'literary conscience' by those with sympathy for his views. His opponents, such as Jörg Haider, see Turrini and other critical writer–intellectuals, such as Elfriede Jelinek and Gerhard Roth, as prominent members of a 'left–wing cultural Mafia', which seeks to undermine traditional Austrian values. The FPÖ's attempts to discredit critical intellectuals produced death–threats against Turrini,[6] and led Jelinek to place a performance ban of her works in Austria, as a protest.

In the context of a high degree of notoriety at home and the exposure of his work abroad, it is rather surprising that there has hitherto been relatively little academic interest in his plays in the English–speaking world. In this chapter I shall focus on one aspect of Turrini's criticism of contemporary society, his depiction of the pernicious affects of the mass media, as manifest in his play *Die Minderleister* (1988). Before examining this play in detail, I shall sketch the contours of Turrini's criticism of the media in the context of his sometimes troubled career and by reference to collections of his essays, interviews and speeches.

---

[3]For a vigorous critique of the myth of Austria's non–involvement see the psychiatrist Erwin Ringel's seminal 'Eine neue Rede über Österreich' in his *Die österreichische Seele. Zehn Reden über Medizin, Politik, Kunst und Religion.* Vienna/Munich: 1994.

[4]A *Contemporary History of Austria*, New York: 1990, p.71f.

[5]See the introduction to the present volume, p.3f.

[6]Personal communication with Turrini's editor, Silke Hassler.

The Theatre as the 'ultimate place of patience'

Peter Turrini has been no stranger to controversy ever since his début at the age of 27 with the dialect plays *Rozzenjagd* (The Rat Hunt – written 1967) and *Sauschlachten* (Slaughtering the Pig), both premièred in January 1971 as part of a showcase for new stage writing by Vienna's 'Volkstheater'.[7] Written partly under the influence of Antonin Artaud's theatre of cruelty, these two plays belong to the tradition of parodic folk theatre or popular theatre ('Volksstück'), which started in the early twentieth century with the dramas of Ödön von Horváth and Marieluise Fleisser, revivals of whose work inspired the first theatrical efforts of other contemporary German–speaking dramatists, such as Franz Xavier Kroetz, Martin Sperr, Rainer Werner Fassbinder and the Tyrolean Felix Mitterer.[8] These 'critical' or 'new' *Volksstücke*, as they became known, were an important trend particularly in the early 1970s.[9]

There followed, in the next two years, the one–act play, *Kindsmord*, and free adaptations of classics such as Beaumarchais' 'The Marriage of Figaro' (*Der tollste Tag*) and Goldoni's 'Mirandolina' (*Die Wirtin*), both of which reveal the influence of Turrini having by now acquired a political theory — socialism — to underpin his political observations. In *Der tollste Tag*, for example, the corrupt Count Almaviva is throttled with a whip by his servant Figaro in a deliberate revolutionary re–writing of Beaumarchais' ending.[10]

As a number of occasional essays from this period testify, however, Turrini was soon to become disillusioned with his chosen medium and turned his back on it. His brief experience of the Austrian theatrical establishment convinced him that it is thoroughly corrupt; little more than a branch of the entertainment industry and, like other sectors of the economy,

---

[7]At this time, the 'Volkstheater' was the most important theatre to champion new work, which was anathema to a conservative public attracted to the high cultural feast of classics served up by the State Theatre (*Burgtheater*) and its associated stages. See Gerhard Scheit, *Theater in Österreich*, in Horst A. Glaser (ed.), *Deutsche Literatur zwischen 1945 und 1995*, Berlin/Stuttgart/Vienna: 1997, p.530f.

[8]See Gabrielle Robinson, 'Slaughter and Language Slaughter in the Plays of Peter Turrini', *Theatre Journal* 43 (1991), p.197.

[9]See Jürgen Hein, 'Formen des Volkstheaters im 19. und 20. Jahrhundert', in *Handbuch des deutschen Drama*, ed. Walter Hinck, Düsseldorf: 1980, pp.489–505, and Justus Fetscher, 'Theater seit 1968 – verspielt?' in Klaus Briegleb and Siegried Weigl (eds.), *Gegenwartsliteratur seit 1968* (= *Hansers Sozialgeschichte der deutschen Literatur vom 16. Jahrhundert bis zur Gegenwart*, vol. 12, ed. Rolf Grimminger), Munich: 1992, pp.491–535.

[10]There is a probable influence here of Horváth's play *Figaro läßt sich scheiden*. See Christopher Innes, *Modern German Drama. A Study in Form*. London/New York/Melbourne: 1979, p.234.

at the mercy of market forces.[11] In such a situation, it is his view that the theatre critic is 'Papst und Hure des Marktes'(GL, 34), and plays a special role by determining which 'products' are served up for the delectation of the tiny minority of the population who actually attend theatrical performances (GL, 30). In an essay entitled 'Kulturkritik', which anticipates his own move away from the theatre, Turrini refers to those of his colleagues who have recognised that they must escape the cultural ghetto where they write works of little interest to the vast majority of society and reach a wider audience (GL, 39f.). In the appropriately titled essay, 'Dilemma', Turrini comes to the conclusion: 'Wir haben eine Massenkultur, aber keine Kultur für die Massen'. It is this insight which led him to abandon the plans he had for two new plays,[12] and to descend from what had become for him a lofty theatrical pedestal. During the next decade or so he wrote almost exclusively for the mass medium of television, revealing a faith, first espoused by an older generation of left–wing thinkers such as Benjamin and Brecht in the context of the cinema, that it could serve as an instrument of social enlightenment in the political class struggle. Turrini justified this decision in the following terms:

> Wer der breiten Bevölkerung wirklich etwas sagen will, muß von seinem Dichterpodest heruntersteigen. Nicht der Künstler ist wichtig, sondern die Menschen, von denen er redet. Nicht die Kunst ist wichtig, sondern die Form, in der man mit möglichst vielen Menschen reden kann (GL, 41).

Both the audience and the medium, therefore, take primacy over the artist and the work of art itself. Behind this conviction is the clearly discernible materialist ideology of a committed socialist and a grasp of the choices which face the 'critical' artist in a capitalist society:

> Entweder macht er [the artist] reine Kunst und kümmert sich nicht um die politische und ökonomische Situation der Massen. Das Elend der Unterdrückten ist für ihn kein Thema. Ihm ist der Reim wichtiger als die Revolution. Dieser Schriftsteller dient den Herrschenden. Der andere Schriftsteller [...] stellt seine Kunst in den Dienst ihrer Opfer, der Ausgebeuteten, der Unterdrückten. Eine Kunst, die sozusagen über den Dingen steht, gibt es nicht, wie die Menschen nicht über den Dingen stehen, sondern das Ergebnis der Dinge sind (GL, 42f.).

With the exception of the short plays *Josef und Maria* and *Die Bürger* (1980/1981), the next phase of Turrini's career thus saw him involved in television film projects with his co–writers, Wilhelm Pevny and Rudi Palla, and an ensemble of trusted producers, directors (Dieter Berner), actors

---

[11]Peter Turrini, *Es ist ein gutes Land. Texte zu Anlässen*, Vienna: (Europa) 1986, p.30. All further quotations carry the abbreviation GL and the page number.

[12]Michael Töteberg, 'Peter Turrini', in Heinz Ludwig Arnold (ed.), *Kritisches Lexikon zur deutschsprachigen Gegenwartsliteratur*, Munich: 1978ff., p.5.

(Helmut Qualtinger),[13] and cinematographers. The mid 1970s to the mid 1980s, yielded major television work. The six–part series, *Die Alpensaga*, for example, was acclaimed by some sections of the public and critics alike, in spite of the predictably negative reaction of official representatives of the Catholic Church, some of whom forbade the filming of scenes on their premises, and of the Austrian Farming Union, which campaigned in the press against the project.[14] The series follows the history of a rural village from the turn of the century and the onset of industrialisation up to the start of the period of postwar reconstruction. It depicts the everyday life and customs of a peasant community and examines the impact of outside developments on it. To the surprise of the broadcasters, *Die Alpensaga* was highly regarded by international critics not only as a televisual chronicle and obituary of a dying social class, the farming communities which had once been so important, but as an Austrian equivalent of Bertolucci's epic *1900*.[15]

The international success of *Die Alpensaga* persuaded the Austrian state broadcasting service ORF, with financial backing from West Germany's ZDF, to commission a six–part sequel in 1983. This set out to portray the history of the industrial working class in Austria and was entitled *Die Arbeitersaga*. Of the six scripts completed, only the last two were ever filmed, receiving plaudits and prizes abroad when shown at film festivals. Opposition was, however, intense and, amid accusations of political censorship, the plug was pulled on the project following the intervention of an unholy alliance of the trade unions, the governing Austrian Socialist Party (SPÖ), by now in a grand coalition with the Conservatives (ÖVP), and employers' associations. The latter were outraged at what they believed to be Turrini's travesty of the so–called Social Partnership, which had been the cornerstone of the postwar economic consensus and the Austrian model of industrial relations. In particular, Turrini and his co–writer were vilified for depicting the unions and the ruling SPÖ as being corrupt and in cahoots with one another to the detriment of the interests of the working classes, which both were committed officially to protecting. A thoroughly distraught, embittered and disillusioned Peter Turrini was left to reassess his artistic future after five years of work on the enterprise, which had ultimately been in vain.[16]

[13] Apart from being an actor, Qualtinger (1928–1986) was a leading satirist and *Kabarettist* who together with his collaborator Carl Merz created the eponymous *Herr Karl*, the prototype of the opportunist petit–bourgeois *Mitläufer*, first performed in 1961.

[14] A similar fate befell Franz Innerhofer's filmed version of his book *Schöne Tage*.

[15] See Sigrid Löffler, "Mehr Senf zum Würstl", *profil*, 28. April, 1980.

[16] Documents of the controversy can be found in Wolfgang Schuch and Klaus Siblewski, (eds.), *Peter Turrini. Texte, Daten, Bilder*, Munich: 1991, pp.119–125.

As his latest collection of essays, speeches and journalism, covering the years 1985–1995,[17] reveals, Turrini's subsequent return to writing stage plays, although clearly influenced by his profound love for the theatre (LM, 111), was a considered response to his own frustrating experience with the prevarication and censorship of the broadcasting authorities. There is, however, a further influencing factor to which he refers: the media and telecommunications revolution which had taken place since his first excursions into television drama. This revolution not only had far–reaching ramifications for an artist with a political message to get across, but also, as I shall now go on to discuss, for the status of the theatre as the medium par excellence for the presentation of social ills.

The once parochial and patriarchal, cosy media landscape in Austria, in which the state broadcaster ORF had a total monopoly, was redrawn in the 1980s as a plethora of transnational, mostly German–based commercial cable and satellite companies entered the market. The advent of over 20 channels and the remote control button, which Turrini dubs the 'Kultgegenstand der achtziger Jahre' (LM, 73) and which fostered the habit of 'hopping' rapidly from one channel to another, have had a deleterious effect on the audience's viewing habits. In recent years, he sees the situation as having been exacerbated by the advent of the home video in general, and the burgeoning popularity of pornographic and horror films, in particular (LM, 85). In Turrini's eyes both these factors have had a far–reaching and irrevocable impact which rendered the medium no longer suitable for his artistic and political ends. Turrini clearly feels that he can no longer count on his TV audience's undivided attention, and concludes that the theatre is 'der letzte Ort der Geduld'; the ultimate place of patience, in which the audience can engage with the action on stage in a more concentrated and uninterrupted way: 'Ich kann mir nicht mehr hinsetzen und ein Drehbuch schreiben, weil ich überzeugt bin, daß niemand die Geschichte mehr von Anfang bis Ende sehen will' (LM, 111f.).

A second and in my view more persuasive reason for his abandoning television was the realisation of the inherent fraudulence of a medium which purports to offer true representations of actual events. He cites as an example the manipulation of the truth in the news coverage of the Gulf War of 1991, in particular the video footage of so–called 'smart bombs', which, as one was led to believe, unerringly destroyed their military targets, without any damage to the civilian population (LM, 42f.). Elsewhere, he suggests that networks which first stimulate and then fill the demand for global news, like the American Cable News Network (CNN), even go as far as to

---

[17]Peter Turrini, *Liebe Mörder! Von der Gegenwart, dem Theater und dem lieben Gott*. Herausgegeben von Silke Hassler und Klaus Siblewski. Munich: (Luchterhand) 1996. All further quotations carry the abbreviation LM and the page number.

fabricate stories for their audience's quick consumption. Belated insights such as these reveal, I think, just how panglossian Turrini was in his earlier faith in television. There is, however, a further dimension to his critique: in an essay with the appropriate title *Wir sind Ertrinkende* of 1993, Turrini discussed the feeling that he was drowning in the plethora of visual images flooding into his home of the war in Bosnia–Herzogovina. He confesses to being no longer moved to empathy and sympathy by them as he was by similar pictures in the 1960s and 1970s from Vietnam (LM, 43). For Turrini, the theatre, precisely because it makes no effort to conceal the fact that it is a masquerade, offers the opportunity of empathy and is a more honest and upright medium for the presentation of social ills:

> Während im Leben ständig vorgegeben wird, man sei ohne Maske, man würde die Wahrheit sagen, man sei ganz bei der Sache, ist in Wahrheit alles Maskerade. Im Theater gibt es trotz der Schminke, das wirklich Ungeschminkte (LM, 111).

Die Minderleister

The first product of the new phase in Turrini's commitment to 'das wirklich Ungeschminkte', an uncompromising depiction of the reality beneath the surface grease paint of Austrian life, was his stage play *Die Minderleister* (1988).[18] This work deals with one of the main political issues of the day: the end of the postwar economic consensus and the restructuring and privatisation of hitherto state–owned heavy industry. Until well into the 1980s the Austrian economy had been a success story of steady improvement in incomes, working conditions and social security, and Austrians considered their country a haven of stability and affluence. Developments ran more or less parallel to the much vaunted 'eonomic miracle' of West Germany to whose currency the Austrian Schilling was officially pegged. Even the impact of the general economic down–turn caused by the 'oil crisis' of the 1970s was able to be contained by a mixture of employment policies often labelled Austro–Keynesianism, which were championed by the ruling SPÖ and the Chancellor, Bruno Kreisky. By the mid–1980s, however, such economic thinking gave way to the new orthodoxy of monetarism which saw the end of big government in most of the states of the West. For an economy with such a large and paternalistic public sector the changes were bound to be uncomfortable.

In an interview to accompany the world première of *Die Minderleister*, Turrini castigated the politicians and their lackeys in the press who defended the economic restructuring; he reaffirmed his commitment to bringing into the public domain the fate of those people 'die zu den Verlieren der

---

[18]Peter Turrini, *Die Minderleister*. Frankfurt/M.. (Luchterhand) 1989. All quotations are from this edition and carry the code M followed by the page number.

ökonomischen und gesellschaftlichen Krise gehören' (LM, 74). In the play, Turrini draws on his own brief experiences as a labourer in the early 1960s at the VOEST–steel plant in Linz to depict the desperate plight of steel workers who lose their jobs.

Die Minderleister is not only Turrini's most overtly topical play to date, it constitutes a significant development in his oeuvre in another important regard: he eschews the dialect of many of his earlier stage plays and experiments with a new form. All of the characters speak standard German, and the workers, like the witnesses for the prosecution in Peter Weiss's famous play about the Auschwitz trials of the 1960s, *Die Ermittlung*, are given free verse in which to express themselves. Almost without exception, representatives of politics and capital and other social functionaries, with whom the author has no sympathies, speak in prose. As Turrini explained in an interview, he had a very specific and experimental intention in choosing this highly stylised form:

> Ich wollte [...] den sogenannten kleinen Leuten große Aufmerksamkeit verschaffen, indem ich ihnen eine große Form gebe. Ich wollte ihnen den Rang von klassischen Figuren verleihen, um ihnen zumindest auf der Bühne jene Wichtigkeit zu geben, die ihnen nach meiner Überzeugung zusteht. In einer Welt, in der ihnen Sprache genommen wird, in der politische Funktionäre angeblich für sie sprechen, ihre innere und äußere Wahrheit aber ausklammern, ist der Versuch, ihnen die größtmögliche Sprache wiederzugeben auch ein Versuch ihrer politischen Rettung (LM, 82).

Apart from being an obvious departure from one of the defining characteristics of the 'Volksstück', this choice of verse also made feasible certain other dramatic inventions which the 'realistic' material did not initially suggest. One of the most important is the chorus–like figure of the works' librarian, William Shakespeare, who opens the play and who functions partly to put the events we are about to see on stage in the wider context of postwar Austrian reconstruction.

The drama is set in and around a steel mill in an unnamed 'Krisenregion' and takes its title from a neologism which had been coined by managers in the real nationalised industries to identify those 'underachievers', who, in the official, euphemistic terms were to be 'let go' from their jobs, that is to say made redundant. It is these people who, Turrini holds, are being scape–goated as the cause of the economic crisis, which is itself effectively being 'privatised' by the state deflecting attention away from the politicians responsible and on to individuals: 'Man nennt sie "Minderleister", als wäre es ihre "mindere Leistung", die zur Krise geführt hat' (LM, 74).

The play's central protagonist is the 29–year–old steelworker, Hans Freiberger, who, like Turrini himself, was raised in the countryside and migrated to the nearby big city in search of employment. After the initial ridicule of his colleagues in his gang of blast furnace workers, he finds their acceptance under the caring eye of his foreman, Schmelzer, the self–styled head of a surrogate 'family', to whose member he refers as his 'sons'. At the start of the play the impact of the re–structuring programme is already being felt: the forge has been closed and the rolling mill has been put on short–time working. One of the supervisors reveals to the men that there are more redundancies in the offing, and very soon we learn that Hans is about to become one of the first casualties.

Hans is very much a conformist, who believes that all that is required for material success is the willingness to toil at the job by which he defines his entire being. He personifies to a considerable extent Turrini's view that Austrian industrial workers had fully identified and acquiesced with the economic system, which was underpinned by the model of Social Partnership, and had reaped their desired material rewarded in the so–called 'fat years' of the postwar recovery. This they did at the expense of their own broader political awareness and class solidarity (LM, 77). Significantly, an earlier threat to his job security had led Hans not to protest but to enrol at his local technical school to gain more marketable skills. Now that the system has entered a phase of real crisis, he is left perplexed that his seemingly modest needs and wants can no longer be met. It is the desperation that ensues which determines the drama of *Die Minderleister.*

The action of the play alternates between the steel mill, where Hans is 'at home' with his band of brothers, and the abode of the play's second family: the house where he lives with his wife, Anna. The central aspects of Turrini's critique of the media emerge in his depiction of the latter's relationship. In Turrini's portrayal, Hans and Anna seek refuge from the increasing insecurity of their situation in a dream world, which offers only temporary alleviation from the reality of their existence. As Anna says at the opening of scene four:

> Wenn man die Augen zumacht
> geht das Schlimme vorbei
> und das Schöne kommt (M,
> 24).

Significantly, this dream world is a prefabricated one, in the sense that it takes its inspiration from the industrialised and commercialised images of television and video. In Anna's case, she loses herself in a diet of glamorous imported American soap operas, like the appropriately titled 'das Traumschiff', with its maritime dreams of instant romance in exotic locations. Similarly, the TV–lottery and quiz games offer the chance of individual wish–fulfilments of a more material kind. Hans, for his part, seeks solace in pornography and alcohol. Turrini draws attention to the extent to which these fantasy images pervade and ultimately undermine even the most intimate of his characters' inter–personal relationships when Hans continues to watch a pornographic video and drink while Anna makes love to him. In an attempt to gain his attention, Anna even adopts the voice and demeanour of the actress on screen. What ensues is a loss of her own identity, when Anna, placing her hand over Hans' eyes, states her willingness to be just what her husband wants her to be (M, 27).

Turrini pursues his theme of fantasy versus reality and refines it to reveal the extent to which the border between the two worlds is not only confused but on certain occasions is also transgressed. This emerges with abundant clarity in scenes eight and nine. Anna, like Hans, loses her job when the washing machine factory which employs her transfers its production to Spain, where labour costs are much lower. With no other source of income in sight, she takes paid work in a pornographic video, which is shot with an unemployed steel worker in the less than salubrious surrounds of the local jeans and general electrical store run by a Yugoslav immigrant. Thus, Anna becomes an active participant in the booming fictionalised, visual world of the sex industry and is herself commodified. In the next scene Hans, who, as we have seen is an habitual consumer of similar products, is put in a situation in which he literally purchases Anna, albeit unintentionally, when he acquires the cheap video in which she has performed. Anna who was compelled to prostitute herself initially when she made the film is now prostituted once more, only this time by her own husband. Turrini is thus able to reveal in a painful and cogent way the real exploitation and cost to human relationships which the manufacture of pornography can entail. A further implication is that the flight into fantasy is not so much a temporary illusion as a self–delusion.

There are a number of other scenes, which depict and highlight the relationship between real and fantasy worlds. For example Hans' work mates, Ringo, Ursus and the group's story–teller, Der Italiener, take refuge, like him, in the world of private fantasy generated by pornography and other media images. In scene three, which takes place in the steel mill's common room, the men relate brief, fantastic tales of their ideal selves — successful racing driver, a peasant, and a Venetian Gondolieri — in the language of the videos which they consume. Under the ever watchful eye of the company's close circuit cameras, the three men even wear the hats and caps of their dream professions at work. Schmelzer, who eschews any head garb, in the ultimately erroneous belief that he has an intuitive sense of where danger lurks, reveals that all the workers regard what is effectively the rejection of the trappings of their jobs as essential to determine and maintain their individual identity. Their bosses recognise this fact and seek to undermine the workers by threatening the withdrawal of their wages for their failure to wear protective headgear. Schmelzer explains this to the Ordner as follows:

Mit einem Schutzhelm
wäre Ursus nicht Ursus
sondern einer
wie jeder andere (M, 20).

The survival strategies which the men have developed, including the assertion of their individuality by clinging on to private fantasies, are ultimately revealed to be insufficient to shield them from a hostile and dangerous environment in which, in Schmelzer's literal and metaphorical words, 'Alle Scheiße kommt von oben' (M, 23). Turrini's stage directions, which describe the hats as being shot through with holes and charred by the heat of the furnace, merely serve to underline this fact.

Turrini is also at pains to show the ideological function of the products of the mass media. They act, like alcohol, as a drug, and not only blind their consumers to the reality of the economic system in which they live, they also dissipate any strength they might have to resist what is happening to them. As such they serve to manufacture consent to the status quo. Turrini refers to this phenomenon in an interview about his play: 'Die Videos, die Quizspiele fressen das Bewußtsein der Menschen und damit ihre Kraft zum Widerstand' (LM, 81). The pernicious potential of the video machine is also underscored by the significant role it plays in the everyday professional life of the furnace workers: it is the technological device by which their every movement, be it at the work–place or during breaks in the canteen, are observed and recorded. Turrini's steel mill is an Orwellian inferno in which all are under surveillance.

It is to this extent that Turrini's critique of the media, in *Die Minderleister*, although obviously written at a time of even greater technological advance, which spawned new media, such as video, and genres, like pornography and horror, has thus much in common with older analyses by thinkers on the left of the political spectrum. In rejecting his earlier belief in the didactic potential of the mass media, for example, Turrini merely rehearses an orthodox tenet. One is reminded, for example, of the seminal critique of the 'Culture Industries' contained in the fourth chapter of Horkheimer and Adorno's *Dialectic of the Enlightenment*,[19] in which the mass media are identified as new agents of social control by which the individual is dominated. Similarly, Turrini's understanding of the individual as viewer is also resolutely traditional: he reveals no interest in more recent theories of the media which highlight how meaning is constructed when

---

[19]See Max Horkheimer and Theodor Adorno's, *Dialectic of Enlightenment*. In particular the essay which makes up the 4th Chapter: 'The Culture Industry: Enlightenment as Mass Deception'. English edition, translated by John Cumming (London: 1973).

individuals engage in a dialogue with 'texts' and of how such meanings can often run contrary to the apparent intentions of their 'authors'.[20]

On a number of occasions in the play, Turrini engineers a collision of the dream world and reality in order to demonstrate both the inadequacy of media–driven fantasies as proof against the vicissitudes of life and their nightmarish potential. In so doing, another level in his critique of the popular media emerges when he deploys what he terms 'die groteske Ästhetik eines Horror– oder Pornofilms' (LM, 85). Typically, this involves sudden interruptions in which the reality of the stage action is transferred into a hyper–reality, which draws on the conventions of such popular film genres. Turrini thus gives himself both the licence and the aesthetic means to exaggerate and distort in order to draw attention to the underlying reality of the economic Darwinism which confronts his characters. Scenes five and seven provide the important action in this regard.

In scene five Hans, who has by now been informed that he is surplus to the steel mill's requirements, visits the Director of Personnel to protest. Under the watchful eye of a security guard, she gives him a lecture in the laws of global capitalism; in two separate and almost identical speeches, the principles of the free market to which the individual's rights are subordinated are elucidated. Significantly, this figure is the one social functionary in the play who is given verse to speak:

> Reden wir noch einmal
> vom Markt.
> Der Markt steht über den
> Menschen.
> Er folgt nicht ihren Gesetzen
> er folgt seinen eigenen.
> Er ist wie die Gestirne
> am Firmament.
> Was immer die Menschen
> den Sternen erzählen
> es erreicht sie nicht.
> Es berührt sie nicht.
> Wir müssen das zur Kenntnis
> nehmen.
> Sie müssen das zur Kenntnis
> nehmen (M, 49–50).

The reality in which we all find ourselves is one in which we are in thrall to the superhuman laws and movements of the free market, which is totally indifferent to our needs. In the modern world, Turrini is saying, God and

---

[20]See for example the introduction to Ulrike Meinhof and Kay Richardson (eds), *Text, Discourse and Context: Representations of Poverty in Britain*, New York: 1994.

history have abdicated their position to the mechanism which is at the heart of global capitalism.

Between the two sermons on the realities of the market, Turrini sandwiches what might be termed a 'video nasty' in which the stage action is transmogrified into a scene reminiscent of a cheap horror film. The Director of Personnel attacks Hans with a whip and then launches into a long and uncontrolled speech during which she verbalises all the hatred, disgust and contempt of a working class woman who has escaped her own environment, only to be constantly confronted with the very people she has tried so resolutely to leave behind her: her loathing is ultimately an expression of her self–loathing. Following a tussle with the security guard, the latter scalps her with a metal letter opener. The metamorphosis then ends as suddenly as it started.

Another example of the collision of the fantasy world of a popular cultural genre with the mimetic reality of the stage action occurs in scene seven. Hans and Anna are sitting in their living room, discussing their situation to the background accompaniment of a TV quiz show. Whilst Anna still holds out hope of getting work, however menial, Hans has invested their last money in a fistful of lottery tickets and dreams of what he will do when he wins the jackpot. Taking a cigarette lighter, he demonstrates his toughness by holding his hand over the flame and proclaims his readiness to fight back. At the same time he echoes the dictum of the Personnel Director upon which the prevailing socio–economic order is founded, thereby failing to realise that he subscribes to the very ethos which has brought about his predicament:

> Nur wer hart ist
> kommt durchs Leben (M, 68).

These words are the cue for the quiz show host and his two female assistants to emerge from the television screen, and the Freiberger's living room is transformed into a glittering studio. Hans is offered the chance to participate in the game of '6 aus 45' in which the figures relate to the proportion of jobs available to those seeking employment.

In a grotesque parody of a celebrated and now defunct light entertainment programme, 'Einer wird gewinnen', Hans is offered the chance of employment, but only on condition that he is willing to trample on his nearest and dearest in a series of knock–out encounters. Having disposed of effigies of a colleague and his brother, he is unable to eliminate his own wife from the competition. Hans may consider himself tough, but learns that he is not sufficiently tough to win the social and economic game of the survival of the fittest.

In all such scenes in which there is a sudden transformation of the stage action to the fantasy world of video, the style of these artefacts is imitated. It is worth emphasising at this juncture that Turrini does this, not out of any postmodern delight in 'quoting' popular cultural forms, as is the case with some of the other authors discussed in this volume,[21] but rather in a conscious attempt to draw attention to the deleterious effects on the lives of ordinary people which the mass media have. Moreover, the sudden halting of the stage action, which accompanies the switch from real to hyper–real, serves, in the best Brechtian tradition, to alienate the audience from it.[22] Such 'distancing' or defamiliarisation is designed to initiate the critical reflection of the audience and to show the brutal reality underlying the events depicted on stage. It is Turrini's aesthetic device by which he attempts to drive home his political message and it amounts to a new formal experiment in his work.

The remaining action of *Die Minderleister* bears out the author's view that individual economic advancement is always at the cost of others. In scene eleven Hans makes a final, desperate attempt to recover his position of employment when he travels to the capital city to throw himself on the mercy of the Employment Minister. This media–conscious figure, whom we first encounter studying videos of one of his speeches and practising facial expressions, senses the opportunity for a grand gesture, which will generate some much–needed good publicity. He arranges for Hans to be given a new job at the plant as one of the overseers who monitor the performance of the shop floor. His chief task is to blacklist those who are deemed to be 'Minderleister'. Hans accepts for the sake of his own and Anna's future, but this act involves the inevitable betrayal of both his father–figure, Schmelzer, and his 'brothers' in the steel plant. Having thus proved himself in their eyes a turncoat, they promptly ostracise him. Hans is confronted with a moral dilemma as he is forced to choose between betraying his wife and betraying his public 'family'. Like the tragic heroes of classical drama whom Turrini deliberately evokes, Hans chooses suicide as the only a way out of his predicament. The further implication is that the supernatural forces of free market global capitalism as described by the Personnel Director act as a new teleological principle (or Nemesis) and crush another victim. This occurs in the brief and apocalyptic scene fourteen, although Hans' fate is clearly adumbrated much earlier in the play in his description of his early days in the steel mill, in scene five:

---

[21]See, for example, the discussion of intertextuality in the contributions by Fiddler and Lanyon.

[22]See Walter Benjamin's seminal essay 'Was ist das epische Theater?' in *Angelus Novus. Ausgewählte Schriften 2*, Frankfurt/M: 1988, p.346–347.

Ich wollte einfach
in den Ofen gehen.
Wenn du nirgends zu Hause
bist
habe ich gedacht
dann wenigstens
da drinnen (M, 42).

The penultimate scene opens with the stage in virtual darkness with Hans standing on the apron in the black uniform of one of the overseers. He adds his own name to those of the 'Minderleister' and the stage is then flooded in light to reveal a steel blast furnace with a gantry above it. All the characters of the play, including those from the hyper–reality of the TV quiz show, now gather on stage so that a veritably serene Hans can bid them his last farewell. In his final speech to Anna, he wistfully declares that he, too, would like to close his eyes and imagine a better way to live, but is no longer able to do so. He now accepts the reality that has deprived him of his public and private home and consigns himself to the furnace. Hans' act, however, is not evidence of Turrini's own acceptance of the status quo, nor is it a sign of resignation or fatalism on his part. The extremity of Hans' demise has a very clear didactic intent, as Turrini explained in an interview:

> Die Bühne ist für mich ein Ort, das Schreckliche noch schrecklicher zu zeigen, um abzuschrecken [...]. Ich denke mir, wenn wir in dieser Welt etwas bewegen wollen, wenn wir Dinge ändern wollen, wenn es nicht so schlimm kommen soll für den einen oder die anderen, dann muß man eben das Schlimmste zeigen, damit das Schlimmste nicht passiert (LM, 92–93).

Conclusion

Peter Turrini's works for the stage, like Friedrich Dürrenmatt's offer us a series of worst–case scenarios, or to use the latter's terms, models of what might happen if events take their 'worst possible turn'.[23] Unlike Dürrennmatt, however, Turrini believes that the world is changeable. He is thus committed to a clearly articulated moral position which has its base in a socialist perspective. He is also aware that his political commitment is open to abuse by the very people he hopes to criticise; however he sees no alternative:

> Die größten Moralisten werden zum Gewissen der Nation erhoben, damit sich der Rest um so gewissenloser verhalten kann. Und trotzdem gibt es keine Alternative zur moralischen Position, oder anders gesagt, zu einer Vorstellung von dem, was Gut und Böse ist. Wäre ein Schriftsteller so ein postmodernes Arschloch, für den

---

[23]Friedrich Dürrenmatt, '21 Punkte zu den Physikern' [Punkt 3], in *Die Physiker*, Zürich: 1992, p. 77.

alles von gleicher Gültigkeit ist, so wäre ihm doch alles gleichgültig, oder? Woher sollte er dann die Leidenschaft nehmen, ein Gedicht, eine Erzählung, ein Theaterstück zu schreiben. (LM, 103)

I hope to have shown how Peter Turrini, following his early success in the theatre, came to regard it as an unsuitable medium for his declared aim of giving a voice to society's disadvantaged and suppressed. Breaking out of what he termed a narrow and elitist 'cultural ghetto', Turrini put his hopes in the power of mass media, as a potential instrument of social enlightenment and change. However, his own experience of television, particularly the hard lessons learned during the aborted *Arbeitersaga* project, together with unease at the impact of technological change and the advent of new media, like video, led him to return to the theatre. One important theme of *Die Minderleister*, the first new play since his self–imposed absence from the stage, is accordingly the exploration of how 'das wirklich Ungeschminkte', the unvarnished reality of life in contemporary Austria, is submerged in a deluge of mass media images. Moreover, *Die Minderleister* also constitutes an important new departure from an aesthetic point of view. In it, an altogether more experimental form enables Turrini to break out of the confines of the often stark realism of his earlier works for the stage.

POLARITY AND BREATHING — ASPECTS OF THOMAS BERNHARD'S PLAYS

RALF JEUTTER

How does one measure the greatness of a writer? By the impact they have on many people? By the impact they have on a few, but 'influential' people? Or by the impact the writer has at an international level which shows that they have something to say which transcends national borders? As a recent publication shows,[1] Thomas Bernhard is by now an international phenomenon, with studies of the critical reception of his works in the Ukraine, Russia, Bulgaria, Hungary, Norway, and, of course, in all the other major European countries. Nevertheless, one cannot say that he is a writer with a broad based appeal; his work cannot be easily used for syllabus purposes in public teaching institutions nor would he appear to keep librarians busy.[2] The sales of his books in the Anglo–American world are, compared with the likes of Grass, Böll, Andersch and other celebrities, negligible.

Thomas Bernhard's status as a prose writer is beyond doubt, and if anything, his reputation is growing. It is by now widely acknowledged that Bernhard's voice as a prose writer is unique and that he added something to the body of world literature which is strictly identified with his name. He has already stylistic followers and plagiarists in various countries. Whether you call what he does *Wortkaskaden*, *Suada–Kunst*, *Dauerpalaver*, *Konversationsmaschinerie*, *Wort–und–Haßmaschinerie*, *Haßlitaneien*, *Quasselterror* or *Partituren*, *Arien*, *Wort--Etüden*, *Kunst der Fuge*. Each of these descriptions, whether positive or negative, make clear that we are confronted with something quite exceptional.

But what about his status as a playwright? Again, if one measures the importance of a writer by his international resonance, one would not

---

[1]Wolfram Bayer: *Kontient Bernhard. Zur Thomas Bernhard–Rezeption in Europa*, Vienna: 1995.

[2]See Ewald Osers as yet unpublished article: 'The Reception of Thomas Bernard's Work in Britain and in America': 'Over the past two years the five Thomas Bernhard titles I have translated were borrowed exactly 1,217 times throughout Britain. In view of the fact that there were, during that time, 606 days on which the public libraries were open, this makes exactly 2 borrowings per day. It is probably unfair to compare literature with non–fiction borrowings, which are generally heavier. But if I compare my 5 Thomas Bernhard translations with my 3 translations of the Czech novelist Ivan Klima — i.e. fiction with fiction — I find that my Klima books were borrowed more than 22 times each day — in other words 11 times more often Thomas Bernhard [...]'.

describe Bernhard as a great playwright. This is reflected in the number of translations which have been made of his plays. While most of his prose works have now been translated into the major European languages, only a small number of his plays have found their way onto international stages. Take Britain as an example: only four of this plays have been performed *Die Macht der Gewohnheit* (1976), *Elisabeth II.* (1992), *Der Theatermacher* (1993) — the last two in the small yet influential 'fringe' theatres, the Gate and the Almeida — and *Vor dem Ruhestand* (1997). *The Force of Habit*, to give it its English title, staged in the Royal National Theatre's Lyttleton, was a complete disaster (both with the audience and the critics). The misunderstandings were both fundamental and instructive, and say probably more about a particular English attitude than about Bernhard. 'What a waste of talent and everybody's time', wrote, for example, Irving Wardle in *The Times* (10.11.76). And Bernard Levin in *The Sunday Times* (14.11.76) judged that *The Force of Habit* was of 'a tedium you could bend forks with. It alternates ghastly neo–Beckettian pseudo–philosophising and no less dreadful reflections on the demands of art [...] with slapstick routine of an acupunctural painfulness [...]'.

In Germany the playwright Bernhard was the darling of the review pages of the serious press or 'Feuilleton'. All of his 18 plays were received with great interest, he never had problems publishing his playlets, or *Dramoletten*, as he called them, in *Theater Heute* or *Die Zeit*. The reactions were however mixed. But Bernhard was a playwright whose works almost invariably provoked a scandal. The critics always had plenty to write about and this often absolved them from the much harder task of being concerned with the art of his writing. The scandal surrounding *Heldenplatz* alone fills a large volume.[3]

Academics were and are divided over his plays. Once can find many of the familiar approaches to literary criticism which are currently fashionable. Typical German concerns are with the 'correctness' or otherwise of his political views. He is seen to be ambiguous, frivolous, yes even scandalous. While some (like Gamper)[4] argue that Bernhard's characters reflect the status quo, there are others who maintain that his protagonists operate in isolation and are not much more than a register of his own idiosyncrasies. Others — again a very German approach — regard Bernhard as somebody who deals in philosophical propositions (for example Klug, who shows how indebted Bernhard is to Kierkegaard),[5] or quite the opposite, philosophical concerns are seen as male projections trying to hide an underlying

[3]*Heldenplatz. Eine Dokumentation*, Burgtheater Wien (ed.), 13.1.1989.
[4]H. Gamper: *Thomas Bernhard*, Munich: 1977.
[5]Christian Klug: *Thomas Bernhards Theaterstücke*, Stuttgart: 1991.

psychological malaise. Others consider Bernhard's plays to be reflections and representations of the Self.

On the pages which follow, I shall explore major themes in Bernhard's writings such as illness, communication and polarity. Bernhard's world of language is that of opposites and oppositions: a 'on the one hand' and 'on the other hand' structure. The opposites in Bernhard's world are endless: the position of man, for example, between the spiritual and the animal realm; genius and failure; sickness and health; creative and destructive; inner and outer; the I and the you. All typical polarities of our Western culture.

Bernhard's language is a clash of opposites, contradictions and paradoxes. Hubert Fichte, a writer very different from Bernhard, expressed his problem with language as follows:

> Gäbe es zwischen dem Wittgensteinschen Schweigen und der Sprache unserer Siegeranalysen und Siegersynthesen eine Sprache, in der die Bewegung sich abwechselnder und widersprechender Berichte deutlich werden könnte, das Dilemma der Empfindlichkeit und Anpassung, Verzweifeln und Praxis — ich würde sie benutzen. Es wäre eine wesentlich andere Sprache.[6]

Bernhard's writing is concerned with the same problem, which is ultimately the problem of polarity, and the impossibility of breaking through polar thinking. Unlike Hubert Fichte, who learned obsessively all the major European languages plus a few non–European ones in the search for this otherness, Bernhard never looked to another language. He uses paradox, juxtaposition (*Einfach kompliziert*) and contradictions to create tension within the langauge he uses. Bernhard, by not providing any exits, creates the desire and even the need for escape routes. Or the desire for the opposite of polarity, namely unity. I shall now move on to examine in more detail the short plays *Claus Peymann kauft sich eine Hose* and *Claus Peymann und Hermann Beil auf der Sulzwiese*.[7]

The first play is centred around the contrast of 'einerseits–andererseits', a contrast well–known in Bernhard's plays and prose works. The contrast here is that of trying on a pair of trousers and bringing a play to the stage. The play is farcical from the outset and sabotages any meaningful discourse. But the equation of trying on a pair of trousers with rehearsing great art is not a forced joke. Bernhard rather exploits possibilities of language to put these activities on the same level: 'probieren' in German fits equally the trying on of trousers and the rehearsing of a play. The effect is comical but, at the same time, Bernhard creates polarities which show both the legitimacy of these polarities

---

[6]Hubert Fichte: *Xango*, Frankfurt/M.:1976, p.109.
[7]Frankfurt/M.: 1990.

(because they are linguistically possible) and at the same time, via this specific example, the ridiculous nature of polarities.

Once the polarity of *Hose* and *Theater* is established (via verbs which cover both areas) the rest follows logically: *Hosenkauf* can now be put on the same level as *Tragödie* (30). Peymann says: 'Hosenkauf ist immer eine Tragödie gewesen/Ich weiß nicht/ist es fürchterlicher Shakespeare zu probieren/oder sechs Hosen Bernhard' (30). By the same token dress sense and artistic development are equated:

> Vor vierzig Jahren sind Sie in Fetzen herumgelaufen/im Winter bei zweiundzwanzig Grad minus/haben Sie nur ausgefranste Blue Jeans angehabt/und ein sogenanntes Cocacolaleibchen/bis Sie Iphigenie inszeniert haben in Stuttgart/nach der Iphigenie waren Sie auf einmal sehr elegant gekleidet/In Paris haben Sie diese Verwandlung durchgemacht (30).

Another well–known polarity in the plays of Bernhard is that of food versus art: 'Bernhard: Wissen Sie was/wir gehen in die Zauberflöte/ ist ein Lokal/indem man erstklassig ißt und wenig bezahlt' (32). After having established the connection between art and buying trousers, Bernhard can now short–circuit and, instead of playing yet another variation on the theme of illness and art, he can explore illness and trying on trousers, more precisely, the dangers of suffering a stroke in one of the 'Probierzellen' (surely an allusion to epilepsy, the holy illness, as Thomas Mann refers to it on his essay on Nietzsche and Dostoyevski).[8] Bernhard has of course already a term for this affliction: the 'Kleiderhausprobierzellenschlag':

> Ich: Die Hosenprobierzellen sind zu eng/in ihnen ist keine Luft/In den Hosenprobierzellen/hat schon so viele der Schlag getroffen/fragen Sie doch die Kleiderinnung/die wird es Ihnen bestätigen/Die Leute gehen in ein Geschäft hinein/und wollen nur eine Hose probieren/und probieren naturgemäß sieben oder acht/und es trifft sie der Schlag/der Kleiderhausprobierzellenschlag ist der häufigste (32).

The connection back to art is made immediately when Peymann says: 'Es ist wie wenn ich/drei Tage und drei Nächte *Wintermärchen*[9] probiert hätte' (33).

We are only a few pages into the play and the term 'Hosenprobe' has the same legitimacy as the term 'Theaterprobe' and carries by now similar connotations and raises similar issues, such as that of male and female differences:

> Interessanterweise ist der Tod/in den Herrenprobierzellen ungleich häufiger/als in den Damenprobierzellen Peymann/die Damen schlüpfen ja auch leicht in ihre Röcke hinein/während es den Herren die größte Mühe macht (35).

---

[8]Thomas Mann, *Neue Studien*, (Stockholm Edition) Frankfurt/M.: 1948, p.73–102.
[9]The German title for Shakespeare's play, *A Winter's Tale*.

No doubt an ironic allusion to the competitiveness between men and women, whereby the man is the creator of artefacts who has to compensate his natural sterility with hard work and suffering, while the woman is the natural creature whose pain endured during child birth the man is so loathe to accept.

What one encounters here and in other examples, is the mimicry of a discourse on art. The 'Probierzelle', whilst being potentially lethal on the one hand, is, on the other, a chamber of inspiration. In such a way the 'Kleiderprobierzelle' is equated with a writer's study:

> Während einer solchen Hosenprobe/habe ich einmal die Idee für einen Roman gehabt/den Roman habe ich auch geschrieben [...]/ Wir machen nur eine Hosenprobe/und wir konzipieren einen Roman/oder ein Bühnenstück' (35).

The ambivalence Bernhard felt towards art, or rather the creation of art, is reflected here in the ambivalent character of the 'Probierzelle'. It is at the same time the source of death and the source of creation. The transposition of a serious topic (a major concern for Bernhard during most of his life) into a farcical setting is Bernhard's way of saying two things at the same time: that art is serious but that it shouldn't be taken seriously; that art is important, albeit only as important as trying on a pair of trousers.

In the same way that he hates the 'Herrenprobierzellen', Bernhard hates the theatre, the actors on the stage, and the theatrical world in general. Peymann and Bernhard are of course constructed as polarities: both are bound to the theatre by fate, but Peymann out of love, and Bernhard out of hate. This polarity peaks in a rhythmic chiasmus: 'Das Theater ist meine Welt', says Peymann, while Bernhard retorts: 'Meine Welt ist es nicht' (36).

Once a polarity is established, Bernhard can develop logical conclusions from it, and, simply by following the path of logic, he inevitably produces exaggerations, hyperbole, and seemingly apodictic judgements: Peymann says: 'Das Theater ist meine Leidenschaft Bernhard/nichts als das Theater'. Bernhard replies:

> Genau umgekehrt ist es bei mir/ ich verabscheue das Theater/ es zieht mich an/ weil ich es verabscheue/ Sie lieben die Schauspieler/ ich hasse sie/ Sie lieben die Bühne/ ich hasse sie/ Alles das sie lieben/ hasse ich/ alles das sie verabscheuen/ liebe ich/ ich liebe alles/ das sie verabscheuen (37)

Bernhard writes in the mode of logical deductions and in the form of chiasmic rhythms. The intertwining of contradictions and the drawing of logical ('sprachlogische') conclusions from a given proposition, often arbitrary, is Bernhard's way of showing unity in the polarities. Bernhard can, for example, develop an important theme out of nothing. Bernhard only needs to say to Peymann: 'Soll ich Ihnen nicht doch die alte Hose abnehmen', in order to provoke the latter into a monologue on the difficulty of being Director of the *Burgtheater*:

> Wo denken Sie hin Bernhard/ wenn ich nicht einmal die Kraft hätte/ meine alte Hose allein zu tragen/ Wie schätzen Sie mich ein/ Schließlich bin ich Burgetheaterdirektor/ da muß ich mehr Kraft haben/ als nur meine alte Hose zu tragen Bernhard/ Als Burgtheaterdirektor/ ist es ja ein fortwährendes Kräftemessen/ da habe ich keine Angst Bernhard/ Schwergewicht ist das Burgtheater/ wie kommen Sie denn überhaupt auf die Idee/ daß ich nicht einmal meine alte Hose tragen kann/ wenn ich Burgtheatredirektor bin/ Der Burgtheaterdirektor hat tagtäglich/ das ganze Burgtheater zu tragen Bernhard/ bildlich gesprochen Bernhard/stellen Sie sich das mal vor/tagtäglich das ganze Burgtheater wie es liegt und steht Bernhard/ dieses ganze vor Schauspielern und Dramaturgen/ überquellende Burgtheater aufzuheben schon in der Früh' und in die Höhe zu stemmen/ und immer höher und höher zu stemmen Bernhard (38f.).

In Bernhard's plays one is always equally distant from any centre or periphery as far as the content is concerned. Topics and themes just seem to be exchangeable elements within a particular formal structure. Austria as a comedy, for example, the best comedy in the world; that all Austrians are Nazis; the eating of the 'Rindsuppe' carries as much importance as directing the world's best plays with the best actors in the world's best theatre, or the writing and production of the *Überstück*, which Peymann had always demanded of Bernhard:

> [...] ein richtiges Burgtheatertheater/ eine richtige große alles verstörende Andernaseherumführkomödie/ bringen Sie einmal Ihre ganze Rücksichtslosigkeit auf der Bühne/ Ihren Ganzen Weltekel/ nicht nur Ihren halben Weltekel sondern Ihren ganzen Weltekel Bernhard/ schreiben Sie so ein Stück Welttheater/ daß es das Burgtheater zerreißt/ so einen richtigen grandiosen Weltscherz Bernhard/ daß das Burgtheater explodiert/ daß die ganze Stadt Wien erzittert/ Sie wissen schon was ich meine/ [...] diesen ganz großen weltumwerfenden Wurf/ diese ganz und gar weltausdenangelnhebende Komödie für alle/ dieses Komödienungeheuer Sie wissen schon Bernhard/ schreiben Sie etwas daß alles andere/ in den Schatten stellt/ schreiben Sie ganz einfach einmal die ganze Weltliteratur nieder/ schreiben Sie sie ganz einfach einmal in Grund und Boden/ (46).

The play ends with Bernhard and Peymann sitting among the Nazis, with Peymann eating his 'Rindsuppe', stretching out his legs, obviously enjoying the experience. There is no hint of any contradictions.

In *Claus Peymann und Hermann Beil auf der Sulzwiese*, the sequel to *Claus Peymann kauft sich eine Hose,* unity appears in the idea of simultaneity: Peymann's dream is to stage the whole of Shakespeare's works in one evening: 'Sturm und Hamlet gleichzeitig/ und alles zusammen nicht länger als fünf Stunden' (57). This play should combine not only all previous stage designs, it should be performed in all the languages and different interpretations in which Shakespeare's work has ever been performed. Moreover, it is regarded as an escape route out of a classical Bernhard situation: 'Ausweglosigkeit'. Peymann:

> Das Theater ist eine einzige Ausweglosigkeit/ dahin kommen all/ die lebenslänglich einen Ausweg gesucht haben/ das Theater hat keinen Ausweg/ außer/ [...] wir führen den ganzen Shakespeare/ an einem Abend auf (57).

This is also an alternative to the polarity of Peymann's obligation to provide a unique theatrical experience in the Burgtheater on the one hand, and Bernhard's fantastical solution on the other: close it down and ship it piece by piece to Mongolia; smash it to bits; turn it into a mental asylum; or convert it into a theatre museum complete with wax figures.

This obligation to create a theatre of superlatives, leads on the other hand (pole) to dreadful nightmares of total and unadulterated failure:

> Weil wir immer nur den höchsten Anspruch im Kopf haben/ und weil wir mit dem höchsten Anspruch nach Wien gegangen sind/ wache ich jede Nacht mit einem Angstschrei auf (70).

A recurrent attempt in Bernhard's work to transcend polarity is to write something down and strike it out in the next moment, to create and destroy in one act. In this case it is Beil, the *Dramaturg*, who, in one of his dreams, deletes the world's entire stock of dramatic works: 'ich strich alle Stücke so lange/ bis von ihnen nichts mehr da war/ ich strich die ganze dramatische Weltliteratur aus' (74).

It is conspicuous how many characters in Bernhard's plays are engaged in the act of eating. There are some plays, for example, whose temporal structure is divided according to meal times; there are others in which the act of eating gives the speeches of characters a particular rhythm. *Claus Peymann und Hermann Beil auf der Sulzwiese* derives its rhythm from one action: the repeated biting into a veal cutlet. Peymann talks about transcending the usual artistic restrictions and limitations, about the *way out*, the ultimate theatre, which leaves all other theatre behind, a theatre he calls the ALL–Theater, the one which is all inclusive. Meanwhile Beil remains seated, eats, and is afraid of being bitten by tics, which can cause meningitis. Bernhard's verdict is that we are schnitzel–eating people and as such disqualified from any form of transcendence. As Peymann remarks to Beil: 'Wenn ich sehe wie Sie in Ihr Schnitzel beißen/ denke ich/ daß es nicht für den ganzen Shakespeare reicht' (63).

The most basic polarity which we all know and experience is that of breathing: it is the most basic rhythm and, at the same time, the foundation for all other polarities; if we are no longer able to breathe, we are dead, and ergo: end of polarities. Breathing has to do with taking in part of the world, we assimilate what we can use of it and return what we cannot. Eating and that which goes with it, namely digestion, involves a similar process. The difference is that digestion is more concerned with the body's physicality, whereas breathing has always had a connection to metaphysics, as is so clearly evident in ancient languages — *spirare/spiritus*; psyche = breath and soul; *mahatma* means great soul and great breath.

The polarity in the physical sub–text is then quite clear; sheer physicality *einerseits* and spirituality *andererseits*. The rule in Bernhard's plays is that the more inauthentic, false and morally despicable the characters, the more they eat (*Die Berühmten* and *Über allen Gipfeln ist Ruh* provide ample evidence of this). But eating is always there, a *memento mori* of sorts, a reminder that we are caught up in a polarity which foils all our attempts to find an escape route (not very dissimilar to the situation of the hunger artist).

Bernhard's ability to condense can be seen in an exemplary manner in the image of Beil eating and at the same time fearing meningitis; the potential loss of his cerebral powers. Der Theatermacher complains: 'Diese Schwüle einerseits/ und dieses Gefühl/ erfrieren zu müssen hier/ andererseits — ' (70). This is the situation in which most of the characters find themselves — a life between extremes, whereby each of the extremes is unbearable, and life is unbearable. Bernhard's morally inspired rage against Nature can be seen in the fact that the characters necessarily fail because they are caught up in the polarity of breathing/speaking and eating/digestion, the two major rhythmic activities 'above' and 'below'. They are failures in Voss' sense in the Wittgenstein play *Ritter, Dene, Voss*: 'Wir können nicht denken/ wenn wir an Menschen und ihre Bedürfnisse gebunden sind' (*RDV*, 178). This statement by Voss encapsulates the paradoxical character of communication in Bernhard's plays, which is undoubtedly one of his core themes. The characters can never bridge the gap between what is said or expressed and that which is felt and experienced. Bernhard is as adamant about the impossibility of bridging this gap as he is about the characters being trapped in a situation they cannot escape: 'Wir entkommen nicht mein Kind' (*Am Ziel*, 21) is a statement which can be found in all manner of variations in all his plays.

At the heart of the communication problem is the assumption of the characters that they are not only being misunderstood but also that they can never be understood. To this extent, they would all appear to be in a position similar to that of the 'Weltverbesserer': he has written a tractate about how to improve the world, for which he has received a medal from the city of Frankfurt — the only problem is that nobody understands it. This insistence on being misunderstood is very often hypostacised as language scepticism in the Wittgenstein mould, but, as Christian Klug has pointed out, there is more to it than this:

Wenn Bernhards Figuren versuchen, ihre Sprachskepsis erkenntnistheoretisch zu untermauern, maskieren und rationalisieren sie nur ihr Problem, Innerlichkeit mitzuteilen. Durch vergröbernde und grotesk zuspitzende Formulierungen gibt der Autor zu erkennen, daß auch er es für ein absurdes Mißverständnis hält, Sprachskepsis auf Schwierigkeiten der Gegenstandserkenntnis zurückzuführen. Tatsächlich geht es nicht um die Adäquanz von Wort und Ding, sondern um die authentische Kommunikation von Innerlichkeit.[10]

It is of course ironic and fitting that Bernhard should choose for his monologues on the impossibility of communication that communicative art form par excellence: the theatre. Moreover, it is symptomatic that Bernhard creates in his plays ideal communicative settings. His characters have nothing else to do but be concerned with themselves; to meditate and work on themselves. Indeed, they are placed in a context where there are no external duties or distractions.

Behind Bernhard's untiring effort to set up polarities, his insistence on showing his characters to be inescapably caught up in contradictions, there lurks an ideal of unity as expressed in the dream of the synchronous staging of all Shakespeare plays in all languages, or Bruscon's daydream of the comedy of all comedies in the *Theatermacher*. Behind Bernhard's characters' failure to communicate can be detected an ideal of communication. For example, characters like Glenn Gould or Roithamer[11] in the prose works come close to this ideal: Glenn Gould *becomes* his music, and does not need any mediators; Roithamer designs and builds a house for his sister which is identical to her. The ideal is art which communicates itself. It is rather like theatre without an audience, without a stage, without actors, or indeed without a script. In Bernhard's prose works, however, very different rules apply by comparison with his plays. Greatness, uniqueness and the genius appear in Bernhard's prose usually in decontextualised quotations and allusions. Through this device, greatness is at least claimed and evoked. On the stage, on the other hand, something very different is represented visually from that which is claimed verbally; stage props, meals, the banality of the mundane. The metaphysical concerns of the protagonists become part of the everyday routine in which they are engaged. Unlike in his early prose, Bernhard does not put his characters into a spiritual landscape, in a symbolically significant space; he provides no mythological framework for the action.

---

[10]Christian Klug, op.cit., p.83.
[11]See *Der Untergeher*, Frankfurt/M.: 1983 and *Die Korrektur*, Frankfurt/M.: 1975.

Elias Canetti's *Rede auf Hermann Broch*[12] is really a meditation on breath, breathing and air. In this essay there is a sentence which describes Broch's fictional characters as follows:

> Seine Gestalten sind ihm keine Gefängnisse. Er entschwebt ihnen gerne. Er muß ihnen entschweben; aber er bleibt in ihrer Nähe. Sie sind in Luft gebettet, er hat für sie geatmet. Seine Behutsamkeit ist eine Scheu vor dem Hauch seines eigenen Atems, der an die Ruhe der anderen rührt.[13]

Unlike Broch's, Bernhard's characters are solid and clearly delineated. They are 'Gefängnisse', defined through, and limited by, their monologues. The separation of the characters from everything outside themselves is absolute. It is touching, for example, that Katharina, the little girl in *Einfach kompliziert* brings the older actor milk at regular intervals. Milk is, of course, the quintessential symbol of nourishing, caring, warmth and nurturing. But for the older actor it is also a reminder that he has broken off all contact with his fellow human beings:

> [...] jeden Dienstag und Freitag/ bringst du dem alten Schauspieler die Milch/ dem alten Schauspieler/ der nicht mehr unter die Menschen geht/ komm herein/ komm herein mein Kind/ Die Menschen sind die Ursache/ immer sind es die Menschen.' (*Einfach Kompliziert*, 256).

Bernhard's main theatrical imagery is closed spaces, limits and sharp linguistic dividing lines. The characters are always busily building walls around themselves, boxing themselves in, or as Rüdiger Görner has put it: 'Bernhard's plays are, essentially, about stalemates.'[14]

Canetti's meditation on air and breath stresses the fact that air delimits, that breathing unites and brings people into contact with each other whether they like it or not. They are united by this substance air and through their breathing. Breath is something which is outside of us, not something which belongs to us. In such a way it is beyond us (the link with metaphysics has been mentioned before): 'Vielleicht ist jeder Atemzug von dir der letzte Hauch eines anderen', writes Canetti in *Alle vergeudete Verehrung*.[15] Thus, breath preserves us from totally cutting ourselves off, from shutting ourselves in to the point of making the frontiers of our 'I' impenetrable. As Thorwald Dethlefsen maintains:

---

[12]Elias Canetti, *Alle vergeudete Verehrung. Aufzeichnungen 1949–60*, Munich:1970.

[13]Ibid., p.201.

[14]Rüdiger Görner: 'The Excitement of Boredom', in W.G. Sebald, (ed.) *A Radical Stage*, Oxford/New York/Hamburg: 1988, p.168.

[15]Op. cit, p.24.

We need to be conscious of the fact that we are breathing in the very same air that our enemies are breathing out. It is the self–same air, too, that the animals and plants are breathing. The breath continually connects us to everything else.[16]

In such a way breath has lot to do with contact and relationships; a notoriously difficult area in the life of Bernhard's characters. This contact between what comes from 'out there' and our own bodies takes place in the lung vesicles (the alveoli). Our lungs have an internal surface area of some seventy two square metres, whereas the surface of our skin measures only one and a half to two square metres. The lungs are therefore our largest organ of contact. Seen in this light it is interesting to note that Bernhard suffered most of his life (from the age of seventeen) from an incurable illness of the lungs, which I think, determined and defined his concerns and life habits. Breathing was a hazardous affair for Bernhard. He could only walk and talk slowly in real life, quite the opposite of his longwinded prose sentences and his highly energetic theatrical monologues. It also determined Bernhard's own approach to illness which was a fundamental one, not concerned with petty 'Zivilisationskrankheiten', although he could also exploit those to great effect. His experience of illness was of a force which struck exactly at the point where liberation should have taken place. When Bernhard, just seventeen, started to walk into the *entgegengesetzte Richtung*, as he calls it,[17] away from his family, just when he thought he could stand on his own two feet, illness forced him back to the point of original departure. Illness destroys our delusions of grandeur, our hubris. The fact of being an individual, an individual with any pretensions, is risible. Bernhard's sentence, 'Es ist nichts zu loben, nichts zu verdammen, nichts anzuklagen, aber es ist vieles lächerlich, wenn man an den Tod denkt',[18] should not be understood as empty rhetoric but as an experience, and also the summary of this theatrical programme. All this characters suffer from afflictions, some clearly symbolic (like those with the dying senses), others farcical. Therefore all of them are seen to be lacking something, of being unwhole, crippled in mind and body. Bernhard's characters do not *become* ill, — there is no process involved — nor do the characters' illnesses possess a teleological dimension; causal relationships which would explain them. Bernhard's characters *are* ill. And one could say that they are ill because they speak. Every act of speaking in Bernhard's world of polarities is an act of becoming unwhole, of self–crippling, of making differentiations and creating divisions, and, in so doing, the characters isolate themselves.

---

[16]Thorwald Dethlefsen: *The Healing Power of Illness*, Dorset: 1990, p.115.
[17]Thomas Bernhard, *Der Keller. Eine Entziehung*, Salzburg:1976, p.7f.
[18]Anneliese Botond (ed.), *Über Thomas Bernhard*, Frankfurt/M.: 1970.

On the other hand, and this is the final and most fundamental paradox, only through speaking can they make themselves whole again: by speaking everything at once, at the same time, exhausting all possibilities of language in one great long speech. The characters' reluctance to share the same language with all those others who have spoilt it, their resistance to share the same air with all those who pollute it, is compensated for by their attempt to say EVERYTHING; to express everything at once, and to have an eternity in which to do so. Behind all the individual plays lies the utopia of the *Überstück*. Whoever wants to stage Bernhard's plays according to this concept would have to create a gigantic hall of voices in which all his characters act at the same time. Only then might we get an idea of the degree to which Bernhard hated to separate his characters off in such an artificial manner.

OPERATING ON A 'LIVING CORPSE':
THE PLAYS OF GERHARD ROTH

UWE SCHÜTTE

In an interview in 1990 Gerhard Roth scoffed at the theatre as 'an outdated form of art. It is nothing but a living corpse.'[1] Prose, according to Roth, is a far more exciting form of literature. Even films are superior to the drama, addressing, he insists, 'a livelier mind'.[2] What drove Roth to pronounce such an apodictic judgement on the insignificance of contemporary German–language theatre? A superficial, though probably not entirely inaccurate, explanation might be the predominantly negative public and critical response that met his own plays. Meanwhile, many of his prose works (and film scripts) won critical acclaim and sometimes even awards. Their quality underscored Ulrich Greiner's praise, expressed as early as 1976: 'there can be no doubt that Gerhard Roth, alongside Thomas Bernhard und Peter Handke, is one of the most important contemporary writers in Austria.'[3]

Yet whereas the genres of drama and novel are of equal significance within the literary production of both Bernhard and Handke, the role of the drama in Roth's complete works is merely a subordinate one: whilst having published well over 20 non–dramatic texts, as well as numerous essays, newspaper articles, and polemics, he has, to date written only four plays.[4] All of these were premièred at the 'Steirischer Herbst', an annual festival of experimental art in Graz, organised by the 'Forum Stadtpark'; a group of authors and artists, closely linked with Roth's early years as a writer. Apart from these first performances, his plays were staged only reluctantly.[5]

The theatre scene of Graz in the seventies was characterised by vibrant anarchy and subversiveness. The young writers' objective was to shake up a society they deemed complacent and repressively bourgeois — and their

---

[1]See Barbara Petsch, 'Moby Dick und die Literatur', *Die Presse* 12.3.1990. This and all subsequent translations of quotes from reviews and dramas are my own.

[2]See Karin Kathrein, 'Der österreichische Kopf ist mein Thema', in: *Bühne* 9 (1991), p.54–9.

[3]See Ulrich Greiner, *Der Tod des Nachsommers*, Munich: 1979, p.163–68.

[4]Roth has also gained a reputation for his essays and various contributions to newspapers, most of which are collected in the two volumes *Die schönen Tage beim Trabrennen*, Frankfurt/M.: 1982 and *Das doppelköpfige Österreich*, Frankfurt/M.: 1995.

[5]See Peter Ensberg and Helga Schreckenberger, *Gerhard Roth. Kunst als Auflehnung gegen das Sein*, Tübingen: 1994, p.147.

undertaking was indeed crowned with success.[6] Probably the greatest stir was caused by Wolfgang Bauer's play *Gespenster*, which portrayed the decadent lives of a bohemian circle of writers and revelled in depictions of alcoholic excess and sexual orgies. Among the audience many, perhaps quite rightly, regarded this to be a realistic self–portrait of the young Graz authors.[7]

When the play was broadcast on Austrian television a nationwide uproar ensued. In a discussion following the transmission, for example, a female viewer called for the 'bark beetle' Bauer to be 'fumigated'. Anonymously authored circulars called on the 'decent' citizens of Graz to use violence against this 'gang' of writers whose 'mental deficiency' could only appeal to 'idiots'. Newspapers were deluged with letters protesting 'smut' and 'degenerate art', while its author, denigrated in a terminology equally reminiscent of Nazi propaganda, was readily referred to as 'vermin'. Yet when Roth, a close friend of Bauer, wrote an open letter in reply to a hostile review of the play, using words like 'Klosettfliegen' ('blowflies') and 'Schmierenkomödiant' ('barnstormer'), he was sued for libel *and* lost the court case. As an added 'bonus' Roth was henceforth subjected to nightly telephone terror from unidentified 'lovers of the arts'.[8]

Roth's own plays have never provoked similar scandal — with the exception of the scenes of rape, murder and the casual shooting of a dog that provide the finale to his second play. This latter unmotivated act of violence prompted an apparently animal loving audience to utter 'displeased shouts' and 'mild whistles' — which in turn provoked the leading actor to turn on the viewers and accuse them of apparently 'not much minding' a woman being strangled while 'getting all worked up' over a dead dog.[9] Unlike Bauer, however, Roth never set out to outrage the public deliberately.

> [Roth's] plays could be termed a 'theatre of the mind'. [...] His characters are artificial, prototypes exemplifying linguistic concepts, ideological positions, and philosophical questions.[10]

This quote sums up succinctly the overriding theme and key concern of Roth's dramatic productions: the difficulty of reconciling the theoretical

---

[6]See Jutta Landa, *Bürgerliches Schocktheater. Entwicklungen im österreichischen Drama der sechziger und siebziger Jahre*, Frankfurt/M.: 1988.

[7]See in this context Anthony Waine's discussion of Bauer's work in Chapter Three.

[8]See Greiner, *Der Tod des Nachsommers*, op. cit., p.204.

[9]Quotes from Hilde Spiel, 'Milde Pfiffe in Graz', in: *Frankfurter Allgemeine Zeitung*, 11.10.1977.

[10]See Ensberg/Schreckenberger, op. cit. p.148.

nature of abstract concepts with stage representation and its demands of concretisation and visualisation.

Roth's prose works can be subdivided into three categories. His experimental phase of the early seventies, represented by novels such as *die autobiographie des albert einstein* (1972); a realistic period launched in 1974 with three works of travel fiction, the most successful being *Winterreise* (1978); and finally the writings published between 1980 and 1991 which eventually constituted his cycle *Die Archive des Schweigens*, with *Landläufiger Tod* (1984) as its centre–piece. This classification into three artistic phases can also be applied to Roth's dramatic production. His first play *Lichtenberg*, was premièred in 1973, the year of the so–called 'Tendenzwende'.[11] Accordingly, it marks the conclusion to Roth's early experimental period which fused a critique of language and the sciences with an abstract style, fragmentary form, and schizophrenic narrative perspective.

The play's protagonist, a scientist, is only remotely connected with the 18th century philosopher, Lichtenberg, although Roth does incorporate some of his aphorisms into the script. The play opens with Herr Wenzel handing over his retarded son, invariably only referred to as 'the object', to the professor for the purposes of 'study' and possible transformation into a 'proper' human being. Shortly afterwards, a widow living nearby is raped and murdered, and the scientist casts suspicion on the virtually mute 'object'. Using the results of his cleverly manipulated experiments, strengthened by the authority of his rational discourse, the professor succeeds in convicting the 'object' of the crime. Yet in the end he himself turns out to have committed the murder. The 'object' meanwhile, distressed by the experiments and the false accusations, grabs a gun and shoots the professor, thus eventually 'verifying' the accusations levelled at him.

The plot bears obvious similarities to Büchner's *Woyzeck*. In *Lichtenberg*, as in his experimental prose, Roth reveals the correlation between power and language, and demonstrates the limits of rational thinking. Roth highlights the process of how language is transformed into power and how the impotent 'object' is subsequently driven to violence as the only means to resist the professor's power of expression. Thematically, there is a close link with the early plays of Peter Handke such as *Kaspar* (1968) or *Das Mündel will Vormund sein* (1969). But in contrast to Handke's formalised experimental theatre, Roth's drama is more traditional in its deployment of characters, dialogue, and stage design. These stylistic

---

[11]This could roughly be translated as 'a change of direction' referring to the change from either predominantly political (in Germany) or predominantly experimental (in Austria) forms of writing in the late sixties to the more autobiographical oriented, subjective, self–reflexive genres of the mid–seventies.

concessions, Roth hoped, would make his theoretical reflections on the nature of language palatable to a wider audience.

Yet it is precisely this compromise that generates the problematic nature of the play. Roth's linguistic critique, rather than being made accessible to the viewers is, in fact, eliminated from the play. This became particularly apparent in the decision made by the director of the Graz première to cast the French clown and mime artist, Pierre Byland, in the role of the 'object'.[12] The reviews clearly show that Byland fascinated the audience with his masterly performance but in so doing, imbued the cretinous 'object' with a degree of individuality and (bodily) expressiveness that he is deliberately denied in Roth's script.

1973 represented a watershed in Gerhard Roth's progress as an author. He was awarded a literary award for his experimental writings and used the prize money to finance a tour of the USA on which he was accompanied by Wolfgang Bauer. Roth experienced the encounter with the country's expansive landscapes and different way of life as something akin to a cultural shock. On his return to Graz, he decided to abandon his experimental and abstract style, fastening a large sign above his writing desk on which he wrote 'KEEP IT SIMPLE!' Within a short period of time he completed two realistic novels set in the United States, *Der große Horizont* (1974) and *Ein neuer Morgen* (1976), both of which rely heavily on the photographs and notes he had taken during his travels. They are, however, far removed from travel fiction in the traditional sense. Similar to Handke's *Der kurze Brief zum langen Abschied* (1972), America serves as a backdrop to Roth's painstaking depictions of social alienation, of futile attempts to escape rigid social conventions, and the desperate human quest for personal identity and a purpose in life.

Very similar themes feature in the two plays premièred in 1977 and 1978 respectively. The protagonist of *Sehnsucht* (1977) is a virtually solipsistic writer, Albert Lindberg. Set in his cottage, the play develops around the angst–ridden gatherings of several characters, who ponder the difficulties in their relationships, and their troubled identities. Lindberg struggles to overcome his loneliness and isolation by relating to three women; his wife Katharina, his lover Ida and the single Sonja, but fails miserably. Ida pinpoints his problem:

> You're always caught up in your own ego, like under a glass dome. You just don't care about other people, they're completely indifferent to you.[13]

---

[12]Byland was also cast in the lead role in a Berlin production of Handke's *Das Mündel will Vormund sein*.

[13]See Gerhard Roth, *Lichtenberg. Sehnsucht. Dämmerung*, Frankfurt/M.: 1983, p.70.

Ida herself, though, is unable to break away from Lindberg, despite being courted by an attractive actor. In view of such emotional imbroglios and complexities, a reviewer rightly disparaged *Sehnsucht* as 'German inwardness of the very worst sort'.[14]

The disputes fought out between the parties in ever changing alliances inflict nothing but hurt; a solution is out of the question and, with the lines rigidly drawn, escape remains an illusion. Lindberg, for example, tells Sonja about fanciful exploits and adventurous travels in foreign countries, only to admit a few moments later that he is incapable of undertaking even the shortest of journeys. When, in the final act, Ida eventually finds the strength to leave, the built–up emotion erupts in a frenzy of brutal and random violence: Lindberg strangles Ida and then shoots his friend's pet dog.

Sehnsucht is also a play about language, demonstrating its potential to obstruct and impair communication. Instead of bridging the distance between humans, it constrains the individual, frustrating any attempts at meaningful interpersonal and social contact. Here Roth takes up the linguistic critique, formulated by the so–called 'Wiener Gruppe' of the 50s and subsequently developed by the young Graz authors, and dresses it in a theatrical plot. Although the play represents an attempt at a truthful reflection of social reality, it remains a sequence of unrelated scenes with no plot progression. Roth himself once admitted that the play had been written at a point of deep emotional crisis, but that his object had been to expose the dilemma of the human condition rather than to express his own personal feelings.[15] Thus the characters were deliberately conceived as artificial types lacking in personality and individual history, intended as embodiments of common human attitudes. But, as a critic shrewdly remarked, 'there is a thin line between general validity and triviality'.[16] *Sehnsucht* is a paradigm of an uninspired studio theatre that simply disappoints, failing, as it does, in its two aims to find an appropriate mode for its linguistic critique, and to offer a convincing portrayal of social reality.

In 1978 a new play by Roth opened the 'Steirischer Herbst'. *Dämmerung* reprises the themes of *Sehnsucht*, yet does so without improving on its predecessor to any considerable degree. The plot develops around a funeral party and the squabbles erupting between the provincial, petit–bourgeois guests torn apart by mutual hatred, resentment, frustration, and ambition. Again the characters are contrived, sketchy clichés: the protagonist, wilfully disengages from the people around him, his frustrated wife whom he betrayed, their rebellious daughter, an impertinent waiter, an

---

[14]See Peter von Becker, 'Gewalt in der Idylle. Gerhard Roth's "Sehnsucht" als Beispiel eines dramatischen Genres', *Theater heute* 11 (1977), p.44.

[15]See Roth, 'Über "Sehnsucht"', *Theater heute* 11 (1977), p.41.

[16]See Ensberg/Schreckenberger, op. cit. p.158.

alcoholic, a fascist engineer, and a submissive accountant. The dramatic dialogues are tedious and, once again, unconvincing. The plot concludes with a thunder storm that lacks symbolic force and merely serves as a means to bring about the characters' return to their dreary homes.

The reviewers unanimously rated *Dämmerung* a disaster. The flaws in Roth's play became especially glaring when contrasted with his award–winning novel *Winterreise*, published that same year. The Austrian critic Hilde Spiel, for example, who had reviewed all of Roth's plays, frankly suggested he give up the drama in favour of his prose writings.[17]

Roth heeded her advice. Asked to give his opinion on the state of contemporary theatre, he gave the sarcastic reply that he had no intentions to write another play in the foreseeable future and justified himself as follows:

> I currently lack the financial resources to subsidise both theatre and audience to see my plays staged. The profits of one production roughly earn me enough money to lead the existence of a sauna attendant for three months and I am a slow writer, I need at least a year to finish a play.[18]

Although Roth only states economic grounds, his disappointment over the critical failures of his plays is unmistakeable. Yet his resolution to turn to prose was expedited by an additional, more personal circumstance: a severe heart condition forced Roth to give up his full–time post at a computer centre in Graz and move to the countryside to recuperate. He rented a cottage in the south–west of Styria, a region nestling on the borders to Slovenia, unspoilt by tourism and virtually untouched by modern industrialisation. Here, in the cultural backwaters of Southern Austria, Roth was suddenly confronted with an archaic and seemingly intact way of life. During his daily wanderings, Roth explored the area in a manner an ethnologist would, noting down impressions, taking thousands of pictures, chatting to peasants and farm labourers.

From the material he compiled, Roth authored two books, both dealing with the countryside, yet in very different ways. While *Der Stille Ozean* (1981) is a semi–autobiographical novel written in the realist genre, *Landläufiger Tod* (1984) developed into a magnum opus of nearly 800 pages, a chaotic conglomeration of heterogeneous textual forms, styles, and points of view, all converging in the schizophrenic mind of the narrator, Franz Lindner.

After the completion of *Landläufiger Tod*, Roth was offered a commission for the 'Steirischer Herbst', which he eagerly accepted.

---

[17]See Hilde Spiel, 'Von den Arten der Sprachlosigkeit', *Frankfurter Allgemeine Zeitung*, 9.10.1978.
[18]See 'Gerhard Roth', *Theater heute* Jahrbuch 1980, p.4.

Erinnerungen an die Menschheit was to be his first play after an eight–year absence from the world of the theatre. This commission was to provide Roth with an opportunity to adapt his concept of a schizophrenic narrative strategy for the stage, thereby breaking with the conventions of traditional theatre, which had previously compromised and diluted his radical critique of language and epistemology.

The result is a sequence of 28 separate and autonomous scenes that defy any plot progression or sense of unity. Populated by eccentric figures such as talking dogs, animate boiled eggs, blind butchers, and mad astronomers, the events on stage include a bizarre wedding ceremony performed in a lunatic asylum, two horses debating nuclear physics, the appearance of the world's tallest dead man (measuring over 18 ft.), and the light of dawn, which embraces planet earth, whilst simultaneously reciting a poetic monologue.

Not surprisingly, it is virtually impossible to summarise the play in words, not least because of its conceptual lack of a consistent plot. Tentatively it might be described as an allegorical kaleidoscope of fragmentary, microcosmic scenes that compose a web of associative references. *Erinnerungen an die Menschheit* does not address the spectators' cerebral faculties but appeals to their sensibility, compelling them to succumb to the poetical logic of the text, whereby they achieve their own meaningful synthesis of its apparently disparate parts.

Roth's imaginative script was matched by a stage set and costume designs of equally vivid extravagance and colourful opulence, devised by the renowned artist, Günter Brus.[19] The collaborative feature of the play should not be underestimated, as Roth's creative concept and Brus' congenial visual realisation combine to an aesthetic unity that transcends the boundaries of standard theatre productions. Naturally this, in turn, raises the question whether it is legitimate, or indeed appropriate, to approach a work of art synthesis such as *Erinnerungen an die Menschheit* from literary criticism's fairly restricted perspective, particularly given the fact that the textual element in Roth's play represents only one part within a much larger project. For this reason the following discussion will focus less on the story of *Erinnerungen an die Menschheit* — this would only yield subjective judgments on individual scenes that were conceived to defy all attempts at objective analysis. Roth's critique of reason, a continuous thread running through his entire *oeuvre,* here leaves behind that tautological discourse

---

[19]Brus, a close friend of Roth's, is one of the main figures of the 'Wiener Aktionismus', a movement that set out to shock a complacent Austrian post–war society. After publicly defecating into the Austrian national flag in 1968, Brus was charged with the defamation of a state symbol. He consequently fled into an eleven–year 'exile' in Berlin to avoid imprisonment.

whereby ratiocination deconstructs rationality; he no longer works with theoretical concepts but with mythological visions.

The tenth scene, appropriately entitled 'Rätsel' (riddle), exemplifies Roth's technique. In an abattoir three blind butchers are chopping meat and pass the time trying to solve riddles, for which they are repeatedly reprimanded by their strict supervisor. Their puzzles oscillate between humorous puns ('Welches ist der höflichste Fisch?/Der Bückling!') and cryptic oracles ['The blind man saw a rabbit, the lame man caught it, and the naked man put it in his pocket. What is it?'].[20] Instantly the reading/viewing audience is drawn into this maze of conundrums and riddles, struggling to unravel the 'meaning' of the scene. Why are the butchers blind? Why are they prohibited to talk? Who or what is symbolised by the supervisor? What is the purpose of the riddles in the first place?

None of these questions, however, can be answered satisfactorily, nor is it feasible to determine the moral by deductive or logical thought. Unlike the parables we all remember from school, there is no model solution. Roth's *Erinnerungen an die Menschheit*, is an achievement in that it surpasses other absurd plays, which also set incidents within an irrational context, only to develop them subsequently with logical consistency and according to dramaturgical rules. It is, for instance, not all that difficult to come up with several ideas as to what Samuel Beckett's Godot might stand for — yet how are we to make sense of such 'haphazard' associations that assemble an abattoir, a supervisor, blindness, and riddles? A satisfactory answer will remain elusive, not least owing to the fragmentary and rudimentary character of the scene that inhibits the unfolding of dramatic development.

Another scene, 'Die Hand', depicts an astronomer gazing through a telescope. To the astronomer the stars in the sky epitomise signs whose secret meaning he is suddenly able to comprehend in one flash of ecstasy. Yet in the very moment the universe transforms itself from a distant object of scientific study into a living system of signs and significance, a gigantic hand reaches out from nowhere to drag the hysterically laughing astronomer off the stage. Arguably this incident, happening halfway into the performance, constitutes the heart to the play. In a manner both concise and intelligible, Roth demonstrates that the price to be paid for a genuine insight into the workings of the universe, the ability to 'read the book of nature', is sanity.

The phenomenon of analogous thought that occurs in the short–circuiting of the mental act of comprehending ('Begreifen') by the physical process of being seized ('Ergriffensein'), is characteristic of the thought patterns of the insane. It results, for example, in their tendency to

---

[20]See Roth, *Erinnerungen an die Menschheit*, Graz: 1985, p.27f.

understand metaphors literally.[21] It can also be found in the mythical world–view of so–called primitive cultures, their 'savage mind', to use Lévi–Strauss' phrase. As the anthropologist expressly noted, this 'pensée sauvage' should not be understood in a narrow sense as native thinking but rather as the 'mind in its untamed state' and consequently 'distinct from mind cultivated or domesticated for the purpose of yielding a return'.[22] It is a thinking pattern which, although working on an entirely different basis, nonetheless leads to accurate conclusions and valid knowledge. Thus it represents not so much a diametrical opposition to our rationalised stringent way of thinking, than a complementing parallel.[23] Western cultures, however, with their science and technology oriented societies, have largely marginalised and banned the 'savage mind' to the creative arts.

To 'understand' the enigmatic scenes in *Erinnerungen an die Menschheit*, we need to submit to Roth's 'savage thinking'. In so doing it soon becomes evident that what formerly struck us as overt nonsense now seems more sensible than the easily fathomable. This paradox was spelt out by Walter Benjamin in his essay on 'Surrealism':

> For histrionic or fanatical stress on the mysterious side of the mysterious takes us no further; we penetrate the mystery only to the degree that we recognise it in the everyday world, by virtue of a dialectical optic that perceives the everyday as impenetrable, the impenetrable as everyday.[24]

Roth's objective in *Erinnerungen an die Menschheit*, however, is not merely to transcend the standard critique of rationality. He aims to revolutionise and revitalise the contemporary German–language stage with the means of his mythical imagery. In his polemical essay 'Das Theater und seine Spielregeln. Eine Philippika', Roth specified the ills that he believes beset playhouses. One of his key targets of criticism are state subsidies and the way theatres are thereby weighed down with bureaucratic interference. As a result, he argued, theatres eschew experimental productions in order to appeal to the prosaic taste of the affluent middle classes who sponsor them.[25] To witness authentic 'theatre', Roth declared, one should not visit the playhouses but rather 'seedy bars, court rooms, abattoirs and lunatic asylums, public toilets, army barracks, prisons, pubs, and tube stations.'[26]

---

[21]See Leo Navratil, *Schizophrene Dichter*, Frankfurt/M.: 1994, p.72ff.

[22]Claude Lévi–Strauss, *The Savage Mind*, London: 1966, p.219.

[23]Lévi–Strauss, op. cit., p.13.

[24]Walter Benjamin, *One–Way Street and Other Writings*, London: 1997, p.237.

[25]A view shared by Austria's most successful playwright, Thomas Bernhard, who once humorously remarked in an interview that he no longer visited the theatre as the heavy smell of perfume of the ladies next to him always made him feel sick.

[26]See 'Das Theater und seine Spielregeln. Eine Philippika', in: Roth, *Das doppelköpfige Österreich*, Frankfurt/M.: 1995, p 129f.

Thus a rejuvenated stage had to be generated apart, and independently from, institutionalised cultural spheres:

> This theatre, initially drafted *without theatre* and only on paper, puts an end to socio–political history painting, these eternally proliferating mammoth pieces, puts an end to state–doctrined imitatory theatre and it also ignores stage *culture* which threatens to suffocate it.[27]

However, Roth acknowledged, this is feasible only once we dissociate ourselves from the methods and principles of rational thought that dominate and structure our society. Hence a theatre based on such anti–cultural and anti–rational premises would inevitably end up being a '*sense*less institution where the individual finds release from societal pressures, where she/he renders her/himself unfit for future exploitation and manipulation'. Its issues would be drawn from those spheres of life where genuine aspects of human nature manifest themselves: 'in Punch and Judy shows, lunatic asylums, secret thoughts, in fears and loneliness, in meta–languages, in violence and sexuality, in fairy–tales and unattainable desires.'[28]

Sentiments of this nature reveal Roth's proximity to the concepts of Jean Dubuffet in the visual arts, specifically the theory of *art brut*. Dubuffet perceived established culture as a bourgeois means to suffocate all kinds of artistic expression that deviate from the norm. As an antidote, he insisted, society needed *art brut* — art that was purposely made poorly. Virtually anticipating the structure of Roth's play, Dubuffet stated:

> A philosophy that would consider fragmentary fields one after the next, without worrying about making connections between them, and that would obstinately apply this technique would undoubtedly come up with some very fertile findings.[29]

Erinnerungen an die Menschheit surely needs to be regarded as a paradigm of the 'theatre on paper' envisaged by Roth, and classified within Dubufft's terminology as *théâtre brut*. Critically, the play was an almost universal failure.[30] One can only speculate whether the scathing responses of reviewers and subsequent indifference of academics is the inevitable fate awaiting any play that seeks to undermine the very foundations on which both professions are built: the enlightenment ideology of reason, institutionalisation, social conformity, and state subsidy.

---

[27]Ibid., p.130f.

[28]Ibid., p.132.

[29]Jean Dubuffet, *Asphyxiating Culture and Other Writings*, New York: 1988, p.42.

[30]Examples of bad reviews are those by Helmut Schödel (*Die Zeit* 11.10.85) and Hans Hahnl (*Arbeiterzeitung* 30.9.85). A positive assessment of the play is Günter Engelhard's (*Weltwoche* 3.10.85). The remaining eleven reviews I have examined were primarily, though not always entirely, negative.

Presumably the 'Steirischer Herbst', an established part of the drama circuit, was not an adequate platform to air such a critique in the first place. It should also be added that the production of Roth's aesthetic attack on the subsidisation of bourgeois theatre actually swallowed up tax money in excess of 3.5 million Schillings (roughly £170,000). But did Roth have any other option? Should he have refrained from staging it in order to preserve one instance of his 'theatre on paper'? Ultimately, Roth's ambitious venture to revolutionise the contemporary stage has failed utterly and completely. This, however, neither proves that German–language theatre is not in need of reform nor does it render the study of plays superfluous. Rather, it is an indication of Roth's artistic and moral integrity that he embarked on a project that he knew right from the outset was doomed to fail, critically and commercially.

DAS THEATER DER VERLICHTETEN ERZÄHLUNG BEI PETER HANDKE UND WIM WENDERS

FRITZ WEFELMEYER

1.

Die Geschichte des Theaters ist ein Spiegel der metaphysischen Verfassung des Menschen. Als ein Wesen, das mit seinem Körper und seinen Sinnen in die physische Welt gehört, aber in Intuition und Denken, in Vision und Einbildungskraft die physischen Grenzen übersteigt, als ein solches Wesen hat der Mensch im Theater nach dem Spielplan gesucht, der seine Zweiweltenbürgerschaft ins angemessene Verhaltnis setzt. In der Antike wußte der Mensch sich in seinen metaphysischen Rechten und Pflichten noch in die Obhut, aber auch in die Willkür göttlicher Wesenheiten gestellt. Götter waren eine Realität und darum erschienen diese auch auf der Bühne. Aber der auf dem Theater in sinnlicher Anschaubarkeit ausgetragene Konflikt zwischen Gott und Mensch oder auch zwischen Gott und Gott ist nur der Widerschein einer metaphysischen Tragödie. Das Theater ist göttliches Spiel, nicht nur weil man die Götterrolle für wahr hält, sondern weil man auch die göttlichen Wesenheiten selbst noch wahrnimmt. Mag diese geistige Wahrnehmung im Vegleich mit früheren Zeiten auch schon getrübt sein, so reicht sie aber immer noch aus, um in der Kunst ein lebendiges Abbild zu schaffen. Mit Recht hat darum in der Antike die Funktion eines Schutzpatrons für das Theater auch ein Gott inne: Dionysos.

Im Mittelalter verwandeln sich diese Wesenheiten dann schon teilweise in bestimmte Tugenden, Seelenqualitäten und Vernunftbegriffe.[1] Allegorische Rollen vertreten äußerlich diese als innerlich erfahrenen Qualitäten. Doch bleibt die Grenze noch fließend, insofern göttliche Wesenheiten, z.B. Engel, zwar fast ausschließlich innerlich erfahren, aber eben doch als von dem *eigenen* Innern getrennt existierend gesehen werden, mit anderen Worten, Engel sind keine Phantasieprodukte menschlicher Einbildungskraft. In der allegorischen Bibelauslegung, aber auch in den Mysterienspielen ist alles letztlich auf eine Vision des Universums gegründet, in dem zwei Welten existieren, die geistige und die physische

---

[1]Zum Verständnis des größeren Zusammenhangs vergleiche E. Cassirer: *Philosophie der symbolischen Formen*, besonders der 1.Teil ('Die Sprache') und 2.Teil ('Das mythische Denken'), Darmstadt: 1994 und O. Barfield: *Saving the Appearances. A Study in Idolatry*, Hannover: 1988.

Welt. Diese korrespondieren miteinander, weil Gott sie geschaffen hat. Die sichtbare Welt ist eine Offenbarung der unsichtbaren Welt, aber diese Offenbarung kommt nur durch göttliche Handlung zustande, es sei denn, sie geschehe auf dem Theater.

Im Barock tritt dann neben die Allegorie noch das Emblem, in dem sich bereits, als Grundstuktur, eine klare Trennung zwischen Physischem und Geistigem vollzieht. Was diese Grundstruktur angeht, so ist sie bis in die elementaren Bausteine der Dichtung nachweisbar. In der Vorliebe des Barocks für die Genetiv–Metapher wird sie sichtbar. Da ist auf der einen Seite das wahrnehmbare konkrete Bild und auf der anderen der rationale abstrakte Begriff, der sich im Unterschied zu anderen Begriffen auf nichts sinnlich Wahrnehmbares mehr bezieht.[2]

Man denke an emblematische Metaphern wie 'ein Ball des falschen Glücks' oder 'ein Totenbuch der Sterblichkeit'. Diese Verbindung von abstraktem Begriff, aus dem die göttlichen Wesenheiten schon ausgewandert sind, und dem sinnlich wahrnehmbaren Bild macht die Künstlichkeit eines Großteils des barocken Theaters aus. Valentin Wember faßt die Entwicklung so zusammen:

> Die ausdrückliche Beziehung von Bild und Begriff in den emblematischen Strukturen ist bei aller Bezugnahme eben doch zugleich ein Separieren der beiden Ebenen. Gerade indem Bild und Begriff ausdrücklich aufeinander bezogen werden, wird ihre Einheit aufgehoben. [...] Die Epoche des Barock ist [...] eine Übergangsepoche, in der die mittelalterlichen Allegorien allmählich in die rationalen Emblemstrukturen zerfallen.[3]

Was dem Zuschauer bleibt, ist der Dualismus von Bild und Begriff. Da die Begriffe aber nur innerlich erfaßt werden können, erwächst jetzt in den Philosophien, bei Descartes, bei Leibniz, bei Pascal, ein neues Selbstvertrauen, ein neues Bewußtsein des eigenen Ichs. Dieses ist ein Ich, das im *eigenen* Denken Begriffe bilden und diese der sinnlichen Welt vorschreiben kann. Noch der zentralperspektivisch angelegte Bühnenraum, dem wir dem Barocktheater verdanken, ist Ausdruck dieser neuen Perspektive, die das Ich jetzt auf die Welt wirft.

Freilich hat das Theater seit dem 18. Jahrhundert den als künstlich empfundenen Dualismus von Bild und abstraktem Begriff zu überwinden versucht. Dennoch ist nicht zu übersehen, daß es, vor allem im 20. Jahrhundert, eine Überwindung der rationalistischen Emblemstrukturen, allgemeiner der Trennung von Bild und Begriff, nicht nur, wenn man es einmal so ausdrücken darf, nach vorn, im Experiment mit neuen

---

[2]Ich folge hier den Überlegungen von V. Wember: 'Bausteine zu einer goetheanistischen Geschichte der neueren deutschen Literatur. Das 17. Jahrhundert. Teil 2', in: Tycho de Brache, *Jahrbuch für Goetheanismus* 1994, 268–286.

[3]Ebenda, S.281.

Ausdrucksmitteln, sondern auch nach hinten, also durch Rückbesinnung auf die allegorische Weltverfassung gegeben hat und gibt. In Österreich, zu Beginn dieses Jahrhunderts, hat Hugo von Hofmannsthal als einzelner diese Rückbesinnung versuchsweise unternommen. In seinem Theaterstück *Jedermann* knüpft er 1911 an das Mysterienspiel des Mittelalters an.[4] In der Postmoderne ist dies aber kein einzelnes Unternehmen mehr. Es wimmelt nur so von Allegorien: bei Umberto Eco, bei Sam Shepard, bei Botho Strauß und bei Joseph Beuys, bei letzterem schon bevor die Postmoderne ganz zur Blüte kam. Die Literaturtheoretiker Peter und Christa Bürger haben gar die Allegorie zu der exemplarischen Kunstform der Postmoderne erklären wollen.[5]

2.

Im Titel dieses Aufsatzes ist die Rede von der 'verlichteten Erzählung'. Diese Formel habe ich gewählt, um eine doppelte Opposition zu bezeichnen. Zunächst einmal soll dieses Theater der Erzählung nicht mit dem *erzählenden* oder *epischen Theater* Brechts oder Piscators verwechselt werden. Im epischen Theater dient bekanntlich die Übernahme von Erzählformen dazu, die Einheit von Ort, Zeit und Handlung aufzubrechen. Stoff und Handlungsvorgang werden so verfremdet, daß der Zuschauer aus der identifikatorischen Anteilnahme und dem direkten Erlebnismitvollzug herausgerissen wird. Der Zuschauer verwandelt sich zu einem kritisch abwägenden Betrachter, der durch Abstand haltende Analyse 'die Probe aufs Exempel' macht.[6] Das klassische Theater und dessen Zuschauer gelten Brecht als Gegner. Interne, aus der Natur des Erzählens selbst stammende Probleme stehen nicht im Vordergrund bei der Adaption von Erzählelementen in die Brechtsche Dramaturgie. Allerdings warnt Brecht vor den ideologischen Interessen, die sich hinter einer bestimmten Erzählung verbergen können, bzw. die durch das Erzählen verwirklicht werden sollen, weshalb ja im epischen Theater nicht nur die Handlung mit Hilfe der

---

[4]An Hofmannsthal wiederum hat Peter Handke mit seinen Stücken, laut K. Kathrein, angeknüpft: 'Die meisten seiner Stücke, so betont der Autor, seien allerdings auch *Jedermann*–Dramen.', in: 'Die herbe Lust, kein Wiederholungstäter zu sein. Einige Überlegungen zur Rezeption von Peter Handkes Bühnenwerken der achtziger Jahre', in: G. Fuchs/G. Melzer (Hg.): *Peter Handke. Die Langsamkeit der Welt*, Graz/Wien: 1993, S.162. Anknüpfungen an die allegorische Schreibweise und Weltauffassung allgemein finden sich auch bei Thomas Mann, Frank Wedekind und anderen, vgl. G. Kurz: *Metapher, Allegorie, Symbol*, Göttingen: 1997, S.54f.

[5]C. Bürger/P. Bürger: *Postmoderne. Alltag, Allegorie und Avantgarde*. Frankfurt/M.: 1987.

[6]O. F. Best: *Handbuch literarischer Fachbegriffe. Definitionen und Beispiele*, Frankfurt/M.: 1972, S.71.

Erzählung kritisch betrachtet werden soll, sondern auch umgekehrt die Erzählung durch eine Handlung oder eine andere Erzählung.

Bei Handke und Wenders dagegen dient das Theater — und ich rechne das Kino als Lichttheater dazu — der Darstellung derjenigen Probleme, die sich aus dem Erzählen selbst ergeben oder zumindest der Situation, in der sich das Erzählen heute befindet. Das Theater wird zu einem Repräsentationsraum für Erzählprobleme. Wo das Erzählen nicht mehr erzählerisch über sich Aufschluß geben kann, muß das Theater einspringen.

Weiterhin ist aber ein Theater der Erzählung auch so zu verstehen, daß hier auf das Theatralische, das Handlungsmäßige beim Erzählen aufmerksam gemacht werden soll. Die linguistische Theorie ist dem vor Jahren schon nahe gekommen, als sie von Sprechhandlungen und Erzählakten gesprochen hat.[7] Dieses, wenn man es einmal so sagen darf, implizite Theater des Erzählens, also jener Handlungsakt, den wir immer wieder ausüben, wenn wir erzahlen, kann explizit gemacht und dann auch auf die Bühne gebracht werden.

Die zweite Opposition, die ich mit dem Begriff eines Theaters der Erzählung aufrufen möchte, ist die zum klassischen Theater. In der klassischen Gattungspoetik bilden Theater und Erzählung, oder Drama und Epos, bekanntlich zwei verschiedene Gattungen. Das Theater ermöglicht es dem Zuschauer, einer Sequenz von Handlungen beizuwohnen, die sich als Geschehen zeitgleich vor seinen Augen entfaltet. Erzählelemente tauchen trotzdem im Handlungsgeschehen auf, sei es, daß die Vorgeschichte des eigentlichen zeitlichen Handlungseinsatzes erzählt werden soll, sei es, daß der biografische oder motivationale Hintergrund einzelner Figuren oder Figurengruppen erzählerisch verdeutlicht wird, oder sei es, daß ein außerhalb der Bühnenhandlung liegendes Geschehen, zeitgleich ablaufend oder nicht, vergegenwärtigt wird.

Gegenüber der eigentlichen Handlung behält die Erzählung jedoch stets eine untergeordnete Rolle: im Mittelpunkt des Theaters steht der Handlungsverlauf und das diesen Verlauf begleitende Miterleben der Zuschauer unter der Klammer einer Einheit von Zeit, Ort und Handlung.[8] An dieser Gewichtung hält nicht nur das antike Theater von Aeschylos, Sophokles und Euripides fest, sondern auch noch das Theater der Neuzeit bis ins späte 19. Jahrhundert hinein. Die Erzählung, vor allem wenn man an das homerische Epos denkt, macht aber ihrerseits auch Gebrauch von Theaterelementen, um zum Beispiel eine der Vergangenheit (die häufigste

[7]J. Searle: *Speechacts*, Cambridge: 1971. Vergleiche auch J. Halstead: 'Peter Handke's Sprechstücke and Speech Act Theory', in: *Text and Performance Quarterly*, 1990 (Juli), 10/3, S.183–193.

[8]Vergleiche M. Fuhrmann: *Dichtungstheorie der Antike*. Darmstadt: 1992, besonders Kapitel 1.

Erzählform) angehörende Episode durch Wiedergabe von Dialogen zu aktualisieren. Mit den wörtlich wiedergegebenen Dialogen zwischen den Erzählfiguren wird zudem beim Zuhörer oder Leser eine größere Anteilnahme am Erzählten, eine größere Vergegenwärtigungsleistung erzielt. Lediglich die Stimme des Eposerzählers, in klassischer Terminologie: des Sängers, schlägt dabei, als akustisches Element, eine Brücke zur gesprochenen Sprache, die zum Theaterhandeln gehört. *Wer* aber handelt und spricht, *wie* die Person gekleidet ist und *wo* genau sie im Raum und *auf welche Weise* dort positioniert ist, das bleibt in der Erzählung einerseits den Beschreibungskünsten des Erzählers und andererseits der Einbildungskraft des Zuhörers überlassen. Theater und Erzählung sind, trotz Überschneidungen, letztlich zwei getrennte Welten.

Peter Handkes und Wim Wenders Theater der Erzählung hält an dieser Trennung zwischen Theater und Erzählung nicht mehr fest, um damit doch noch nicht zum epischen Theater Brechts oder Piscators zurückzukehren. So setzt der Film *Himmel über Berlin* (*Wings of Desire*), für den Handke und Wenders zusammen das Drehbuch geschrieben haben[9], scheinbar mit einer Erzählstimme ein, die in geradezu klassischer Manier die Präliminarien für eine Märchengeschichte im Ton der Brüder Grimm macht:

> Als das Kind Kind war, ging es mit hängenden Armen, wollte, der Bach sei ein Fluß, der Fluß sei ein Strom und diese Pfütze das Meer. Als das Kind Kind war, wußte es nicht, daß es Kind war, alles war ihm beseelt, und alle Seelen waren eins. Als das Kind Kind war, hatte es von nichts eine Meinung, hatte keine Gewohnheit, saß oft im Schneidersitz, lief aus dem Stand, hatte einen Wirbel im Haar und machte kein Gesicht beim Fotografieren.[10]

Doch handelt es sich hier keinesfalls um den traditionellen Erzähler, denn die Kamera zeigt die simultan geschehende Niederschrift dieser Worte auf ein Stück Papier mit Hilfe eines von einer Hand gehaltenen Füllers. Im weiteren Verlauf des Films wird klar, daß die Stimme dem Engel Damiel gehört, dessen Aufgabe oder Natur es ist, sich schriftliche Notizen über das Geschehen auf Erden zu machen. Nach der eben zitierten Eröffnungsszene, taucht in der zweiten Kameraeinstellung dann aus der Vogelperspektive das Bild einer Stadt auf, es handelt sich hier um Berlin. Überblendet wird dieses Bild vom Bild eines Auges: der Zuschauer sieht das folgende Geschehen mit dem Blick von oben, aus der Perspektive der beiden Engel, die zu den Hauptakteuren des Films zählen. Es stellt sich mithin eine 'personale Erzählsituation her', wenn ich hier einmal Franz Stanzels mittlerweile

---

[9]Zu Peter Handkes Anteil an dem Film siehe C. Fusco: 'Angels, History and Poetic Fantasy. An Interview with Wim Wenders', in *Cineaste*, 1988, 16/4, S.17.

[10] W. Wenders/P. Handke: *Der Himmel über Berlin. Ein Filmbuch* Frankfurt/M.: (Suhrkamp) 1992, S.4.

legendäre Kategorisierung der Erzählsituationen benutzen darf.[11] Der
Zuschauer erhält Einblick in die Innenperspektive der engelischen Weltsicht.
Was aber sofort die Erzählsituation verkompliziert, ist der Umstand,
daß die Standortgebundenheit einer personalen Perspektive, in der die Welt
ja subjektiv wahrgenommen wird, daß diese Standortgebundenheit sich
auflöst, weil die Engel mit objektiver Richtigkeit gerade die
Innenperspektive aller menschlichen Wesen einnehmen können. Die Engel
können in anderen Worten die menschlichen Gedanken und Gefühle, auch
als unausgesprochene oder überhaupt unausgedrückte wahrnehmen. Der
Zuschauer sieht sich in die Position des auktorialen oder traditionell
olympischen Erzählers versetzt. Er sitzt, wie einst Homer, der als Erzähler
unter den Göttern des Olymps saß und von oben herab, vom Olymp aus,
beides erkannte und künstlerisch wiedergab: nämlich die
schicksalswirkenden Gedanken der Götter einerseits und das Handeln and
innere Denken und Fühlen der trojanischen und griechischen Helden
andererseits.

Weiterhin verkompliziert sich die Situation noch dadurch, daß
Momente der Ich–Erzählsituation aufgenommen werden, insofern die
beobachtenden Engel nicht nur die innere Gedankenwelt der Menschen
wahrnehmen können, sondern diese bis zu einem gewissen Grade auch
beeinflussen können.[12] Damit ist die traditionelle Rolle der Engelwesen
angesprochen, die schon seit vielen hunderten, ja tausenden von Jahren
bekannt ist: Engel gelten als Schutzengel und höheres Selbst des Menschen.
Es ist hier nicht der Ort, in eine Debatte einzutreten, inwieweit bei Wenders
und Handke Motive aus der Bibel, aus theologischem und mystischem
Schrifttum und aus der Volkslegende übernommen worden sind.[13]
Entscheidend ist vielmehr festzuhalten, daß der Zuschauer in eine
Sichtweise eingeführt wird, in der Innen– und Außenperspektive,
Seinsbereich des Erzählers und Seinsbereich der Erzählfiguren, Subjekt und
Objekt, ständig als getrennt, aber doch wieder als identisch erfahren
werden.[14] Diese Sichtweise gleicht in manchem der des Kindes. Die schon
zitierten Zeilen über die Weltsicht des Kindes, mit denen der Film einsetzt,
erweisen sich daher eben auch als eine Initiation, als eine Anweisung, sich
wieder in die Welt des Kindes zu versetzen, wo weder die klare Trennung

---

[11]F. K. Stanzel: *Theorie des Erzählens*, Göttingen: 1985.
[12]Weitere Komplikationen der Erzählsituation werden aufgezeigt bei D. Berghahn:
""...womit sonst kann man heute erzählen als mit Bildern?" Images and Stories in Wim
Wenders' "Der Himmel über Berlin" and "In weiter Ferne, so nah!" in: J. Morrison/F.
Krobb (Hg.): *Text into Image: Image into Text*, Amsterdam: 1994, S.329–338.
[13]Vergleiche E. Gauldie: Flights of Angels, in: *History Today* 1992
(Dezember), S.13–20.
[14]Vergleiche vor allem die Kapitel 4, 5 und 6 in: F. K. Stanzel, op. cit.

der Welt in Subjekt und Objekt, noch die in individuierte, vereinzelte Seelen existiert. Was aus der Sicht des Engels Damiel eine Beschreibung des Wesens des Kindes ist — und nur was die Essenz, das Wesen der Dinge ausmacht, halten die Engel ja fest — das ist für den Zuschauer die Anweisung, wieder die Wahrnehmungsweise des Kindes einzunehmen. Nur mit den Augen des Kindes läßt sich scheinbar dieser Film verstehen, läßt er sich überhaupt erst sehen. Die sich gleich anschließenden Szenen bestätigen übrigens die Nähe zwischen Engeldasein und Kinddasein: es sind in der Regel eher Kinder, nicht Erwachsene, die die Engel wahrnehmen können. Im Kontext der eingangs gemachten Überlegungen läßt sich aber die filmische Wiedergabe der Niederschrift jenes Textes, der die Sehweise des Kindes vorführt, genauer verstehen als Sehanweisung oder Einschreibung in den Film, eben in der Art einer *Inscriptio*, wie man sie an allegorisch–emblematischen Kunstwerken findet. An sich ergibt es ja keinen Sinn, einen geschriebenen Text abzufilmen, es wäre so, als wenn man auf der Bühne den Sprechtext auf eine Tafel schreibt, anstatt ihn als Teil der Bühnenhandlung sprechen zu lassen. Sinnvoll wird dieser Vorgang aber vielleicht doch, wenn man ihn eben als *Inscriptio* versteht, als begriffliche Aussage, die ihrerseits das Bild verständlich macht und die vom Bild aus veranschaulicht wird. Die insgeheim allegorische Verfassung des Films *Himmel über Berlin* zeigt sich bereits in der Eingangsszene. Aber nicht nur dieser Film, sondern auch eine Reihe von anderen Filmen und Theaterstücken, für die Wim Wenders und Peter Handke verantwortlich zeichnen, sind allegorischer Natur.

Für die engelhafte Wahrnehmung sind die Menschen lebende Allegorien. Nicht die absolute Individualität nehmen die Engel an einzelnen Menschen oder auch an einzelnem Geschehen wahr, sondern den Typus, das Typische, das ewige Wesen, die unvergängliche Gestalt. So wird auch nicht ein Kind als einzelnes charakterisiert, sondern in seiner Kindlichkeit, eben als der Typus Kind. Wird Physisches erfaßt, dann bleibt es als solches bestehen, wie folgende Aufzeichnung der Engel verdeutlicht:

> Eine Passantin, die mitten im Regen den Schirm zusammenklappte und sich naß werden ließ ... Ein Schüler, der seinem Lehrer beschrieb, wie ein Farn aus der Erde wächst, und der staunende Lehrer ... Eine Blinde, die nach ihrer Uhr tastete, als sie mich spürte ... Es ist herrlich, nur geistig zu leben und Tag für Tag für die Ewigkeit vor den Leuten rein, was geistig ist, zu bezeugen.[15]

Die Engel kennen nicht den Umweg einer Erfassung des Wesens der Dinge, des Geistigen, über eine Zusammenstellung und Analyse von Erfahrungen und Sinneseindrücken, die schließlich die Bildung eines Begriffes erlauben. Für die Engel ist die Essenz *sofort* einsehbar, in ihrer

---

[15]W. Wenders/P. Handke: *Der Himmel über Berlin. Ein Filmbuch*, op. cit., S.19.

Welt herrscht Simultanität im Verhältnis zur Erkenntnis. Die Engel sehen auf einen Blick, was sich für den Menschen nur in der Abfolge von Blicken und der oft mühsamen Analyse des Erblickten ergibt.[16] Sukzessive Enthüllung der Wahrheit als Stückwerk beim Menschen steht gegen simultane Offenbarung der ganzen Wahrheit, wie es nur den Engeln möglich ist. Die Engel unterliegen nicht den Bedingungen der Zeit, für den Menschen ist die Zeit absolute Bedingung der Wahrheitsfindung, denn das Erkennen der Wahrheit ist ein prozessuales Geschehen; die Erkenntnis der Wahrheit braucht Zeit, und die Bibel sagt ja auch mit Recht vom Meister der Lüge, also dem Gegensatz der Wahrheit auf Erden, daß 'der Teufel keine Zeit habe.'[17]

Die Schwierigkeit, die sich hier allerdings für den Filmtheatererzähler ergibt, besteht darin, daß eine Geschichte der Engel nicht gezeigt werden kann, weil Engel eben keine Geschichte haben. Was der Film denn auch in der ersten Hälfte vorführt, scheint nichts anderes zu sein, als eine lose Versammlung von Episoden und Dialogen, aber, was die Engel anbelangt, nicht die Entwicklung eines Themas oder 'Plots'.

Daß später dennoch Entwicklung geschieht, ist just dem Zustand der Geschichtslosigkeit zu verdanken. Einer der beiden Engel wird der Ewigkeit überdrüssig und entwickelt Verlangen nach einer irdischen Verkörperung.[18] Dieses wachsende Verlangen hebt aber nur umso schärfer den Unterschied zwischen engelischer und menschlicher Wahrnehmung und Existenz hervor.

Der Zuschauer wird, gleich von Anfang an, in eine variable Wahrnehmungsweise, die verschiedenste Erzählhaltungen übergangslos miteinander verknüpft, gleichzeitig wird ihm aber der Zusammenhang zwischen den von den Engeln wahrgenommen Phänomenen vorenthalten. Lediglich das erwähnte Thema des wachsenden Verlangens macht hier eine Ausnahme. Ansonsten scheinen die Engel ziellos von einer Begegnung zur nächsten zu wandeln, stets auf die innersten Gedanken der Menschen hörend. Was immer Gegenstand des menschlichen Bewußtseins werden kann, es wird von ihnen erfaßt. Und wie auch immer trivial der Anlaß sein mag, der dieses Bewußtsein eines Menschen zum inneren Sprechen oder Monologisieren bringt, in diesem Sprechen erscheint etwas vom Wesen dieses Menschen. Besondere Aufmerksamkeit aber erweisen die Engel diesen Selbstgesprächen und Gedankenfolgen im menschlichen Bewußtsein

---

[16]Vergleiche auch W. Wenders: *The Logic of Images. Essays and Conservations* London/Boston: 1991, S.79: 'And if anyone lies, the angel can right away hear the difference between the thought and the spoken word.'

[17]Vergleiche H. Blumenberg: *Lebenszeit und Weltenzeit*, Frankfurt/M.: S.71.

[18]Zu der Natur dieses Verlangens vgl. A. Kuzniar: Suture in/Suturing in Literature and Film. Handke and Wenders, in: I. Hoesterey/U. Weisstein: *Intertextuality. German Literatue and Visual Art from the Renaissance to the Twentieth Century*, Columbia: 1993, S.213 [201–217].

nur dann, wenn sich zeigt, daß der betreffende Mensch in eine schwierige oder ernst zu nehmende Situation geraten ist. Ein Verweilen der Engel, so scheint es, setzt voraus, daß etwas Wesentliches im Menschen in Gefahr geraten ist. Hier gilt dann: So wie der erste Teil des Films in schwarz und weiß gedreht worden ist, so liegt für den Zuschauer Einsamkeit, Sorge und Verzweifelung auf der einen und Hoffnung und neue Zuversicht auf der anderen Seite, wie schwarz und weiß, offen vor ihm. Die engelische Perspektive, die vom Zuschauer eingeübt wird, ist daher nicht eine unter vielen, sondern stets die Totale. Das innere Wesen der Menschen soll betrachtet werden, nicht sein Auftreten in der Zeit ist entscheidend. (Selbst bei der Figur des Peter Falk, einem früheren Engel, wird das noch spürbar: Er zeichnet sein Gegenüber in genauer Beobachtung, um das Wesentliche der Erscheinung festzuhalten.) Der Zuschauer wird angehalten zu einer ständigen Verinnerlichungsleistung; das physisch Erfaßte gibt Raum für das innerlich Erfaßte, den wahren inneren Menschen. Traditionell gesehen ist eine solche Sichtweise, nach dem Zeugnis der großen Religionen, erst möglich nach dem Tode, wenn die vom Körper befreite Seele, ohne physische Restriktionen und den Umweg über die Sinne, die Wahrheit erfaßt.

3.

In Handkes am stärksten von Österreich geprägtem Bühnenstück, dem lyrischen Drama *Über die Dörfer*, übrigens 1982 von Wim Wenders in der Bühnenfassung uraufgeführt, hält die Figur der *Nova* die Zuschauer wie folgt an:

> Immer wieder wird einer von euch der lebende Tote sein müssen: [...] Schließt die Augen, und aus dem Nachbild der Sonne entsteht der neue Kontinent [...]. Gehend versäumt nicht die Schwellen zwischen dem einen Bereich und dem nächsten: erst mit der Erkenntnis der Übergänge erhebt sich der Wind des anderen Raums, und die kreisenden Raben sind keine Unglücksvögel, sondern bringen euch die Speise.[19]

Während die Engel den Ausgang von der physischen Sonne nicht brauchen, um ins Zentrum der inneren Wahrheit zu treten, braucht die menschliche Einbildungskraft und Wahrheitserkenntnis durchaus diesen Ausgang: 'Schließt die Augen, und aus dem Nachbild der Sonne entsteht der neue Kontinent.'[20] Während die leibfreie, übernatürliche Erkenntnis schon im Licht wandelt, muß die menschliche, erdgebundene, über die Sinne vermittelte Erfahrung ins Licht gebracht, eben verlichtet werden.

---

[19]P.Handke: 'Über die Dörfer', in: ders. *Theaterstücke in einem Band*, Frankfurt/M.: 1992, S.447.
[20]Ebenda.

214 – Fritz Wefelmeyer

Das Bühnenstück *Über die Dörfer* kann im Ganzen als eine solche Verlichtungsschule, als ein Übungsfeld, als eine ermahnende Handlungsanweisung verstanden werden, die darin besteht, den geistigen Zusammenhang zwischen den Menschen, aber auch deren Zusammenhang mit den physischen Weltereignissen zu suchen. Die menschlich irdische Welt soll so in das Reich der geistigen Wahrheit überführt werden.[21] Das Bühnenstück läßt an dieser dem Menschen wesensmäßig zukommenden, nur innerlich zu vollziehenden Aufgabe der Vergeistigung oder Verlichtung keinen Zweifel. Schon die Gattungsbestimmung, die Handke seinem Stück mitgegeben hat, läßt diese Richtung erkennen: er nennt das Stück im Untertitel *Dramatisches Gedicht*, um im dramatischen Handeln jene Innerlichkeit und Subjektivität zum Vorschein zu bringen, für die gemeinhin das Gedicht, vor allem in der Form des *lyrischen Ichs*, zum Statthalter wird. Man könnte auch sagen, daß das Handeln auf der Bühne zu einer Verdichtungsleistung führt, die als inneren Vorgang der Zuschauer übernehmen muß, wenn er überhaupt das Stück, Handke würde wohl sagen, wenn er überhaupt sein Leben verstehen will.

Der Film *Himmel über Berlin* läßt jedoch den Zuschauer, zumindest in der ersten Hälfte, in einer gewissen Ratlosigkeit zurück, weil er in der Teilnahme an der Wahrnehmung der Engelwesen nur die Differenz zu der eigenen, den Umweg über die sinnliche Erfahrung gehende Erkenntnis sieht. Nebenbei bemerkt, diese Ratlosigkeit drückt sich auch im Zweifel an der wahrscheinlichen Existenz solcher Wesen aus, eben weil beim heutigen Stand der Bewußtseinsentwicklung Engelwesen nicht mehr wie noch im Mittelalter und auch noch in der Renaissance direkt wahrgenommen werden können. Die Darstellungen der Engel in der bildenden Kunst dieser Zeit geben ja ein eindringliches Zeugnis davon, wie sehr noch die Präsenz dieser Wesen im Leben empfunden wurde. Die heutige Geisteserkenntnis nimmt in der Regel den Umweg über die Analyse sinnlicher Erfahrungen, sie kann nicht mehr auf Empfindungen aufbauen, die heute nur noch von einer Minderheit geteilt werden.

4.

Während nun der Zuschauer die Filmereignisse nicht mehr als Erzählung wahrnimmt, sondern nur noch als Aufreihung beispielhafter Situationen, die die Erkenntnisweise der Engelwesen sinnfällig machen sollen, wird er genau mit jener Figur konfrontiert, die als Erzähler geradezu exemplarisch die Geschichte des Zusammenhanges von überirdischen und menschlichen

---

[21]Man hat daher das Stück auch zurecht in die Nähe der Mysterienstücke gerückt, vgl. E. Hammer: 'Rätsel fürs Fest. Zu Peter Handkes dramatischem Gedicht 'Über die Dörfer', in: G. Melzer/J. Tükel (Hg.) *Peter Handke. Die Arbeit am Glück*, Königstein/Ts: 1985, S.99.

Wesen aufgezeichnet hat: nämlich der Erzähler und Sänger Homer. Dieser führt den Zuschauer direkt in das Erzählproblem, mit dem der Zuschauer sich indirekt bei der Beobachtung der von den Engelwesen ausgeführten Handlungen beschäftigt hat, nämlich in das Problem, wo der Zusammenhang zwischen den einzelnen Szenen und Kameraeinstellungen gegeben ist. Allerdings wird der Zuschauer dabei auf den größeren sozialen und politisch historischen Kontext gestoßen, der das den Menschen vorbehaltene Erzählen heute schwierig macht. Die Entfremdung in den Lebensverhältnissen und die Vereinzelung der Menschen in der Gesellschaft hat dem Sänger die Schar der Zuhörer gestohlen, die sich einst um ihn ringten, um seinem Vortrag zu lauschen. Stellte sich früher in gemeinsamem Zuhören das durch den Sänger vermittelte Band einer gemeinsamen Geschichte und geschichtlich vermittelten Identität her, so ist der moderne Zuhörer zum vereinzelten Leser geworden, dessen Prototyp die für sich dahin studierenden Leser in einer großen öffentlichen Bibliothek sind. Es ist denn auch bezeichnend, daß der Zuschauer dem Erzähler Homer zum ersten Mal in einer solchen Bibliothek begegnet, wo niemand seinen Worten zuhört und seine Rede nichts anderes ist als ein murmelndes Selbstgespräch, das nur zu den Engelwesen durchdringt. Und ebenso bezeichnend ist es, daß diese Wesen, die doch sonst den gefährdeten Menschen, denen sie im Film begegnen, die Kraft zur inneren Aufrichtung verleihen, dem Sänger keine Hilfe geben können.

Aber Homer ist noch mit einer weiteren Schwierigkeit konfrontiert: die äußere, also physische Realität von Berlin erlaubt dem Erzählen keinen Anhalt mehr, um von Erzählstation zu Erzählstation einen Faden zu spinnen. Die Nazizeit, der 2. Weltkrieg und die Teilung der Stadt nach dem Krieg haben wichtige Spuren zerstört, denen der Erzähler folgen könnte. So räsonniert der Sänger, während er in der Nähe des Potsdamer Platzes an der Mauer entlang durch desolates, unwegsames Gelände wandert, wie folgt:

> Ich kann den Potsdamer Platz nicht finden! Nein, ich meine hier ... Das kann er doch nicht sein! Denn am Potsdamer Platz, da war doch das Cafe Josti. Nachmittags habe ich mich da unterhalten und einen Kaffee getrunken, das Publikum beobachtet, vorher meine Zigarre geraucht bei Löhse und Wolff, ein renommiertes Tabakgeschäft, gleich hier gegenüber. Also, das kann er hier nicht sein, der Potsdamer Platz, nein! Man trifft keinen, den man fragen kann.[22]

Und so geht es in diesem zwischen Erinnerung und Desorientierung schwankenden Räsonnement weiter. Doch will Homer sich trotz Eingeständnis des verlorenen Postens, auf dem das Erzählen steht, von der Suche nicht abhalten lassen:

---

[22]W.Wenders/P.Handke: *Der Himmel über Berlin. Ein Filmbuch*, op. cit., S.58.

Aber ich gebe so lange nicht auf, bis ich den Potsdamer Platz gefunden habe! Wo sind meine Helden! Wo seid ihr, meine Kinder? Nenne mir, Muse, den armen, unsterblichen Sänger, der, von seinen sterblichen Zuhörern verlassen, die Stimme verlor ... wie er vom Engel der Erzählung zum unbeachteten oder verlachten Leiermann draußen an der Schwelle zum Niemandsland wurde.[23]

Was hier über Berlin gesagt wird, ließe sich auch auf ähnliche Weise über die Landschaftszerstörung in den österreichischen Alpen sagen, die in *Über die Dörfer* thematisiert wird. Während aber die Figur der Nova in *Über die Dörfer* noch die Kraft hat, sich durch ihre Rede eine Zuhörerschaft zu schaffen, wird der Sänger Homer im *Himmel über Berlin* aus der menschlichen Gesellschaft an die 'Schwelle zum Niemandsland' gedrängt. Der 'Engel der Erzählung', eine an das Barock gemahnende Genetivmetapher, ist vom Sänger an das Filmtheater übergegangen. Es allein scheint noch die Kraft zu haben, eine Zuschauerschaft zu versammeln. Und es scheint auch der Ort zu sein, wo die Krise des Erzählers dargestellt werden kann. Denn nicht nur vereinsamt der Erzähler, er kann auch den Zusammenhang, den Erzählfaden, nicht mehr herstellen. Statt Handlungen zu erzählen, werden die Handlungen nun gezeigt. Im Falle des Erzählers durchaus als tragische Handlung, denn der Film endet mit Homers Aussage, daß die Menschen den Erzähler brauchen, 'wie sonst nichts auf der Welt.' Nicht zufällig ist der Film daher auch von den Autoren in Akte aufgeteilt worden — was im übrigen noch einmal den Charakter des Kinos als (Licht)Theater unterstreicht.

Freilich verliert, paradoxerweise, das Filmtheater doch auch seine andere Kunstform nicht: die der Erzählung. Denn wie der Erzähler zum Handelnden wird, so wird er, so werden seine Erzählprobleme genausogut zum Erzählgegenstand. Der Erzähler wird erzählt — neben einer ganzen Palette anderer Gegenstände. Der Zuschauer im *Himmel über Berlin* wird im folgenden nämlich mit einer Vielfalt von historischen Dokumenten und Einzelszenen konfrontiert. Gezeigt wird die wachsende Liebe zu einer Trapezkünstlerin, die der Engel Damiel hegt; daneben treten Stadtansichten und dann Szenen, die sich um die Erstellung eines Films über die Nazizeit drehen. Der Schauspieler Peter Falck, ein früherer Engel, tritt auf, und schließlich verfolgt die Kamera noch den Sprung in die Zeit, zu dem sich der Engel Damiel entschlossen hat, um, versuchsweise, ein menschliches Dasein zu führen. Gleichzeitig wird der Zuschauer aber immer wieder auch aufgefordert, die Totalperspektive des im rein Geistigen verbleibenden anderen Engels einzunehmen.

Während also dem Zuschauer durch die Engelperspektive immer wieder die Möglichkeit geboten wird, das innere Nachdenken und Erleben

---

[23]Ibid., S.59.

der menschlichen Akteure kennenzulernen, bleibt er völlig ohne Hilfe der Engel, wenn es darum geht, den Handlungszusammenhang zu erfassen: der Zuschauer ist auf sich selbst verwiesen. Das Erzählen nämlich, das Zusammenhang stiften kann, gehört ganz in den menschlichen Bereich: der Mensch selbst ist, wie Handke und Wenders sagen, der 'Engel der Erzählung'. Doch besagt die Metapher auch, daß durch das Erzählen dem Menschen eine engelgleiche Qualität zukommt. Der Erzähler erhebt sich über die materiell physische Geschichte, so wie es die Engel in ihren Wahrnehmungen tun. Fakten und Ereignisse stammen aus der irdischen Welt, deren Zusammenhang aber sieht nur, wer mehr sieht als Fakten und Ereignisse.

Diese Bestimmung eins Engels der Erzählung ließe sich als eine Eingrenzung, wenn nicht gar Alternative, der Konzeption eines 'Engels der Geschichte' deuten, die Walter Benjamin entwickelt hat und die der Film ausdrücklich zitiert.[24] Benjamin sehe, so besagt das Zitat im Film, einen Engel, genauer den *Angelus novus* des Paul Klee, als 'Allegorie des Rückblicks auf die Geschichte'. Bei Benjamin führt die Totalperspektive, in der der Engel mit Schrecken auf die Geschichte zurückblickt, noch direkt auf einen, wenn auch bitteren Sinn der Geschichte. Dieser Engel ist aber laut Diagnose des Sängers Homer im *Himmel über Berlin* an den Rand gedrängt worden. Der Film ist eher die Suche nach einem Sinn, denn dessen Aufweis. Sinn und Zusammenhang sind nicht gegeben, sondern müssen gestiftet werden.[25]

Der Kontext, in dem das Zitat über Benjamins Engel auftritt, unterstützt diese Deutung ebenfalls. Das Zitat endet nämlich mit einem Doppelpunkt, der durch ein neues Zitat gefüllt wird. Dieses Mal mit dem poetischen Text eines anderen Autors, allem Anschein nach aus einer Erzählung genommen. Der Text nimmt inhaltlich überhaupt keinen Bezug auf Benjamins Thema. Diese beiden Texte wie auch eine Reihe anderer Texte werden jeweils von einem anderen Besucher der Berliner Staatsbibliothek still gelesen. Lediglich die Engel, die von einem Leser zum nächsten weiterstreichen und deren innerliches Lesen wahrnehmen können, bilden den Zusammenhang zwischen den Texten.

---

[24]Vergleiche auch den Hinweis auf Benjamin in W. Wenders: *The Logic of Images*, a.a.O., S.77.

[25]Insofern der Film nicht einen Sinn aufweist, sondern zur Sinnsuche anregt, teile ich auch nicht J. Habermas' Bedenken: 'Verklärt der Film nicht das Außeralltägliche auf Kosten der trivialeren Erfahrungen, aus denen wir lernen? Entwertet er nicht zugunsten eines Seinsgeschicks die Kontingenzen, die die Kräfte des Ich herausfordern? Verwischt er nicht den Unterschied zwischen Benjamin und Heidegger — zwischen profaner Erleuchtung und einer gegen das Profane gerichteten Erweckung?' in J. Habermas, *Die nachholende Revolution. Kleine Politische Schriften VII*, Frankfurt/M: 1990, S.17.

Die die Geschichte umfassende, die Körpergrenzen überspringende Zusammenschau aller Zeiten und die Einsicht in die Motive und das Nachdenken der Zeitgenossen spannt im Zuschauer die Kräfte an, nach einem Zusammenhang zu suchen. Der Film muß zwangsläufig den Zuschauer überfordern, doch entläßt er ihn keineswegs aus der Pflicht, nach jenen verbindlichen Elementen zu forschen, die das Geschehen in die Einheit einer verstehbaren Geschichte bringen können. Der Film endet, wie am Anfang, mit einer Notiz, einer Einschreibung, die den Film lesbar machen kann, ohne jedoch zu verraten, wie dies tatsächlich auch geschehen soll. Die Notiz des zum Menschen gewordenen Engelwesen lautet, am Ende des Films: 'Ich weiß jetzt, was kein Engel weiß.' Obwohl sich die Aussage zunächst auf die Liebesbeziehung zwischen Mann und Frau bezieht, kann sie doch vielleicht auf die Filmhandlung übertragen werden: Nur als menschliche Verkörperung ist dem Engel die Erfahrung möglich geworden, daß zwei so unterschiedliche Wesen wie Mann und Frau, so unterschiedlich wie die einzelnen Begebenheiten im Film und auch so unterschiedlich wie Stücke einer zerbrochenen und mit sich zerfallenen Gesellschaft und Geschichte, sich zu einem ganzem verbinden, zu *einer* Geschichte verbinden können.[26]

5.

In Handkes Bühnenstück Das *Spiel vom Fragen oder Die Reise zum Sonoren Land*, etwa zwei bis drei Jahre nach dem *Himmel über Berlin* geschrieben, wird dieses Motiv einer Suche nach Zusammenhang noch weiterentwickelt. Hatte der Film den Zuschauer in die Anthropologie der menschlichen Erkenntnisweise eingeführt, indem er diese durch den kontrastiven Vergleich mit der der Engelwesen deutlich herausstellte, so wird jetzt in diesem Bühnenstück die dem Menschen gemäße Weise des Fragens untersucht, denn die Frage ist ja der Beginn einer Suche nach Erkenntnis.[27] Was ist der Mensch, wie verbindet er sich mit anderen, persönlicher gefragt, wer bist du, wer bin ich, wie kann eine Verbindung

---

[26]Kritisch dagegen sehen R. P. Kolker and P. Beicken die Erfahrung des zum Mensch gewordenen Engel: *The Films of Wim Wenders. Cinema as Vision and Desire* Cambridge: 1993, S.157 ff.

[27]In einem Interview aus demselben Jahr, in dem *Himmel über Berlin* ins Kino kam, hat Handke deutlich gemacht, daß ein Theater des Fragens auf den Verlust der Zuschauerschaft, wie sie das antike Theater noch kannte, reagiert. Der Film konstatiert diesen Verlust im Hinblick auf die antike Zuhörerschaft: 'Die Übereinstimmung des attischen Publikums, dieser gemeinsame Traumraum — das haben wir nicht mehr. Wir sind kein Kreis von Zuschauern mehr. [...] Wenn man das aber nicht mehr erreichen kann, dann muß man es im Grunde fast aufgeben. Oder man muß ganz, ganz von vorne anfangen, man muß anfangen zu fragen.' Zitiert nach T. Hennig: *Intertextualität als ethische Dimension. Peter Handkes Ästhetik 'nach Auschwitz'* Würzburg: 1996, S.78.

zwischen uns, wie kann eine Verbindung zwischen mir und der Welt hergestellt werden?

Wieder tauchen allegorisch verfaßte Rollen auf, so heißt zum Beispiel eine Figur 'ein Spielverderber' und eine andere 'ein Mauerschauer' und eine dritte 'ein Einheimischer', aber während diese Figuren zunächst noch durch ihre Bezeichnung oder Namen dem Leser eine Inskription vor Augen halten, mit deren Hilfe sich die Handlungen dieser Figuren im Stück aufschlüsseln und verstehen lassen, so zeigt sich bald, daß gerade die besonderen Rollen, die diese Figuren spielen sollen, so ambivalent und vielschichtig sind, daß die Namen nur in die Irre zu führen scheinen. So wird zum Beispiel die Opposition zwischen Mauerschauer und Spielverderber, also zwischen dem, der über die eingemauerte Wahrnehmung sich erheben kann und der dem Ernst und der Spielunlust der anderen entkommen ist, und jenem anderen, der jedes Spiel verderben muß und der das Spielerische im Dasein, das Leichte und Freie nicht ertragen kann, später gerade umgedreht. Das Wechselspiel zwischen beiden Seiten lautet zunächst so:

> Mauerschauer: Die Fichte dort, sie lebt!
> Spielverderber: Die hat man sicher nur gepflanzt, um sie sterben zu sehen [...]
> Mauerschauer: Aber schau doch, die Mitternachtssonne. Die Inseln im Strom. Das Wacholderland. Ist es denn nicht auch für dich schön hier?
> Spielverderber: Ja, vorderhand noch ist es schön. Schön wie an letzten Tagen. Aber was kommt dann? Stell Dir einmal vor: die ganze Zeit hier. Der Winter, der Frost, der Schnee ...
> Mauerschauer: Wie ist es schön, wenn es schneit: auf die Stirn, die Lippen, den Puls.
> Spielverderber: Der Zug, in dem wir unterwegs sind, wird stecken bleiben. Die Heizung ausfallen. Die Füße Frostbeulen bekommen [...]
> Mauerschauer: Dort sind zwei richtige Liebende. Und mit ihnen wiegt sich die Welt.
> Spielverderber: Ja, vorderhand noch.
> Mauerschauer: Und wie schön sie lachen.
> Spielverderber: An ihrem Lachen sieht man schon ihr baldiges Weinen.[28]

Im weiteren Verlauf des Stückes zeigt sich dann aber, daß die eine Figur auch ihre Oppositionsfigur in sich enthält und über kurzem erlebt der Zuschauer eine völlige Rollenumkehrung, die aber mitnichten zu einer Aufgabe der allegorisierenden Rollenbezeichnungen 'Mauerschauer' und 'Spielverderber' führt. Diese bleiben erhalten. Der Zuschauer erkennt, daß

---

[28]'Das Spiel vom Fragen oder Die Reise zum Sonoren Land', in: P. Handke: *Theaterstücke in einem Band*, Frankfurt/M.: 1992 S.491 ff.

die typisierende Bezeichnung ihren Gegentypus schon mit sich bringt, so daß die Trennung zwischen beiden nicht absolut ist.[29]

Die Fragen allerdings, die der eine Typus an den anderen richtet wie in dem eben zitierten Beispiel, sind Fragen, mit denen dem Gesprächspartner die eigene Sichtweise aufgezwungen wird. Dies geschieht bisweilen auf recht subtile Weise wie zum Beispiel durch Lenkung der Vorstellungskraft des Partners in eine bestimmte Richtung, oder durch eine Frage, die auf eine Bestätigung der eigenen Position abzielt:

> Mauerschauer: Ist es denn nicht auch für dich schön hier?
> Spielverderber: Ja, vorderhand noch ist es schön. Schön wie an letzten Tagen. Aber was kommt dann? Stell Dir einmal vor: die ganze Zeit hier. Der Winter, der Frost, der Schnee ...[30]

Handke beläßt es aber dabei nicht. Er leitet seine Zuschauer an, nach solchen Fragen zu suchen, die Figuren vom Typus des Mauerbeschauers oder des Spielverderbers wirkliche Selbsterkenntnis und Erkenntnis der Welt ermöglichen würden. Durch die richtige Frage würde eine solche Figur ins Licht der Erkenntnis gestellt, würde ihr Weltverhältnis verlichtet. Hierbei ist allerdings genau darauf zu achten, daß die Erkenntnis des eigenen Selbst und der Welt nicht durch die Frage vereinseitigt wird: Eigenheit des Selbst und Anderssein der anderen sollen einander nicht ausschließen, sondern ergänzen. Der, der die Fragen richtig stellen will, muß wissen, daß es zwei Seiten zu berücksichtigen gilt. Jede Frage steigt aus der Persönlichkeit des Fragenden auf, ist mit dessen Interessen, Neugier und Wissenwollen verbunden. Die Antwort aber kommt dem Fragenden von außen zu, als etwas, daß er noch nicht in seinem Selbst hat. Während er also die Dinge ins Licht seiner Frage, seiner Erkenntnis zieht, anerkennt er den Kontrast, gar Widerstreit von Dunkel und Hell, den seine Frage gerne zu Gunsten der Helle, des Lichts beilegen möchte. Der Fragende bestätigt ja indirekt das Dunkel der Welt, die Andersheit und Fremdheit der Dinge, von denen man sich in Unkenntnis getrennt sieht. Durch die Antwort macht man sie aber zum Teil des eigenen Selbst. Kein größerer Gewinn als die richtige Antwort auf die gestellte Frage. Und doch führt diese Antwort oft wieder zu neuen Fragen: die Antwort wird fraglich oder fragwürdig und damit ist das Dunkel wieder hergestellt.

Wer aber an der Antwort einfach festhält und sich weigert, sie zu befragen, also ihre Fraglichkeit zu bedenken, der begibt sich in Gefahr. Er läßt die Dinge, auf die durch die Frage das Licht der Erkenntnis und

---

[29]Für weitere Überlegungen zu den beiden Typen vergleiche K. Wagner: 'Ohne Warum. Peter Handkes *"Spiel vom Fragen"*, in: G. Fuchs/G. Melzer (Hg.): Peter Handke. *Die Langsamkeit der Welt* Graz/Wien: 1993, S.207ff.

[30]*Das Spiel vom Fragen*, a.a.O., S.492.

Aufmerksamkeit gerichtet wurde, völlig in diesem einen Licht aufgehen. Die Antwort, die gegeben wurde, ist die endgültig letzte. Die Aufklärung ist perfekt. Die Verlichtung der Lebensverhältnisse endet in der Totalauflösung durch Licht. Zwischen dem eigenen Selbst und der Welt gibt es schließlich keinen Unterschied mehr. Der Mensch, der die Befragung aufgegeben hat, verliert seinen Weltbezug. Wie die Fliege ins Licht der Kerze stürzt, so verbrennt er schließlich in der geschichtslosen, erzählfreien und absolut unbedingten Lichtwelt, die keine Gegensätze mehr kennt. Verlichtung wird zu Verlöschen, Vergehen, Verschwinden. Die Verführung, in diese Lichtwelt zu versinken, ist groß, und es sei hier daran erinnert, daß Lucifer nicht nur der gefallene Engel ist, sondern auch der Verführer, der als strahlender Engel in gleißendem, blendendem Licht erscheint.

In Figur des 'Einheimischen" im *Spiel vom Fragen* hat Handke eindrucksvoll diese Gefahr der Verlichtung auf die Bühne gestellt. Dieser 'Einheimische' — der Name ist bereits eine allegorische Inskription — ist in manchem das Klischee des österreichischen Hinterwäldlers — und doch mehr, weil er die Verführung zum fraglosen Einverständnis mit der Welt durch subtile Veränderung der ästhetischen Wahrnehmung erzielen möchte. Die Muse einer postmodernen Poesie ist dabei behilflich:

> Fragefrei werden. Fraglos ausharren. Wie die Blätter von den Bäumen fallen, ohne Fragezeichen. Einfach wie die alten Statuen mit der verhüllten Hand das Buch halten und mit der anderen darauf zeigen. Die Lösung des Problems des Fragens erkennst du am Verschwinden dieses Problems. Keine Zwischenräume mehr — also auch keine Fragen mehr. Bäume, wiegt mich mit euch. Der Schmetterling geht ab in Gestalt eines Mädchens. Der Wahnsinnige tritt auf mit dem Blütenzweig der Jahreszeit im Haar. Die kirschgroßen Regentropfen treffen, ohne ihn aufzuwirbeln, auf den Staub des Feldweges und die Strohhalme der verlassenen Felder. Helles Bild nähert, dunkles entfernt sich.[31]

Der Einheimische wünscht, keine Differenz mehr zwischen sich und der Welt zu empfinden. Er will, anders als der Fragende und Reisende, zu Hause sein. Er möchte seine Heimstatt gefunden haben. Fraglos will er sein und mit sich einverstanden. Die ästhetische Wahrnehmung seiner Welt wiegt ihn in einem Zustand narzißtischen Genusses und archaischer Geborgenheit.[32] Der reine Selbstbezug wird schließlich durch das Selbstzitat, hier Wahrnehmungen und Versatzstücke aus früheren Handketexten, hergestellt. Man ist bei sich selbst angekommen und doch scheinbar ganz woanders: die punktförmigen Erfahrungen, die hier an einer

---

[31]Ebenda, S.541.

[32]Dieser Zustand ist Teil jener 'Gnaden– und Erlösungsszenarios', die P. Strasser untersucht: Aufeinander zu, aneinander vorbei. 'Über Bedingungen der Möglichkeit des rechten Verstehens und Liebens, fragmentarisch dargelegt aus Anlaß von Peter Handkes fragwürdigem 'Spiel vom Fragen', in: *Manuskripte* 29 (1989), S.8ff.

poetischen Perlenkette aufgezogen werden, erinnern nicht zufällig an die Aufzeichnungen, die die Engel im *Himmel über Berlin, zu* Beginn des Films, miteinander austauschen.

Dennoch gelingt es dieser Figur nicht, das Bewußtsein davon zu unterdrücken, wie fragwürdig die wahrgenommenen Dinge eigentlich sind. Sei dies nun die Idiotie eines Sängers, der, wenn er nur einen Hammer hätte, von morgens bis abends hämmern würde, oder sei es die Reduktion des Fragebewußtseins auf das vegetabile Bewußtsein einer Rose. Die letzten Worte lauten:

> Wo ist der Hund, der dem armen Lazarus die Schwären des Fragens ableckt? *Ich hämmert' in der Nacht* ... Warum? Warum? Warum? Die Rose ist ohne Warum. Und du? Und du? Und du?[33]

Für einen Moment wird an dieser Theaterfigur eine sich nie beruhigende Postmoderne sichtbar, in der, zusammenhanglos und als Zitat, alles und jedes nebeneinander steht: der Popsong *If I had hammer* so gut wie eine Naturbeobachtung und ein Zitat aus der Bibel. Dies alles, nicht anders als die Figuren selbst, sind allegorische Erscheinungen auf der Suche nach ihrer Inskription, ihrem Begriff, ihrem geistigen Wesen, ihrem Engel.

---

[33]*Das Spiel vom Fragen*, a.a.O., S.541.

FROM GERMAN PAGE TO ENGLISH STAGE: A TRANSLATOR'S VIEW

PENNY BLACK

I have chosen the title of my talk deliberately in order to reflect its content: I shall reflect on my own experience and discuss the practicalities of translating two plays by Peter Turrini, *Sauschlachten* (1971) and *Tod und Teufel* (1990). I would like to state at the outset that the simple fact the latter play has yet to be performed on an English stage is an eloquent comment on the difficulties encountered when one wishes to translate a German–language play, particularly by an Austrian writer, for the theatre in Britain.

My career as a translator started with *Tod und Teufel*. At the time I was living at home with my young son and was approached by Michael Kingsbury, the artistic director of London City Theatre who suggested that I might translate a Turrini play. I had a keen interest in Turrini's work dating back to the period of six years, which I had spent in Austria; I find nearly all his plays immensely theatrical and exciting, and his television series *Die Alpensaga* profoundly influenced my view of Austria. At the time I was approached the latest play he had written was indeed *Tod und Teufel*, and it seemed for that reason an obvious point of departure. Anyone can in fact translate any play they wish although it can only then be performed or even shown to anyone else if one has secured the rights from the author's publisher. Most rights to a translation are for a fixed period of time — usually three years. The reason for this is that a third party may request to do a further translation and if this happens to be some illustrious playwright, for example, such as David Hare or Christopher Hampton, then the publisher would obviously not wish to squander such a possibility. To my great surprise I was granted an option to translate one of Austria's most important living playwrights following my submission of a draft translation of two scenes. As far as I could gather, the decision seemed to be based on my having lived in Vienna, a rather spurious training as an actress at the *Schauspielschule Krauss*, but most importantly an absolute lack of interest from anybody else.

So I started. Needless to say I received no payment. You cannot claim to be a translator of plays until you have actually translated one! It was also much more difficult a task than I had envisaged, and I almost abandoned the project after the very first scene because I realised that even the seemingly most simple text from a linguistic point of view posed an entirely different set of problems from a dramatic point of view.

I shall now deal with some of the decisions that have to be made before translating a play. The first relates to setting: should it be transferred and located in a British context or should one retain the original, in this case Vienna? Fortunately, unlike his earlier work, *Tod und Teufel* is not a dialect play and this obviously made matters easier. The next question I asked of myself was whether I should stick like a magnet to the original text, or make it as appealing, accessible (and dramatic!) in English. This I wanted to do but not at the price of sacrificing accuracy. My personal aim when I translate a play is that I want it to read as if it were an English–language play, so that an English–language audience would not be able to guess that it had been written originally in another language. At the same time, I also hope that any German speakers in the audience would be able to work out what the original was. On occasions a German speaker has approached me after a performance, saying something to the effect that they had a good idea of what the German text was, and this I view as the greatest compliment. It is also very important to remember a simple fact when translating a play: it is very different from translating prose. What I mean by this is that it is essential to get the dialogue right.

After I had been working on, or should I say, ploughing through *Tod und Teufel* for about eighteen months, I was very fortunate to receive a bursary from the British Centre for Literary Translation, at the University of East Anglia, Norwich. This was wonderful! A month of peace and quiet away from my family and an opportunity to discuss with many people my rather non–academic approach to translation. I was relieved to discover, having read several very frightening books on the theory of translation, in articles on actual translator's practice, that many have an even less academic approach than I do. Ranjit Bolt, who has had his translations performed at the Royal National Theatre sometimes does not even read the play to the end before he commences translation! My idiosyncrasy is that I feel I have to get something, anything, down on paper, even if it is initially not very good at all. I do this until I can hear the voices of the characters, then when I can hear them, I go back to the beginning and start afresh.

It is a common experience when translating a play that things appear to run smoothly until you hit a small point but one which can cause no end of trouble. Titles of plays are notoriously difficult, as the following brief example will demonstrate. In one play, by the East German playwright, Christian Martin, it took me more than four weeks to translate the entire script — I heard the characters' voices immediately — however the title took me a further six weeks, involving several telephone calls to Germany. The play was called *Lulle und Pulle*, slang words for *fags* and *bottle* (i.e. nicotine and alcohol). Clearly the author had chosen these two lexical items, not least because they rhymed. After much deliberation I finally settled on *Ciggie and Swiggie*.

Tod und Teufel caused no problems as far as its title was concerned, but I did encounter great difficulties in one particular scene, namely the ninth. This scene is set in the penthouse apartment of the arms–dealer, Walter Leschitzky, who demonstrates to the defence minister, Erwin Fischer, a new gun with 'smart' technology, which guarantees one hundred per cent accuracy by targeting and then seeking out a pigment in the victim's iris. Because this pigment differs slightly, depending on ethnic background, it is even possible to select one's 'target' on a racial basis. Seven shots are fired through an open window onto the street below, the defence minister promptly signs Leschitzky's application to export the weapon, and then the seven corpses are fetched by attendants and laid out on the stage so that their murderer can 'honour' the kill in the traditional fashion of an Austrian huntsman. In so doing, the equally traditional litany of 'Weidmannsheil!' – 'Weidmannsdank!' is heard three times. My problem was that I did not have the first idea of how to translate these words, although I was convinced that there must be some form of English equivalent.

Research in the library into hunting practices, however, drew a blank: it would appear that there is no tradition of honouring the kill in this way in Britain. I delved deeper and consulted books on Victorian and Edwardian hunting ways and customs. In the end, all that I could ascertain was that, whilst in Austria they have feasts and ceremonies and honour the kill at the end of a day's hunting, in Britain it appears that a huntsman comes home on his own, wipes his gun, cleans his dog, has a tot of whisky and goes to bed. Of course none of this information was of the slightest of help with the translation of 'Weidmannsheil!' – 'Weidmannsdank!'. The best that a number of dictionaries could offer was *good hunting* and *thank you*, but these lexical items, I felt, did not express the celebration of the event. The solution I settled on was the hunter saying *Good Hunting!* and the fraternity replying *Hurrah!* — along the lines of Hip Hip Hurrah! I felt that these at least expressed the sentiment and celebration of the scene. However, six weeks spent researching *Good Hunting!* and *Hurrah!* is not necessarily good time management.

Death and the Devil is a particularly long play and my work on it underwent constant revision — this is, of course, potentially an endless process but there comes a point where one has to decide on a final draft and submit it to the publishers, which is where I will now leave Turrini's play for the time being so that I can turn my attention to *Sauchlachten*[1], or as I imaginatively translated it, *Slaughtering the Pig*.

---

[1]Quotations are from the following volume: *Turrini Lesebuch. Stücke, Pamphlete, Filme, Reaktionen etc.* Ausgewählt und bearbeitet von Ulf Birbauer. Vienna/Zürich:

The publishers needed to be convinced that this was the best rendition of the title and were initially very keen on *Pigslaughter*, but I was fortunate to be able to get my way and persuaded them that *Slaughtering the Pig* was a more active title, in keeping with the context of the play. Again, my reason for wishing to translate this early work, which is in the tradition of the so–called critical *Volksstück*[2] was because I had been attracted by its undeniable theatrical impact. I commenced work at the start of 1994. By this time I had a few plays under my belt, and so London City Theatre and I approached the Arts Council of Great Britain for a commissioning grant to translate the play. We presented our case and made the point, not least, that the play was very pertinent to the situation in the former Yugoslavia. We received a grant to the princely sum of £2000.

Some theatres, the more mainstream ones with money to spare, often commission a 'rough' translation of a play for a couple of hundred pounds, to see if they really want to produce it or not. If they do, then obviously a full translation is commissioned. This is hardly an ideal situation for the translator, as one clearly puts every possible effort into the 'rough' version in order to 'sell' the play. However it does have the benefit of avoiding some of the problems at a later stage in the process. I had provided Michael Kingsbury, London City Theatre's Director with a resumé, but I had not done a 'rough' translation. This was to cause a few difficulties, as we shall see a little later.

Slaughtering the Pig is a very different play to *Death and the Devil*: not only was it written almost twenty years earlier it also reveals the inexperience of a young playwright and, for example, there are several passages which are overwritten. A greater difficulty was posed by the obvious fact that it was written in dialect. Peter Turrini introduces the play with the words 'Die Sprache dieses Stückes ist österreichisch mit Anklängen ans Kärntnerische'. The inference of this is that we are not dealing with a 'pure' dialect; it is not what any real peasant might speak, rather it is what I would call a 'Künstlersprache' all of its own, as the following example demonstrates:

BAUER: Aber die Goschen aufmachen, kannst wohl? (liest weiter) MEIN SÜSSES KLEINES ZUCKERGOSCHERL!
SEPP: Jo, wer kann denn so was Süsses schreiben?
BÄUERIN: Die Keuschnigg Maria an unseren Volte.
SEPP: A was, hätt o mir net gedacht, wo die so ein saubres Gestell hat.
BAUER: Euch gehört ein Stoppel in Oasch und einer in Mund gsteckt, sonst ist da nie Ruh.

(Europaverlag) 1978 [third edition 1989], pp.83–125. Subsequently abbreviated as S followed by the page number.
[2]Turrini even gives his play the subtitle 'Ein Volksstück'.

BÄUERIN: Net so unfeine Ausdrück. Der Seppl hat schon recht. Die Maria hat ihre dünnen Haxen von der Kinderlähmung, hätt net so auf unseren Hof gepaßt.
FRANZ: Das wär ja noch schöner, noch a Krüppel am Hof (S, 109).

Because of the content of the play and the fact that there are no equivalent rural peasant communities in Britain, I kept to the Austrian setting but used a sort of artificial West Country dialect to get across the robustness of the speech. The above section I translated as follows:

FARMER: But you can open that mouth, can't you. (He continues to read) My dear sweet honeymouth.
SEPP: An' who from around here can write like that?
WIFE: Maria Keuschnigg can, and to our Volte.
SEPP: Her with the dodgy undercarriage, would you believe it.
FARMER: One day I'll shove a bung up your arse and one in your mouth, just to get a moment's peace.
WIFE: Don't be vulgar. But Sepp's right. That Maria wouldn't have fitted in on the farm — she's got such thin legs from when she had polio.
FRANZ: Oh great, now there's a cripple on the farm.

Apart from the dialect, *Slaughtering the Pig* contains many difficulties — if not traps — for the translator. There are, for example, a number of songs, poems and even the national anthem, all of which I decided were essential.

There is another facet to *Slaughtering the Pig*, to which one grows accustomed when one has been working 'close–up' to it for a longer period of time: it is simply a very shocking play. It has been my experience that British directors are often uncomfortable when they encounter the more aggressive kind of German–language play and they can get cold feet. It is my view that this is not least because contemporary English–language theatre is often about what is not said on stage — one thinks of Harold Pinter, for example. Publishers have approached me with potential commissions for Austrian works for the stage which might deal, for example, with such savoury matters as cannibalism, and I have to inform them that I have my doubts as to their suitability for a British audience, even though the publishers themselves might find them hilariously funny.

In a situation such as this, one becomes more than just a translator; one becomes a *mediator* between two cultures. It was in this context that I made a mistake, one that I hope never to repeat; I sent the director a first draft of my translation (and I ask you to remember that he had not previously seen a 'rough' translation before he commissioned it). The draft was, frankly, dreadful in the way that first drafts often are: half was written in my artificial West Country dialect, the other half in Received English. He was horrified! Contractually obliged to stage the play, all he could discern in it was torture, vulgarity and racism — in an appalling translation. He wanted to change and cut out whole sections, but I refused. I felt that *Slaughtering the Pig* has a very strong message that warranted the violence. I took the translation away and thoroughly revised it as I had always planned to do. I kept the director abreast of further drafts, and the fourth became the final one. It was agreed contractually that I would have access to rehearsal and I also was involved in the casting. This brings me to a group of people who are crucial to the transfer of a German–language play to the British stage; the actors.

In my experience, the minute you have anything to with German–language theatre, actors approach you and ask if the play is 'Brechtian'. I have found it easiest to allay their fears and answer simply in the affirmative. They then usually take this to mean that they have to worry less about a character's psychologial motives and are able to concentrate more on what the director wants. I have also found that my contact with actors in the process of rehearsal is quite probably the best way to check the quality of my translation: if an actor is unable to get a line right, then it usually indicates that there is something wrong with the translation.

My translation of *Slaughtering the Pig* was performed in London to critical acclaim and full houses in February 1995. Almost simultaneously, the original was revived in Vienna. I took pleasure in the reviews which revealed that the impact on audiences had been the same in English as it was in Austrian. Writing in the *Kurier* (10.2.1995) newspaper, Caro Wiesauer came to the following conclusion:

> Was in den 70er Jahren ein Skandal war, bringt heute schrecklich, aktuelle Brisanz auf die Bühne. Ein Stück, das man vielleicht nicht gerne sieht, aber nicht bereut, gesehen zu haben. [...] Eine Aufführung, die man auch die Muntersten noch eine Spur wacher macht. Weil es an die Wurzeln der Faschismus–Bewegungen aller Zeiten führt, tief hinein in die menschlichen Seelen.

The review of the English production by Antonia Quirke in *The Stage* (21.2.1995) concurred:

> Austrian playwright Peter Turrini's deeply squalid one act play is more effective a screech against fascism than a legion of documentaries concerning the outrages of Hitler's ethnic cleansing [...].

I think that both of these reviews provide one answer to the question as to whether there is room for plays by Austrian writers, such as Peter Turrini. But there is a further question. Why is it that Turrini plays are performed around the world but only seldomly in Britain. All his plays have been published in translation in the United States of America but there is, sadly, little hope of that happening in my own country; anyone wishing to stage Turrini in Britain in translation and who approaches the publishers will get a print–out from my computer! I shall return to *Death and the Devil* in this context. At the moment, no one seems to want the play. London City Theatre are unable to mount a production in their own small theatre, as

Turrini's publishers have stipulated a 250–seat auditorium, as they are well within their right to do. We have done a rehearsed play reading of the work with some wonderful actors and it proved a great success. Despite being a thoughtful and at times funny play, which is visually exciting and has a number of strong roles for female actors the likelihood of it being staged is at best remote. My own view is that there is something of an unwillingness to take a risk with a play of this kind, not least because German–language works tend to get lumped together and are regarded, sometimes with justification, as earnest, turgid and unlikely to be a popular success.[3] In such a situation, I think that the translator, via judicious choice of material, has an important role to play in the encouragement of interchange between two theatrical traditions.

---

[3]See in this context the critical reception of English–language translations of Thomas Bernhard's plays, as discussed by Ralf Jeutter in the present volume.

SELECT BIBLIOGRAPHY

Note:
Full references for primary texts and their editions are given in the footnotes to each of the respective chapters. Detailed bibliographies on the individual playwrights are contained in *Kritisches Lexikon zur deutschsprachigen Gegenwartsliteratur* (KLG), edited by Heinz Ludwig Arnold (Munich: 1978ff.). What follows is a selection of secondary literature.

Arnold, Heinz Ludwig (ed.): *Wolfgang Bauer*, Munich: (text + kritik) 1978.

Aspetsberger, Friedbert, Norbert Frei and Hubert Lengauer (eds.): *Literatur der Nachkriegszeit und der fünfziger Jahre in Österreich*, Vienna: (Österreichischer Bundesverlag) 1984.

Aspetsberger, Friedberg and Hubert Lengauer(eds.): *Zeit ohne Manifeste? Zur Literatur der 70er Jahre in Österreich*, Vienna: (Österreichischer Bundesverlag) 1987.

Aspetsberger, Friedbert (ed.): *Österreichische Literatur seit den zwanziger Jahren. Beiträge zu ihrer historisch-politischen Lokalisierung*, Vienna: (Österreichischer Bundesverlag) 1979.

Aspetsberger, Friedbert (ed.): *Traditionen in der neueren österreichischen Literatur*, Vienna: (Österreichischer Bundesverlag) 1980.

Auckenthaler, K. (ed.): *Lauter Einzelfälle. Bekanntes und Unbekanntes zur neueren österreichischen Literatur*, Bern: (Peter Lang) 1996.

Barnouw, Dagmar: *Elias Canetti*, Stuttgart: (Metzler) 1979.

Barry, T. F.: 'The Weight of Angels. Peter Handke and 'Der Himmel über Berlin''', *Modern Austrian Literature*, 1990, (3/4), pp.53-64.

Barthofer, Alfred: 'Vorliebe für die Komödie: Todesangst. Anmerkungen zum Komödienbegriff bei Thomas Bernhard', *Vierteljahresschrift des Adalbert Stifter-Institutes des Landes Oberösterreich* 31 (1982), pp.77-101.

Bauschinger, S. and S. L. Cocalis (eds.): *Vom Wort zum Bild: Das neue Theater in Deutschland und den USA*, Bern: (Francke) 1992.

Bayer, Wolfram: *Kontinent Bernhard. Zur Thomas Bernhard-Rezeption in Europa*, Vienna: (Böhlau) 1995.

Bortenschläger, Wilhelm: *Der Dramatiker Fritz Hochwälder*, Innsbruck: (Wagner Universitätsverlag) 1979.

Briegleb, Klaus and Siegried Weigl (eds.): *Gegenwartsliteratur seit 1968* (= *Hansers Sozialgeschichte der deutschen Literatur vom 16. Jahrhundert bis zur Gegenwart*, vol. 12, ed. Rolf Grimminger), Munich: (Hanser) 1992.

Brinkler–Gabler, Gisela (ed.): *Deutsche Literatur von Frauen. Zweiter Band: 19. und 20. Jahrhundert*, Munich: (Beck) 1988.

Bushell, Anthony (ed.): *Austria 1945–1955. Studies in Political and Cultural Re-emergence*, Cardiff: (University of Wales Press) 1996.

Caldwell, D. and P.W. Rea: 'Handke's and Wenders's "Wings of Desire". Transcending Postmodernism', *The German Quarterly*, 1991, pp.46–54

Case, Sue–Ellen: *Feminism and Theatre*, Basingstoke: (Macmillan) 1988.

Connor, Steven: *Postmodernist Culture: An Introduction to Theories of the Contemporary*, Oxford: (Blackwell) 1989.

Conrad, Peter: *Modern Times, Modern Places. Life and Art in the 20th Century*, London: (Thames and Hudson) 1998.

Demetz, Peter: *Die süße Anarchie. Deutsche Literatur seit 1945. Eine kritische Einführung*, Frankfurt/M./Berlin: (Ullstein) 1970.

Dietrich, Margret: *Das moderne Drama. Strömungen, Gestalten, Motive*, 2. erw. Aufl. Stuttgart: (Kröner) 1963.

Dietze, Gabriele: *Die Überwindung der Sprachlosigkeit: Texte aus der neuen Frauenbewegung*, Frankfurt/M: (Luchterhand) 1979.

Dittmar, Jens (ed.): *Thomas Bernhard. Werkgeschichte*. Aktualisierte Neuausgabe, Frankfurt/M.: (Suhrkamp) 1990.

Donald, G.: 'Fritz Hochwälder's Range of Theme and Form', *Modern Austrian Literature* 18 (1985), Nr.2, pp.31–45.

Ensberg, Peter and Helga Schreckenberger: *Gerhard Roth. Kunst als Auflehnung gegen das Sein*, Tübingen: 1994.

Esslin, Martin: *The Theatre of the Absurd*, 3rd edition, Harmondsworth: (Penguin) 1980.

Fiddler, Allyson: *Rewriting Reality: An Introduction to Elfriede Jelinek*, Oxford: (Berg) 1994.

Fiddler, Allyson: 'Postwar Austrian Women Writers', in Chris Weedon (ed.) *Postwar Women's Writing in German*, Providence/Oxford: (Berghahn) 1997, pp. 243–268.

Fiddler, Allyson: 'Reading Elfriede Jelinek', in Chris Weedon (ed.) *Postwar Women's Writing in German*, Providence/Oxford: (Berghahn) 1997, pp. 291–304.

Firda, R. A.: *Peter Handke*, New York: (Twayne) 1993.

Fuchs, G. and G. Melzer (eds.): *Peter Handke. Die Langsamkeit der Welt*, Graz/Wien: (Literaturverlag Droschl) 1993.

Fuchs, Christian (ed.): *Theater von Frauen: Österreich*, Frankfurt/M.: (Eichborn) 1991.

Glaser, Horst A. (ed.) *Deutsche Literatur zwischen 1945 und 1955*, Bern/ Stuttgart/Vienna: (Haupt) 1996.

Gößling, Andreas: *Thomas Bernhards Frühe Prosakunst. Entfaltung und Zerfall seines ästhetischen Verfahrens in den Romanen 'Frost'- 'Verstörung' - 'Korrektur'*, Berlin/New York: (de Gruyter) 1987.

Greiner, Ulrich: *Der Tod des Nachsommers. Aufsätze, Porträts, Kritiken zur österreichischen Gegenwartsliteratur*, Munich/Vienna: (Hanser) 1979.

Grimm, Reinhold: *Nach dem Naturalismus. Essays zur modernen Dramatik*, Kronberg/Ts.: (Athenäum) 1978.

Gürtler, Christa (ed.): *Gegen den schönen Schein: Texte zu Elfriede Jelinek*, Frankfurt/M.: (Neue Kritik) 1990.

Halter, R.: 'Peter Handkes "Über die Dörfer"', in R. Weber (ed.) *Deutsches Drama der 80er Jahre*, Frankfurt/M.: (Suhrkamp) 1992, pp. 287-305.

Haslinger, A.: *Peter Handke. Jugend eines Schriftstellers*, Salzburg/Vienna: (Residenz) 1992.

Hassel, Ursula and Herbert Herzmann (eds.): *Das zeitgenössische deutschsprachige Volksstück*, Tübingen: (Stauffenberg) 1992.

Hennig, T.: *Intertextualität als ethische Dimension. Peter Handkes Ästhetik 'nach Auschwitz'*, Würzburg: (Königshausen and Neumann) 1996.

Höller, Hans: *Kritik einer literarischen Form. Versuch über Thomas Bernhard*, Stuttgart: (Heinz) 1979.

Huber, Martin, and Wendelin Schmidt-Dengler (eds.): *Statt Bernhard. Über Misanthropie im Werk Thomas Bernhards*, Vienna: (Verlag der Österreichischen Staatsdruckerei) 1987.

Huntemann, Willi: *Artistik und Rollenspiel. Das System Thomas Bernhard.* Würzburg: (Königshausen & Neumann) 1990.

Hutcheon, Linda: *A Poetics of Postmodernism: History, Theory, Fiction*, London and New York: (Routledge) 1988.

Innes, Christopher: *Modern German Drama. A Study in Form*, London/ New York/Melbourne: (CUP) 1979.

Janke, P.: *Der schöne Schein. Peter Handke und Botho Strauß*, Vienna: (Holzhausen) 1993.

Janz, Marlies: *Elfriede Jelinek*, Stuttgart: (Metzler) 1995.

Jeutter, Ralf: *Im Fliegenglas. Krankheit, Gesundheit, Wahnsinn und Vernunft in der Prosa Thomas Bernhards*, Amsterdam: (Rodopi) 1999.

Jung, Jochen (ed.): *Glückliches Österreich. Literarische Besichtigung eines Vaterlands*, Salzburg: (Residenz) 1978.

Klocker, Hubert (ed.): *Wiener Aktionismus 1960-1971* (two volumes). In cooperation with Graphische Sammlung Albertina, Vienna and Museum Ludwig, Cologne: 1989.

Klug, Christian: *Thomas Bernhards Theaterstücke.* Stuttgart: (Metzler) 1991.

234 – *Select Bibliography*

Koebner, Thomas (ed.): *Tendenzen der deutschen Gegenwartsliteratur*, Stuttgart: (Kröner) 1984.

Koepnick, L.P.: 'Negotiating Popular Culture: Wenders, Handke, and the Topographies of Cultural Studies', *The German Quarterly*, 1996, (69/4) pp. 381–400.

Kunne, Andrea: *Heimat im Roman: Last oder Lust? Transformation eines Genres in der österreichischen Nachkriegsliteratur*, Amsterdam: (Rodopi) 1991.

Laemmele, Peter and Jörg Drews (eds.): *Wie die Grazer auszogen, die Literatur zu erobern. Texte, Portäts, Analysen und Dokumente junger österreichischer Autoren*. Munich: (edition text + kritik) 1975.

Landa, Jutta: *Bürgerliches Schocktheater. Entwicklungen im österreichischen Drama der sechziger und siebziger Jahre*, Frankfurt/M.: (Athenäum) 1988

Landa, Jutta: '"Königskomödien" oder 'Fäkaliendramen'? Zu den Theaterstücken von Werner Schwab', *Modern Austrian Literature* 26 (1993), pp. 215–229.

Magris, Claudio: *Der habsburgische Mythos in der österreichischen Literatur*, Salzburg: (Otto Müller Verlag) 1966.

Malkin, J.: *Verbal Violence in Contemporary Drama. From Handke to Shepard*, New York: (CUP) 1992.

McGowan, Moray and Ricarda Schmidt (eds.): *From High Priests to Desecrators. Contemporary Austrian Writers*, Sheffield: (Sheffield Academic Press) 1993.

Menasse, Robert : *Das Land ohne Eigenschaft. Essay zur österreichischen Identität*. Frankfurt/M.: (Suhrkamp) 1995.

Melzer, Gerhard: *Wolfgang Bauer: Einführung in das Gesamtwerk*, Königstein/Ts: (Athenäum) 1981.

Melzer, G. and J. Tükel (eds.): *Peter Handke. Die Arbeit am Glück*, Königstein/Ts.: (Athenäum) 1985.

Mittermayer, Manfred: *Ich werden. Versuch einer Thomas Bernhard Lektüre*, Stuttgart: (Heinz) 1988.

Pavis, Patrice: 'The Classical Heritage of Modern Drama: The Case of Postmodern Theatre', *Modern Drama*, no. 1 (1986), pp. 1–22.

Pfister, Manfred: *The Theory and Analysis of Drama*, transl. John Halliday, Cambridge: (CUP) 1988.

Piel, Edgar: *Elias Canetti*, Munich: (Beck = Autorenbücher 38) 1984.

Preece, Julian: 'The Uses of Language in the Dramas of Werner Schwab: Towards a Definition of "das Schwabische"', in Arthur Williams, Stuart Parkes, and Julian Preece (eds.), *Contemporary German Writers, their Aesthetics and their Language*, Bern/Berlin/Frankfurt/New York/Paris/Vienna: (Peter Lang) 1996, pp.267–82.

Ringel, Erwin: *Die österreichische Seele. Zehn Reden über Medizin, Politik, Kunst und Religion.* Vienna/Munich: (Europaverlag) 1994.

Robinson, Gabrielle: 'Slaughter and Language Slaughter in the Plays of Peter Turrini', *Theatre Journal* 43 (1991), pp.195–208.

Roelcke, T.: *Dramatische Kommunikation: Modell und Reflexion bei Dürrenmatt, Handke und Weiss*, Berlin: (de Gruyter) 1994.

Schlaffer, Hannelore: 'Der Dramatiker Werner Schwab', *Merkur* Heft 3, 1994, pp. 265–71.

Schmidt–Dengler, Wendelin: 'Vorwort' in Petra Nachbaur and Sigurd Paul Scheichl (eds.), *Literatur über Literatur. Eine österreichische Anthologie*, Graz: (Styria) 1995.

Schmidt–Dengler, Wendelin: *Bruchlinien. Vorlesungen zur Österreichischen Literatur 1945 bis 1990*, Salzburg and Vienna: (Residenz) 1995.

Schmidt-Dengler, Wendelin: *Der Übertreibungskünstler. Studien zu Thomas Bernhard*, 2. Aufl., Vienna: (Sonderzahl) 1989.

Schnell, Ralf: *Geschichte der deutschsprachigen Literatur seit 1945.* Stuttgart: (Metzler) 1993.

Schödel, Helmut: *Seele brennt. Der Dichter Werner Schwab*, Vienna: (Droschl) 1995.

Schuch, Wolfgang and Klaus Siblewski, (eds.): *Peter Turrini. Texte, Daten Bilder*, Munich: (Luchterhand) 1991.

Schütte, Uwe: *Auf der Spur der Vergessenen. Gerhard Roth und sein 'Archiv des Schweigens'*, Wien: (Böhlau) 1997.

Sebald, W.G.: *Beschreibung des Unglücks. Zur österreichischen Literatur von Stifter bis Handke*, Salzburg and Vienna: (Residenz) 1985.

Sebald, W.G. (ed.): *A Radical Stage. Theatre in Germany in the 1970s and 1980s*, Oxford/New York/Hamburg: (Berg) 1988.

Sebald, W.G.: *Unheimliche Heimat. Essays zur österreichischen Literatur*, Salzburg & Vienna: (Residenz) 1991.

Sieg, Katrin: *Exiles, Eccentrics, Activists: Women in Contemporary German Theater*, Ann Arbor: (University of Michigan Press) 1994.

Spiel, Hilde (ed.): *Kindlers Literaturgeschichte der Gegenwart* Bd. 2; Frankfurt/M.: (Fischer) 1980.

Suchy, Viktor: *Literatur in Österreich von 1945 bis 1970. Strömungen und Tendenzen*, Vienna: (Dokumentationsstelle für neuere österreichische Literatur) 1973.

Sully, Melanie: *A Contemporary History of Austria*, New York: (Routledge) 1990.

Szondi, Peter: *Theorie des modernen Dramas*. Frankfurt: (Suhrkamp) 1963.

Vogelsang, Hans: *Österreichische Dramatik des 20. Jahrhunderts. Spiel mit Welten, Wesen, Worten*, Vienna: (Wilhelm Braumüller Universitätsverlag) 1981.

Waine, Anthony: 'Recent German Writing and the Influence of Popular Culture', in Keith Bullivant (ed.), *After the "Death" of Literature: West German Writing of the 1970s,* Oxford/New York/Munich: 1989.

Walter-Buchebner-Gesellschaft (ed.): *Die Wiener Gruppe.* Walter-Buchebner–Literaturprojekt, Vienna/Cologne/Graż: (Böhlau) 1987.

Weedon, Chris (ed.): *Postwar Women's Writing in German,* Providence/Oxford: (Berghahn) 1997.

Wefelmeyer, F.: 'Beyond Postmodernism. The Late Works of Peter Handke', in: Moray McGowan and Ricarda Schmidt (eds): *From High Priests to Desecrators. Contemporary Austrian Writers,* Sheffield: (Sheffield Academic Press) 1993, pp. 45-62.

Weigl, Sigrid: *Die Stimme der Medusa. Schreibweisen in der Gegenwartsliteratur von Frauen,* Reinbek bei Hamburg: (Rowohlt) 1987.

Weinzierl, Erika and Anton Pelinka (eds): *Das große Tabu. Österreichs Umgang mit seiner Vergangenheit.* Vienna: (Österreichische Staatsdruckerei) 1987.

Weiss, Walter: 'Die Literatur der Gegenwart in Österreich', in Manfred Durzak (ed.), *Die deutsche Literatur der Gegenwart. Aspekte und Tendenzen.* Stuttgart: (Reclam) 1971, pp. 386-399.

Wenders, W.: *The Logic of Images. Essays and Conservations,* London/Boston: (Faber and Faber) 1991.

Williams, Arthur et. al. (eds.): *'Whose Story?' — Continuites in Contemporary German–language Literature,* Bern: (Peter Lang) 1998.

Wittstock, Uwe (ed.): *Roman oder Leben. Postmoderne in der deutschen Literatur,* Leipzig: (Reclam) 1994.

Wischenbart, Rüdiger: *Der literarische Wideraufbau in Österreich 1945-1949. Am Beispiel von sieben literarischen und kulturpolitischen Zeitschriften,* Königstein/Ts.: (Hain) 1983.

Zeyringer, Klaus: 'Das Elend des Vergleichens? Literatur und Film – Handke und Scharang', *Wirkendes Wort,* 1993 (43/2), pp. 301-317.

Zeyringer, Klaus: *Innerlichkeit und Öffentlichkeit. Die österreichische Literatur der achtziger Jahre,* Bern and Munich: (Francke) 1992.

INDEX

NOTES ON THE CONTRIBUTORS

Penny Black moved to Vienna on completion of her German studies, where she trained as an actress. In recent years, she has established a reputation as an author (e.g. the radio play *Leda's Birth*), producer, adaptor and translator of German–language plays. She has received a bursary from the British Centre for Literary Translation and has had commissions to translate a number of plays, including *Yes, My Fuehrer* (Brigitte Schwaiger), *Slaughtering the Pig, Death and the Devil* (Peter Turrini) and *Ciggie and Swiggie* (Christian Martin).

Allyson Fiddler is Lecturer in German Studies at Lancaster University, having previously taught at the University of Wales (Swansea) and the University of Nottingham. Her research interests in contemporary Austrian literature are reflected in a number of articles, in her book *Rewriting Reality: An Introduction to Elfriede Jelinek*, and her editing of *Other Austrians: Post–1945 Austrian Women's Writing*.

Frank Finlay is Senior Lecturer and Head of German Studies at The University of Bradford, having previously taught English at the Wirtschaftsuniversität, Vienna, and German at the Manchester Metropolitan University. As a student, he produced a number of plays by Austrian writers at the Gulbenkian Studio, Newcastle upon Tyne. He has published a monograph on Heinrich Böll and articles on German literature, culture and aesthetics.

Silke Hassler studied Comparative and German Literature in Vienna. She is the author of numerous articles and conference papers on Austrian and exiled writers, and contemporary Austrian drama. She is currently preparing an edition of Peter Turrini's work.

Ralf Jeutter is Senior Lecturer in German at The Manchester Metropolitan University (UK). He is the author of the volume *Im Fliegenglas. Krankheit, Gesundheit, Wahnsinn und Vernunft in der Prosa Thomas Bernhard*, as well as essays on a range of other writers.

Jenny Lanyon has recently completed a PhD at Oxford Brookes University on contemporary women's writing.

Victoria Martin studied German at the universities of Exeter and Cambridge before starting her career at the Manchester Metropolitan University. She is a Fellow of St Anne's College and Lecturer in German at Oxford University. Her publications are in the area of sociolingusitics and Austrian German.

Julian Preece has a wide range of research interests in German and Austrian literature and has published, for example, on Bernhard, Canetti, Brecht, Grass, Kafka and Schwab. He held lectureships at Queen Mary and Westfield College of the University of London and Huddersfield University before moving to the University of Kent. He is editor with Arthur Williams and Stuart Parkes of *Contemporary German Writers, Their Aesthetics and Their Language* and *'Whose Story?'* — *Continuities in Contemporary German–language Literature*.

Mike Rogers is Lecturer in German at the University of Southampton. He has a particular interest in theatre and poetry, and in Austrian literature. He has published on Nestroy, Karl Kraus, and various themes germane to the theatre.

Axel Schalk combines freelance writing (especially theatre) with teaching at the University of Potsdam and employment as a *Dramaturg*. He has worked at the Deutsches Schauspielhaus in Hamburg and the Schillertheater in Berlin. He is the author of numerous articles on contemporary German drama.

Uwe Schütte holds a doctorate from the University of East Anglia and is currently at Aston University. He is the author of the monograph *Auf der Spur der Vergessenen. Gerhard Roth und sein 'Archiv des Schweigens'*.

Anthony Waine has published extensively on twentieth century literature and has recently explored the impact of popular culture on German writers such as Rolf–Dieter Brinkmann, Jörg Fauser, and Peter Härtling. In the area of modern theatre, he is the author of several articles (e.g. on Weiss, Dürrenmatt, Zuckmayer); a monograph charting Martin Walser's development as a dramatist, and he is co–editor, with Graham Bartram, of the volume *Brecht in Perspective*. He is Lecturer in German Studies at Lancaster University.

Fritz Wefelmeyer is Reader in German Studies at the University of Sunderland. His main publications are in the area of 18th to 20th century culture.

Julie Wilson is a theatre director/choreographer, having recently completed a PhD thesis. Directing credits include a new musical adaptation of 'Alice in Wonderland' with designer Mark Hinton, for the Lawrence Batley Theatre; 'Street Scene' an American Opera by Kurt Weill, and 'The Navigator', a one man show for a virtual theatre environment.